The Beijing Olympiad

Who will benefit from the Beijing Olympiad?

What value will the 2008 Games be to the people of China?

The 2008 Olympic Games have been the source of considerable controversy since long before their announcement, and seem destined to become the most keenly scrutinized sporting extravaganza ever. While its legacy is yet to emerge, there is little doubt that the Beijing Olympiad will have major implications for a stream of concurrent matters, including the rise of China as a superpower, international relations, human rights developments, the future of Olympism and the Olympic Movement, the East–West clash, the North–South divide, and the processes of globalization.

The Beijing Olympiad: The Political Economy of a Sporting Mega-Event considers the global and local impact of the Games, and provides valuable insight into contemporary China, its culture, society, economy and politics in the build-up to the 2008 Olympics.

The Beijing Olympiad examines key questions, providing a range of original insights of interest to scholars, researchers and students from Sports Studies to Sociology, Politics, Economics, International Relations and Legal Studies.

Paul Close is Director of the Amity Centre for Globalization Research (ACGR), Jaipur, India. **David Askew** is Associate Professor of Law, and **Xu Xin** is Associate Professor of International Relations, both at Ritsumeikan Asia Pacific University.

The Beijing Olympiad

The Political Economy of a Sporting Mega-Event

Paul Close, David Askew and Xu Xin

Routledge
Taylor & Francis Group

LONDON AND NEW YORK

First published 2007
by Routledge
2 Park Square, Milton Park, Abingdon, Oxon OX14 4RN

Simultaneously published in the UK
by Routledge
270 Madison Ave, New York, NY 10016

Routledge is an imprint of the Taylor & Francis Group, an informa business

Typeset in Goudy by RefineCatch Limited, Bungay, Suffolk
Printed and bound in Great Britain by
Cromwell Press, Trowbridge, Wiltshire

British Library Cataloguing in Publication Data
A catalogue record for this book is available from the British Library

Library of Congress Cataloging-in-Publication Data
Close, Paul.
The Beijing Olympiad : the political economy of a sporting
mega-event / Paul Close, David Askew and Xu Xin.
     p.   cm.
  Includes bibliographical references and index.
  1. Olympic Games (29th : 2008 : Beijing, China)
2. Olympics–Political aspects–China.   3. Human rights–China.
4. Civil rights–China.   I. Askew, David.   II. Xu, Xin.   III. Title.
GV7222008.C56   2006
796.48–dc22   2006018425

ISBN10: 0–415–35700–4 (hbk)
ISBN10: 0–415–35701–2 (pbk)
ISBN10: 0–203–00301–2 (ebk)

ISBN13: 978–0–415–35700–5 (hbk)
ISBN13: 978–0–415–35701–2 (pbk)
ISBN13: 978–0–203–00301–5 (ebk)

To Shigeo and Sachiko Kido and the memory of
Sydney Alexander Close and Sadao Ohki

Contents

List of illustrations and tables

Illustrations

Tables

List of contributors

Paul Close is Director of the Amity Centre for Globalization Research (ACGR), Jaipur, India.

David Askew is an Associate Professor (Law), Ritsumeikan Asia Pacific University, Japan.

Xu Xin is an Associate Professor (International Relations), Ritsumeikan Asia Pacific University, Japan.

Acknowledgements

We wish to thank the following for their help and support during the writing of this book: Daiwa Anglo-Japanese Foundation; European Commission; Ministry of Education, Culture, Sports, Science and Technology (Japan) (MEXT); Japan Society for the Promotion of Science (JSPS); Lincoln Allison; Rethinam Arul; Soundaram Arul; John Brennan; A. G. Geddes; Selmin Kaska; Ohkubo Atsushi; Margaret Teremetz; To Chinh; Gwen Wallace; and Yoshimoto Keiichi.

Abbreviations

AAA	All-China (Amateur) Athletic Association
ACHPER	Australian Council for Health, Physical Education and Recreation
AHD	*American Heritage Dictionary*
AC	Answers.com
AGF	Asian Games Federation
AI	Amnesty International
AIDS	Acquired Immune Deficiency Syndrome
AIOWF	Association of the International Olympic Winter Sports
ANOC	Association of National Olympic Committees
ANOCA	Association of National Olympic Committees of Africa
ASF	All-China Sports Federation
ASIAD	Asian Games
ASOIF	Association of Summer Olympic International Federations
BBC	British Broadcasting Corporation
BIBICO	Beijing 2008 Olympic Games Bid Committee
BOCOG	Beijing Organizing Committee for the Olympic Games (Beijing Organizing Committee for the Games of the XXIX Olympiad)
BOA	British Olympic Association
BQ	Brainy Quote
BRIC	Brazil, Russia, India, China
BRICSAM	Brazil, Russia, India, China, South Africa, ASEAN, Mexico
CAS	Court of Arbitration for Sport
CBA	China (or Chinese) Basketball Association
CFA	Chinese Football Association
CIA	Central Intelligence Agency
CIIC	China Internet Information Center
CNOC	Chinese National Olympic Committee
COC	Chinese (National) Olympic Committee
COD	*Concise Oxford Dictionary of Current English*
CPC	Communist Party of China

CRIA	China, Russia, India and ASEAN
CSHRS	China Society for Human Rights Studies
CSL	China (Football) Super League
CSO	civil society organization
CU	Columbia University
DESA	Department of Economic and Social Affairs of the United Nations Secretariat
EOC	European Olympic Committees
ETIC	East Turkistan Information Centre
EU	European Union
EXPO	World Exposition (World's Fair)
FBI	Federal Bureau of Investigation
FEAAF	Far Eastern Amateur Athletic Federation
FEER	*Far Eastern Economic Review*
FIEP	Fédération Internationale d'Education Physique
FIFA	Fédération Internationale de Football Association
GCS	global civil society
GCSO	global civil society organization
GDP	gross domestic product
GHRR	global human rights regime
GMD	Guomindang (Chinese Nationalist Party)
GNGO	global non-governmental organization
GPE	global political economy
HIV	human immunodeficiency virus
HPAE	high-performing Asia economy
HRW	Human Rights Watch
ICC	International Criminal Court
IDRC	International Development Research Centre
IF	International Federation (of a sport on the programme of the Olympic Games)
IFs	International Federations
ILO	International Labour Organisation
IMF	International Monetary Fund
IOA	International Olympic Academy
IOC	International Olympic Committee
IPC	International Paralympic Committee
KMT	Kuomintang (Chinese Nationalist Party)
LAOOC	Los Angeles Organizing Olympic Committee
LDP	Liberal Democratic Party (Japan)
MNC	multi-national company
MOCOG	Manchester Organizing Committee for the Olympic Games
MSN	Microsoft Network
MSP	Member of the Scottish Parliament

NAFTA	North American Free Trade Agreement
NBA	National Basketball Association (USA)
NBS	National Bureau of Statistics (PRC)
NGO	non-governmental organization
NIE	newly industrializing economy
NOC	National Olympic Committee
NPC	National People's Congress (of China)
NSDTs	nation-states *and* dependent territories
NZOC	New Zealand Olympic Committee
OAP	Olympic Action Plan (of BOCOG)
OC	Olympic Charter
OCA	Olympic Council of Asia
OCOG	Organising Committee of the Olympic Games
OGKS	Olympic Games Knowledge Services
OHCHR	Office of the High Commissioner for Human Rights (UN)
ONOC	Oceania National Olympic Committees
PASO	Pan-American Sports Organisation
PLA	People's Liberation Army
PMTH	*Postmodern Therapies*
PPP	purchasing power parity
PRC	People's Republic of China
PU	Princeton University
REC 2008	Report of the IOC Evaluation Commission for the Games of the XXIX Olympiad in 2008
REC 2012	Report of the IOC Evaluation Commission for the Games of the XXX Olympiad in 2012
ROC	Republic of China (or Taiwan)
SCPCS	State Commission for Physical Culture and Sports
SOCOG	Sydney Organising Committee of the Olympic Games
SPJ	Socialist Party of Japan
SSG	State Sport General Administration
SLP	Scottish Labour Party
SNP	Scottish National Party
TNC	trans-national company
UDA	Union des Annonceurs
UDHR	Universal Declaration of Human Rights
UN	United Nations
USFSA	Union des Sociétés Françaises des Sports Athlétiques
USNOC	United States National Olympic Committee
WADA	World Anti-Doping Agency
WDEL	Webster's Dictionary of the English Language
WEF	World Economic Forum
WHO	World Health Organization
YMCA	Young Men's Christian Association (YMCA)

Preface

China has long held a prominent position in the Western imagination. From Marco Polo onwards, China – or, as otherwise called, *the Middle Kingdom* – has been viewed as a mystical, unknown and unknowable place. Whether Sinophile or Sinophobe, early European merchants, missionaries and ambassadors, such as Lord George Macartney, have bequeathed fascinating accounts of the China they encountered, while telling us just as much about their Western prejudices as about China itself (see Robbins 1908; see also Jones 2001). Many notable Western scholars have been drawn to the exotic features of Chinese civilization. For instance, Baron de Montesquieu (1689–1755) is one of many Western thinkers who have looked to China for inspiration in trying to make sense of and advances in politics and governance among other areas of social life. Equally significant has been the cultural and aesthetic impact of China on the West, with *Chinoiserie* as *objets d'art* having been transported to the West for many centuries to great critical acclaim. Indeed, from *Chinoiserie* and Orientalism (Said 1978) to the Yellow Peril and US containment, China has loomed large in the Western psyche.

The perceived wealth, luxury, eroticism and depravity of the East has variously attracted and repelled, while the Eastern political order has been depicted by some as despotic and tyrannical, but by others as an expression of enlightened totalitarianism – as a utopian polity, in which mandarins (philosopher kings) ruled benevolently. From the *philosophes*, such as Voltaire, to twentieth-century intellectuals, such as Jean Paul Sartre, the Chinese *state of affairs* has been regularly idealized in the West. Eastern sensuality has been contrasted with, and indeed viewed as a threat to, Western virility. The decadent, emotional and irrational East has been *feminized* and counter posed to the virtues and masculinity of the West, providing in the process a justification for European imperialism. This myopic Orientalism continues to figure strongly in Western writing, thinking and attitudes about the East in general and China in particular, colouring, shaping and determining the Western approach to everything concerning that part of the world (*ibid.*). The question arises, therefore, 'what will be the impact of China's treatment of that Western inspired mega-event, *the modern Olympiad?*'

As a team of insiders and outsiders, we have been both caught up in the Western fascination with China and intrigued by this fascination as a topic in itself. Herein lies the cocktail of influences that inspired our decision in the early weeks of 2004 as the Athens Olympic Games approached to research and write about the follow-on event, the Beijing Olympiad, the four-year period starting with the closing ceremony of the Athens Games and ending with the closing ceremony of the 2008 Beijing Games. We would write a book about the sport involved, but in the broadest sense, and in the widest possible context – that of the global developments within which all sport is embedded and in relation to which sport plays an important, formative role.

The authors take great delight in sport in general and many of the sports that make up the Olympic Games in particular. We also admire the extravaganza of the Olympic Games, just as we do similar mega-events, such as the FIFA World Cup. However, the appeal for us of sport, it has to be said, is less as active participants (beyond some walking and cycling), and more as spectators, observers and social scientists. The Beijing Olympiad has presented us with an opportunity to study a subject which we enjoy personally but which, at the same time, has immense significance in relation to our respective, overlapping areas of scholarly research as well as to major social developments at the global level.

We hope that our pleasures, interests and also concerns surrounding the Beijing Olympiad will come over to the readers of our book. We are *China watchers* in the popular sense, while being more precisely *China scholars*, who have endeavoured to come up with an *objective* examination of the Beijing Olympiad along with much else besides. At the same time, we recognize the limitations of any work which seeks to be scholarly and objective. We are committed to a critical approach to what we study, which for present purposes means being critical both of China and of those who are critical of China from the standpoint of Western society, culture and continuing (if only for the time being) hegemony. What follows is not a simple, crude attack on Chinese society, governance, human rights record and the like from a narrow, taken-for-granted Western point of view. Our approach is far more cautious and, we trust, more balanced, scrutinizing as far as possible Western-based notions, interests and motives, such as those that underpin the Olympic movement, which after all may be regarded as yet another vehicle of Western imperialism, albeit of the *latter-day* variety. Our critical approach also entails taking to task our own scholarly disciplines for their limitations, bias and somewhat imperious tendencies. We hope to have contributed to the conceptual, analytical and theoretical strengths of such disciplines as Sociology, Political Studies, International Relations, and Legal Studies. We are empiricists wanting to inform both the general reader and our academic colleagues. We are an interdisciplinary team of social scientists hoping to advance the study of such things as the Olympic Games, mega-events, China, East Asian social relations and developments, and global social patterns, processes and trends.

Each of us is committed in his own way to wishing well the Beijing Olympiad, along with the city of Beijing in hosting the event, and the Chinese people in their attempt to put on a good display. We are in no doubt that the Beijing Olympiad will turn out to be a highly impressive and memorable occasion. At the same time, we are conscious of the issues, concerns and controversies surrounding the Games, such as those of whether Beijing should have been selected in view of the People's Republic of China's (PRC's) human rights record, the prospect of so-called terrorist attacks during the Games, and so on. However, notwithstanding these considerations, we are looking forward to a mega-event which will prove to be an outstanding sporting and scholarly experience of the kind to which we have tried to do justice in this book.

Paul Close, David Askew and Xu Xin, October 2006

Introduction

This book is about sport, and in particular about a sporting mega-event, the Beijing Olympiad. Sporting events in general are social occasions, and Olympic Games have become the sports meetings with the greatest social presence in the world today. A modern Games is the climax of a social process which begins many years earlier, passing through on the way a four-year long Olympiad which starts with the close of the previous Games. Not only the 2008 Olympics, but also the 2004 to 2008 Olympiad will be a high profile jamboree with major social, cultural, political and economic implications. What occurs in and around the 28 sports of the Games in which many thousands of athletes will compete between 8 and 24 of August 2008 in the vicinity of Beijing will attract a huge amount of attention throughout the world, helped by massive media interest. But furthermore, what occurs as part and parcel of the build-up to the Games will be an impressive sporting, social and economic spectacle in itself; will substantially shape what happens at, through and beyond the Games; and will have considerable consequences for China, and for the future of the Olympic movement.

The unfolding of the Beijing Games, Olympiad and legacy will be played out as a complex social matter in the context of a broad array of concurrent social, cultural, political and economic developments at and between the local (including the nation-state), regional (East Asian), and global levels. Above all, the character, course and consequences of the Beijing Olympiad can be grasped only by viewing and interpreting these things in relation to the encompassing political economy, that area of social life where the political and economic spheres merge, and are increasingly doing so on the global plane. Olympiads are *global-reach* events, as elucidated in Chapter 1, which also lays the basic conceptual and theoretical framework for studying, analyzing and making sense of the Beijing Games and Olympiad, and indeed of all mega-events of whatever genre. Chapter 1 spells out the book's main argument, aspects of which are then further elaborated in Chapters 2 and 3.

We argue that there is an *extraordinary convergence*, or *elective affinity*, between modern Olympism and *the ideals and tendencies* of modern market capitalism; and that this particular *mutual attraction* throws considerable light on the Beijing Olympiad, an examination of which in turn strongly illuminates the relationships between the Olympic movement and various other modern social phenomena, including the growing appeal of liberal democracy and individualism, the spread of *the Western cultural account*, the progress of globalization, and the rise of China as a major political-economy player on the world stage. An examination of the Beijing Olympiad reveals that, as with all elective affinities in human and social life, while the mutual attraction between the ideals and tendencies of Olympism and those of modern market capitalism is great, it is by no means simple, total and unsullied. The attraction between Olympism and the Olympic movement, on the one hand, and capitalism and the capitalist mode of production, on the other, is incomplete and somewhat contradictory. Indeed, the movement's relationships with all the modern social phenomena with which it has elective affinities will appear far from smooth, untroubled and guaranteed when viewed through the lens of the 2004 to 2008 Olympiad, culminating as this is likely to do in the greatest mega-event, sporting or otherwise, of all time.

In our view, the Olympic movement and, more specifically, the International Olympic Committee (IOC), by virtue of its responsibility for and influence through the Olympic Games, is not only furthering the cause of Olympism, but also playing a major role in the global social network, or compact, which is using its collective power to steer the processes of globalization. The latter is occurring along three basic social dimensions – the economic, the political, and the cultural – in a way which has so far largely reflected Western values combined with *Northern power*, or hegemony, increasingly rooted as this is in the evolving global political economy (GPE). Given recent developments in the GPE, however, it is possible, even probable, that a fundamental shift has been taking place since the early 1990s, in the distribution of GPE power and configuration of GPE power players towards East Asia and especially China, as signalled and further secured by the 2008 Games going to Beijing.

There are grounds for assuming that the Beijing Olympiad may act as a catalyst in the re-alignment process within the GPE and, not unconnectedly, will provide a spur to important changes inside Chinese society itself, not least in the area of human rights. After all, the Olympiad will be a convergence point or focal event for a cluster of major developments at and between the local, regional and global levels of social life, and between which there is a formidable array of elective affinities. The developments involved include the deepening institutionalization of Olympism at the global level; the global spread of the Western cultural account around the doctrine of individualism; the advance of market capitalism and liberal democracy on the global plane; the progress of globalization in conjunction with the consolidation of global society; and the rise of China as a regional and global political economy player and superpower. It is because of the way in which the Beijing Olympiad will draw together in a highly concentrated, dense and intense fashion these developments that the 2008 Games are likely to be not merely another sporting mega-event, but moreover the greatest ever mega-event, at least for the time being, with unprecedented internal and external social, economic, political and cultural consequences.

A prominent thread running through the book is that of exposing the driving intensions behind and interests served by the Olympic Games. In this regard, Chapter 5 examines the Asian discourse on the Olympics. Guided by Japan's acquisition of the Games, first South Korea and then the PRC have been intent on mobilizing the Olympic extravaganza in pursuit of an abiding set of internal and external political-economy goals. By hosting the Games, Japan was admitted to an exclusive club in celebration of its coming of age. The event then provided the means not only of showcasing its economic success and of enhancing its prestige on the world stage, but also of boosting the governing regime's domestic credibility. Subsequently, South Korea followed by the People's Republic of China have been motivated by an urge to up-stage their regional rival, Japan, through even more successfully hosting the Games. Paradoxically, however, this very ambition, stiffened as it is in the case of the PRC by deep-seated and highly assertive Chinese nationalism, poses a not inconsiderable threat to Beijing's dream of an unblemished 2008 spectacular.

In Chapter 6 our account of the Beijing Olympiad turns to an outline of the historical path leading to the 2008 Games, with similarities being drawn with the *Long March* which eventually led to the establishment of the PRC approximately 60 years earlier. There is an examination of the various internal and external political considerations involved, intimately associated as these are with a range of crucial economic factors and forces. In Chapter 7, *Conclusion*, we conclude by pulling together the threads and arguments of the book and speculating on the eventual outcome of the years of preparation that have gone into the 2008 Games given the gathering evidence. Will the Games reflect, and perhaps reinforce, substantial social progress in China and further afield as judged with reference to the kind of Olympic ideals articulated by Baron Pierre de Coubertin, the founder of the modern movement? Alternatively, will they be little more than window dressing for the kind of political oppression and economic exploitation which many associate with the global advance of market capitalism – the driving force behind globalization – as indicated by China's capitulation to the West in this among other areas of social life?

Chapter 1

Toward an analytical framework

The symbol for the Olympic Games, the five rings, is the most readily identified image in the world. The rings are recognized by over 90% of the world's population, which is even higher than the logos of megabrands such as Shell and McDonald's [Morgan and Pritchard 1998].[1]

(Andranovich et al. 2001: 114)[2]

The Olympic movement's symbol of five interlocking rings was designed by Baron Pierre de Coubertin, the founder of the modern movement, in 1913; was adopted by the Olympic movement at its sixth world Congress held in Paris in June 1914; and was first displayed at an Olympic Games,[3] gracing the Olympic flag, at Antwerp in 1920.[4]

Coubertin explained in the August 1913 edition of *Revue Olympique*:

The emblem chosen to illustrate and represent the world Congress of 1914 [is] five intertwined rings in different colours – blue, yellow, black, green, red – [. . .] placed on the white field of the paper. These five rings represent the five parts of the world which now are won over to Olympism and willing to accept healthy competition [. . .]. Moreover, the six colours thus combined reproduce those of all the nations without exception. The blue and yellow of Sweden, the blue and white of Argentina, the French, British, American, German, Belgian, Italian, and Hungarian tricolours, the yellow and red of Spain lie next to the new Brazilian and Australian flags, and the old Japan and the young China. This is really an international emblem.

(Coubertin, 1913; quoted in Barney 1992a; see also Durry 1997)[5]

The origins and meanings of the five-ring emblem, or symbol, as it has come to be called by the International Olympic Committee (IOC), has long been the subject of scrutiny, debate and controversy (see Barney 1992a; Grombach 1980; Lennartz 2001; MacAloon 1981; Poole and Poole 1963; Young 1985). Robert Knight Barney, in one of the most influential accounts, claims that the inspiration for the five-ring symbol came from Coubertin's 'personal sport involvement in France', in particular after he became in 1890 the founding President of the *Union des Societes Francaises des Sports Athlétiques* (USFSA) (Barney 1992a: 628). The USFSA was formed by the merger of Coubertin's *Comite Jules Simon* with Georges de Saint Clair's *Union des Sociétés Francaises de Courses a Pied*, and the 'logo of the USFSA, created to symbolize the union' of the 'two sports bodies, was the simple interlocking of two rings' (*ibid.*). The USFSA's two-ring symbol was displayed on the uniforms of its athletes from 1893, and so at least a year before Coubertin convened the Conference at the Université Paris-Sorbonne at which the modern Olympic movement was launched (*ibid.*). Barney claims that it is 'obvious, therefore, that Coubertin's affiliation with the USFSA led him to think in terms of interlocked rings or circles' when he turned his mind to creating 'a logo for his commemorative conference of 1914', the result being a *ring-logo* to symbolize the Olympic movement's 'success up to that point in time, just as the interlocking of two rings had signified the successful marriage of two distinct societies into one, the USFSA' (*ibid.*).[6]

But, why did Coubertin choose five rings for the Olympic movement? Barney notes that while 'Olympic literature has long held that they signify the five continents of the world', Coubertin 'never spoke of "continents" ' during the 1913–14 period, 'only of specific areas of the world "désormais acquises á l'Olympisme" ' – areas that had been *won over to Olympism* (*ibid.*). Instead, Barney argues, the explanation lies in the fact that Coubertin designed the symbol as 'a logo for the 20th anniversary congress celebrating the IOC's establishment', so that Coubertin's five rings denoted the number of Olympic Games events that had been 'staged before the time of the 1914 Paris proceedings' (see also Young 1985), something which in turn accounts for the choice of the particular ring colours. Coubertin 'did not think in terms of each colour representing a continent'; for Coubertin 'the white background of the flag, together with the green, red, yellow, black and blue rings, represented at least one of the colours present in the flag of each nation represented in the Games of the first five Olympiads' (Barney 1992a: 629).[7]

Be that as it may, there is a widely held belief that the five rings do stand for the continents of Africa, the Americas, Asia, Europe and Oceania, as exemplified by the claims that 'the interlocked Olympic rings were designed by Coubertin in 1914 as a representation of the five continents and the colors of their many national flags' (Guttmann 2002: 2); and 'the five interlocking rings, represents the union of the five continents and the meeting of the athletes of the world at the Olympic Games' (World Atlas 2006; see also Znamierowski 2005). What is more, the five-continents interpretation can be found in statements that have been made for some time in various Olympic movement documents, including in at least one written by Coubertin himself:

The five rings represent the five continents. They are interlaced to show the universality of Olympism and the meeting of the athletes of the whole world during the Olympic Games [. . .]. Pierre de Coubertin [. . .] explains the meaning of the flag: 'The Olympic flag [. . .] design is symbolic; it represents the five continents of the world, united by Olympism, while the six colours are those that appear on all the national flags of the world at the present time' [Coubertin 1979, originally 1931; quoted in Coubertin 1986b: 470]. Combined in this way, the [. . .] colours of the flag [. . .] represent all nations.

(Museum Lausanne 2002: 3)

As if to underscore the point, the Olympic Charter (OC) – the codification of the Fundamental Principles of Olympism, Rules and Bye-Laws (IOC August 2004: 7) – now evidently endorses the view that the rings represent continents. In the edition of the Charter which came into force on 1 September 2004 (*ibid.*), three days into the 2004–8 Beijing Olympiad, heralded by the closing ceremony of the 2004 Athens Games,[8] the IOC declares that the 'five interlaced rings' represent 'the union of the five continents and the meeting of athletes from throughout the world at the Olympic Games' (*ibid.*: 8).

The Olympic symbol seems to have gathered ever growing significance for the Olympic movement. Both the symbol and the other Olympic icons[9] are deemed to convey the 'meaning and the values of Olympism', and to 'give the Olympic movement and the Games an identity' (Museum Lausanne 2002: 2). Olympism, as 'a life philosophy or a code of conduct to follow' (*ibid*: 6),[10] is said on behalf of the movement to be encapsulated in the Olympic motto *Citius, Altius, Fortius*, or *Faster, Higher, Stronger*, in that:

These three words encourage the athlete to give his or her best during competition, and to view this effort as a victory in itself. The sense of the motto is that being first is not necessarily a priority, but that giving one's best and striving for personal excellence is a worthwhile goal.

(*ibid.*: 6)

Although it has been suggested that the Olympic motto 'in the present context of moral relativism can mean anything that one wishes it to mean' (Lucas 1992; quoted in Staun 2003), the Olympic movement formally interprets the motto as implying the Olympic creed, or movement's main article of faith, according to which:

The most important thing in the Olympic Games is not to win but to take part, just as the most important thing in life is not the triumph but the struggle. The essential thing is not to have conquered but to have fought well.

(Museum Lausanne 2002: 6)

As befits Coubertin's original intentions, the Olympic movement remains firmly committed to *winning over*, or converting, the world to Olympism, which is being 'disseminated throughout the world' primarily by National Olympic Committees (NOCs). More specifically, the task, or mission (IOC 19 February 2006a), which has been assigned by the IOC to NOCs is 'to disseminate Olympic values on a national level' (IOC 20 February 2006a), such as through educational programmes:

> The National Olympic Committees (NOCs) promote the fundamental principles of Olympism at a national level within the framework of sports. NOCs are committed to the development of athletes and support the development of sport for all programs and high performance sport in their countries. They also participate in the training of sports administrators by organising educational programs.
>
> (IOC 19 February 2006a)

Aided by each NOC's activities, the IOC tells us, the Olympic movement is playing an ever greater part in not merely the development of sport, but also in overall social *development*, and doing so in a way which is sensitive to the particular, local circumstances involved:

> The Olympic movement is constantly expanding and is an extraordinary factor in development. Today it represents a major world phenomenon in the development and promotion of sport on every level, as well as in sectors related to education, individual rights, cultural diversity, improvement of society in general and sustainable development. One of the missions of the NOCs is to develop and promote the Olympic ideals in their respective countries. According to the Olympic Charter, Olympism, blending sport with culture and education, seeks to create a way of life based on the joy found in effort, the educational value of good example and respect for universal fundamental ethical principles [. . .]. The [. . .] programmes at the disposal of the NOCs within the framework of the promotion of Olympic values [. . .] make an important contribution [to social development by] enabling the NOCs to carry out actions related to the values conveyed by the fundamental principles of Olympism according to their need, their individual situation and their culture.
>
> (IOC 18 February 2006)[11]

The *constant expansion* of the Olympic movement is reflected in a range of concrete indicators, including the increase in the number of NOCs within the Olympic movement, the rise in the number of cities bidding for the Games, and the growing interest being shown in Olympic Congresses.

The NOC membership of the Olympic movement has expanded steadily over the years, and has been augmented most recently during the Beijing Olympiad. On 9 February 2006, just before the opening of the 2006 Winter Games in Torino, Italy,[12] it was announced that, in accordance with a decision taken by the 118th Session of the IOC, the Marshall Islands had 'become officially the 203rd member of the Olympic movement' (IOC 9 February 2006). This accession to the Olympic movement is highly significant in that, as a result, the Marshall Islands became 'the 16th country in Oceania with IOC recognition, leaving only one other – Tuvalu – still seeking Olympic status' (Associated Press 2006). Indeed, consequently, Tuvalu gained the dubious distinction of being not just the only country – in the sense of an independent nation-state, as recognized by the United Nations (see Chapters 2, 3 and 4) – in Oceania still outside the Olympic movement, but moreover the only country apart from one other anywhere in the world outside – the other being the Holy See, or Vatican.

The way in which the NOC membership of the Olympic movement has swelled to cover all the world's independent nation-states apart from two of the smallest, and all of them except for the only current one which can be expected to eventually join, namely Tuvalu, is indicative of how the movement had managed before the 2008 Games to successfully win over, at least in a sense, to Olympism close on the whole world. Other indicators of the advance of Olympism include the rise in the number of cities bidding for the Games, especially since the 1980s (Short 2003). The first bidding competition was for the 1904 Games between the two US cities of Chicago and St Louis (Games Bids 22 February 2006; see also Matthews 2005). The first Games to be held after the First World War attracted nine bid cities before being won by Antwerp, but those of 1928 attracted only two, with Amsterdam winning, and those of 1932 only one, Los Angeles (Games Bids 22 February 2006). Los Angeles had first bid for the 1924 Games, won by Paris. As John Short explains:

> the City of Los Angeles [. . .] made a bid for the Games as early as 1923, initiated by an IOC member from Los Angeles, William May Garland. He was chairman of the local Community Development Association and worked closely with the city's business and political elite, especially Harry Chandler, owner of the LA Times. Garland was also president of the Chamber of Commerce, so the impetus for the Games came from local boosters, business leaders and real estate interests, a constellation of interests referred to as the 'urban growth machine' [Jonas and Wilson 1999; Molotch 1993]. The 1932 Games explicitly were employed to boost the city's image, economy and business fortunes. Proposed at the time of boom, they also were used to stimulate the local economy as the economic recession turned into the Great Depression.
>
> (Short 2003; see also Barney et al. 2002; Short 2001, 2004;
> Tomlinson and Young 2005)

There was a sharp increase in the number of bid cities to 13 for the 1936 Games, hosted by Berlin (see Krüger and Murray 2003), a figure almost equalled later by the number of bids for the 1952 Games, won by Helsinki, and the 1956 Games, won by Melbourne. But, a marked decline in the number of bid cities then followed: four for the 1964 Games (Tokyo); four for the 1968 Games (Mexico City); four for the 1972 Games (Munich); three for the 1976 Games (Montreal); two for the 1980 Games (Moscow); and only one for the 1984 Games (Los Angeles). Just two cities bid for the 1988 Games, when Seoul (South Korea) beat Nagoya (Japan); but six bid for the 1992 Games, which went to Barcelona, six for the 1996 Games (Atlanta), five for the 2000 Games (Sydney), 11 for the 2004 Games (Athens), ten for the 2008 Games (Beijing), and nine for the 2012 Games (London) (see Games Bids 22 February 2006). What this rollercoaster pattern seems to reflect above all is the way in which, after the Second World War, 'the cost of hosting the Games became a prohibitive factor in cities bidding for the Games', especially 'before the advent of substantial revenues from major corporate sponsoring and broadcasting rights' (Short 2003). There has been a dramatic increase in the cost of staging the Games. For the 1960 Rome Games, US$50 million was spent 'on public works' (*ibid.*; see also Davies, E.L. 1996); the 1972 Munich Games cost US$850 (see Brichford 1996); the 1976 Montreal Games cost US$1.5 billion (see Iton 1978); and those held in Moscow in 1980 are estimated to have cost between US$2 billion and US$9 billion (Short 2003; see also Barrett 1980). The spiraling costs were not being covered by income from traditional sources of revenue – that is, from the sale of tickets, coins, stamps and mascots; and it took some time for the 'increasingly lavish Olympics' to be rescued in part by higher income from the sale of broadcasting rights, in particular to television companies, as the Games became 'a global media event' (Bernstein and Blain 2003; see also Barney et al. 2002), but then more decisively by a major infusion of funds through corporate sponsorship deals, especially starting in the 1980s (Short 2003; see also Barney et al. 2002; Cai and Yang 2004; Cashman and Hughes 1999; Ferrand and Torrigiani 2005; Preuss 2000, 2004).

The 1976 Montreal Games were responsible for exposing the gulfs that had opened up between a host city's 'programmatic aspiration', the 'high cost' of staging a Games, and 'actual revenue' (Short 2003). After taking into account 'the cost of all infrastructural investments', the city suffered an estimated net loss of US$1,228 million (calculated at 1995 prices; see Preuss 2000, 2004), with the loss falling to local and regional taxpayers (Short 2003). Montreal's experience fed the reluctance of other cities to bid for the Games, until Los Angeles 'charted a new course' (*ibid.*). Being the only bid city for the 1984 Games, Los Angeles 'had a strong negotiating position with the IOC', and crucially the US's NOC 'set up a private non-profit corporation', the Los Angeles Organizing Olympic Committee (LAOOC), 'to make the arrangements so that the city taxpayers were not responsible for the costs' of the Games (*ibid*.). While LAOOC's costs were only US$467 million, it made U$300 million from the sale of television broadcasting rights, and signed deals with 34 corporate sponsors – including Coca-Cola, Mars, and Anheuser Busch – each of which paid between US$4 million and US$15 million 'for the exclusive right to market their products with the Olympic logo' (*ibid*.). The result was total revenues of US$1123 million (*ibid*.), and LAOOC 'made a profit; corporations achieved global penetration as the Games were broadcast to 156 countries; local businesses made money and the city became the center of world attention without accruing long-term costs or heavy debt burdens' (*ibid*.; see also Andranovich et al. 2001; Burbank et al. 2001; Van Riper 2006).[13]

In these respects, the 1984 Games were successful, and so much so that the experiment in corporate sponsorship deals which took place 'became a model for a marketing program introduced by the IOC' (Short 2003), called *The Olympic Program* (TOP), whereby 'the IOC receives long term financing while the sponsors get access to a world wide audience in an association with the Olympics, one of the most recognized and positively perceived "brands" on the planet' (*ibid*.; see also Johnston, A. 1999). Under this scheme, the IOC 'drew up long-term agreements [with] large corporations', including during 2001 to 2004 with Coca-Cola, John Hancock, Kodak, McDonald's, Panavision, Schlumberg Sema, Time, Visa, and Xerox.

Also as a result of the financial success of the Los Angeles Games, other cities were encouraged to follow suit, including more and more from beyond Europe and the USA. Between 1896 and 2004, the Games were held on 25 occasions in 17 different countries, but only four were held outside of Europe and North America (Short 2003). It was not until the 1956 Melbourne Games that they were held outside of Europe and the USA for the first time (*ibid*.); and it was not until 1964 that they were held in Asia. When the Games are held in Beijing in 2008, it will be only the third time that they have been held in Asia (*ibid*.; see also Horton 1998; McClain 1990). However, this does not accurately reflect the degree of interest which seems to have been shown by non-Western cities in hosting the Games, including quite early on. Alexandria in Egypt bid for the 1916 Games, cancelled because of the First World War; Alexandria, Buenos Aires and Rio de Janeiro joined in the bids for the 1936 Games; Buenos Aires and Mexico City for the 1956 Games, won by Melbourne; Mexico City and Tokyo for the 1960 Games; Tokyo for the 1964 event; Mexico City for the 1968 Games; Nagoya and Seoul for the 1988 Games; Beijing and Istanbul for the 2000 Games, won by Sydney; Cape Town, Buenos Aires, Istanbul, Rio de Janeiro and San Juan, Puerto Rico, for the 2004 Games; Beijing, Istanbul, Osaka, Bangkok, Cairo, Havana and Kuala Lumpur for the 2008 Games; and Rio de Janeiro, Istanbul and Havana for the 2012 Games (Games Bids 22 February 2006).

What the relative paucity of bids from non-Western cities and, perhaps more to the point, of successful bids reflects is how hosting the Games requires 'infrastructural investments that only few countries in the world can afford or are willing to undertake' (Short 2003), especially when there is the possibility of a major shortfall opening up between the cost of hosting the Games and the revenues that will be accrued. Even now, there is nothing like a guarantee that the host will avoid a loss and incurring debts. According to Tom Van Riper, the cities of Montreal (1976), Barcelona (1992), Sydney (2000) and Athens (2004) were still paying off debt well into the Beijing Olympiad, 'due mainly to splurging on sports venues that don't have much after life' (Van Riper 2006). Although Montreal achieved 'an operating profit', as of 2006 the city was still 'paying off the last of its debt on the Olympic Stadium', with the help of a '17-cents-per-pack cigarette tax' (*ibid.*). Barcelona was 'populated with a host of arenas left over from 1992 that [sat] mostly empty'; Sydney's Super Dome had gone into receivership, and the city's taxpayers were burdened with a bill of £57 million per annum for the upkeep 'on a new rail system' that had been greatly under-used since the Games (see Gordon 2003; Madden 2002); and Athens, which according to Van Riper had paid £6.8 billion (US$12.0 billion) to take the Games *back to their roots*, representing 5 per cent of Greece's annual GDP, was burdened with 'venues built for baseball, basketball and other sports' that carried 'a £57 million annual price tag, and an £82 million sailing facility [all of which went] mostly unused' (Van Riper 2006). The final overall cost of the Athens Games was an Olympic record. In November 2004, Greece's Finance Minister, George Alogoskoufis, announced that the total cost of the Athens Games had reached nearly 9 billion euros, or US$11 billion, 'almost double the amount forecast just a year before the Games' (Reuters 13 November 2004): the 'socialist government that lost elections five months before the August Games had insisted [that] the total cost would not significantly exceed 4.6 billion euros', but 'years of delays in construction and a huge rise in the security budget dramatically inflated the cost' (*ibid.*). The security budget alone for what was the first Games since the 11 September 2001 *terrorist* attacks on the USA, and so the first during the *War on Terror*, had surged from the projected US$125 million in the 1997 bidding file to over US$1.2 billion in practice (*ibid.*).

Van Riper puts the blame on the IOC, claiming that it 'has encouraged gigantism; spending massive amounts on sports that come around every four years', the result being that host cities 'typically spend billions on venues, infrastructure, security and other assorted necessities for the privilege of bringing in tens of thousands of guests for 17 days', when 'often, tourism revenue, job creation and ticket sales' do not meet expectations, burdening local taxpayers with *the Winner's Curse* (*ibid.*). Still, Beijing is 'set to smash the spending record' in 2008 for hosting a Games, as flagged at the outset by the way in which as a bidding city it had budgeted to spend £13.2 billion, or US$23.2 billion, 'nearly twice what Athens laid out' in 2004 (*ibid.*). Before and during the Beijing Olympiad, estimates of both the overall likely cost of the 2008 Games and the amounts to be shouldered by the city of Beijing, the Beijing Organizing Committee for the Games of the XXIX Olympiad (BOCOG) and other contributors varied considerably and seemed to change constantly. Shortly after the close of the 2004 Athens Games, it was reported that BOCOG was 'working on a budget of some US$1.6 billion', which together with the 'additional major expenditure in environmental protection, in improving highway and railway links, and in the construction of Olympic venues', resulted in an expected 'total outlay' for the Games of around 131 billion yuan, or US$16 billion (Shao Da 17 September 2004). Then, in 2005 BOCOG increased its budget for the Games to US$2 billion (*China View* 3 March 2006; Reuters 3 March 2006), while as long ago as 2002, 'Beijing's leaders announced that the [total] price tag for the "the best-ever Olympic Games in history" ' would be as high as US$37 billion (Patterson 15 February 2005; see also Owen 2005). The rising costs have been attributed in part to the 'increase of security expenses' compared with what was anticipated when Beijing 'competed to host the Olympic Games [and a] possible terrorist threat was not considered' (*China View* 3 March 2006), the election of Beijing having taken place in Moscow in July 2001 (see IOC July 2001a).

Whatever the causes, some in China began to worry about the rising costs, including members of the National People's Congress (NPC), the top legislature in the People's Republic of China (PRC) (*China View* 3 March 2006). Zhang Guiyu, an NPC deputy from Shandong Province in eastern China, suggested that Beijing's 'ambition to host a first-class Olympics' did not mean an 'unreined budget: "The organizers of the event should exert all efforts to show a best-ever Games to the world with the minimum amount of expenditure" ' (*ibid.*). Zhang pointed out that in China there were ' "still many people living under the poverty line, especially in the countryside. We can not afford an extravagant event" ' (*ibid.*). Subsequently, at the March 2006 NPC in Beijing, China's Prime Minister, Wen Jiabao, promised 'to take measures to close the divide between the new rich and numerous poor' (BBC 5 March 2006), and in particular pledged 'extra money for rural areas and farmers, to spread growing wealth to the impoverished countryside' (*ibid.*). He told the conference that building 'a "new socialist countryside" is a major historic task', and that the government planned to spend 340 billion yuan (US$42 billion; £24 billion) during 2006 'upgrading agriculture, and billions more on rural social services', as China's economy was set to grow by 8 per cent during 2006 and by an average of 7.5 per cent during 2006–10. The government's policy had been spurred by 'growing rural unrest [among] the hundreds of millions of rural poor' who were being 'left behind by China's surging urban economy'. The government was aware of '87,000 protests and other incidents of discontent' during 2005 (*ibid.*). According to Wen Jiabao, 'some deeply seated conflicts that have accumulated over a long time have yet to be fundamentally resolved, and new problems have arisen that cannot be ignored'. China must 'pay more attention to social equity and social stability so that all the people can enjoy the fruits of reform and development,' he said (*ibid.*). The amount which the government intended to spend during 2006 on helping build a *new socialist countryside* through upgrading agriculture was similar to what by March 2006 was the 'estimated $40 billion [that would] be spent on improving Beijing's infrastructure before the opening ceremony' of the Olympic Games in August 2008 (Reuters 3 March 2006).

Those who had steered and supported Beijing during its successful bid to host the Games were convinced that the costs would be greatly outweighed by the benefits. Speaking four days after Beijing's 2001 election to host the Games, Ye Zhen, a spokesperson for the National Bureau of Statistics, 'predicted that over the next seven years, Olympic effects would add an average of 0.3 to 0.4 percentage points a year to national gross domestic product (GDP)'; and the Beijing Municipal Statistics Bureau expected 'the city itself to benefit to the extent of no less than 2 percentage points a year' (Shao Da 17 September 2004). A 'big pre-Olympic investment boom' was anticipated, with the State Statistics Bureau estimating 'new investment [totaling] 280 billion yuan', 64 per cent of which would be in 'infrastructure construction' (*ibid.*). The Beijing municipal government claimed that by 2008, 'the Olympic economy will have created as many as 2.1 million new job opportunities' (*ibid.*). In particular, the city would work strenuously to attract *inward investment* from abroad:

> Beijing is baking a huge 'Olympic cake'. On April 18 and 19 [2004], it hosted 'Invest Beijing', a conference aimed at market promotion for the Olympic economy [. . .]. The conference attracted many of the world's top 500 enterprises including General Electric, Nortel Networks, Boeing, Volkswagen, Eastman Kodak, and Wal-Mart. Domestic players were also well represented by such names as Lenovo, Huawei and the Sinopec Group. All of the participants were eager to get their slice of the Olympic cake.
>
> (*ibid.*)

While for 'many host cities, the curse has overshadowed the blessing' (Van Riper 2006), it would seem that an ever-growing stream of cities are drawn to bid by the imagined benefits and gains (see Allen et al. 2000; Cashman and Hughes 1999; PriceWaterhouseCoopers 2000; Department for Culture, Media and Sport 2002), the result being a major contribution to 'the more general trend for many cities seeking to make the global connection' (Short 2003; see also Hall and Hubbard 1998, Roche 1992, Short 1999; Wilson 1996). As Short has put it, the 'increasing competition between cities to host the Games is part of the growing competition between world cities for global spectacles' (Short 2003); and indeed, the Games do 'provide an important platform for place marketing as cities seek to achieve international recognition and world city status' (*ibid.*), even though this entails an expensive and risky 'rewriting and reshaping' of the cities (*ibid.*; see also Andranovich et al. 2001):

Hosting the Games provides a significant opportunity to recontextualize cities by connecting them to a global space of flows and reconstituting them internally. New and improved links with the wider world plug the city more effectively into the global flows of capital, people and ideas.

(Short 2003)

Certainly the process of bidding and preparing for the Games tends to be persuasively rationalized and justified in terms of a discourse, meta-narrative, or grand account (Lyotard 1984, 1999), which envisages 'the creation of the global city, well connected to the outside world, [and] presenting a positive image to millions of viewers around the world, all [of whom are] potential visitors, tourists and investors' (Short 2003). The image 'presented is one of modernity and multiculturalism, part of the shared global discourses of democracy and liberalism while also adding a touch of the uniquely local' (*ibid.*). In the case of the Beijing Games, for instance:

BOCOG's general goal is to host high-level Olympic Games and high-level Olympics with distinguishing features, [in particular] Chinese style, cultural splendour, contemporary spirits and mass participation. The Beijing Olympic Games will be a perfect occasion to fully display China's 5,000-year history and its resplendent culture, a grand ceremony that will gather athletes from all over the world and present diverse and brilliant cultures. The Beijing Olympic Games will fully express the common aspiration of the Chinese people to jointly seek peace, development and common progress together with the peoples of the world, and it will highlight the fact that the 1.3 billion Chinese people of 56 ethnic groups, along with 50 million overseas Chinese, are all most enthusiastic participants in the Beijing Olympic Games.

(BOCOG 4 March 2006)

A city will be presented as a 'distinctive place connected to a shared global space' (Short 2003). But, the 'biggest winners of the Olympic windfall' will be 'the political regimes running the city that have the opportunity to reshape the city's desired image'; while most of 'the negative costs' will be 'borne by the weaker groups in the city, especially those inhabiting prime inner city sites' (*ibid.*). Generally, preparations for the Games 'have been associated with a spatial removal of the poor and the marginal, which can be both temporary and permanent', and which is one of the main sources of 'the resistances to both hosting and bidding for the Games' (*ibid.*; see also Abbs 2005; Lenskyi 2002; News24 4 March 2006).

The trend whereby more and more cities are trying to make *the global connection* – to become *world cities* (Beaverstock et al. 2000; Gold and Gold 2005; Sassen 1991) – is part and parcel of the processes of globalization (Short 2003; Short and Kim 1999). This trend is reflected in the increasing number of cities bidding to host not just the Games, but also other Olympic events, some of which are themselves becoming *global spectacles*, a development which in turn is yet a further indicator of the *constant expansion* of the Olympic movement. Growing interest is being shown in Olympic Congresses, each of which is a 'gathering of all international sporting bodies (associated, affiliated, and recognised by the IOC) [in order] to reflect upon the future of sport in our society' (IOC 22 February 2006; IOC 23 February 2006). These events 'bring together representatives of all the parties that make up the Olympic movement', namely the IOC, the NOCs, the International Sports Federations (IFs), the Olympic Games Organising Committees (OGOCs), 'the athletes, coaches, judges and the media, as well as other participants and observers' (IOC 8 February 2006; see also Games Bids 4 February 2006). A Congress's 'role is consultative'; it is convened by the IOC President (IOC August 2004:14); and 'is a rare event held on average every fifteen years' (IOC 23 February 2006).

The first Olympic Congress, held on 23 June 1894 at the Université Paris-Sorbonne, attracted 78 delegates representing 37 sports federations from nine countries and territories. The sixth Congress, held in Paris in 1913, at which Coubertin introduced the Olympic symbol and flag, was attended by 140 participants, including 120 delegates representing 29 NOCs plus 20 IOC members. The eleventh Congress held in Baden-Baden, Germany, in September 1981, the first under the IOC's new president, Juan Antonio Samaranch, was attended by 469 official delegates from 144 countries and territories, including 310 representing 143 NOCs, 67 representing 26 IFs, and 85 IOC members (see Miller, D. 2004; Müller 2004; Wagner 2006).[14] The twelfth Congress saw a return to Paris, opening 100 years to the day after the inaugural event (IOC 23 February 2006), and at a time when the number of NOCs was approaching 200, there being 197 that sent teams two years later to the 1996 Games in Atlanta (Paul 1996).[15]

It would be 15 years before the next Congress, called on the initiative of President Jacques Rogge (IOC 28 October 2005).[16] Just over a year into the Beijing Olympiad, on 28 October 2005, the IOC Executive Board 'confirmed the following cities, proposed by their respective National Olympic Committees, as candidates to host the 13th Olympic Congress in 2009': Athens (Greece), Busan (South Korea), Cairo (Egypt), Copenhagen (Denmark), Lausanne (Switzerland), Mexico City (Mexico), Riga (Latvia), Taipei (Chinese Taipei; Taiwan), and Singapore (*ibid.*).[17] The decision as to which of these cities would host the event was to be made at the 118th session of the IOC, scheduled to take place in Turin as a prelude to the 2006 Winter Games; and on 8 February 2006, one of the front runners, Copenhagen, was chosen to host the 2009 Congress, the declared purpose of which was 'to study and discuss the current functioning of the movement and define the main development axes for the future' (IOC 8 February 2006).

In addition, Copenhagen would simultaneously host the meetings of the IOC's Executive Board and the 121st session of the IOC (*ibid*.).[18]

For some observers, the result was destined to be the most important meeting ever in the history of sport:

> IOC members will [have chosen] the location for what is perhaps the most important Olympic meeting in years to come [. . .]. The large number of interested cities is probably a surprise to the IOC [. . .]. Perhaps the high-profile 2012 Olympic Games bid election held [in 2005] at the IOC session in Singapore raised the overall appeal for hosting IOC meetings. Not only did that meeting attract a record number of delegates and members of the media, but it hosted internationally famous people and world leaders such as British Prime Minister Tony Blair, Hilary Clinton and David Beckham among dozens of others [. . .]. For 2009 the stakes will be higher. Early conservative estimates suggest that 7,500 people will attend the congress including IOC members, NOC and sports federation representatives, and members of the media [. . .]. The meeting could be the most important in sports history to date. On the meeting agenda will be the election of the next IOC president or the acceptance of current President Jacques Rogge for an additional term; a vote on what sports will be added or dropped for the 2016 Summer Games; and the election of the host city for the 2016 Summer Games which is already shaping up to be a battle similar to the 2012 bid. Special congress agenda items will cover issues important to the future of sport and the Olympic movement. It's no wonder that several cities want to be part of this event. In many cases countries that aren't yet capable of hosting the Olympic Games will take this opportunity or others like it to participate and raise their profiles within the Olympic movement. [It] is clear that the IOC needs to reform the site selection process for official meetings now that they are becoming almost as glamorous as the Games themselves.
>
> (Games Bids 4 February 2006)[19]

The changing character and importance of Olympic Congresses is indicative of how the Olympic movement appears to be successfully converting the world to Olympism, and may be seen to reflect and reinforce the presence on the world stage of those Olympiads in which they occur, although the 1913 Congress may hold onto its place among the leading pack given that it saw the début of the Olympic movement's symbol, just as the 2004–8 Olympiad may prove hard to dislodge as the greatest mega-event, sporting and otherwise, of all time, as discussed later in this chapter and in Chapters 2, 3 and 5 (see also Wang 2005).

As Robert Knight Barney has noted, 'most people in the world now recognize the Olympic five ring symbol. It appears on products we eat, drink, drive, wear, and otherwise use in our daily lives' (Barney 1992a: 628). When the Olympic movement's symbol is, with the permission of the IOC,[20] integrated in a design 'with another distinctive element', the result is described as an Olympic emblem (IOC 8 August 2004). For instance:

> The official emblem of Beijing 2008 entitled 'Chinese Seal – Dancing Beijing' cleverly combines the Chinese seal and the art of calligraphy with sporting features, transforming the elements into a human figure running forward and embracing triumph. The figure resembles the Chinese character 'Jing', which stands for the name of the host city and represents a particularly significant Chinese style. The artwork embodies four messages: Chinese culture; the color of red China; Beijing welcomes friends from all over the world; [and] the Olympic motto of 'Citius, Altius, Fortius' (Faster, Higher, Stronger).
>
> (IOC 24 February 2006; see also BOCOG 29 October 2005)

An extensive amount has been written about the Olympic movement's symbol, emblems and other icons, or graphic devices, as well as those of other bodies, including on their purpose, impact and categorization. For instance, while some, such as Greg Andranovich (Andranovich et al. 2001: 114) and Robert Knight Barney (Barney 1992a: 629), refer to the Olympic movement's five-ring symbol as a *logo*, others – and especially *purists* – will not regard it as a *logo* because it is not a *word* or *letter* graphic. The *Concise Oxford Dictionary of Current English* defines a *logotype* as *an emblem or device used as the badge of an organization*, while pointing out that the etymology, root or origin of the term can be traced to the Greek word 'logos', meaning *word* (Allen 1990: 698). A logotype, or logo, is a *textual* graphic device used to identify an entity, such as an organization, and to distinguish this from other entities. A graphic device which is *non-textual* or which is a combination of textual and non-textual elements is not a logo. Still, logos, non-textual graphic devices and combinations of the two are all used in a similar way to help identify and distinguish organizations, including in the form of, for example, company-marks, brand-marks and trade-marks. These marks, or marques, are the graphic devices by which commercial enterprises identify, distinguish and draw attention to themselves and their products, goods and services in connection with the process of marketing – of promoting, selling and exchanging their goods and services on the market in the pursuit of returns, revenues and profits. The McDonald's *golden arches* emblem is one of the best known and most widely recognized commercial logos (see Watson 1997), but others are those of Budweiser, Coca-Cola, General Electric, Johnson and Johnson, Kodak, Panasonic, Samsung, VISA and Volkswagen, all of which are *sponsoring corporations* of the 2008 Beijing Olympic Games. They will make financial contributions to the funding of the event, or more precisely of the Olympic movement, in return for securing privileges, such as 'marketing rights to the 2008 Olympic Games, the Chinese Olympic Committee and the Chinese

Olympic Teams' (BOCOG 21 February 2006). The sponsoring corporations also include Lenovo, a Chinese company the commercial logo of which is becoming increasingly well known due to the company's elevation to the position of the world's third biggest personal computer maker, helped by its purchase of IBM's personal computer division in April 2005 (BBC 10 May 2005), IBM having once been an Olympic sponsor. The 2008 Games sponsors also include companies with widely recognized commercial marques that entail non-textual elements, such as Adidas and Omega. Interestingly, however, they do not include any companies with commercial marques that are purely non-textual, of the kind used by such well-known multinational, transnational or global-reach corporations as Apple, Mercedes, Nike, Rolex and Shell.

The recognition enjoyed by the marques, or promotional graphic devices, of such major commercial enterprises – or mega-brands (Andranovich et al. 2001: 114)[21] – as McDonald's, Coca-Cola, Nike and Shell seems to extend to a few other bodies, including the Red Cross, the United Nations and the Olympic movement, each of which is a mega-organization of the non-commercial kind, at least in principle, formally or notionally. In practice, it is difficult to escape the conclusion that some if not all of this category of organizations are themselves largely commercial in orientation, as a result of which their promotional graphic devices will qualify as commercial marques. This applies to the Olympic movement. After all, as one NOC has pointed out, the 'only source of financial support the IOC [has] is private funding', through mainly 'the sale of television rights and marketing programmes' (BOA 21 February 2006). For instance, the US television company NBC alone paid the IOC US$456 million for the US rights to the 1996 Atlanta Games, US$705 million for the US rights to the 2000 Sydney Games (ibid.), and US$793 million for the US rights to the 2004 Athens Games, when it proceeded to broadcast over 1200 hours of coverage, three times the number four years earlier (Crawford 30 August 2004).

The marketing programmes are even more lucrative. Corporate sponsorship has become a major source of revenue for the Olympic movement, especially since the 1984 Los Angeles Games and even more so since 1985 when the IOC launched TOP, its 'world-wide sponsorship programme', the intention being 'to establish a diversified revenue base for the Olympic Games and the Olympic movement', in return for which 'TOP sponsors, all multinational corporations', enjoy various rights, including that of being able to use the Olympic symbol on their products (BOA 21 February 2006). The Olympic movement generates revenue through five distinct programmes, partly managed by the IOC and partly by the Organising Committees for the Olympic Games (OCOGs). The IOC manages broadcast partnerships and the worldwide sponsorship programme, whereas the OCOGs manage the domestic sponsorship, ticketing and licensing programmes, albeit under the direction of the IOC. In these ways, the Olympic movement received over

US$4 billion during the 2001 to 2004 period, overlapping as this did with the start of the 2004 to 2008 Beijing Olympiad. Grasping its turn, the Beijing Organizing Committee for the Olympic Games of the XXIX Olympiad (BOCOG) has been quick off the mark in *marketing Beijing 2008* (BOCOG 22 February 2006). Thus:

> Through the Games, China and the world will be bound closer together than ever. Looking ahead to 2008, it is clear that the opportunities are vast. In staging [the] most memorable Games in history, the Beijing Organizing Committee (BOCOG) will provide its corporate partners with an opportunity to invite the world in and introduce China to the world. A poll conducted by the Beijing 2008 Olympic Games Bid Committee showed that 94.6% of the Chinese people supported the bid. This huge good will and enthusiastic support of the Games will translate into exceptionally high levels of recognition and support across the country for those companies who sponsor the Games. For international entities looking to expand into the thriving Chinese marketplace, a partnership with the 2008 Olympic Games will deliver a powerful business opportunity for growth, and product/service showcasing while serving to strengthen and build ties of friendship throughout China. For Chinese firms, the Olympic Games provide an honorable opportunity to enhance their image and demonstrate their strengths in key technologies, products and services while gaining recognition for their commitment to China's national quest for professional excellence in all realms of business. The journey begins here. It is a journey toward unbounded opportunities, toward the most dynamic economy and most promising marketplace in the world.
>
> (BOCOG 21 February 2006)

While the declared, or overt, mission of the Olympic movement with the help of NOCs, such as the Chinese National Olympic Committee (COC) – which describes itself as 'a non-governmental, non-profit national sports organization of a mass character' (see COC 2006) – is to promote Olympism, it is difficult not to conclude that the movement has other equally, if not more, important missions. In particular, there are those goals that are being pursued in conjunction with the 'increasing corporatization of the Games' (Short 2003), a development which has been neatly summarized as follows:

> Corporatization of the Olympics accelerated after 1983. Professional athletes were allowed to compete, and the Olympic logo was allowed to be associated with corporations. This change in Olympic policy opened the market floodgates. As a result selling the corporate sponsorship rights to the Games has become big business.
>
> (Abbs 20 June 2005)

For John Short, the corporatization of the Olympic Games is both, as he puts it, implicit and explicit. It occurs implicitly, or incidentally, 'through the interlinked directorships and [other] connections of the IOC members' (*ibid.*; see also Barney et al. 1999, et al. 2002; IOC 25 February 2006). What Short identifies as 'developers and financiers' make up the bulk of the membership of the IOC, 'and their business interests mesh seamlessly with their Olympics position' (Short 2003; see also Jennings, A. 1996). More explicitly, or directly, the corporatization of the Olympics is attributable to the 'role of corporations in the funding and directing of the Games', especially since the 1984 Los Angeles event, but also ever since 1896, when the Games 'relied upon a businessman, George Averoff, to finance the refurbishment of the Olympic stadium in Athens' (Short 2003; see also Coubertin 1978). More recently, the 1960 Rome Olympics were supported by '46 private sponsors' (Short 2003 see also Davies, E.L. 1996); the 1976 Montreal Games were associated with '168 official products'; and the 1980 Moscow event benefited from the endorsement of 200 products (Short 2003; see also Barrett 1980). At the same time, however, the part played by corporate sponsorship in the staging of the Games has 'changed dramatically' since 1984, having become 'more dominant' (Short 2003). As Short puts it, the 1984 Los Angeles Olympics were 'the first truly corporate Games', with 20 per cent of the US$1124 million in total revenues coming from corporate sponsorship. These Games 'marked the beginning of an upward trend in corporate funding', so that in the case of the 1996 Atlanta Games, almost 30 per cent of the US$1686 million in total revenues came from corporate sponsorship (*ibid.*).

Subsequently, a significant feature of the corporatization process of the Olympics is the way in which it 'has involved a narrowing of the business interests to a few giant, global corporations' (*ibid.*). In 1976, 742 business 'enterprises advertised with the Olympic Games', but in 2000 at Sydney the number had fallen to less than 100 (*ibid.*). For Short, this development has important implications:

> There has been a narrowing and deepening of corporate sponsorship. For the top corporate sponsors, the global coverage of the Olympic Games provides the opportunity to spread global recognition and appreciation of their products and services. The Games have become an important vehicle of economic globalization, a platform for the penetration of selected corporations into global markets and global consciousness. The increasing importance of major corporations to the IOC has affected IOC policies [. . .]. The corporate sponsorship has also influenced the siting of the Games. The major corporations have been very eager to get the Games into China as a strategy of promoting their products and name recognition to one of the largest faster growing markets in the world. Beijing came very close to getting the 2000 Games, which went to

Sydney. From the corporate standpoint there are only 17 million consumers in Australia but over a billion in China. It came as a relief, but
not much of a surprise, to the sponsors that Beijing was successful in
landing the 2008 Games.

(ibid.)

Essentially, one way of looking at the choice of Beijing to host the Games
is that it 'was in large measure driven by the need to find an entry into the
vast Chinese market' for corporate sponsors (ibid.). This interpretation of
the IOC's decision in favour of Beijing would seem to lend itself to the
conclusion of many observers that the main mission of the Olympic movement is not the professed one of promoting Olympism, at least for its own
sake, but instead that of pursuing the aims of the movement's corporate
stakeholders, and above all of the biggest of these, those stakeholders that
have acquired a controlling share in the movement as a commercial enterprise and corporate body. For instance, Maryann Abbs argues that those
'who promote the Olympics are interested in power, prestige and profit'
(Abbs 20 June 2005), their prizes for (politically) organizing and (economically) sponsoring an event. The pursuit of power, prestige and profit will be
the covert mission of the Olympic movement; will be the sub-text, sub-
narrative or sub-plot underlying the Olympic motto and creed, the doctrine
of Olympism, and the overall Olympic project. The overt mission will be
something of a ruse, deception or smokescreen, facilitating the ability of the
organizers and sponsors to realize their own sectional interests, aims and
rewards whatever the costs to others, local inhabitants, taxpayers, and so on.

In a similar way to Abbs, Jean-Marie Brohm suggests that the 'primary aim
of the organizers of sports or Olympic competitions is not sport for its own
sake but sport for capitalist profit; or rather, their aim is capitalist profit
through sport' (Brohm 1978: 137; quoted in Toohey and Veale 2000; see also
Staun 2003). Brohm, described as 'one of the most influential of the Marxist
sports critics' (Staun 2003), has portrayed the Olympic Games as 'a symbol
of "the capitalist sport-industry" ', and has set in motion an anti-Olympic
movement which 'seeks to aid all comrades, all trade union and political
organisations to develop the necessary anti-Olympic activity and expose the
Games for the masquerade they are' (Brohm 1978; quoted in Staun 2003).
He argues:

The Olympics serve to camouflage the class struggle. They are the
highest expression of the moronic sports spectacle, hammering home
the ideology of the ruling class. They are the most spectacular example
of the repressive functions of the institutions of sport which is a brake
on the struggle of workers everywhere against their bourgeoisies and
bureaucracies.

(ibid.)

For Brohm, the Olympic movement is a tool in the hands of the *ruling class* – the capitalist bourgeoisie and state bureaucrats – used to pursue the ruling class's interests, centred on profit and power, contrary to the interests of the working class. If so, then the ruling class would appear to have become (perhaps reflecting the circumstances of the post-Cold War *new world order*) quite open, carefree and even blasé about revealing its interests and *ideology*, at least if the following list of tributes is anything to go by:

> From building global participation, to creating financial stability, to providing opportunities for the world's best athletes – regardless of race, gender, or economic status – to compete in fair competition, President Samaranch's contributions have been truly remarkable.
>
> The Olympic Games – combining the world's best sporting performance, global participation, in close co-operation with the private sector and the media – have become the greatest event on earth, and contribute to the promotion of world peace. Your leadership and dedication were instrumental in achieving this.
>
> During your presidency, the creative collaboration of sports and business was expanded and intensified. It is alliances like these that will continue to advance the Olympic idea and ideals of peace and prosperity in the new millennium.
>
> During your historic tenure you have taken the Olympic Games to levels of recognition and respect which were almost incomprehensible at the time you assumed the Presidency of the IOC.
>
> Thanks to your support during the past fourteen years, our company has been able to achieve its objective, that is, to serve society on a global scale through our Audio and Video Technology. It has been an honour for us to contribute in the spirit of partnership, and we are pleased to continue to support the Games for the coming years.
>
> Among your contributions to the Olympic movement, the most remarkable one is, while maintaining the long-established tradition and prestige of the Olympic movement and on the other hand, to have brought success to it on a commercial base.
>
> Your impressive actions were all aimed at fortifying and positioning the Olympic Brand as a high-class, strong, moral, emotional brand with a clear message of peaceful, happy, healthy world competition in an international, tolerant and wonderful example for the youth of our planet and also for mankind in general.
>
> The IOC, under President Samaranch, has used sport as a means of making a more inclusive world. Sport and the resulting media attention has, by far, the most influential effect on the youth of the world and the IOC has used the Olympic Games to bring hope and a sense of belonging to all its inhabitants, specifically those engaged in warlike acts.
>
> (IOC July 2001b)

This highly flattering, if not obsequious, praise – from respectively Douglas Daft, Chairman and Chief Executive Officer of Coca-Cola Company; Yutaka Narita, President of the Dentsu corporation; Juergen Schrempp, Chairman of the Board of Management of Daimler Chrysler; George Fisher, retired Chairman and CEO of Kodak; Kazuhiko Sugiyama, Executive Vice President, Member of the Board, Matsushita Electric Industrial Company; Yoshihiro Yasui, Chairman of Brother Industries; Nicolas Hayek of the Swatch Group; and R. Stephen Rubin, President of the World Federation of the Sporting Goods Industry – was heaped upon Juan Antonio Samaranch on his retirement after 20 years as President of the IOC in 2001 (*ibid.*).[22] It indicates the strong ties of mutual interest that had developed between the Olympic movement and *big business* (see Sklair 2002a); how the movement had itself assumed the mantle of a business enterprise, and indeed a mega-enterprise; how the five-ring Olympic symbol had become a leading commercial logotype (see Barney et al. 2002); and how the Olympic Games and Olympiads had become *mega-events*.[23]

By the start of the twenty-first century, the Olympic Games were economic mega-events,[24] but not only this. They had also become political and cultural mega-events. As with all mega-events,[25] the Games have three principal social aspects, or dimensions: the economic, the political and the cultural.[26] Social phenomena in general have three basic dimensions, globalization being an example:

> The existence, extent, meaning and measurement of economic, political and cultural globalization have provided a rich and argumentative agenda for contemporary social theorising [see Short 2001]. A discussion of the Games provides an opportunity to consider a very concrete example of globalization. The Games not only actualize some of the forces and many of the paradoxes of globalization, they also exemplify the complex intersections of cultural and political, as well as the more commonly studied, economic globalization.
>
> (Short 2003; see also Axford 1995;
> Baylis and Smith 2004; Held et al. 1999)

The economic, political and cultural dimensions of Olympic Games as social events intersect in a complex manner, especially so due to the way in which they 'are embodied in at least three scales: global, national and local', while since 'their inauguration in 1896, they have become increasingly global' (Short 2003), and indeed above all *global*. Short is mainly concerned with how the 'modern Summer Olympic Games are global spectacles, national campaigns and city enterprises' (*ibid.*), at one and the same time; and thereby in the way in which the Games are the focus of 'connections between the global and the local' in an era of globalization (*ibid.*). The challenge for anyone trying to study, analyze and make sense of the Games will be to clarify the *complex intersections* of their economic, political and cultural dimensions at and between the different levels at which they are *embodied*, while taking into account how – in accordance with the progress of globalization – they are becoming more globalized (see Chamerois 2002). A notable contribution has been made by Greg Andranovich and his colleagues through their examination of the relationship between the 'global economy', and in particular 'increasing global economic competition', and 'urban politics' by way of, what they refer to as, 'a new and potentially high-risk strategy of stimulating local economy growth', namely 'the mega-event strategy' (Andranovich et al. 2001: 113). Their analysis draws on a comparison of 'the approaches taken by [. . .] three cities to bidding for and staging an Olympic mega-event': Los Angeles, 1984; Atlanta, 1996 (see also Bragg 1997; French and Disher 1997; Lenskyj 2001; Maloney 1996; Pingree 1996); and Salt Lake City, which hosted the Winter Games of 2002 (see also McKay and Plumb 2001; Preuss 2000). Further commendable work has been conducted by Maurice Roche, whose focus has been largely on the political and cultural dimensions of mega-events, but again in the context of broader social developments and in particular in relation to globalization.[27]

However, while there is a steadily expanding array of accounts addressing mega-events, so far there are next to none that have tried to tackle the issues of how to *theorize* them, how to relate mega-events both in general and by type, or genre, to globalization, and how best to clearly and consistently define 'mega-event' for the purpose of studying, analyzing and making sense of this social phenomenon (see, for example, Andranovich and Burbank 2004; Andranovich et al. 2001; Horne and Manzenreiter 2002, 2004; Manzenreiter and Horne 2004). Among the few exceptions in these respects is the work of Maurice Roche. In *Mega-events and Modernity* (Roche 2000), he 'explores the social history and politics of "mega-events" ' from the late nineteenth century to 'the current crisis of the Olympic movement in world politics and culture' (Roche 2000; see also Da Costa 2002; Lenskyj 2002; Senn 1999; cf. Hobermann 1986), such as by examining 'the ways in which these kinds of events have contributed to the meaning and development of "public culture", "cultural citizenship" and "cultural inclusion/exclusion" in society, at both the national and the international levels' (Roche 2000: 1). For Roche:

> The concept of 'mega-events' refers to specially constructed and staged international cultural and sports events such as the Olympic Games and World's Fairs (hereafter Expos). Mega-events are short-lived collective cultural actions ('ephemeral vistas'; [Greenhalgh 1988]) which nonetheless have long-lived pre- and post-event social dimensions. They are publicly perceived as having an 'extra-ordinary' status, among other things, by virtue of their very large scale, the time cycles in which they occur and their impacts [. . .].
>
> (Roche 2003: 99)[28]

This definition of 'mega-event' is a useful starting point – such as for studying the Beijing Olympics and Olympiad – while nevertheless presenting major difficulties when it comes to identifying mega-events in practice, empirically, given the problems of deciding what qualifies as 'very large', or for that matter 'large', and of establishing an event's *publicly perceived extra-ordinary status*. Essentially, these problems are about how to distinguish mega-events from non-mega-events other than intuitively and arbitrarily; and they bring to mind the question of whether Roche's approach to defining 'mega-event' is the *best* one. While, of course, there cannot be a *correct* definition of 'mega-event', there may be a *best* definition for the particular purpose at hand, such as that of studying, analyzing and making sense of Olympic Games. In so far as the aim is, for example, to understand the Beijing Olympics and Olympiad in relation to those matters that are integral to such things as globalization and *modernity* (*ibid.*: 100–1), then the question arises of whether Roche's approach to defining 'mega-event' best suits the purpose, or whether another approach would be better and even best.

Roche himself gives clues as to an alternative, perhaps more fruitful notion. He tells us, if somewhat tautologically, that mega-event 'genres have had an enduring mass popularity in modernity since their creation in the late 19th century and continue to do so in a period of globalization' (*ibid.*: 99). Here, Roche touches on an issue of major importance to the task of making sense of mega-events within *modernity*, if only because of its relevance to the quest for the best way of defining 'mega-event'. This is the issue of how to represent the relationship between possible mega-events such as Olympic Games, on the one hand, and concurrent social events, processes and developments that are likely to qualify as 'mega' simply by virtue of their *embodiment* (Short 2003) at the global level, and perhaps connectedly of their part in the processes of globalization, on the other.

Roche draws attention to the relationship between mega-events and globalization, including the relationship's temporal character. For Roche, it would seem, 'the mega-event phenomenon' (*ibid.*: 101) pre-dates globalization (*ibid.*: 99). Subsequently, it has endured under globalization, and indeed has been (positively or *eu-*) *functional* (*ibid.*: 100) in relation to this process, or set of processes, along with such accompanying phenomena as 'contemporary society' and 'modernity', and in particular 'late modernity' (*ibid.*: 100–1; see also Beck et al. 1995; Close 1995; Fornäs 1995; Giddens 1991). Here, there is a reminder of Short's point that the Olympic Games offer corporate sponsors an opportunity for greater product recognition, appreciation and sales; provide corporations with a platform for the greater *penetration of global markets and global consciousness*; and thereby act as a vehicle for economic globalization (Short 2003). Roche argues that mega-events, due to especially, 'but not exclusively, their temporal characteristics and what can be called their "dramaturgical" features and appeal' (Roche 2003: 101), constitute 'resources for sustaining personal time structure in contemporary conditions that threaten this' (*ibid.*: 101). For Roche, 'the main structures of meaning that continue to be associated with mega-events in modernity' (*ibid.*: 101) are *functional* in relation to personal and interpersonal 'identity' (*ibid.*: 101). Roche claims that these *structures* are highly 'relevant to the understanding of mega-events' (*ibid.*: 101) in that they help account for the way in which mega-events functionally relate to, facilitate and support the 'microsocial' processes (*ibid.*: 100) of 'what phenomenological sociology refers to as the "life world" ' (*ibid.*: 100), on the one hand, and the ' "macrosocial" systems' that entail, for instance, globalization processes, on the other. Mega-events have become *functional* in relation to both, and so bridge the microsocial and macrosocial spheres from within the intermediary ' "mesosocial" sphere in contemporary society' (*ibid.*: 100; see also Kelle 2001).[29]

Roche tells us:

> Mega-event genres were born in the late 19th century during a period of national building and empire building in the industrializing capitalist societies of the USA and Western Europe. This period has been [. . .] portrayed by Eric Hobsbawm (1992) as being characterized by a wave of 'inventions of tradition', and he refers to sports and expositions as leading examples of such cultural invention [. . .]. [The] enduring popularity and institutionalization of mega-event genres in national societies and in international and global society since that 'early modern' period derives from their social functions for elites and mass publics [. . .]. [The] periodic production of particular mega-events can be usefully understood as the production of intermediate 'meso-sphere' processes, involving sociotemporal 'hubs' and 'exchanges' in the economic, cultural and [other] 'flows' and 'networks' which can be said to contribute to the current development [. . .] of culture and society at the global level. It is on this basis that [. . .] mega-event movements such as the Olympic [movement] can be usefully understood as important [. . .] roles in the cultural aspects of contemporary global-level governance and institution building [see Roche 2000: Chapter 7].
>
> (Roche 2003: 100–1)

The ' "mesosocial" sphere in contemporary society' is 'the intermediary sphere through which the life world, and its "microsocial" processes, is connected with "macrosocial" systems [. . .] and change' (*ibid*: 100), where the 'life world' is the sphere of in particular 'personal identity formation' (*ibid*: 100); and the macrosocial sphere includes the activities and processes of 'global-level governance and institution building' as befits 'global society'. Within the mesosocial sphere, mega-events constitute *exchange hubs* in the economic, political and cultural networks and flows of social life within and between the microsocial and macrosocial spheres. Here, however, in so far as mega-events will not be the only exchange hubs within the mesosocial sphere, the question arises of how to distinguish mega-events from the rest. For Roche, it would seem, the answer is that mega-events are of a *very large scale* and, connectedly, are *publicly perceived as having an 'extra-ordinary' status* (ibid.: 99). But, given the problems of confidently deciding which events qualify as 'very large' and which are *perceived as extra-ordinary*, what about distinguishing and defining mega-events in some other, perhaps more sociologically pertinent, sound and valuable way? What about, for instance, defining them as being those, and only those, events that are so large that they themselves have a global status, reach or scope? As such, mega-events will be distinctive by being the only mesosocial sphere events which also have a presence within the macrosocial sphere. Mega-events defined, distinguished and identified as global – or *globalized* – events will not merely accompany globalization; instead, they will be integral features of globalization.

The *globalizational* approach to the mega-event notion has been alluded to by a range of writers, including Alan Tomlinson and Christopher Young in their account of the relationship between politics, culture and national identity, on the one hand, and what they refer to as *global sports events*, in particular the Olympics and the World Cup, on the other (Tomlinson and Young 2005); and John Horne and Wolfram Manzenreiter in the introduction to their assessment of the impact of the 2002 FIFA World Cup finals on the host countries, Japan and Korea. Here we are told: 'three aspects are discussed: the specific regional political economy of the 2002 World Cup; the role of sports mega-events in identity construction and promotion; and how such events are both constituted by and constitutive of globalization' (Horne and Manzenreiter 2002: 187). If mega-events are *constitutive* of globalization, then it follows that they will be global events, and can be identified, distinguished and defined as such. Essentially, an event will be a mega-event if it is, in the first place, a 'global event' (Short 2003).

Mega-events may be functional in relation to or may have a symbiotic relationship with globalization, but as global events themselves. They will be *concrete examples*, or *embodiments*, of globalization (ibid.). In particular: 'Sport, like English, has become a global language and globalization is embodied in such international sport practices as the Olympic Games' (ibid.). Accordingly, mega-events will resemble a range of other macrosocial entities, including the United Nations (UN), World Health Organization (WHO), International Criminal Court (ICC), International Labour Organization (ILO), World Bank, International Monetary Fund (IMF) and World Trade Organization (WTO). Sporting mega-events will belong to a particular macrosocial genre; as mega-events, they will represent yet other macrosocial phenomena. World Cup competitions as mega-events will represent FIFA as a globalized organization; and Olympic Games will represent the IOC as a globalized organization, the Olympic movement as a globalized social movement, and Olympism as a globalized world view, doctrine or philosophy.

But, adopting the *globalizational* approach to mega-events may result in some of the events which Roche takes to be mega-events being left out of the frame. It may mean excluding all Expos as well as some FIFA World Cup finals, and even some Olympic Games. It cannot be assumed, as Roche appears to do, that events qualify as mega-events merely because they aspire to qualify as such, or because their successor events qualify, or because their antecedents were mega-events. In whatever way 'mega-event' is defined, whether a particular event can be counted as a mega-event will be an empirical matter, and this may mean that the earliest Olympic Games were not mega-events, in that they did not have the required global status, reach or scope. Indeed, even when judged with reference to the *operational criteria* specified by Roche, the earliest Games are far from obvious candidates for the accolade 'mega-event'.

For Short, it was only at the 2000 Sydney Games, when 'there were athletes from 199 countries', and so 'most countries of the world competed', that the Olympic Games 'had become truly global' (*ibid.*). Although the first modern Olympic Games 'was an important national event', the event 'had limited international impact (*ibid.*). In the early years, the Games 'were not then a global phenomenon', an 'early limiting factor to the global diffusion of the Olympic Games [being] the cost and difficulty of international travel' (*ibid.*). According to Short, it 'took a long while for the Games to become global spectacles and the process is intertwined with [the] development of mass media, particularly television' (*ibid.*). Thus:

> The growth of the Games and their increasing globalization was connected closely to television coverage that could transmit the images worldwide. For the 1960 Rome Games, CBS paid $660,000 for the right to fly film from Rome to New York, while Eurovision transmitted the first live coverage of the Games. The Italian IOC earned $1.2 million from the deal. There has been a steady increase in the coverage ever since. Only 21 countries saw television coverage of the Rome Games, but by Atlanta in 1996, this had increased to 214. Few countries in the world are unable to see the Summer Olympics. More than 3.7 billion people watched the Sydney Olympics from 220 countries. The typical viewer watches the Games 11 times, resulting in a combined viewing audience estimated at 36 billion. Selling television rights has become an increasingly important part of funding the Games. In Munich in 1972 less than 10% of the revenue of the Games came from television companies, but by Atlanta in 1996 this had increased to almost 40%. The absolute amounts have grown on average 30% each Olympiad, from $40 million in 1972 to $556 million in Atlanta. In a package deal, the NBC paid $3.5 billion to cover the Sydney Olympics, Athens, and Beijing as well as the winter Games of 2002 and 2006. Television revenues currently provide 55% of all IOC's marketing revenue. US TV companies, in particular,

account for 60% of the total world-wide rights. The Summer Games are now thoroughly corporatized, providing a huge global audience of consumers and a global opportunity to sell goods and services around the world.

(*ibid.*)

Even now, the global-spectacle notion of the Games 'needs to be treated with some care'. This is because the Games will be 'seen differently in different parts of the world' through the eyes of many different 'national audiences' (Tomlinson 1996). For example, while an audience in Hungary 'can see hours of fencing', in the USA, this sport 'scarcely merits much attention'. In each case, the television 'coverage concentrates on [the local] national teams and representatives', so that 'people in different countries [will] quite literally see different Olympics' (Short 2003). The Olympic Games 'are a global spectacle', but 'a nationally biased' and, connectedly, 'commercially driven global spectacle' (*ibid.*). There is a sense in which the Games have become highly globalized, mega-events and spectacles while, at the same time, remaining deeply localized events, and not just within the places, cities and countries where they are being hosted, but also within every place and 'nation' where they are being observed through local, national and otherwise parochial *spectacle lenses*.

Not unconnectedly, there is a sense in which by having become globalized, the Games if anything 'intensify national feelings rather than transcend them' (*ibid.*). In that the 'Games celebrate national identity' (*ibid.*), and do so in an intensely competitive manner, as mega-events and global spectacles they will do more than merely channel nationalism; they will emphasize, exaggerate and reinforce nationalism. Moreover, they will do this contrary to any tendency under the sway of globalization towards a global society, or more to the point a 'global community' (*ibid.*), of the kind presumably sought by those who want to convert the world to Olympism (see Chapters 2, 3 and 4 of this book).

If the early modern Olympic Games fell short of qualifying as mega-events, then this may reflect the way in which globalization either had still to get underway (as inferred by Roche) or was still in its relatively early stages. For some, while globalization has a long, centuries-old history, it nonetheless took off and rapidly progressed on a significantly higher plane during the 1960s, which therefore mark the start of the distinctive *era of globalization*.[30] If so, then the earliest mega-events, sporting or otherwise, will have occurred at around the same time, during the 1960s. The first mega-event of any genre may have been the 1964 Tokyo Olympics, and the second may have been the 1966 FIFA World Cup.[31] Moreover, it could be that the Olympic Games and FIFA World Cup competitions remain the only events that warrant being called 'mega-events', with each of these examples vying with the other for the lead position. While the Games are probably the biggest mega-events,[32] World Cup competitions are certainly the biggest single-sport mega-events;[33]

and there seems little doubt that the Beijing Games will be the greatest mega-event of all time, at least for a while (see Chapters 2, 3 and 4).

The *globalizational* approach to defining mega-events is a way of more accurately registering the parts played by Olympic Games among other events in the processes of globalization, and so of helping to ensure that these events receive the kind of recognition and status they deserve as *hallmark events* of globalization (Roche 2003: 120; see also Syme et al. 1989), and indeed as *the* hallmark – or flagship (Roche 2000) – events of globalization. Mega-events, sporting and any other genre, will symbolize, signal and substantively embody the progress of globalization as a set of processes along three basic social dimensions: the economic, the political and the cultural (Axford 1995; Baylis and Smith 2004; Held et al. 1999; Short 2003); and the way this progress has gathered momentum and gained greater impact in a *tsunami-like* manner.

What is more, the *globalizational* approach lends itself to a re-conceptualization of the boundaries around mega-events; and, more specifically, to counting portions of the *temporal space* around Olympic Games and FIFA World Cup finals as inclusive parts of the mega-events involved. According to Roche, *mega-events are short-lived but have long-lived pre-event and post-event social dimensions* (Roche 2003: 99). If so, then what about regarding these social dimensions as links within mega-events; links whereby an Olympic Games or a World Cup final is so intimately entwined with its prequel, say, that both constitute integral parts of a particular mega-event? What about taking the start of any World Cup mega-event to coincide with the opening of the pre-finals knockout competition; and the start of any Olympic Games mega-event to coincide with the opening of its Olympiad? Greg Andranovich has hinted at treating Olympic Games as integral parts of more inclusive mega-events:

> A mega-event strategy unfolds over a considerable period of time; typically there is a decade between launching a bid and the closing ceremonies and, of course, the legacy of the event can last for many more years. To facilitate comparison [. . .], we divide the Olympic mega-events into three periods: the bid process, the organization period, and the legacy of the Olympics.
>
> (Andranovich et al. 2001: 118)

An Olympiad is the four-year period between the close of one modern Summer Olympic Games and the closing of the next, as exemplified by the interval between the closing ceremony of the 2004 Athens Games and the closing ceremony of the 2008 Beijing Games. If Olympiads rather than just the Games of Olympiads are viewed as mega-events, then this will mean of course that Olympiads will follow on from each other in tandem, as an unbroken chain of abutting sporting mega-events, at least in so far as and for as long as Olympiads remain global in their status. The evidence so far is that the 2004–8 Olympiad will serve to further consolidate and enhance the global status of Olympiads; and the initial signs are that the subsequent Olympiad culminating in the 2012 London Games will do the same. If the *globalizational* approach to defining 'mega-event' is adopted, then the Beijing Olympiad may well turn out to be the greatest, most spectacular mega-event, sporting or otherwise, of all time. If so, then the question arises of whether the Beijing Olympiad's standing in this regard will be long lasting or merely short lived; of whether the Beijing Olympiad is destined to be up-staged by the follow-on London Olympiad, as might be expected given the prevailing thrust of globalization.

While the relationship between the Olympics (the collective term for Olympic Games, Olympiads, the Olympic movement, and Olympism) and globalization will not be a unidirectional, functional one, but instead a two-way, mutually supporting, symbiotic inter-action, the Olympics will be far more reducible to globalization than vice versa. The Olympics will be largely shaped by globalization, and perhaps especially economic globalization, and so in turn by those considerations, factors and forces that underpin, drive and determine globalization processes. In this regard, Roche tells us that the 'enduring popularity and institutionalization of mega-event genres in national societies and in international and global society since [the] "early modern" period derives from their social functions for elites and mass publics' (Roche 2003: 100). Here, Roche touches on what could be the key to making sense of mega-events in whatever way they are defined. It may be that the form, content and development of mega-events, on the one hand, are largely explicable in terms of prevailing distributions of power, configurations of power players, relationships between *elites* and mass publics, and social class systems, on the other. While mega-events 'are large-scale cultural (including commercial and sporting) events which have a dramatic character, mass popular appeal and international significance', they 'are typically organized by variable combinations of national governmental and international non-governmental organizations and thus can be said to be important elements in "official" versions of public culture' (Roche 2000: 1). For Roche, mega-events are managed by the combined forces of state apparatuses and non-state, civil society organizations (CSOs), such as the IOC, in a manner which suits the cultures, world views and missions with which they are associated. While mega-events 'provide ordinary people with opportunities to connect with and affirm or contest collective identities', the same events also – and perhaps primarily – 'provide power elites with "flagships" and catalysts to promote their visions of society and of the future' (Roche 2000).

There is a reminder here of the argument that while the declared mission of the Olympic movement is to promote Olympism, the more important missions are those being pursued through the 'increasing corporatization of the Games' (Short 2003), attributable as this is to the 'role of corporations in the funding and direction of the Games' (*ibid.*) and, not unconnectedly, the consequences of the 'interlinked directorships and [other] connections of the IOC members' (*ibid.*). As Short has put it, the Olympic Games were originally 'organized along elitist, masculinist principles' (*ibid.*). The Games 'were initially organized along exclusionary principles'; were 'biased in both class and gender terms' (*ibid.*). Membership of the IOC was 'by invitation from a small pool of rich, white men' and was 'consciously insulated from any electoral process' (*ibid.*). The result was a 'governing body' of men who were 'rich, titled or well-connected', and 'preferably all three' (*ibid.*). Although by 2002, 'the membership had widened to 123 members from 82 countries' and there was 'only a smattering of the titles' – a Princess, a Princess Royal, a Dona Infante, and a Grand Duke – there were 'still only seven women', and it was still 'dominated by the rich and the connected' (*ibid.*). Thus:

> The biographies listed at the IOC website reveal a membership dominated by rich business people: corporate lawyers, presidents of business groups and company directors figure largely [see IOC 25 February 2006]. The IOC is not a representative body: it is a rich man's club in which personal and business connections wrap around Olympic business [Jennings, A. 1996; Jennings and Sambrook 2000]. One example: Juan Antonio Samaranch, from Barcelona, became President of the IOC in 1980. In October 1986 Barcelona was awarded the 1992 Summer Olympic Games. In 1987 [Samaranch] also became president of the largest Catalan financial institution *La Caixa* and three years later became president of the expanded institution, *La Caja de Ahores de Barcelona*.
>
> (Short 2003)

Especially since the end of the Cold War, 'the discourse of democratisation has swept the world, but the IOC remains largely insulated from democratic accountability' (*ibid.*). In a similar way to the IMF, World Bank and WTO, 'the IOC stands as an important, undemocratic, unaccountable globalizing organization' (*ibid.*). The IOC 'remains an elitist organization' (*ibid.*). With its headquarters in Lausanne Switzerland, the IOC resembles 'an unelected para-state, insulated from reform' (*ibid.*). This is not to ignore the way in which there 'has been some minor reform in recent years, prompted by the scandals of corruption discovered in the bid of Salt Lake City' (*ibid.*). As cities became more 'desperate to land the Games' and each member of the IOC 'held an all-important vote that they could cast in secret', the cities became more 'lavish with their hospitality, and many delegates [. . .] eager to cash in on their voting power' (*ibid.*). It emerged that the IOC neither made 'checks on members visiting the cities' nor had any 'ethical guidelines in place' (*ibid.*; see also Calvert 2002). Consequently:

The system was corrupt endemically, with delegates leveraging more and more lavish gifts from cities' boosters increasingly eager to lubricate their bid with generous 'hospitality'. One IOC member was routinely referred to as the 'human vacuum cleaner' for his ability to suck up money, gifts, holidays, flights and medical attention for him and his family.

(Short 2003)

In November and December1998, it was alleged that bids for the 1992 Winter Games had been supported by 'massive corruption', with 'as many as 25 IOC members [having] had their votes bought by [the] bid cities' (*ibid.*). Consequently, an 'IOC Commission was quickly formed in response to media pressure and especially to the worries of corporate sponsors that their products would be tainted with the label of corruption' (*ibid.*). In 1999:

the Commission reported that seven IOC members were to be expelled, including Jean-Claude Ganga of the Congo, General Gadir of Sudan, Sergio Fantani of Chile and Augustin Arroyo of Ecuador. Ten more IOC members were warned about their behaviour; two were exonerated. The scandal brought the scrutiny of media attention to the lavish life style of IOC members who, it was revealed for the first time, were given business class flights to the Games and full time drivers and luxury cars during their stays. They were installed in luxury accommodations with specific requirements for fresh flowers to be placed in their rooms each day of their residence. These requirements are in heavy contrast to the more Spartan accommodations and basic conditions afforded to the athletes of the Games. The penchant for President Samaranch to be referred to as 'His Excellency' was symptomatic of an unelected, unaccountable para-state grown heavy and fat with excessive entitlements. The IOC members expected and were granted the privileged lifestyle of the global elite.

(*ibid.*)

Perhaps the members of the IOC acted and were feted as if they were members of *the global elite* simply because that is precisely what they were. Certainly, there were elites at the 'local' and global levels that ran, managed or governed Olympic Games and Olympiads by virtue of their control over the Olympic movement, including through their membership of 'local' NOCs and especially of the *global* IOC, 'the supreme authority of the Olympic movement' (IOC 25 February 2006). In the first instance, these will have been *political elites*, although their power will have been rooted in both political spheres and economic spheres at the 'local' and global levels. Certainly also, there are still *power elites* that govern Olympic Games and Olympiads by virtue of their control of the Olympic movement, just as there will be power elites that govern any other early twenty-first century mega-events; and the evidence suggests that, above all, there is an evolving and strengthening *global power elite*, an elite the power of which is rooted in the advance of the *global political economy* in accordance with the progress of globalization.

Guided by Maurice Roche and John Short, power elites govern, even dictate, Olympic Games and Olympiads; and, with the help of these events, also enjoy and exercise power and control over *the rest*, the *non-elites*, or *the ordinary people*. While these elites may be doing this in part to convert the world to Olympism, they will also be doing it in pursuit of the corporatization of the Games, and so in support of globalization, and of their own interests, and so in order to retain, consolidate and augment their power. But, in that their power is rooted in the political economy, then the question arises of how these elites relate to other social factions whose power sources are the same; and in particular to that social faction which Jean-Marie Brohm has referred to as the *ruling class*, given its dependency upon and so interests in such things as *capitalist profit*, *capitalist profit through sport*, *the capitalist sport-industry*, and *capitalist ideology* (Brohm 1978; see also Staun 2003; Toohey and Veale 2000).

When Roche suggests that the analysis of mega-events can 'benefit from perspectives that emphasize their explicitly ideological aspirations and potentially hegemonic impact' (Roche 2003: 100; see also Roche 2000; Rydell 1984, 1993), might he have added that the ideology and hegemony involved reflect and reinforce the interests of a ruling class, or a set of *interlinked* (Short 2003) ruling classes, the power of which can be traced to political economy patterns, processes and trends, and so increasingly to the evolving global political economy?[34] Are some if not all power elites, in particular those that govern mega-events, actually ruling classes whose power derives from their ownership and control of the means of production at various social levels, but increasingly their ownership and control at the global level by way of such devices as multinational, transnational and global-reach corporations? It is possible that the power elites which govern Olympic Games and Olympiads are the same social factions, and in particular the same ruling classes, that are mainly in charge of steering globalization in accordance with the imperatives of economic globalization, the more central and most influential dimension of globalization relative to the political and cultural processes (see Axford, 1995; Baylis and Smith, 2004; Held et al. 1999):

> Globalization is the set of processes, whereby – facilitated by enhanced global flows of such things as industry, investment, individuals and information (Ohmae 1990, 1995) – the world is becoming structurally (economically and politically) more integrated (see Baylis and Smith 2004) and culturally (ideationally) more homogenized (cf. Berger and Huntington 2002). The world is becoming, in other words, a 'borderless' (Ohmae 1990), 'single place' (Robertson 1992; Scholte 2000).

> Ideationally, globalization is the vehicle whereby the 'Western cultural account' [Axford 1995; Meyer et al. 1987] is being globally diffused, if somewhat unevenly and erratically. Western cultural forms, expressions and items are being adopted, albeit at different speeds, more or less everywhere including throughout East Asia (see Kim 2000). The growing popularity of football (otherwise known as *soccer*) in East Asia matches what is occurring elsewhere in the world, and provides a highly instructive example of how the Western cultural account is being presented, or purveyed, to and acquired by a significant non-Western *Other* [. . .]. In East Asia as elsewhere, the Western cultural account is interacting with local cultures [. . .]. The results are syntheses of the global and the local [. . .].
>
> (Close and Askew 2004b: 243–4)

This statement about globalization and its relationship with culture, the Western cultural account, local cultures and football should not be read as if the various, contending definitions of, discourses on and debates about globalization are being ignored. Close and Askew recognize how the process of cultural globalization through the interaction between the Western cultural account and local cultures entails not only acceptance and compliance, but also rejection and resistance. At the local level, there is a range of responses and results, including conformity and homogenization, on the one hand, and localization, playback and *glocalization*, on the other (see Lechner and Boli 2005).

Close and Askew's statement about globalization was written about football in general, but with the 2002 FIFA World Cup co-hosted by Japan and Korea in mind in particular. Something very much like it could be said about many other sports and sporting events,[35] including perhaps above all about the 2008 Beijing Olympic Games and the 2004–8 Beijing Oympiad (see Chapters 2, 3 and 4).[36] It is to be expected that the distinctive 'local' culture, or cultures, of China will be far from simply swept aside and away by globalization and the Western cultural account with the assistance of the Beijing Games. Instead, the 'local' will make an appearance at, will make its presence felt during, and will impose itself upon this sporting extravaganza; will ensure that the Western cultural account content of globalization is somewhat localized; and will to some extent be played back on, influencing, globalization through the process of *glocalization* (see De Moragas Spa et al. 2004).

But also what cannot be ignored is how the processes of globalization, localization and glocalization will take place in the context of determining distributions of power and, connectedly, property, whereby Chinese cultures may be sacrificed by the powerful and propertied in their own factional interests. This would be consistent, after all, with that global pattern whereby globalization is being steered by power elites, or ruling classes, largely in pursuit of their own specific interests at the expense of many local cultures, world views and sensitivities, environmental and ecological needs, and reduction of global inequalities, deprivations and associated ominous divisions:

> Extreme poverty remains a daily reality for more than 1 billion people who subsist on less than $1 a day. Hunger and malnutrition are almost equally pervasive: more than 800 million people have too little to eat to meet their daily energy needs [. . .]. More than a quarter of children under age 5 in developing countries are malnourished. [In] the worst-affected regions – sub-Saharan Africa and Southern Asia – the number of hungry people has increased by tens of millions [. . .]. Most of the world's hungry live in rural areas and depend on the consumption and sale of natural products for both their income and their food. Hunger tends to be concentrated among the landless or among farmers whose plots are too small to provide for their needs [. . .]. Hunger and poverty [. . .] can provide fertile ground for conflict.
>
> (DESA 2005: 6–9)

It is likely that few, if any, of the global poor will be among those who will participate in the 2008 Beijing Olympics, if only as television viewers. As Short has pointed out, in the early years, the 'Coubertin international project was restricted to few countries, essentially the richer countries of Europe and the US' (Short 2003). At the global level, the 'partial nature of the early Olympics was [very much] due to differences in wealth' (*ibid.*). While the Games 'have broadened in participation', still 'both athletic success and the hosting of the Games reflect the global inequalities in wealth' (*ibid.*). Quite simply, 'richer countries can send more athletes and can afford the necessary expenditure in sports development and training that ensures success' (*ibid.*), the result being their disproportionate success at the Games when judged in terms of their medals tally. Of the 927 medals won at the 2000 Sydney Games, 357 were won by just five countries: 96 by the USA, 88 by Russia, 59 by China, 58 by Australia and 56 by Germany. Fifty per cent (463) of the medals were won by competitors from Europe and North America; while just over 2 per cent (50) were won by those from sub-Saharan African countries (*ibid.*). In effect:

> Success at the Olympic Games reflects wealth and national spending on sports. Countries with few resources and little spending are less successful [. . .]. Even as participation in the Games becomes more global, success at the Games becomes more uneven. In effect, the Games reinforce the unequal distribution of resources in the world by the unequal participation of different countries and their unequal success in standing on the medal podium.
>
> (*ibid.*)

Likewise, many or most of the poor of sub-Saharan Africa and the rest of the world will be excluded from participating in the Games by their poverty and by all that contributes to and helps explain and sustain their poverty. Even if they are interested, they will not be able to see or otherwise follow the Games either at all or to anything like the degree to which the more privileged, propertied and powerful parts of the world are able to do. Still, the aims, missions and interests of those who variously run the event will be served, with many of these factions becoming yet more propertied and powerful in the process. The *North–South* divide will remain, and may even become wider, deeper and more entrenched, not helped by the way in which certain one-time Third World countries have achieved considerable gains within the post-Cold War, *new world order* distributions of property and power at both the regional and global levels. This applies to India and, even more so, to China, which has experienced a dramatic rise in its standing relative to other global political-economy power players, its re-entry onto the world stage as a global superpower seemingly all but guaranteed. What was the Third World and is now the South has lost a significant coterie of principal, front-line advocates in the competition, confrontation and conflict which continues to characterize the evolving global political economy. It would not be surprising to discover that those who remain trapped in the South's cycle of poverty will lament China giving in to the global march of market capitalism and, not unconnectedly, being seduced by the lure of the Olympics.

It is to be expected that the shifts in the pattern of political economy relations, including of so-called international relations, that have marked the end of the Cold War – and, for some, the victory and vindication of the West[37] – and the subsequent unfolding of the *new world order* in step with the onward march of globalization will be variously reflected in the character, course and consequences of the 2004–8 Beijing Olympiad.[38] The Beijing Olympiad will present an *extra-ordinary* opportunity to study, analyze and make sense of these developments, an opportunity exploited in the rest of this book.

Chapter 2

Olympism, individualism and nationalism

When astronaut Yang Liwei rocketed into space on China's first manned spaceflight, he carried with him the 2008 Beijing Olympic Games banner and China's national flag. Just like the spaceflight, China's award of the Olympic Games represents the coming of age for this growing world superpower. On this historic flight the Olympic Games logo was flown high. But the Chinese government fears that the banner will be dragged through the dirt by protestors when the Games begin. 'Free Tibet' and human rights agitators are gearing up to protest, and the government does not want their glorious sports epic sullied by dissent at home or abroad. Face matters to the Chinese government. Looking good for the Olympic Games is one of the reasons why the Tibetan 'exile government' in the Indian Himalayan hill station of Dharamsala believes that there is a chance of winning a deal that will allow the Dalai Lama and his exiled people to go home.

(Gearing 23 December 2003)

For some, the 2008 Olympic Games may turn out to be not only *a celebration of China's coming of age as a growing world superpower*, but also a springboard for China's coming of age more broadly, including through its greater compliance with the ideals of the Olympic movement – with, that is, Olympism; and connectedly, with the values enshrined in *universal human rights*, and so the principles embodied in the *global human rights regime* (see Close and Askew 2004a).[1] David Black and Shona Bezanson, for instance, examine the 'liberalising potential' of the Olympics, with reference to the impact of the 1988 Seoul Games and the possible consequences of the Beijing Games; consider the ways in which the 2008 event 'may affect prospects for human rights improvements and political liberalisation' in the People's Republic of China (PRC); and argue that while 'the outcomes of this process are likely to be quite different from the western-style liberal democratisation that occurred in South Korea, the process of engagement between 21st Century China and 21st Century Olympism holds the possibility of stimulating a fruitful, dialogic, and progressive exchange on rights issues' (Black and

Bezanson 2004; see also Black and Van Der Westhuizen 2004). Another observer, Stephen Sullivan, suggests that the Beijing Games and Olympiad may become a vehicle for, in particular, influencing the 'negotiations concerning Tibet' and enhancing the human rights of 'the Uygur people and other ethnic and religious groups' in China (Sullivan 26 February 2004),[2] especially in that, according to the *Olympic Charter*, Olympism is 'a philosophy of life, exalting and combining in a balanced whole the qualities of body, will and mind. Blending sport with culture and education, Olympism seeks to create a way of life based on the joy found in effort, the educational value of good example and respect for universal fundamental ethical principles' (*ibid.*; see also IOC 1 September 2004).[3] Sullivan interprets Olympism's *exaltation to respect universal fundamental ethical principles* as a requirement on those who host the Olympic Games to respect *universal human rights*, and therefore on China during the Beijing Olympiad to improve its 'stance on human rights' (Sullivan 26 February 2004).

Sullivan notes that *giving Beijing the Olympics may have been* wrong, but assumes that the decision provides 'very real opportunities to elicit change' in China because the central government is 'fearful that it will lose face in front of the world if the Beijing Olympics is used to highlight [its] human rights violations' (*ibid.*). This is not to say, however, that the government will necessarily grasp the opportunities. China's greater compliance with universal human rights is possible, but not inevitable. As Sullivan puts it, either the government will address its 'shortcomings in a positive manner or it will employ extreme measures to make sure that the likes of the "Uygur and Tibetan Questions" ' do not raise their ' "ugly heads" and spoil the show' (*ibid.*). If the government takes the *extreme* approach, then this could be 'brutal', with 'mass detentions' of anyone thought likely to be disruptive; and with Tibet and Xinjiang being 'locked down', so that travel by Uygurs or Tibetans outside of their respective areas is forbidden during and in the run up to the Games, and travel to these areas by foreigners is prohibited 'on the basis of a jumped up "terrorist threat" '(*ibid.*). Sullivan suggests that such measures would not be 'in the spirit of the Olympics', and so should be avoided: 'We have a marvelous opportunity here that should not be squandered. We can, if we do it right, make the Beijing Olympics a celebration of a Brave New World. If we don't we will expose the whole Olympic ideal as a mockery and a sham' (*ibid.*). Sullivan argues that what he calls 'the "free" world' should use the Beijing Olympiad 'to press for change in Beijing's policies towards [its] ethnic minorities and religious groups' (*ibid.*).

Sullivan's discussion draws attention to a number of important considerations to be taken into account when assessing the Beijing Olympiad. First, there are the *discourses* on the award of the 2008 Games to Beijing, an example being Sullivan's own.[4] His somewhat equivocal reaction to the choice of Beijing reflects a *critical* stance towards the PRC, or at least the PRC's government, and a commitment to a specifically Western world view, meta-narrative,[5] or set of values, concerns and interests. Second, there is the relationship between, on the one hand, the award of the Games and the unfolding of the Beijing Olympiad and, on the other hand, power, and in particular that power rooted in the evolving global political economy (GPE) as exercised by GPE players such as China, the Olympic movement, and the International Olympic Committee (IOC). In this context, there is the issue of how external power players may try to use their influence during the Beijing Olympiad to bring about social change within China, and how in response the government of the PRC may react and try to resist. Third, there is the way in which GPE power and power-play mediates between Olympism, the Olympic movement and the Olympic Games, on the one hand, and further, concurrent social *philosophies*, movements and events, on the other. Fourth, there is the way in which the notion of *elective affinity* as used by Max Weber among others may be useful in studying, analyzing and making sense of the character, course and consequences of the Beijing Olympiad.

As Joel Elliott has said, in *The Protestant Ethic and the Spirit of Capitalism*, Weber's argument is that 'there was an extraordinary convergence, an "elective affinity", between the ideals and tendencies of early modern capitalism and of Protestant Calvinism, especially in the guise of Puritan Christianity' (Elliott 1998: 14; see also Kim, S.H. 2004; Lehmann et al. 1995; Shanahan 1992).[6] In a similar manner, it can be argued, there is an extraordinary convergence, or elective affinity, between *the ideals and tendencies* of modern capitalism and those of modern Olympism; and that this particular *mutual attraction*[7] throws light on the Beijing Olympiad, an examination of which in turn illuminates the relationships between the Olympic movement and various other modern social phenomena, including the advance of market capitalism (see Dunning 2003), the growing appeal of liberal democracy and individualism (see Inglehart and Welzel 2005),[8] the spread of *the Western cultural account* (Meyer et al. 1987), the progress of globalization (Baylis and Smith 2004), and the rise of China as a major political-economy player on the world stage (see Chapters 3 and 4). An examination of the Beijing Olympiad reveals that, as with elective affinities in human and social life in general, while the mutual attraction between the ideals and tendencies of Olympism and those of modern capitalism is strong, it is by no means simple, complete and unsullied. The attraction between Olympism and the Olympic movement, on the one hand, and capitalism and the capitalist mode of production, on the other, is partial and accompanied by complicating aversions. Indeed, the Olympic movement's relationships with all the modern social phenomena with which it has elective affinities will appear far from smooth, untroubled and categorically assured when viewed through the lens of the 2004 to 2008 Beijing Olympiad, culminating as this is likely to do in the greatest mega-event, sporting or otherwise, of all time (see Chapters 4 and 5).

Olympism like Protestantism is a package of ideas, principles and (prescribed) practices, to which a social movement adheres and around which this movement, the Olympic movement, coheres. Protestantism is a form of Christian 'faith and practice that originated with the principles of the Reformation', and out of which two distinct branches grew (Columbia University 2003; see also Bell and Sumner 2002; McGrath and Marks 2004). The evangelical churches in Germany and Scandinavia were followers of Martin Luther, while the reformed churches elsewhere were followers of John Calvin and Huldreich Zwingli. In spite of their differences, these two branches of Protestantism were united around one fundamental principle, that of rejecting the primacy of the Pope and embracing the 'doctrine that the individual conscience is the valid interpreter of Scripture' (Columbia University 2003). Protestantism is commensurate with the 'belief in the primary importance of the individual', or, that is, with *the doctrine of individualism* (AHD 2004a). Indeed, for many, Protestantism is the original source of what has been otherwise called *Western individualism* (Dunning 2003; Ignatief 2003; Jacobsen 2000; Miyanaga 1991; Wenshan 2001), *modern liberal individualism* (Shain 1994) and *classical individualism* (Machan 1998: xiv), according to which 'each human individual [is] of supreme importance both for that person and for the polity in which human beings make their home' (*ibid.*: xiv).

Broadly speaking, individualism is a doctrine (or ideology, philosophy or meta-narrative) which stresses the value of 'individual liberty [and] the virtues of self-reliance and personal independence. It embraces opposition to authority and to all manner of controls over the individual, especially when exercised by the state or society. It is [. . .] directly opposed to collectivism' (AC 3 November 2005; see also Beck and Beck-Gernsheim 2002; Shanahan 1992; Van Harskamp and Musschenga 2001). In *Habits of the Heart*, Robert Bellah and his colleagues distinguish between *expressive individualism* and *instrumental individualism*, where the former 'refers to the deep abiding concerns that Americans', in particular, 'have with personal self-fulfillment, with the idea that one of life's missions is to maximize personal happiness by discovering who you "really" are' (Bellah et al. 1985, quoted in O'Brien and Newman 2004: 40–1). Expressive individualism 'fosters self-absorption', readily becomes *excessive*, and 'undermines commitment to community' (O'Brien and Newman 2004: 41). Instrumental individualism is in a sense more specific or narrow, in that it refers to 'the freedom to pursue financial and career success' (*ibid.*: 41); and so to that doctrine (or sub-doctrine) according to which individual liberty, independence and self-reliance are of mutual benefit to both the individuals involved and the economies in which (to draw on Tibor Machan's phrase) *the individuals make their home* (Machan 1998: xiv). Here, individualism is 'the doctrine that individuals best serve the public interest by pursuing their own self-interest' (AHD 2004a), in particular within the economic sphere of social life. This is 'the doctrine that government should not interfere in commercial affairs', the synonym for individualism in this regard being *laissez faire* (PU 2001). *Laissez faire* is an 'economic doctrine that opposes governmental regulation of or interference in commerce beyond the minimum necessary for a free-enterprise system to operate according to its own economic laws'; while also being, more inclusively, a political (economy) doctrine that advocates 'non-interference in the affairs of others' in general (AHD 2004b; see also Boland 1995; Infantino 1998).

For some, individualism is *the* key to understanding the origins of modern Western capitalism, as it is to the subsequent evolution, consolidation and advance of the capitalist mode of production and capitalist social formations on the world stage. According to Martha Gimenez, for instance, the 'rise of the abstract individual, the bearer of economic, political, civil and human rights, is both a prerequisite for the development of capitalism and a continuing capitalist structural effect that contributes to its ongoing reproduction' (Gimenez 2002; see also Lukes 1973: 73). For Gimenez, feminism is one of the 'expressions of Western individualism' (*ibid.*; see also Fox-Genovese 1992). Another expression is Olympism. But, as with feminism, Olympism is not exclusively an expression of Western individualism. It also expresses, paradoxically, collectivism. Olympism, perhaps like all manifestations of Western individualism, is somewhat contradictory in character, and so sustains complex relationships with other doctrines with which it shares Western and, increasingly, global *social space* (see Bell 1996).[9]

According to Allen Guttmann:

> Coubertin's vision of a better world was liberal in the sense of classic nineteenth century liberalism [. . .]. Individual liberty was the highest good. Like other prophets of nineteenth century liberalism, however, Coubertin was torn between a belief in individualism and the conviction that nationality is the indispensable core of individual identity. His internationalism was never cosmopolitan. Although the Olympic Charter proclaims that games are contexts between individuals, not between nations, the IOC created an institutional structure based on national representation: no athlete can compete as an individual; every athlete must be selected by his or her country's national Olympic committee; every athlete [. . .] must wear a national uniform; when a victor is honored, a national flag is raised and a national anthem played. There have been many attempts to replace these symbols of nationalism with the Olympic flag and the Olympic hymn, but they have always failed [. . .]. In other words, the political vision institutionalized in the Olympics has always been inconsistent and contradictory.
> (Guttmann 2002: 2; see also Barney 1992b; Metcalfe 1994)

What the Olympic Charter (OC) actually says is that the Games 'are competitions between athletes in individual or team events and not between countries. They bring together the athletes selected by their respective NOCs, whose entries have been accepted by the IOC' (IOC 8 August 2004: 16). As if to underline the point, the IOC declares that it 'does not recognize [the] global ranking per country' by Olympic Games medals won, while none-theless – as if also to confirm Guttmann's argument – publishing *medals tables by country* for, it claims, 'information only', and even referring in the process to *medals awarded to countries* (IOC 11 March 2006). Of the 202 *countries* that competed in the 2004 Athens Games, 74 won medals, with three – the USA, the PRC and Russia – dominating; and with four – Eritrea, Trinidad and Tobago, Syria and Mongolia – propping up the table, each winning one bronze medal. In the case of the Athens Games, the IOC singles out for a special mention the PRC's achievement: in 'preparation for hosting the 2008 Games, China had its most successful Olympics ever, with Chinese athletes winning 63 medals including 32 gold medals' (*ibid.*). Halfway through the Beijing Olympiad, Torino in Italy hosted the 2006 Winter Games, at which, by 'winning the bronze medal in the luge event', Martins Rubenis brought 'the first Olympic Winter medal to Latvia'; and at which Enrico Fabris 'skated to a bronze medal in the 5000m speed skating event bringing Italy not only its first medal of the Turin Games but its first ever Olympic medal in that discipline' (IOC 19 February 2006b).

Guttmann's argument may be regarded, however, as somewhat misleading. As it stands, it warrants at least four correctives. First, the contradiction within the Olympic movement is between an emphasis placed on individual-ism and not only that placed on countries, or *nations* (IOC 11 March 2006), but also an emphasis placed on a range of other collectivities; second, this contradiction is but one example of a general feature of the Western cultural account, replete as this is with contradictions (see Bell 1996); third, Coubertin's contradictory approach to Olympism merely, or faithfully, reflects the contradictory character of the culture and society into which he was trying to introduce this doctrine; and fourth, Olympism's contradictory endorsement of both individualism and collectivism may be conducive, if not the key, to its widespread appeal, functionally facilitating its globalization.

Coubertin was more explicitly contradictory than perhaps Allen Guttmann indicates. An individual competitor is advised to temper *his* individualism, individuality and individual pursuit of Olympic glory in the interests of realizing certain other important purposes. First, in relation to self, 'the important thing in life is not to triumph but to compete'; 'the important thing in life is not victory but combat, it is not to have vanquished but to have fought well'; 'the essential thing in life is not conquering but fighting well'; 'the most important thing in the Olympic Games is not winning but taking part' (Coubertin, quoted in BQ 2005). Second, in relation to other individuals and to collectivities, 'if he is knocked out of the competition, [the Olympic athlete] encourages his brothers with his words and presence'; 'may joy and good fellowship reign, and in this manner, may the Olympic Torch pursue its way through ages, increasing friendly understanding among nations, for the good of a humanity always more enthusiastic, more courageous and more pure' (*ibid.*).

The pursuit of friendship, fellowship, what is *good for humanity* and other collective concerns is a principle which is now widely asserted within the Olympic movement, such as in the Olympic Charter:

> The goal of Olympism is to place sport at the service of the harmonious development of man, with a view to promoting a peaceful society concerned with the preservation of human dignity [. . .]. The practice of sport is a human right. Every individual must have the possibility of practising sport, without discrimination of any kind and in the Olympic spirit, which requires mutual understanding with a spirit of friendship, solidarity and fair play.
>
> (IOC 8 August 2004: 9)

The principle is emphasized at not only the global, IOC level, but also at the more 'local' level. For instance, the United States Sports Academy, the International Coaches Association, and the International Association of Sports Academies have collectively declared that the 'goal of Olympism is to contribute to building a peaceful and better world by educating youth through sport practiced without discrimination of any kind and in the Olympic spirit, which requires mutual understanding with a spirit of friendship, solidarity and fair play' (United States Sports Academy 2001); and the New Zealand Olympic Committee tells us:

> By blending sport with culture and education, Olympism promotes a way of life based on: the balanced development of the body, will and mind; the joy found in effort; the educational value of being a good role model; respect for universal ethics including tolerance, generosity, unity, friendship, non-discrimination and respect for others. Olympism uses sport to promote the balanced development of people as an essential step in building a peaceful society that places a high value on human dignity.
>
> (NZOC 2005)

Just as, to recall John Lucas' suggestion, the Olympic motto 'in the present context of moral relativism can mean anything that one wishes it to mean' (Lucas 1992; quoted in Staun 2003; see Chapter 1 of this book), so the contradictory character of Olympism allows this *philosophy of life* (IOC 1 September 2004) to *mean anything that one wishes it to mean*, something which helps to ease the tasks of converting the world to Olympism, generating greater interest in the Olympic Games and of serving thereby the commercial, corporate and class interests whether pursued at the local, regional or global level (see Chapter 1). Olympism and the Games appeal to a wide range of audiences, societies and cultures, and crucially of power elites and governments, while being – because of their paradoxes, inconsistencies and contradictions – a source of considerable confusion and conflict among the Games' various participants (see Chapters 3 and 4). This is not to ignore how the origins of the modern Games, the Olympic movement and Olympism lie in the West due to the prior origins in the West of individualism. Just as Protestantism may well be the source of Western individualism, so in turn the latter is the source of Olympism. This link is then reflected in the core values of Olympism, whereby it is primarily conducive to an individualistic approach to sport and life in general, and appealing to those who assume such an approach.

While the origins of individualism are Western (Berger, 2002: 9; see also Lukes 1973; Morris 1991; Shain 1996; Shanahan 1992), or more precisely European (see Gurevich 1995), and the doctrine persists as a pivotal feature of the Western cultural account, its reach has been greatly extended.[10] The doctrine of individualism in relation to the economy and to society as a whole has been successfully exported as an aspect of globalization from and by the West to become far more widely entrenched, such as in East Asia (see Goldman and Lee 2002; Miyanaga 1991; Wenshan 2001). Western individualism, together with liberal democracy and market capitalism, has been firmly endorsed by various East Asian political leaders, including Kim Dae Jung, the former President of South Korea and the Nobel Peace Prize Laureate of 2000:

> Globalization is by no means restricted to the economy. It is happening in the areas of transportation, communication and culture. It is happening everywhere. Korea, for its part, should not shy away from the challenge of adapting to this global trend [. . .]. The only way for our nation to move forward is to participate actively in the world's trend toward 'globalization' and to embrace the challenges of the new millennium. I believe that, in the 21st century, all nations of the world will be able to enjoy the benefits of democracy. In order to participate fully in globalization, I believe, it is necessary to practice genuine democracy and allow a free exchange of ideas and information. Korea will follow this path [. . .]. I propose each of us become an advocate of democracy and a market economy – not only by advocating these concepts as ideals, but by practicing them so as to achieve the ultimate objectives of democracy and a market economy, namely, individual freedom and social justice.
>
> (Kim Dae Jung 1999; see also Kim Dae Jung 1994, 1998)

In a sense, South Korea is an exceptional case due to Protestantism having become firmly established over many decades. According to official estimates, the country's 'Protestant churches have more than 10 million members', representing more than 20 percent of the entire population (Office of the Prime Minister 2005). In China, according to official estimates, no more than 4 per cent of the population is Christian, never mind Protestant. Even so, this would still mean that there are around 50 million people (out of a total population of 1.3 billion) who are Christian, or about the same number as the total population of South Korea (CIA 1 November 2005). According to unofficial estimates, there are substantially greater numbers of Christians in China – as many as 90 million, made up of 40 to 70 million Protestants and 15 to 20 million Catholics – and moreover increasing numbers, 'exacerbating [their] perceived threat and causing the authorities to clamp down still further on unregistered churches. The perception that China's Christians have close links with the West adds to their plight' (McGeown 9 November 2004):

> Both Catholics and Protestants have long complained of persecution by the Communist authorities, and human rights groups claim the problem is getting worse. According to the Jubilee Campaign, an inter-denominational lobby group, about 300 Christians are in detention in China at any one time, and that number is set to rise. 'China's new generation of leaders are trying to consolidate control of the country as it goes through rapid social and economic changes,' said Wilfred Wong, a parliamentary officer for the Jubilee Campaign. 'The Communists feel threatened by any popular ideology which is different from their own', he said. China's Christian population – especially those who refuse to worship in the tightly regulated state-registered churches – is seen as one such threat [. . .]. Human rights groups have documented an increasing number of arrests of Chinese Christians since the beginning of 2004. According to the charity Christian Solidarity Worldwide, persecution is becoming more systematic and targeted at large-scale Christian gatherings. Since June the charity has documented three mass arrests of unregistered Christians. In each case more than 100 people were detained.
>
> (ibid.; see also Hunter and Chan 2004)

If Protestantism is becoming increasingly popular in China, then this could be linked to its elective affinity with and the spread of Western individualism, the appeal of which in China has been explained as follows:

> 'China is looking for something to take the place of a failed Marxism,' [William] de Bary, the John Mitchell Mason Professor Emeritus of [Columbia] University and Provost Emeritus, told The Wall Street Journal [in 1994]. 'Money worship is eroding the body of society, [and] morality has lost its sacred meaning,' said an editorial in the People's Daily [in the same] year. The appeal of Communist ideology [has] long since waned among the populace. Coupled with a surge of interest in

entrepreneurship and market economics, a moral and philosophical vacuum has evolved to a degree that worries Communist party officials [sic], the paper's editors wrote. 'They are confronting the specter of an unrestrained individualism, and their worry is articulated in the form of an attack on Western individualism,' said de Bary, in [an] interview published in the *South China Morning Post*. 'The complaints about Western individualism actually reflect a concern about a Chinese individualism that is running rampant,' said de Bary. 'It's the consequence of the failure of Marxism or Maoist morality. Their idea is to try to shore up public morality somehow by going back to Confucianism.'

(Columbia University 1994)

The appeal to Communist Party of China (CPC) officials of Confucianism as opposed to Protestantism and Western individualism becomes clear by noting what Confucianism has to say about *human relations*. The key to unlocking Confucian ethics is the notion of *jen*, meaning 'love', 'goodness', 'humanity' or 'human-heartedness' (MSN Encarta 4 November 2005). *Jen* is a supreme virtue, which in human relations is concretely expressed in *chung*, 'or faithfulness to oneself and others' (*ibid.*), and in *shu*, or altruism, as expressed in the golden rule: 'Do not do to others what you do not want done to yourself' (*ibid.*) Other virtues include righteousness, propriety, integrity and filial piety, and anyone (or more precisely any man), who has all the Confucian virtues is a *chün-tzu* (or perfect gentleman) (*ibid.*). But, most important for CPC officials, in the political realm, Confucius 'advocated a paternalistic government in which the sovereign is benevolent and honorable and the subjects are respectful and obedient' (*ibid.*).

Basically, Confucianism seeks 'cosmic harmony through well-ordered relationships', as a result of which Confucianism and Protestantism 'are at odds'. Whereas Confucianism 'esteems *we*-ness', Protestantism 'emphasizes *individual* election and salvation', the result being a 'faith where theology is individualistic, and praxis is self-serving' (Lee 2004). Relatedly, Confucianism is at odds with Western individualism and *laissez faire* market capitalism. Of course, Confucianism has its origins in China, while having established deep roots in other parts of East Asia, and especially in Japan, Korea and Vietnam (see Eastman 1999). However, the differences and tensions between Confucianism, on the one hand, and Protestantism, Western individualism, liberal democracy and market capitalism, on the other, means neither that Confucianism is equally at odds with all forms of capitalism (Beeson 1999) nor that Confucianism as practised, or *Confucianist societies*, cannot accommodate Western market capitalism as practised.

Laissez faire is a doctrine in favour of an ideal, or pure, type of free market economy, and more precisely of a free market *capitalist* economy, something which is achieved only approximately in practice. In market-capitalist societies, the *laissez faire* doctrine tends to give way to sizeable, if highly variable, government (or state) interference and regulation, administration or management. The economy and other areas of social life are generally managed, or governed, to a not inconsiderable degree from the political centre, or core, by the state. Indeed, the governance of market-capitalist social formations resembles the kind of internal management which characterizes organizations in general, as exemplified by the IOC and the Olympic movement overall in particular. The Olympic movement is managed in a highly regulated, top-down and centralized manner, even increasingly so, as can be illustrated by referring to the way in which it handles the use of performance enhancing drugs:

> Drug abuse is considered to be the deliberate or inadvertent use by athletes of substances or methods that may enhance performance. In 1967, the International Olympic Committee became the first sports organisation in the world to establish a Medical Commission, together with the international Cycling Union. Their mission was to put in place a medical control service for the 1968 Olympic and Olympic Winter Games. Competitors who participate in the Olympic Games are governed by the Eligibility Code. This Code states that competitors must abide by the IOC Medical Code. The Code provides for the prohibition of doping; establishes lists of the classes of prohibited substances and procedures; provides for the obligation of competitors to submit themselves to medical controls and examinations and makes provisions for the sanctions to be applied in the event of a violation of the Code. In addition, a list of permissible products is also published.
>
> (BOA 3 November 2005; see also IOC 23 July 2004)[11]

The way in which the Olympic movement is managed in practice is consistent with the highly top-down approach to social governance associated with Confucianism and traditional Chinese culture and society, just as it is at one and the same time with such principles as 'For each individual, sport is a possible source for inner improvement'; 'The Olympic Games were created for the exaltation of the individual athlete'; and 'The Games were created for the glorification of the individual champion' (Coubertin, quoted in BQ 2005). Here, Coubertin's individualism shines through, just as it echoes around more recent views of the Games' guiding *philosophy*, such as when Richard Bell in the United States Sports Academy's *Sport Journal*, tells us that Olympism 'is about the pride in yourself gained through the glory of participation and the quest for achievement' (Bell 2001). For Bell, the 'five ideals that should guide your life are embodied in the concept of Olympism: Vision, Focus, Commitment, Persistence and Discipline' (*ibid*.). Olympism is 'being the best you can be and gaining life's tools to build self-confidence, self-esteem, personal effectiveness and the spirit of adventure' (*ibid*.). For others, Olympism has even deeper significance for individuals *qua individuals*:

The Olympic movement, sometimes referred to as Olympism, is a universal concept that is not defined simply. It is a philosophical ardor for life and the uncompromising pursuit of excellence. Just as individuals operate with a personal philosophy that guides their decision-making, Olympism, too, is philosophically directed through the elevated dimension of quality in how an individual conducts his/her life. Olympism is an inner faith of a man in himself, a constant effort of physical and intellectual enhancement [. . .]. It is a general concept which emphasizes not only development of bodily strength, but generally healthier individuals with a happier attitude and a more peaceful vision of the world [. . .]. Olympism recognizes and extols individual effort and accepts no discrimination among nations, races, political systems, classes, etc. [. . .].

(Hunterformer 2001)

While Olympism may not be a religion in the same sense as Protestantism, it is regularly described by adherents in religious terms, such as when Deborah Hunterformer, the Director of Education Development, Programs and Services for USA Volleyball, claims that *Olympism is an inner faith of a man himself*. Even more directly, Pierre de Coubertin declared: 'For me sport was a religion [. . .] with religious sentiment' (Coubertin, quoted in BQ 2 November 2005). The relationship between sport and religion, equating sport with religion, and going as far as to elevate sport to the status of a religion have been the focus of much attention, such as at the 2004 *International Conference on Sport and Religion*, when Joan Chandler – in a manner which lends support to Maurice Roche's argument about the *functionality* of mega-events in late modernity (see Chapter 1) – stated:

The glue holding a good many diverse (American) groups together is sport. It offers you the illusion of control in a time of uncertainty. Religion, though sometimes divisive, also offers a sense of overarching purpose. This is an interesting juxtaposition. There is some reason that sport is a glue and religion is a glue.

(Chandler 2005; see also Hoffman 1992; Magdalinski and Chandler 2002)

For some observers, the Olympic Games exemplifies how sport can assume something akin to a religious dimension due to the way in which the Games draw on, tease out and provide a focus for other, underlying sentiments and attachments:

The danger of rabidly nationalistic partisanship was there from the start. No wonder, then, that the history of the Olympics has been a mixed one in which the glories of individual athletic achievement have been accompanied by frenzies of chauvinism. To witness the spectator's emotions when *their* national representative mounts the victor's podium, when *their* flag is raised, when *their* national anthem is played, is to wonder if nationalism – or sport – is not the true religion of the modern world.

(Guttmann 2002: 2)

While individualist principles lie at the core of Olympism, collectivist ones, somewhat paradoxically and contradictorily, characterize the *philosophy*, and perhaps especially those which sit well with national sentiments, attachments and identities; with national chauvinism, which may be – rather than sport as such – *the true religion of the modern world.* Accordingly, despite Hunterformer's wishful thinking, sport, like religion, cannot be guaranteed to act like a glue and only like a glue in all situations, as has been variously noted and lamented, including famously by George Orwell in his December 1945 article for *Tribune* on 'The Sporting Spirit' (Orwell 1945; cf. Camus 1962).[12] Following the visit of the Dynamo association football (soccer) team from Moscow to Britain in 1945, Orwell concluded that 'sport is an unfailing cause of ill-will [. . .] typical of our nationalistic age' (Orwell 1945). Orwell tells us:

> I am always amazed when I hear people saying that sport creates goodwill between the nations, and that if only the common peoples of the world could meet one another at football or cricket, they would have no inclination to meet on the battlefield. Even if one didn't know from concrete examples (the 1936 Olympic Games, for instance) that international sporting contests lead to orgies of hatred, one could deduce it from general principles.
>
> (*ibid.*)

In effect, Orwell declares, at 'the international level sport is frankly mimic warfare' (*ibid.*), although 'the significant thing is not the behaviour of the players but the attitude of the spectators: and, behind the spectators, of the nations who work themselves into furies over these absurd contests, and seriously believe – at any rate for short periods – that running, jumping and kicking a ball are tests of national virtue' (*ibid.*). Orwell singles out certain places and peoples as being especially susceptible to the attitude he has in mind:

> In England, the obsession with sport is bad enough, but even fiercer passions are aroused in young countries where games playing and nationalism are both recent developments. In countries like India or Burma, it is necessary at football matches to have strong cordons of police to keep the crowd from invading the field. In Burma, I have seen

the supporters of one side break through the police and disable the goalkeeper of the opposing side at a critical moment.

(ibid.)

It is of interest to speculate on whether Orwell would have classified China around 60 years later as a *young country* in the sense indicated. He would have been able to cite evidence from the Asian Cup football competition held in China shortly before the 2004 Athens Olympic Games, and in particular of the *passionate nationalism* of the supporters of China's team before, during and after the final match when, in Beijing, China's team played Japan's team. On 7 August 2004, 'police set up a blockade near the Japanese Embassy to stop angry soccer fans from gathering there following Japan's 3–1 Asian Cup victory over China' (Jennings, R. 2004). Earlier, at the stadium, Chinese fans had 'shouted anti-Japanese epithets and [thrown] objects on the field' following China's defeat (*ibid.*). Frank Ching reports how just before the match got underway Chinese fans 'booed so loudly that they drowned out the strains of the Japanese national anthem' (Ching 2004); and how 'when Japan won, the spectators pelted the Japanese players' bus with soda bottles and broke the window of a car carrying a Japanese diplomat' (*ibid.*). In Ching's view, while 'soccer hooliganism' occurs elsewhere, 'the hate focused on the Japanese was so vehement that it was clear [that] the soccer match simply provided an occasion for the venting of deeply held anti-Japanese sentiments in China' (*ibid.*). Ching explains:

> Sino-Japanese discord ranges from a territorial dispute over a few uninhabited islands to competition for an oil pipeline from Siberia [and] to Tokyo's military alliance with Washington. However, the most serious problem stems [. . .] from history. For although almost 60 years have passed since the end of World War II, the seeds of hostility sown in the 1930s and '40s continue to poison the relationship. The Japanese invaded and occupied much of China and treated the population with much brutality. From Beijing's standpoint, the Chinese are the victims and Japan has not yet made amends.
>
> (ibid.)

The fans (or fanatical supporters) of China's football team used the Asian Cup to demonstrate their *passionate nationalism* through displays of their *deeply held anti-Japanese sentiments*, rooted as these are in the experience of the way in which much of China was brutally invaded and occupied by Japan during the 1930s and 1940s (see Chapter 6). For them, *the Second Sino-Japanese War* (the first having taken place from 1894 to 1895, mainly over the control of Korea), which took off in 1937, had not been concluded by Japan's surrender in 1945. The legacy of what in China is otherwise known as *the Anti-Japanese War of Resistance, the Chinese People's Anti-Japanese War of Resistance, the War of Resistance*, and *the Eight Years' War of Resistance* entails persistent hostility, resentment and anger, fuelled by how Japan has far from unequivocally acknowledged, never mind atoned for, its wartime atrocities and *crimes* – centred as these are on the Nanjing Massacre, *comfort women*, and Unit 731 (the medical unit set up for conducting research into biological warfare and other things with experiments on live human beings). Many in Japan remain in denial (see Kingston 2006; Saaler 2005; Yamazaki 2005); and for many in China, *the war* has still to be resolved (see Kim 2003; Pempel 2005; Rozman 2004). The Asian Cup was an opportunity to exact revenge, to inflict defeat on Japan, to humiliate the Japanese at a major sporting occasion on the field of play and to abuse them off (see also McClain 1990).

The co-author of *The Japan That Can Say No (No to ieru Nihon)*, originally published in 1989, Shintaro Ishihara, is notorious for his 'unapologetic view of Japan's militarist past' (McAvoy 2004) and his tirades on this and other matters, such as when as Governor of Tokyo he was interviewed for the *Japan Times*:

> China is 'very dangerous', he thunders. Japan's critics are 'just jealous'. Tokyo's bloody conquests of the 1930s and '40s saved Asia from colonization by 'white people' [. . .]. Riling others in Asia, Ishihara insists that Tokyo need not apologize for its bloody wartime invasions of neighbors and argues that Japan did Asia a favor by delivering it from Western imperialism. 'If Japanese hadn't fought the white people, we would still be slaves of the white people. It would be colonization,' he said. 'We changed that.' While such blunt talk embarrasses some Japanese, supporters say Ishihara is simply saying out loud what many people believe but hesitate to say.
>
> (*ibid.*; see also Ishihara 1991; cf. Zhang 1996)

Ishihara was first elected as the Governor of Tokyo in 1999, and then re-elected in 2003 by 70 per cent of the vote (McAvoy 2004), an indication of how Ishihara's views and strident nationalism enjoy a resonance throughout Japanese society. But, returning to the 2004 Asian Cup, for many Japanese, the Chinese fans' conduct had serious implications, including for Beijing's suitability as the host city for the 2008 Olympic Games:

> It began as a sporting event that pitched the greatest talents of Asian football against each other on an international stage. But the Asian Cup is in danger of ending in an international crisis tomorrow when old enemies Japan and China face each other in the final to settle scores that have been brewing for more than 60 years. Resentment over Japan's wartime aggression runs deep among many Chinese and the country's football fans have booed and jeered Japan's side in their cup matches.

The controversy widened yesterday when Japanese media questioned Beijing's qualifications to host the 2008 Olympic Games [. . .]. Some Japanese politicians believe the situation is out of control and members of the ruling Liberal Democratic Party have called for stronger protests to Beijing and even reportedly suggested a boycott of the 2008 Beijing Olympic Games if the situation is not improved.

(Ryall and Robertson 2004)

It seems that football matches in East Asia in the build-up to the 2008 Olympic Games were sometimes afflicted by the passionate nationalism which surrounded football matches and other sporting events in Europe and Asia as witnessed by George Orwell during the 1930s and 1940s:

Even when the spectators don't intervene physically they try to influence the game by cheering their own side and 'rattling' opposing players with boos and insults. Serious sport has nothing to do with fair play. It is bound up with hatred, jealousy, boastfulness, disregard of all rules and sadistic pleasure in witnessing violence: in other words it is war minus the shooting. Instead of blah-blahing about the clean, healthy rivalry of the football field and the great part played by the Olympic Games in bringing the nations together, it is more useful to inquire how and why this modern cult of sport arose. Most of the games we now play are of ancient origin, but sport does not seem to have been taken very seriously [until] the nineteenth century.

(Orwell 1945)

Of course, since 1945, the crowds at football matches and other sporting events have been swelled by *armchair audiences*, occasionally on a huge (or *mega-*) scale, due especially to the development of such mass media as television and, more recently, the Internet.[13] Moreover, the evidence suggests that these *remote spectators* are no less partisan in the way they watch, perceive and respond to the events; and, echoing Orwell, 'that the whole thing is bound up with the rise of nationalism – that is, with the lunatic modern habit of identifying oneself with large power units and seeing everything in terms of competitive prestige' (*ibid.*). Orwell does not 'suggest that sport is one of the main causes of international rivalry' (*ibid.*). For Orwell, 'big-scale sport is itself [. . .] merely another effect of the causes that have produced nationalism' (*ibid.*).

Guided by Orwell, the explanation for *inter-national* sporting occasions, including what are now called sporting *mega-events*, lies in nationalism and the underlying *causes* of nationalism during nineteenth-century social developments. For Orwell, while sporting events in themselves may not be as such the *cause* of nationalism, they do serve to 'make things worse' in that they entail 'sending forth a team [. . .], labelled as national champions, to do battle against some rival team, and allowing it to be felt on all sides that whichever nation is defeated will "lose face" ' (*ibid.*). Orwell is in no doubt that 'sport is an unfailing cause of ill-will'; that 'international sporting contests lead to orgies of hatred'; that at 'the international level sport is [. . .] mimic warfare', especially among 'the spectators [. . .] of the nations' involved; that 'the obsession with sport [and the] passions [. . .] aroused in young countries where games playing and nationalism are both recent developments' are greater than in *old countries*; and that, rather then being a substitute for war, serious sport 'is war minus the shooting' (*ibid.*; see also Goodhart and Chataway 1968).

In Orwell's view, the *surrogate wars* surrounding *inter-national* sporting events are to be understood as surface manifestations of underlying nationalism, nationalist sentiments and *inter-national* hostilities. Indeed, the very creation, staging and popularity of these events are explicable in terms of the same factors. Accordingly, sporting mega-events like the FIFA World Cup and the Olympic Games are not *substitutes* for war. They are not as such safety-value outlets for *inter-national* rivalries, tensions and conflicts. On the contrary, if anything they may not only reflect, but also reinforce deep-seated *inter-national* belligerence. After all, as touched on by Orwell, the 1936 Berlin Games were quickly followed by Germany's annexation of Austria (on 12 March 1938), occupation of Czechoslovakia (the western part by mid-March 1939, and the whole by September 1944), and invasion of Poland (on 1 September 1939), three participating countries in the Games, the result being the greatest, deadliest and costliest war in human history: the Second World War.

Guided by Orwell, instead of contributing to *inter-national harmony*, sporting mega-events can easily reveal and may well accentuate *inter-national dissonance*, where in music *dissonance* is 'a combination of notes that, when played simultaneously, sounds displeasing and needs to be resolved to a consonance', and where the term's synonyms include *discord*, *dissension* and *conflict* (MSN Encarta 2006). Contrary to Coubertin's *sport-as-religion* sentiment, the way in which neither religion nor sport necessarily help glue together *nations* in a *harmonious* manner is no more poignantly demonstrated than by an incident at the Games of the XX Olympiad:

> On September 5, 1972, one day before the commencement of the Munich Olympic Games, eight Palestinian terrorists entered the Olympic Village and killed two members of the Israeli team and took nine other hostages. These nine were killed during failed attempts to rescue them. The terrorists requested the release of 234 Palestinians being held captive in Israel. Five of the terrorists were killed and three were wounded during rescue attempts, along with one West German policeman. The following day a memorial service was held and the Olympic flags were flown at half staff. The Opening Ceremony was delayed one day. The IOC decision to

continue with the Olympic Games after the terrorist attack was thought of as controversial to some. The IOC president, Avery Brundage, proclaimed that 'the Games must go on'. After the attacks, a Palestinian spokesman said, 'that sport is the modern religion of the western world; So we decided to use the Olympics, the most sacred ceremony of this religion, to make the world pay attention to us.'

(Seevak 2002; see also Brasher 1972; Brichford 1996; Czula 1978a; Diem and Knoesel 1974; Groussard 1975; Guttmann 1984; Mandell 1991)

Of course, the Palestinian *terrorist attack* at the Munich Games is far from being the only example of how the Olympic Games have been variously politicized over the years. While one of the main objectives, as stated in the Olympic Charter, of the Olympic movement under the leadership of the IOC is to 'oppose any political abuse of sport and athletes', the Olympic Games have been regularly 'influenced by politics' (BOA 18 November 2005; see also Kanin 1981; Lapchick 1978; Spots 1994). For instance, three Games have been cancelled due to the two world wars; in 1920, Austria, Bulgaria, Germany, Hungary and Turkey 'were not permitted to participate because of their role' in the First World War (BOA 18 November 2005; Dyreson 1999; Lucas 1983; Renson 1985, 1996); the 1936 Berlin Games were used by Adolf Hitler and the National Socialists in Germany 'as a display of political strength' (BOA 18 November 2005), so much so that they have been labelled *the Nazi Olympics* (Guttmann 1988b, 1998; Guttmann et al. 2000; Murray, G.E. 2003; Rosenzweig 1997; see also Hart-Davis 1988; Herz and Altman 1996; Kass 1976; Murray, B. 1992); in 1948, Germany and Japan 'were not invited due to their roles' in the Second World War (BOA 18 November 2005; see also Baker 1994; Buschmann and Lennartz 1998; Voeltz 1996); in 1952, Taiwan withdrew from the Helsinki Games in protest against the PRC being allowed to compete (see Chapter 7; see also Hornbuckle 1996; Maxwell and Howell 1976); at the 1956 Melbourne Games, due 'to the Israeli-led take-over of the Suez Canal, Egypt, Iraq and Lebanon did not take part', and Spain and Switzerland did not as well in protest against the Soviet Union's invasion of Hungary (BOA 18 November 2005; see also Cashman 1995; Jobling 1996; Kent and Merritt 1984; Soldatow 1980); in 1958, the PRC 'withdrew from the Olympic movement and all International Federations', and subsequently was not reinstated by the IOC until 1971 (BOA 18 November 2005; see also Chapters 3 and 6; Adams and Gerlach 2002); in 1960, South Africa was 'banned from the Olympic Games due to its political policy of Apartheid', and then was not reinstated by the IOC until 1991, just in time for it to participate in the 1992 Games (BOA 18 November 2005; see also Quick 1990); at the 1968 Mexico City Games, the US athletes Tommie Smith and John Carlos protested as they collected their medals by raising 'their fists in the sign of black power' (BOA 18 November 2005; see also

Arbena 1996; Gissendanner 1996; Wiggins 1992); the Soviet Union's invasion of Afghanistan in 1979 disrupted both the 1980 and the 1984 Olympic Games, due to a 'number of non-communist nations' withdrawing from the 1980 Moscow Games, and then to 'the Soviet Union and other communist countries' deciding not to attend the 1984 Games in Los Angeles (BOA 18 November 2005; see also Chorbajian and Mosco 1981; Crossman and Lappage 1992; Giller 1980; Guttmann 1988a, 2002; Hill 1999); and at the 1988 Games in Seoul, North Korea, Cuba, Ethiopia and Nicaragua did not participate as a political gesture (BOA 18 November 2005; Guttmann 1988a, 2002).

More recently, and especially since the 11 September 2001 attacks on the World Trade Center and the Pentagon in the USA, attributed (including in the final report of the National Commission on Terrorist Attacks Upon the United States, published in 2004) to *terrorists* affiliated with the Islamic Al-Qaeda network (see Baylis and Smith 2004, Chapters 1, 6, 13, 21 and 33), the possibility of the Olympics being the target of *Islamic terrorism* has been raised. While the 2004 Athens Games were spared attacks, as of around that time *anti-terrorist* preparations were already well underway for the Beijing Games:

> Beijing organizers have begun security projects for the 2008 Olympic Games. Qiang Wei, head of the coordination group, says Beijing will give top priority to anti-terrorism. Qiang says Beijing will provide a detailed security plan in advance to all the participants of the 2008 Games. This will make Beijing's security job much more challenging than past Olympics. Under the plan, Beijing will complete the construction of security organs and training of some security personnel by the end of June [2005]. Beijing has signed agreements with universities in Britain and Australia to train Chinese police.
>
> (*China Daily* 25 March 2005)

Indeed, anti-terrorist co-operation with external security agencies had gone significantly further:

> Some Chinese security personnel will receive FBI's special agents training in the United States for the 2008 Beijing Olympics. US Federal Bureau of Investigation (FBI) made the announcement at a press conference, reported China Radio International. The FBI said that it will train Chinese trainees to ensure the security of 2008 Beijing Olympics. An official of the FBI said that the training for Chinese trainees will be the same to other countries' trainees. After the 9/11 terrorist attack, the United States has enlarged the cooperation with China against terrorism, and this time it will take the cooperation up to a new stage.
>
> (*China Daily* 20 October 2004)

The Chinese government's participation in the US-led *War on Terror* has been viewed critically and cynically, such as by Stephen Sullivan in his account of the consequences for the Uygur (or Uighur), an *ethnic minority* of around 8.5 million people living mainly in the Xinjiang Uygur Autonomous Region (XUAR) located in the north-west border area of the PRC (Sullivan 15 January 2004). Sullivan tells us that the Uygur 'are Caucasian, mostly Muslim and speak a Turkic language'; and that the inclusion of the name 'Uygur' in the autonomous region's title reflects 'the situation in 1955 when the Uygur were by far the largest ethnic group in the region' (*ibid.*). Until the early 1960s, the Uygur 'lived a fairly insular and relatively politically free existence' due to Xinjiang's geographical remoteness and 'apparent economic barrenness' (*ibid.*). Subsequently, however, 'things have changed dramatically in Xinjiang' due to the discovery of 'rich reserves of natural resources and the increasing strategic importance of the area' (*ibid.*). These developments have led the central government 'to populate the region' with 'Han "migrants" ' (*ibid.*), as a result of which there has been a considerable decline in the relative presence of the Uygur in Xinjiang. In 1949, the Uygur numbered about 3.3 million people and comprised about 74 per cent of Xinjiang's total population. But, by 1990, while they numbered around 7.2 million, the Uygur made up only 45 per cent of the region's total (*Uygur Worlds* 15 August 2005). Moreover, the central government's policy of *Han expansion* has been complemented by its policies of assimilating the Uygur along with all other ethnic minorities into a homogenized PRC and suppressing any dissent. In response, the Uygur have 'demonstrated a remarkable resilience' (Sullivan 15 January 2004). They have 'refused to be assimilated', and indeed have come to 'stand out like a sore thumb on the hand of Chinese homogeneity' (*ibid.*) in the eyes of the outside world. In turn, the PRC's central government has responded by firming up its strategy of trying to assimilate and suppress the Uygur while, at the same time, rationalizing this strategy in terms of its participation in the *War on Terror*.

Sullivan reports that prior to the Uygur riots in the city of Gulja in 1997, the PRC's *assimilation policy* had gone largely unnoticed in the outside world, but that these riots drew the outside world's attention to and concern about this policy. Following the riots, the resulting 'government recriminations' and ensuing world attention, the government began to replace the words 'separatist' and 'splitist' with 'terrorist' to all those seeking independence from the PRC (*ibid.*). Following the events of 11 September 2001, the 'propaganda machine' was put to work. The PRC government initiated a 'propaganda and lobby programme' in which its hardline policies were rationalized in terms of the *War on Terror*. The government was hoping to mask the actions it was taking designed to break the will of the Uygur people (*ibid.*). Since the 1990s, 'some ugly and fatal clashes with Chinese authorities' along with other 'alleged events' have been used as a rationale 'for continuing "strike hard" crackdowns on Uygur freedoms of religion' and association that have resulted in detentions, prison sentences and executions; in conjunction with 'a relentless international propaganda campaign' in support of their policies and practices against the Uyghur people as a necessary response to 'Uighur Islamic Terrorism' (*Uygur Worlds* 15 August 2005; see also Chase 2002; ETIC 2002). As already noted (above), according to Sullivan, the PRC's government may now take advantage of the overlap between the global *War on Terror* and the Beijing Olympiad to further tighten its grip over the Uygur, such as by imposing a travel and human rights clamp down 'on the basis of a jumped up "terrorist threat"' (Sullivan 26 February 2004; see also Liew and Wang 2003; Safron 1998; Shi and Shi 2002; Starr 2004).

Whether the Beijing Games actually suffers a terrorist attack or not, the possibility of the Games being a terrorist target during the *War on Terror* could be used by the Beijing-based central government to shore up its political hold over the PRC. Clearly, the relationship between the Olympics and politics, like that between – not unconnectedly – the Olympics and religion, is *both* multi-faceted and complex *and* prominent and pervasive. Apart from anything else, the devotion of many of Olympism's followers appears to be similar to the piety, or religiosity, of many Christians, if not of many other religious faiths, contributing to the impression that Olympism along with such concurrent doctrines as individualism – or, perhaps more precisely, *excessive individualism* (Bellah et al. 1985) – and consumerism exemplify distinctively *modern*, or arguably *post-modern*, religions. Viewed as a religion or at least as religion-like, Olympism, as with Protestantism, has its *scripture* – its sacred or authoritative statement. This is the Olympic Charter, the codification of the Fundamental Principles of Olympism, Rules and Bye-Laws as adopted by the IOC (IOC 1 September 2004). The Charter 'governs the organisation, action and operation' of the Olympic movement and 'sets forth the conditions for the celebration' of the Olympic Games. The Charter serves three main purposes: first, it is 'a basic instrument of a constitutional nature', documenting the Fundamental Principles and 'essential values of Olympism'; second, it 'serves as statutes' for the IOC; and third, it defines the 'rights and obligations' of the Olympic movement's main bodies: the IOC, the International Federations, the National Olympic Committees, and the Organising Committees for the Olympic Games (*ibid.*).

The Charter proclaims that *modern Olympism*, as conceived by Pierre de Coubertin, is (as noted at the start of this chapter) a *philosophy of life*, 'exalting and combining in a balanced whole the qualities of body, will and mind'. As summarized in the Charter:

> The Olympic movement is the concerted, organised, universal and permanent action, carried out under the supreme authority of the IOC, of all individuals and entities who are inspired by the values of Olympism. It covers the five continents. It reaches its peak with the bringing together of the world's athletes at the great sports festival, the Olympic Games.

Its symbol is five interlaced rings. The practice of sport is a human right. Every individual must have the possibility of practising sport, without discrimination of any kind and in the Olympic spirit, which requires mutual understanding with a spirit of friendship, solidarity and fair play [. . .]. Belonging to the Olympic movement requires compliance with the Olympic Charter and recognition by the IOC.

(*ibid.*)

The core ideas, values and principles lying at the heart of Olympism, and so driving the Olympic movement, ensure there are elective affinities between it and several other, contemporary ideational packages, including those of individualism, liberal democracy, the Western cultural account, and market capitalism; those associated with the processes of globalization, through which the world is becoming a single, borderless social space entailing 'ever-intensifying interconnectedness and interdependence' (Axford 1995: 25; see also Chapter 1 of this book); and consequently those that are being assumed by the broad sweep of (in particular the elites of) societies around the world during the twenty-first century. This is reflected in how the 2004 Athens Games 'hosted 11,099 athletes, the largest number ever and also the most women athletes ever. According to Athens 2004 (October 2005), representatives of 202 countries took part, more than any other sport event'. Impressive as these records may be, however, they are likely to be broken by the participation results for the Beijing Games, underscoring how the modern Games have become *the* sporting mega-event, and how the Olympic movement and Olympism are achieving global reach, a theme to be pursued in the next chapter.

Chapter 3

The Olympics, the nation-state and capitalism

Formally, as already noted (see Chapter 2), athletes taking part in an Olympic Games do not represent *countries*, but instead represent National Olympic Committees (NOCs). NOCs are constituent bodies of the Olympic movement, as are the IOC, the International Federations (IFs) of sports on the programme of the Olympic Games, and the Organising Committees of the Olympic Games (OCOGs) (IOC 26 October 2005). The Olympic movement is an umbrella organization which 'groups together all those who agree to be guided by the Olympic Charter and who recognise the authority' of the IOC (*ibid.*). The IOC is the 'supreme authority' of the Olympic movement (*ibid.*), which otherwise describes itself as 'an international non-governmental non-profit organisation and the creator of the Olympic movement' (*ibid.*). It 'exists to serve as an umbrella organisation' of the Olympic movement; it 'owns all rights to the Olympic symbols, flag, motto, anthem and Olympic Games'; and its 'primary responsibility is to supervise the organisation of the summer and winter Olympic Games' (*ibid.*). While the IOC 'guarantees the promotion of Olympism and the smooth running of the Games' in accordance with the Olympic Charter (*ibid.*), the NOCs are responsible for promoting 'the fundamental principles of Olympism at a national level within the framework of sports' (*ibid.*). Furthermore:

> Another objective of the National Olympic Committees is to ensure that athletes from their respective nations attend the Olympic Games. Only an NOC is able to select and send teams and competitors for participation in the Olympic Games. National Olympic Committees also supervise the preliminary selection of potential bid cities. Before a candidate city can compete against those in other countries, it first must win the selection process by the NOC in its own country. The National Olympic Committee can then name that city to the IOC as a candidate to host the Olympic Games. Although most NOCs are from nations, the IOC also recognises independent territories, commonwealths, protectorates and geographical areas. There are currently 202 NOCs, ranging from Albania to Zimbabwe.
> (*ibid.*; see also ANOC October 2005)

Informally, in practice, NOCs and athletes are identified within the Olympic movement as belonging to particular *nations*, or perhaps more accurately to particular *countries*, and even more accurately still to particular *countries and territories*, depending on how the terms 'nation', 'country' and 'territory' are defined (see Smith, A. 1995a, 1995b; Treanor 1997). For Joseph Stalin, a 'nation' was 'a historically constituted community of people' (Stalin, quoted in Hutchinson and Smith 1994); for Fred Halliday, it is a 'group of people who [share] a common identity, with a focus on a homeland' (Halliday, quoted in Baylis and Smith 1997); for Benedict Anderson, it is 'an imagined political community' (Anderson 1983); and for Max Weber, it is 'a community of sentiment which would adequately manifest itself in a state of its own: hence a nation is a community which normally tends to produce a state of its own' (Weber, quoted in Hutchinson and Smith 1994). What Weber has in mind by a *state* is what can be otherwise, and perhaps preferably, referred to as a *nation-state*. According to Anthony Smith, 'states [are] autonomous, public institutions of coercion and extraction within a recognised territory. States are not communities' (Smith, A. 1995b; see also Tivey 1980). Or, according to Iain McLean and Alistair McMillan, *the state* is a 'distinct set of political institutions whose specific concern is with the organization of domination, in the name of the common interest, within a delimited territory' (McLean and McMillan 2003: 512). In other words, a *state* is a set of institutions, or apparatuses, of geo-political governance, management or administration. While a state may be thought of as being the political mainstay at the core of a society, or social formation, it will necessarily be accompanied by much else within that society. It may be accompanied by, for example, *civil society*, defined by McLean and McMillan as 'the set of intermediate associations which are neither the state nor the (extended) family; civil society therefore includes voluntary associations and firms and other corporate bodies' (*ibid.*: 82). In that McLean and McMillan include firms within civil society, they take an *inclusive approach* to the notion. The alternative is to take an *exclusive approach*, whereby firms, or profit-oriented organizations, and *the market* are not counted within civil society. This is the approach of the Centre for Civil Society at the London School of Economics and Political Science:

> Civil society refers to the arena of uncoerced collective action around shared interests, purposes and values. In theory, its institutional forms are distinct from those of the state, family and market, though in prac-tice, the boundaries between state, civil society, family and market are often complex, blurred and negotiated. Civil society commonly embraces a diversity of spaces, actors and institutional forms, varying in their degree of formality, autonomy and power. Civil societies are often populated by organisations such as registered charities, development non-governmental organisations, community groups, women's organisa-tions, faith-based organisations, professional associations, trades unions,

self-help groups, social movements, business associations, coalitions and advocacy groups.

(Centre for Civil Society 2004)

Not all social formations entail civil society in the *exclusive* sense, at least if Yu Keping's analysis is accurate. For Yu Keping, the head of the Centre for Chinese Government Innovations and the former Director of the China Center for Comparative Politics and Economics, Peking University, 'civil society is the intermediate sector between the state and business enterprises' (Yu 2000; see also Glasius and Kaldor 2002). It 'consists of civil organisations which protect citizens' rights and political participation or civic engagement' (Yu 2000). What Yu refers to as 'civil society organisations (CSOs)' display a set of four distinguishing features. First, they are 'non-official, that is, they are civil, and do not represent the position of the government or the state' (*ibid.*). Second, they are 'non-profit, that is, they do not regard profit-making as the main objective of their existence, but perceive [the main objective] to be the provision of public welfare and services' (*ibid.*). Third, they are 'relatively independent, that is, they have their own organisational and management mechanisms and independent sources of funding, and are independent of the government to some extent in terms of politics, management and finance' (*ibid.*). Fourth, they are 'voluntary, that is, members are not compelled to join CSOs, and they do so voluntarily' (*ibid.*). For Yu, as civil society develops, CSOs 'play an increasingly important role in social management'; or, that is, in governance 'independently or in cooperation with the government' (*ibid.*).

Yu examines civil society and CSOs in China, pointing out that these things have made only a recent appearance. Civil society 'has a short history' in China; or, that is, the 'emergence of a relatively independent civil society' is 'a product of modern China' (*ibid.*). Even now, civil society is slow to develop and remains rudimentary. Yu tells us, perhaps somewhat contradictorily, that China's civil society is 'a typical government-led one and has an obvious official–civil duality', so that consequently China's CSOs 'are not institutionalised' (*ibid.*). In China, the CSOs, if they can be counted as such, are not institutionally independent of the state. Instead, 'most of the civil organisations are [heavily] dependent on the Party and government organs of political power', the result being that they have 'a strong official nature' (*ibid.*). Their 'activities [tend to be] under the direct control' of the state; and 'most of their leading cadres and major members are Party members and accept the leadership' of the Party' (*ibid.*). Therefore, 'the functions which many civil organisations claim to perform [. . .] fall far short of their actual roles which are often restricted by local Party and government organs' (*ibid.*). Here, Yu is claiming that there is a discrepancy between how the so-called CSOs represent themselves in principle and how, by virtue of their relationships with and control by the state, they operate in practice. While the

members of CSOs join and participate in the activities of these organizations 'on a voluntary basis', in China 'civil organisations' have 'mandatory
obligations which their members must perform' (*ibid.*). Guided by Yu,
such things as 'self-governance, independence and voluntary service amongst
civil organisations are not very high in China' (*ibid.*), if only for the time
being.

Yu explains that recently, and especially since the end of the 1970s,
the government has been 'adopting a socialist market economy featuring
diversified ownership, [but] with public ownership playing a dominant
role', and with an emphasis on 'government intervention' (*ibid.*). The political system, and indeed the political economy, still pivots around 'the
authority of the Party Central Committee and the leadership of the Party'
(*ibid.*); and accordingly the emerging civil society 'inevitably has a serious
official nature and government leadership. In fact, it often [is] a tool of
the Party and the government' (*ibid.*; see also Wang 2003; Zhang Ye 2003).
Currently, as Elizabeth Wishnich puts it in her assessment of *China as
a Risk Society*, 'the Chinese leadership continues to restrict the development of civil society, especially the role of NGOs, which have proven
crucial elsewhere in the world in promoting environmental awareness',
for example, because the leadership is 'concerned with the prospect of
domestic instability' (Wishnich 2005).

What in other social formations, and especially in Western ones, would be
civil society and CSOs, or non-governmental organizations (NGOs), are in
China largely extensions of the state or integrated within the state. They are
little more or nothing less than state apparatuses, through which the state is
largely in control of overall social administration, management or governance. China remains a *statist* society, one in which *statism* as a doctrine is
highly, or supremely, influential in shaping government policies and practices
in relation to the economy as well as to other spheres of social life. Statism
is the 'doctrine of giving a centralized government control over economic
planning and policy', so that in a statist society the 'government implements
a significant degree of centralized economic planning, which may include
state ownership of the means of production, as opposed to a system where
the overwhelming majority of economic planning occurs at a decentralized
level by private individuals in a relatively free market' (AC 3 November
2005). The term 'statism' can 'refer to various dissimilar ideologies that
share the commonality of having centralized economic planning conducted
by the state. Statist economies are also referred to as *command economies*'
(*ibid.*). Furthermore 'statism' is 'sometimes used to refer to government
intervention in civil as well as economic matters' (*ibid.*).

While China is statist in relation to the economy, it appears to be even
more so in relation to other areas of social life, and in particular to China's
rudimentary civil society and so to what purport to be China's CSOs. This
applies to sport, sports organizations in general, and the Chinese Olympic

Committee (COC) in particular. It is reflected in the manner in which, since the early 1990s, 'sports reform has made significant headways. A long-term plan for sports promotion was worked out and put into practice, and with the promulgation of the Sports Law in October 1995 a breakthrough was made in the institution of a legal system for sports in the country' (COC 31 December 2004; see also Chapter 7 of this book). The COC claims:

> With the deepening of reforms in sports, a new pattern has formed with sports being managed by both [the] state and society as a whole. As a result, more than 20 national sports administrative centres have been set up to govern various competitive sports originally under the direct administration of the State Sport General Administration. A considerable portion of funds to sports training, competition and facilities construction comes from enterprises and individuals instead of exclusively from government budgets. Sports industry is flourishing. The National Fitness Programme has witnessed a vigorous development throughout the country, as the Chinese sports authorities have paid equal attention to raising athletic standards and promoting sports among the masses of people.
>
> (ibid.)

There may have been a shift in the management, or governance, of sport to more of a hybrid system in China, but the participation of the state remains paramount, including in relation to the COC, in spite of the way in which the Committee refers to itself as 'a non-governmental, non-profit national sports organization of a mass character, with the objective of developing sports and promoting the Olympic movement in the country' (COC 3 November 2005). Purportedly, what might be referred to as the *tasks and functions* of the COC include 'giving publicity to the basic principles of the Olympicism [sic] and ensuring the observation of the Olympic Charter in China' (ibid.). Still, the COC's commitment to and success in achieving its self-declared tasks and functions depend upon its relationship with the state, both direct and indirect, given the tasks and functions which in the first place the state assumes in relation to the COC, Chinese society overall, and the wider world.

The way in which the state remains firmly in control over sport in general, and over the COC in particular, is especially evident in China's external sporting participation, in spite of the claim by the COC that it 'represents China in handling international affairs related to the Olympic movement', as 'the sole representative of the whole country's Olympic movement in its relations with the International Olympic Committee (IOC), the Olympic Council of Asia (OCA) and other international sports organizations, as well as all National Olympic Committees (NOCs)' (ibid.). Crucially, it was *why did they do this?*

the government which, by restoring the PRC's participation 'in international sports organizations in the late [1970s,] paved the way for the country to play an active part in the global Olympic movement' (COC 31 December 2004). In turn, following the IOC's meeting in Nagoya in 1979, the PRC has resumed its membership of or has been newly admitted to many international sports organizations in accordance with the IOC *model* (*ibid.*), which allows for the separate participation of Taiwan, otherwise known as the Republic of China (ROC), the main island of which is also known as Formosa (after the Portuguese *Ilha Formosa*, meaning 'beautiful island'). Following a resolution adopted by all IOC members on 26 November 1979, the COC's 'legal status was reinstated in the IOC', while the Olympic Committee in Taipei, the capital of Taiwan, was allowed to remain in the IOC under the name of *the Chinese Taipei Olympic Committee* (COC 7 November 2005). The issue aside of how, if at all, this compromise represents a rejection of 'the two Chinas plot fabricated by the IOC leader' which led to the COC severing 'relations with the IOC' in August 1958 (*ibid.*), it underscores how in practice the COC's activities, both internal and external, are greatly controlled by the state (see Chapter 6 of this book; see also Bush 2005).

In practice, the COC's relationship with the Olympic movement is far from consistent with the features, or criteria, that for Yu Keping define and distinguish CSOs; and is far closer and tighter than the relationships that are sustained by NOCs with their respective states elsewhere in the world. All NOCs will be constrained by state interference and control, but many are far less constrained than the COC. This can be illustrated with reference to the case of the US-led boycott of the Games of the XXII Olympiad held in Moscow in 1980. The USA and 64 other NOCs boycotted the Games, as a result of which the event attracted the lowest number of teams since 1956. None the less, Moscow still managed to host 80 teams, including one from Britain, much to the annoyance of Margaret Thatcher, the Prime Minister of Britain at the time. In retaliation, 'a revenge boycott led by the Soviet Union depleted the field in certain sports' at the 1984 Los Angeles Olympics (IOC 9 November 2005). Still, a record 140 NOC teams took part (*ibid.*), and the 14 NOCs that were persuaded not to participate came solely from the Soviet bloc, where civil society was largely absent. While the PRC did not participate in the 1980 Games, it did do so in the 1984 event, gaining fourth place in the final medals table, behind West Germany, Romania (which notably resisted Moscow's call for a boycott), and the USA.

If and when NOCs do qualify as CSOs, then they will operate as such within civil society at the 'local' *countries and territories* level, whereas the Olympic movement and the IOC are CSOs (or NGOs) that operate within civil society at the global level (see Glasius and Kaldor 2002). The Olympic movement and the IOC are global civil society organizations (GCSOs) or global non-governmental organizations (GNGOs). In between, there is a set of regional, or continental, organizations:

> The NOCs come together at least once every two years in the form of the Association of National Olympic Committees (ANOC) to exchange information and experiences in order to consolidate their role within the Olympic movement. In this way the ANOC helps the NOCs to prepare for their meetings with the IOC Executive Board and Olympic Congresses. The ANOC also makes recommendations to the IOC regarding the use of funds deriving from the television rights intended for the NOCs. These recommendations focus on the implementation of the Olympic Solidarity programmes in particular. The ANOC is currently made up of the 202 NOCs and is split among five continental associations: Africa: ANOCA (Association of National Olympic Committees of Africa); America: PASO (Pan American Sports Organisation); Asia: OCA (Olympic Council of Asia); Europe: EOC (European Olympic Committees); Oceania: ONOC (Oceania National Olympic Committees).
>
> (IOC 7 November 2005)[1]

At whatever level it occurs – whether the local, the regional or the global – civil society will be a social sphere which is distinct from and to some extent independent of the state, however rudimentary the state might be. The existence of the state does not require the existence of civil society, but the existence of civil society requires, by definition, the existence of the state. If the state does not exist in a particular place or at a particular level, then civil society will not exist in that place or at that level. Whether the state and civil society exist at either the regional level or the global level is a contentious matter, but the argument that they do exist at the regional level in, for example, Europe by virtue of the European Union (EU), and at the global level – by virtue of such organizations and institutions as the United Nations (UN), the World Trade Organization (WTO), the World Bank, the International Monetary Fund (IMF), and the International Criminal Court (ICC) – warrants serious consideration (see Close 1995; Close and Ohki-Close 1999; see also Leonard 2005). In so far as the state does exist at the global level, within global society, then the claim that global civil society (GCS) and GCSOs exist becomes plausible, as does the view that the IOC is a GCSO, and indeed is a prominent and influential GCSO due to the status of the Olympic Games as a mega-event and connectedly to the immense appeal that the Games have throughout the world, in particular at the local, or *country and territory*, level.

At the local level, the Games seem to have a strong appeal to the state, and especially to those states within geo-political entities that qualify as *nation-states*. Evidence here is to be found on and through various Internet websites, including the official ones of the Olympic movement and of the host city organizing committees, such as those for Sydney, Athens, Beijing, and London.[2] The appeal in this case may be explicable, if only in part, in terms of nation-states being quite new, somewhat contrived, and variously unstable, especially relative to and, more to the point, in relation to *nations.* As Graham Evans puts it, nation-states 'are not always composed of ethnically homogeneous social, cultural or linguistic groups. The nation-state, which is commonly regarded as the "ideal" or "normal" political unit, is in fact a particular form of territorial state – others are city-states and empires' (Evans 1998: 344). What is more, the twentieth century 'has witnessed what appears to be a growing trend towards supranational forms of political organization, especially on a regional basis' (*ibid.*). The 'nation-state is still a potent force in international relations. However, its detractors have argued that [. . .] the nation-state is an artificial, not a natural, construct [which] despite its near-universality' may be 'something of an anachronism' (*ibid.*). In similar vein, James Paul reports that Canada, Belgium, Britain, Spain and Italy along with 'many other well-established' nation-states 'face separatist claims', in response to which they 'are ceding increasing autonomy to regional' – in the sense of sub-nation-state – bodies (Paul 1996):

> In some cases, regional languages and cultures are enjoying a renaissance. Even regional economies are proclaiming their independence from central authority. Cataluna in Spain has revived the Catalan language, set up its own parliament and claims a unique economic status linked to France and the Mediterranean as well as to Spain. Quebec, Flemish Belgium, Scotland and Northern Italy have staked a claim to special status, too, and some of their citizens favor complete national separation. Meanwhile, France grapples with independence forces in Corsica, China has indigestion over Tibet, Mexico faces insurgency in Chiapas. States are not just under pressure 'from below'. They are also under pressure 'from above' – losing some of their sovereignty to larger entities like the European Union and the North American Free Trade Association [sic] at the regional level, and the World Bank, the IMF and the WTO at the global level. Multinational institutions like NAFTA and the WTO are beginning to nullify [domestic, nation-state] laws in areas like the environment, human rights, labor [sic] protection and the like. In recent polls, even citizens of the United States have expressed doubt that their powerful [country] is capable of solving problems independent of others.
>
> (*ibid.*)

Existing, embryonic and prospective supranational organizations, or regimes, at the regional and global levels may be putting both direct and indirect pressure on nation-states, the indirect pressure being by way of the encouragement these organizations give to sub-nation-state nations, national identity, nationalism, nationalist movements, and separatism in relation to nation-states, albeit some more than others (see also Close 1995, 2000; Close and Askew 2004a; Close and Ohki-Close 1999: Chapter 6). China, for instance, is composed of a quite extensive, diverse and complex set of *ethnically heterogeneous social, cultural or linguistic groups* and, moreover, *nations*, some of which have separatist tendencies. In China, while 91.9 per cent of the population is Han Chinese, there are sizeable proportions of not only Uygur (see Chapter 2), but also Zhuang, Hui, Yi, Tibetan, Miao, Manchu, Mongol, Buyi, Korean 'and other nationalities' (CIA 1 November 2005). The Chinese state officially recognizes, apart from the Han Chinese, 55 *ethnic groups* (CIIC 20 November 2005). However, the cultural, ethnic and national mix of the Chinese population is in practice far greater than this indicates, as Xu Yuan has pointed out:

> As an empire-turned modern state, the [PRC] has sought to integrate peoples within its territory under the banner of common citizenship. The subsequent state project implemented policies based on subjects' *minzu* identity. The PRC constitutionally proclaims itself 'a unitary, multi-*minzu* socialist state' – the Chinese nation (*zhonghua minzu*) comprised of the Han majority and 55 other officially recognized 'nationalities' [. . .]. Popularised in the early twentieth century by Sun Yat-sen, the founder of republican China, the term *minzu* can variously be translated as nation, nationality, ethnic group, ethnic minority (or minority nationality) or people. The state-sponsored project of '*minzu* identification' *(minzu shibie)* from 1953 to 1979 identified 55 minority *minzu* out of over 400 applicant groups seeking official status. With the identification of the Jinuo Zu in 1979, the PR's population of 56 *minzu* was fixed; unidentified groups were placed under the umbrella of other groups.
>
> (Xu Yuan 2004)

For some writers, the cultural, ethnic and national diversity of China not only raises the possibility of certain parts of the PRC, such as the Xinjiang Uygur Autonomous Region (XUAR) (Sullivan 15 January 2004), breaking away, but also poses a threat to the PRC's overall security and survival. As Dru Gladney puts it, China 'is officially a multi-national country with 56 recognized "nationalities" ', but 'recent events suggest that China may well be increasingly insecure regarding not only these nationalities, but also its own national integration' (Gladney 2000). In Gladney's view:

> China is now seeing a resurgence of pride in local nationality and culture, most notably among southerners such as the Cantonese and Hakka who are now classified as Han. These differences may increase under

economic pressures such as inflation, the growing gap between rich and poor areas, and the migration of millions of people from poorer provinces to those with jobs. Chinese society is also under pressure from the officially recognized minorities such as Uyghurs and Tibetans. For centuries, China has held together a vast multicultural and multiethnic nation despite alternating periods of political centralization and fragmentation. But cultural and linguistic cleavages could worsen in a China weakened by internal strife, inflation, uneven growth, or a post-Jiang struggle for succession. The recent National Day celebrations in October, celebrating 50 years of the Communist Party in China, underscored the importance of China's many ethnic peoples in its national resurgence.

(*ibid.*)

It is claimed that, alongside its *Taiwan problem*, the Beijing government faces separatist, or secessionist, movements on the mainland, not only in Xinjiang, but also in Guangxi, Hong Kong, Inner Mongolia, Macau, Manchuria, Tibet and Yunan (see Liew and Wang 2003; Safron 1998; Shi and Shi 2002; Starr 2004), although its tussle in Xinjiang with the East Turkistan Islamic movement has been the most violent. During 2003:

The authorities continued to use the international 'war against terrorism' to justify harsh repression in Xinjiang, which continued to result in serious human rights violations against the ethnic Uighur community. The authorities continued to make little distinction between acts of violence and acts of passive resistance. Repression was often manifested through assaults on Uighur culture, such as the closure of several mosques, restrictions on the use of the Uighur language and the banning of certain Uighur books and journals. The crack-down against suspected 'separatists, terrorists and religious extremists' intensified following the start of a renewed 100-day security crack-down in October [2003]. Arrests continued and thousands of political prisoners, including prisoners of conscience, remained in prison. Concerns increased that China was putting pressure on neighbouring countries to forcibly return Uighurs suspected of 'separatist' activities, including asylum-seekers and refugees.

(AI 25 May 2004)

While, in the end, the Chinese state will resort to armed force against separatists, its strategy will entail trying to otherwise diminish the threat of separatism and sub-nation-state nationalism by promoting 'national' identity, sentiment and commitment at the nation-state level. It will try to do this around *the flag*, literally and figuratively, on various occasions, including at sporting events, and especially those events entailing competition with teams from other countries and territories. The Olympics and especially the 2008 event offer the Chinese state the greatest of opportunities in this respect, hence a source of its enthusiastic support for Beijing's quest to host the Games starting in the early 1990s. Of course, the use of the Olympics in this way is double-edged, and the tactic could backfire. Chinese people may identify more with athletes who belong to their own (sub-nation-state) nations than with athletes of other Chinese nations, including that of China overall, in so far as a Chinese 'nation' exists. Rather than being a rallying point for the Chinese people, the Chinese 'nation' and the Chinese nation-state, or the PRC, in relation to the rest (the people of other countries and territories), the Beijing Olympics could turn out to be just as much, if not more, of a rallying point for China's various nations in relation to each other and the Chinese state, the result being the yet further sharpening of China's sub-nation-state national identities and separatist tendencies.

[Handwritten margin notes: "Promoting the Chinese team to the people of China as a means of bringing so many different nationalities together" / "might backfire"]

A state together with everything else within its territory constitutes a nation-state. A nation-state does not necessarily contain just one nation. Instead, a nation-state may contain a number of nations, as well as parts of nations. Each nation which is contained within a nation-state or which straddles several nation-states has a tendency (following Weber) to strive for its own distinct, separate state (set of apparatuses of social governance) and concomitantly for its own distinct, separate nation-state. If a 'nation' is a *community*, and moreover an *imagined political community*, based on a *shared identity*, and with a tendency to *produce a state of its own*, then it is more accurate to say that NOCs and athletes are identified by the Olympic movement with countries, although the accuracy of this is also questionable. According to one interpretation, *countries* are distinct *geo-political entities* that can be sub-categorized into either (a) independent, sovereign nation-states or (b) non-independent, integral parts of more inclusive countries or, that is, nation-states. For instance, the United Kingdom of Great Britain and Northern Ireland (usually shortened to the United Kingdom or the UK), off the North-western coast of continental Europe, is a country which is in turn composed of three constituent countries – England, Scotland, and Wales – on the island of Great Britain, and the province of Northern Ireland on the island of Ireland.

The UK is a country and a nation-state, but one which in turn contains three countries (and a province) and several nations. Contenders for the nations are the English, the Welsh, the Scots, the Irish and the Northern Irish, not to mention the British, as reflected in the strong, often fanatical, support which is given to the separate England, Scotland, Wales and Northern Ireland *national* teams in a range of sports, including football and rugby, and at various sporting events, such as the Commonwealth Games. Indeed, there has been a 'demand for Scotland to field its own Olympic team when London hosts the 2012 Games' from Linda Fabiani, a Scottish National Party (SNP) member and Member of the Scottish Parliament (MSP). She 'made the call by urging politicians from all parties to get behind the suggestion' (BBC 27 July 2005), adding:

> Let's see Scotland's politicians get behind Scotland's athletes and let's make sure we have a Scotland team at the London Olympics. Scotland can compete internationally in sport, as our Commonwealth Games teams have shown over the years [. . .]. Scotland is recognised as a sporting nation by many international sporting organisations and there is no reason why the Olympic movement should be any different. The Olympic medals picked up by Scotland's sporting heroes over the years indicate a sporting strength that can be built on in Scotland [. . .]. National flags were first carried into an Olympic stadium at the 1908 London Olympics, and it would be good if the Scottish Saltire [flag] could finally join those flags at the London Olympics of 2012.
>
> (ibid.)

Opposition to Fabiani's suggestion has been voiced by Jamie McGrigor, the Conservative Party MSP for the Highlands and Islands. He has accused 'nationalists of playing political football' (ibid.), claiming that SNP members 'care more about their own narrow nationalism than the country's sporting status' (ibid.). A Scottish Labour Party (SLP) spokesman agreed, claiming that SNP members are 'so obsessed with divorcing Scotland from the UK they are willing to jeopardise Scottish Olympic success for their own narrow political ends' (ibid.). The SLP spokesman added, when 'the SNP say they want a Scottish Olympic team to be like those of Hong Kong, Guam and the British Virgin Islands, [do] they not realise that only one of these countries won a medal at the most recent Olympics' (ibid.).

The British Virgin Islands is a UK *overseas territory*, Guam is a US *unincorporated territory*, and Hong Kong is a *special administrative region* of China. The UK has several *overseas territories*, or *dependent territories*, each of which is not part of the UK while being subject to the UK's sovereignty and formal control. *Dependent territories* can be distinguished from *nation-states* in that, unlike the latter, they do not possess full political independence; as well as from countries at the sub-nation-state level in that they are of not integral parts of the governing, sovereign nation-state. Dependent territories, or simply dependencies, are *unincorporated*, non-integral, non-independent appendages of nation-states, and are recognized as such by the UN for the purpose of deciding which geo-political entities are eligible for membership of the UN. Quite simply, dependencies cannot become UN Member States. Only those geo-political entities, or countries, that are recognized by the UN as independent, sovereign nation-states can become UN Member States. Indeed, it is reasonable to argue that a place is only a nation-state if it is recognized as such by the UN, or more precisely through the UN, within the UN General Assembly, by the UN's Member States, all of which will already be UN recognized nation-states. As of the start of the Beijing Olympiad at the end of August 2004, the UN had recognized 192 nation-states, 191 of which had become UN Member States, the exception being the Holy See, or Vatican. While only those geo-political entities that are recognized by the UN as nation-states can become UN Member States, a few other geo-political entities have been granted UN observer status, including the Palestinian Authority (or simply Palestine) and the European Union (EU). As observers, like the Holy See, these non-nation-state UN participants can attend but cannot vote at UN General Assembly meetings.

Just as almost all of the world's nation-states are UN Member States, so almost the same proportion of the world's collection of nation-states *and* dependent territories (NSTDs) have become IOC members. Nearly all NSTDs were represented by NOCs at the 2004 Athens Games, just as they were at both the 2000 Sydney and the 1996 Atlanta events. As James Paul has observed, there 'were 197 "countries" participating in the 1996 Summer Olympics in Atlanta. All were invited by the International Olympic Committee and none invited failed to attend. At the same time, there were 185 "member states" of the United Nations' (Paul 1996). By the 2004 Athens Olympics, a further six countries had become UN Member States: Kiribati, 14 September 1999; Nauru, 14 September 1999; Switzerland, 10 September 2002; Timor-Leste, 27 September 2002; Tonga, 14 September 1999; and Tuvalu, 5 September 2000. At the time of the 1996 Atlanta Olympics, the 16 *Olympians* (as James Paul refers to those NSTDs with NOCs) that were not UN Member States – there being four UN Member States that were not *Olympians* or, that is, IOC members – were American Samoa, American Virgin Islands, Aruba, Bermuda, British Virgin Islands, Chinese Taipei (or Taiwan), Cook Islands, Guam, Hong Kong, Nauru, Netherlands Antilles, Palestine, Puerto Rico and Switzerland. Of these IOC members, the two that were recognized by the UN as independent, sovereign nation-states had become UN Member States by 2005: Nauru in September 1999 and Switzerland in September 2002. American Samoa, American Virgin Islands, Guam and Puerto Rico were dependent territories of the USA; Aruba was a dependent territory of the Netherlands, as was the Netherlands Antilles; both Bermuda and the British Virgin Islands were dependent territories of the United Kingdom; Cook Islands were 'self-governing in free association with New Zealand' (CIA 5 October 2005); Hong Kong was a special administrative region of the PRC; and Chinese Taipei was claimed by the PRC as an integral part – not *country*, but *province* – of that nation-state:

> Taiwan is the island which has for all practical purposes been independent for half a century but which China regards as a renegade province that must be re-united with the mainland. Legally, most [nation-states] – and the UN – acknowledge the position of the Chinese government

that Taiwan is a province of China, and as a result Taiwan has formal diplomatic relations with only 26 countries and no seat at the UN.

(BBC 22 September 2005)

On this reckoning, whereas the PRC is a nation-state, Taiwan either is not a nation-state or is a nation-state, but equivocally and questionably. At best, currently, Taiwan is probably the most marginal nation-state of all the countries and territories in the world.

Having acquired 191 members by the 2004 start of the Beijing Olympiad, the UN was unlikely to further expand its membership during the four years to the opening of the 2008 Games (which is not to ignore that expansion of sorts due to Montenegro's accession on 28 June 2006 following its separation from Serbia on 3 June 2006). On the other hand, there was some scope for an enlargement of the IOC's membership during the Beijing Olympiad. By the 1996 Atlanta Olympics, four UN Member States were not IOC members: Eritrea, Marshall Islands, Micronesia and Palau. Of these, three – Eritrea, Micronesia and Palau – had joined the IOC by the time of the 2000 Sydney Olympics, bringing the membership to 200. During the Athens Olympiad, Kiribati and Timor-Leste joined in anticipation for the 2004 Games, raising the IOC's membership to 202. This left just Marshall Islands plus one other nation-state which by the start of the Beijing Olympiad were UN Member States but not members of the IOC, the other nation-state being Tuvalu, it having joined the UN in 2000. On the other hand, in that IOC membership is not confined to nation-states – it being open in particular to recognized dependent territories – then there was the technical possibility of the number of IOC members increasing by substantially more than two during the period 2004–6, although by how many is difficult to pin down precisely (see ILO December 2004). In practice, at the start of the Beijing Olympiad, no further dependent territories seemed to be on their way to joining the IOC independently of their governing nation-states prior to the 2008 Games, and during the Olympiad just one further nation-state acceded. On 9 February 2006, Marshall Islands became the 203rd member of the IOC, leaving Tuvalu the only UN Member State which was not participating in the Olympic movement, at least by way of an NOC, the only other UN-recognized nation-state in the world without an NOC being the Holy See, or Vatican (see Chapter 1).

By the start of the Beijing Olympiad, with the closing of the Athens Games at the end of August 2004, the memberships of both the UN and the IOC appeared to have reached plateaus, dictated by the limit of their potential memberships within the prevailing global framework of countries, nation-states and dependent territories. In this sense, the UN and the IOC had reached their saturation points or, to put it another way, had attained global-reach status in a manner consistent with the *ideals and tendencies* associated with the progress of globalization, whereby the world is becoming a *single social space*. The global reach of the UN and the IOC as judged with reference to their memberships may be viewed as a manifestation of those (globalization) processes whereby a single, inclusive *global society* is being forged around the policies, principles and practices of the UN and the IOC as global organizations and institutions.

Concomitantly, *global society* is also being constructed around the principles and practices of modern market capitalism, and moreover perhaps principally around this particular package of principles and practices. Indeed, perhaps the parts being played in the construction of *global society* by the UN and all that it stands for (such as a global human rights regime; see Close and Askew, 2004a; and see below), on the one hand, and the Olympic movement, on the other, are themselves largely attributable to the prior part being played by the ideals and tendencies of modern market capitalism. Perhaps, that is, the parts being played by the UN and the Olympic movement are largely explicable in terms of their elective affinities with these particular, underlying ideals and tendencies.

Capitalism has been defined as an 'economic and political system in which a country's trade and industry are controlled by private owners for profit, rather than by the state' (*Concise Oxford English Dictionary* [COD]); and as an 'economic system in which the means of production, distribution and exchange are privately owned and operated for profit' (*Webster's Dictionary of the English Language* [WDEL]). If so, then *market capitalism* can be defined as an 'economic system in which all or most of the means of production are privately owned and operated and where the investment of capital, and the production, distribution and prices of commodities (goods and services) are determined mainly in a free market, rather than by the state. The means of production have generally been operated in pursuit of profit' (Wikipedia 31 October 2005). For McLean and McMillan, capitalism is a 'term denoting a distinct form of social organization, based on generalized commodity production in which there is private ownership and/or control of the means of production' (2003: 62). Within this *form of social organization*, production is driven by 'the profit motive' (*ibid.*: 63); and in so far as the production involved is 'for markets with the desire for gain' (*ibid.*: 63), then the appropriate term to use for this *form of social organization* will be *market capitalism*. McLean and McMillan note that, although 'the world market has always formed the backdrop for the development of capitalism, a number of recent changes, associated with both the "globalization of capital" ' and 'the demise of the Soviet Union, have strengthened the claim that capitalism should now be viewed as a world system' (*ibid.*: 65).

The development of market capitalism as a *world system*,[3] or that is the globalization of market capitalism, has been aided by the demise of the Soviet Union between 1989 and 1991, and with it the 'collapse of Marxist socialism in the Soviet empire' (*ibid.*: 496). For McLean and McMillan, socialism is a 'political and economic theory or system of organization based on collective or state ownership of the means of production, distribution and exchange' (*ibid.*: 496–7). In contrast with market capitalism, market socialism is the 'doctrine [which maintains that] while capital can and should be owned cooperatively, or in some cases by the state, decisions about production and exchange should be left to market forces and not planned centrally' (*ibid.*: 335). If so, then consistency requires 'market capitalism' to be identified not as a *system* or as a *form of social organization*, but instead as a *doctrine*. Consistency requires, more specifically, market capitalism to be distinguished as that doctrine which maintains that the means of production should be partly, mainly or wholly owned privately, and that decisions about production, distribution and exchange should be left mainly to market forces, rather than to central planning by the state. As such, market capitalism is a package of (doctrinal) ideas, principles or prescriptions in favour of a particular *form of social organization*, that form which can be referred to as *capitalist*. Just as Marx 'preferred to speak of the capitalist mode of production' (*ibid.*: 62), so it is preferable to speak of the capitalist form of social organization, of capitalist social formations, and of capitalist societies in order to identify what (the doctrine of) capitalism prescribes; and of the market capitalist form of social production, of market capitalist social formations, and of market-capitalist societies in order to identify what (the doctrine of) market capitalism prescribes.

The doctrinal, or ideational, approach to the conceptualization of capitalism is consistent with the way the term has been used by Max Weber among others:

> Werner Sombart [. . .] describes capitalism in terms of a synthesis of the spirit of enterprise with the 'bourgeois spirit' of calculation and rationality [. . .]. On this basis, Weber (in *The Protestant Ethic and the Spirit of Capitalism*) charts how the 'spirit of capitalism' transformed other modes of economic activity designated as 'traditionalist' [. . .]. Although Weber stops short of suggesting that the Protestant ethic produced capitalism, he believes that the origins of the capitalist spirit can be traced particularly to the ethics associated with Calvinism. Capitalism is [. . .] the consequence of a new spirit of entrepreneurial enterprise [. . .]. The spirit of rational calculation fosters a capitalist economic system in which [for instance] wage-labourers are legally 'free' to sell their labour power [. . .] in the market place [. . .]; and there is a clear separation of home and workplace.
>
> (*ibid.*: 62; see also Sombart 2001)

An *ethic*, or *ethical code*, is a package of principles or standards of (right and wrong) human conduct, whereas the term spirit as used by Sombart and Weber infers such notions as *soul, life force, vital force, vitality, heart* or simply *attitude*. For Weber, the spirit of capitalism can be traced to capitalism's elective affinity with the Protestant, and more specifically the Calvinist, ethic, where capitalism as such is (like Protestantism and Calvinism) a doctrine, or that is a package of principles, dogma or instructions for the purpose of conducting economic and related affairs, activities and relationships.

Under the sway of (the doctrine of) market capitalism, the market-capitalist form of social production has become the dominant form around the world, and at all levels: the local, the regional, and the global. Market capitalism and the market-capitalist form of social production have achieved global reach, and have spearheaded the progress of globalization overall, and thereby of *global society*. This is not to ignore the possibility of counter-vailing factors, forces and considerations, such as resistance, localization and *glocalization*, and in particular of alternative capitalisms and capitalist forms of social production. For instance, McLean and McMillan distinguish Anglo-Saxon capitalism, or 'the "liberal market" model of capitalism', from 'the Rheinish version' of capitalism in which there is an emphasis on the intervening part to be played by 'social democracy' (McLean and McMillan 2003: 16–17), and so by the state, in the processes of the production, distribution and exchange of goods and services. Anglo-Saxon capitalism is that doctrine which favours 'a system of capitalism characterized by extensive market coordination by economic actors and relatively neutral patterns of governmental market regulation aimed at maintaining property right institutions without privileging particular social actors [. . .]. Non-market or associational patterns of economic coordination are weak within Anglo-Saxon capitalism', which is mainly 'associated with the United Kingdom and the United States' (*ibid.*: 16).

Other observers have distinguished Asian capitalism (see Kristof 1998) or East Asian capitalism (see Orru et al. 1996). Nicholas Kristof has contrasted the 'harsh reality of free-market capitalism' as found especially in the United States with Asian capitalism. In Asia, 'some nations [have] followed [an] economic model [which emphasizes] not markets but government planning and long-term relationships' (Kristof 1998). However, in 1998 the Asian 'version of capitalism, particularly the variety developed in Japan and adopted by South Korea, [had become] widely regarded as a problem' in view of 'the Asian financial crisis', which consequently was 'driving governments and businesses alike toward a more Adam Smith, market-oriented version of capitalism' (*ibid.*). For Kristof, writing in the immediate aftermath of the Asian financial crisis, while 'many aspects of East Asia's community ethos [would] remain', the 'region's economies [would] emerge from the financial crisis looking a bit more like the American economy', fashioned as this is primarily by 'the "liberal market" model of capitalism' (McLean and McMillan 2003: 16). The 'changes that diplomats and business executives' wanted would mean that governments would 'control economies less than before', so that in particular finance ministries would 'no longer [tell] the banks whom to lend to', and would lose their 'capacity to determine the fate of banks and securities houses'; labour markets would 'become a bit more flexible, and unemployment rates [would] rise'; lifetime employment and 'rigid seniority systems [would] become less important, and layoffs [would] increase'; relationships 'in general [would] become less important'; the 'system of linked companies, called keiretsu in Japan and chaebol in South Korea, doing business with one another on the basis of loyalty rather than price, [would] gradually give way to a somewhat more open system'; and companies would 'make less effort to build market share and more effort to make money' (Kristof 1998).

The topic of *competing capitalisms* (Beeson 1999), especially between the West and East Asia, in particular in the wake of the Asian financial crisis of the late 1990s, has continued to attract much scrutiny and many publications (see, for instance, Johnson 2001; Tomba 2002), although the focus has tended to shift towards China's version of capitalism in comparison with and in relation to the West's (see Narine 2005). Thus, in Shaun Narine's view, China is in 'a state of transitional capitalism', in that 'it has not yet defined a distinctive approach to capitalist development' (*ibid.*: 2):

> Nonetheless, the approach that it has adopted to date is quite compatible with the American approach to state–economy relations. Indeed, the form of capitalism at work in China is a much rawer and more socially destructive form of capitalism than anything advocated by modern Anglo-American capitalism. At the same time, however, China's acceptance of basic capitalism does not necessarily compromise its ability to wield influence over its neighbours or to develop institutions that promote alternative forms of economic development. This is because China's commitment to capitalism is actually a commitment to economic nationalism. Economic nationalism characterizes the approach of all other regional states to development, providing a common ground on which China and its neighbours can meet and organize institutional arrangements. Ultimately, China will challenge American influence at the regional and international levels not because it is pursuing a radically different economic or political philosophy but because it is adopting and adapting the predominant economic discourse to its own needs.
>
> (*ibid.*: 2–3)

In Narine's view, China 'has no alternative model of capitalism that it wishes to promote or enhance', and instead 'has mostly bought wholeheartedly into the existing economic models and has been utilizing these to considerable effect' (*ibid.*: 27), motivated by *economic nationalism* (see also Blecher 2005; Blume 2003; Guthrie 1999; Helleiner 2002; Yeung 2004). As of the Beijing Olympiad, the PRC, or the state on behalf of the PRC, had embraced and was increasingly embracing market capitalism, and more specifically had opted for the Anglo-Saxon (or liberal market) model of capitalism, as distinct from the Rheinish (or social democratic) model. The PRC had adopted and was applying the Anglo-Saxon model increasingly at the expense of what has been distinguished as the Asian or East Asian model. The PRC had become committed to that form of social production which was becoming the dominant form around the world, and through which the overall globalization package was being spearheaded and global society was being constructed. In turn, the PRC was contributing to the processes whereby a globalized world was evolving in accordance with the ideals and tendencies, or principles and practices, of modern market capitalism, and in particular that version of market capitalism which was associated with the United States and the US's status as the sole global superpower, or global-reach hegemon (cf. Wallerstein 2003). This is not to say, of course, that the balance of global political economy power will inevitably remain tipped in favour of the US at least over the long term, perhaps especially in view of the possibility of China being distinctively motivated by *economic nationalism*, as Narine calls it.

As capitalism, and especially the liberal market model, albeit motivated by economic nationalism, takes hold, it might be expected that civil society will evolve in China, becoming more and more firmly established as a bridge between the economy and the polity, centred as the latter will be on the state. It is likely that organizations will emerge which more fully qualify as civil society organizations (CSOs), in particular by being able to operate in a relatively independent manner in relation to the state (see Wang Yizhou 2003; Yu 2000; Zhang Ye 2003), and that among these CSOs will be the Chinese Olympic Committee (COC). It is reasonable to assume that the choice of Beijing to host the 2008 Games will give a boost to these developments, so that the COC's status as a CSO will become increasingly evident during the period of the Beijing Olympiad as well as afterwards. The COC, or, that is, the COC's relationship with the state, may well emerge as a highly reliable indicator of China's overall political economy progress, both with respect to its internal development and its standing in relation to other political economy players on the world stage, in the increasingly globalized world (see Zheng Yongnian 2004).

The principles and practices, or ideals and tendencies, of modern market capitalism, and in particular of modern liberal market capitalism, will sustain elective affinities with a raft of contemporaneous packages of principles and practices, whereby the globalization of modern market capitalism is further facilitated, consolidated and assured. Indeed, the parts being played by such organizations as the UN and the Olympic movement in the construction of *global society* may be largely understandable in terms of their elective affinities with the prior, underlying ideals and tendencies of modern market capitalism. If so, then these elective affinities will be important in accounting for what would seem to be the high degree of correspondence, or harmony, between the principles and practices of the UN, on the one hand, and those of the Olympic movement, on the other; and in shedding light on the way in which the UN and the IOC show considerable support for each other. For instance, on 31 October 2003, at the 58th session of the UN General Assembly (agenda item 23a), a draft resolution was passed on Sport for Peace and Development: Building a Peaceful and Better World through Sport and the Olympic Ideal (UN 31 October 2003). In doing this, the Assembly recalled its resolution (56/75) of 11 December 2001, in which it decided to include in the 'agenda of its fifty-eighth session the item' on Building a Peaceful and Better World through Sport and the Olympic Ideal, and 'its decision to consider this item every two years in advance of each Summer and Winter Olympic Games' (*ibid.*). The Assembly also recalled its resolution (48/11) of 25 October 1993, 'which, inter alia, revived the ancient Greek tradition of *ekecheiria* ("Olympic Truce"), calling for a truce during the Games that would encourage a peaceful environment and ensuring the safe passage and participation of athletes and others at the Games and, thereby, mobilizing the youth of the world to the cause of peace' (*ibid.*). The Assembly 'noted the inclusion in the United Nations Millennium Declaration of an appeal for the observance of the Olympic Truce now and in the future, and to support the International Olympic Committee in its efforts to promote peace and human understanding through sport and the Olympic ideal' (*ibid.*). The Assembly 'welcomed the initiative of the [UN] Secretary-General to establish the Task Force on Sport for Development and Peace', and 'recognized the important role of sport in the implementation of the internationally agreed development goals, including those contained in the United Nations Millennium Declaration' (*ibid.*).

The General Assembly acknowledged that the support between the UN and the Olympic movement was not just one way. It 'recognized the valuable contribution that the appeal launched by the International Olympic Committee for an Olympic Truce, with which the National Olympic Committees of the Member States are associated, could make towards advancing the purposes and principles of the Charter of the United Nations' (*ibid.*). It 'noted with satisfaction the flying of the United Nations flag at all competition sites of the Olympic Games, and the joint endeavours of the International Olympic Committee and the United Nations system in fields such as poverty alleviation, human and economic development, humanitarian assistance, education, health promotion, gender equality, environment protection and human immunodeficiency virus/acquired immune deficiency syndrome (HIV/AIDS) prevention' (*ibid.*). The Assembly 'welcomed the establishment by the International Olympic Committee of an International Olympic Truce Foundation and an International Olympic Truce Centre to promote further the ideals of peace and understanding through sport, on whose Board the President in office of the General Assembly sits and the Secretary-General and the Director-General of the

United Nations Educational, Scientific and Cultural Organization are represented' (*ibid.*).

[The resulting draft resolution 'urged Member States to observe, within the framework of the Charter of the United Nations, the Olympic Truce, individually and collectively', during the Games of the XXVIII Olympiad, to be held at Athens from 13 to 29 August 2004 (*ibid.*); welcomed the decision of the IOC 'to mobilize all international sports organizations' along with the NOCs of the Member States 'to undertake concrete actions at the local, national, regional and world levels to promote and strengthen a culture of peace based on the spirit of the Olympic Truce' (*ibid.*); called upon all Member States to cooperate with the IOC 'in its efforts to use the Olympic Truce as an instrument to promote peace, dialogue and reconciliation in areas of conflict during and beyond the Olympic Games period' (*ibid.*); welcomed 'the increased implementation of projects for development through sport', and encouraged Member States and 'all concerned agencies and programmes of the United Nations system to strengthen their work in this field', in co-operation with the IOC (*ibid.*); requested the UN Secretary-General 'to promote the observance of the Olympic Truce' among Member States, to support 'human development initiatives through sport', and to co-operate with the IOC 'in the realization of these objectives' (*ibid.*); and confirmed that it had been decided 'to include in the provisional agenda of its sixtieth session the item entitled "Building a peaceful and better world through sport and the Olympic Ideal" and to consider this item before the XX Olympic Winter Games' (*ibid.*), to be held at Turin during February 2006. There is little doubt that a similar resolution will be presented to and passed by the UN General Assembly during the Beijing Olympiad in preparation for the 2008 Games.

Whatever the impact in practice of any such resolution on the course of the XXIX Olympiad and its Games will be, it seems reasonable to conclude that the UN and the Olympic movement will be working in concert to achieve similar goals in accordance with their support for similar principles, practices, ideals and tendencies in the modern world. It seems reasonable to conclude also that this collective, or unified, approach to global development is likely to enjoy considerable success, if only because it will be at one with the approach assumed by other, perhaps more influential, agencies of change, and in particular those that are committed to modern market capitalism. Just as the principles and practices of Olympism and the Olympic movement are not wholly identical with nor singularly determined by, and so simply reducible to, the principles and practices associated with the UN, so they are not wholly identical with nor singularly determined by the principles and practices of modern market capitalism. None the less, the part being played by Olympism in the construction of the globalized world – and thereby of *global society* – may be primarily dependent upon its elective affinity with modern market capitalism. Olympism's contribution to the construction of *global society* may hinge mainly upon the way in which the principles, values and ideals it enshrines coincide with, are compatible with, and help consolidate the principles and practices associated with modern market capitalism; and so upon the way in which they are conducive to the advance of modern market capitalism as the main driving force behind the overall progress of globalization.

There is a general, all-encompassing elective affinity between the *ideals and tendencies* of modern market capitalism, those of modern Olympism, and those of the broad sweep of (especially the leaders and elites of) modern societies at all levels, including that of the global level as reflected in the decisions and initiatives of the UN, and that of the local, nation-state level. At the local level, a raft of illustrative case studies are available, such as those of the nation-states that participated through their NOCs in the 2004 Athens Games or that will participate in the 2008 Beijing Games; the nation-states that have applied to host Games; and perhaps especially the nation-states that have successfully applied.

Chapter 4

Beijing and the Olympic social compact

> The Queen was accused last night of undermining London's Olympic bid by saying that she thought Paris rather than her own capital would win the right to host the 2012 Games. In a private conversation during a Buckingham Palace reception last month, the Queen reportedly ventured the opinion that Parisians were more committed to their bid than Londoners were and that when the IOC made its choice of venue, Paris would win.
>
> (Hamilton and Hoyle 13 January 2005)

During the Beijing Olympiad, there was one successful application to host an Olympic Games. On 6 July 2005, it was announced in Singapore that the host city for the Games of the XXX Olympiad would be the city of London (IOC 6 July 2005). Initially, nine cities submitted applications to host the 2012 Olympic Games: Havana, Istanbul, Leipzig, London, Madrid, Moscow, New York, Paris, and Rio de Janeiro (IOC 27 October 2005). These *applicant cities* were 'assessed by a group of experts who presented a report to the IOC Executive Board', which then – on 18 May 2004 – selected the five candidate cities (Games Bids 29 July 2005), these being London, Madrid, Moscow, New York and Paris. The candidate cities were selected, as the IOC puts it, 'after a study of their application was made by a working group comprising IOC administration members and external experts' (IOC 27 October 2005). This working group assessed each applicant city's 'ability to stage high-level, international, multi-sport events and their ability to organise quality Olympic Games in 2012, against a set of 16 technical assessment criteria', these being Olympic Games Concept and Legacy, Political and Economic Structure, Legal Aspects and Guarantees, Custom and Immigration Formalities, Environment and Meteorology, Finance, Marketing, Sports and Venues, Paralympic Games, Olympic Village, Medical Services, Security, Accommodation, Transport, Media Operations, and Olympism and Culture (*ibid.*). The five candidate cities for the 2012 Games submitted their candidature files to the IOC in January 2005 (*ibid.*). These files were scrutinized by the IOC Evaluation Commission, which went on to carry out on the spot inspections of the candidate cities before issuing a report on 6 June 2005 (*ibid.*; see also IOC 6–9 July 2005), precisely one month before the final decision on the host city for the XXX Olympic Games was made by the full IOC membership during the 117th Session of the IOC in Singapore on 6 July 2005 (IOC 27 October 2005). Following four rounds of voting by the IOC members, London was eventually elected by receiving 54 votes out of a possible 104 (see Figure 4.1).

It may be noted, however, that London's victory was controversial. It was tarnished by the claim that it was a mistake. In December 2005, Alex Gilady, an Israeli member of the IOC and of the IOC's London 2012 Co-ordination Commission, said 'that London only won the 2012 Olympics because of a misplaced vote [in] the third round of voting in Singapore' (BBC 23 December 2005). The mistake occurred when 'a vote was cast for Paris instead of the intended recipient, Madrid'. Gilady suggested that if this particular vote had gone as intended, then Madrid 'would have finished level with Paris on 32 votes apiece in the penultimate round, behind London'; and Madrid 'would have won a head-to-head vote with Paris and gone on to beat London in the final round' (*ibid.*).

Still, according to the IOC's post-election overview, the London 2012 Olympic Games 'vision [was] underpinned by four main themes: delivering the experience of a lifetime for athletes, leaving a legacy for sport, benefiting the community through regeneration', and supporting the IOC

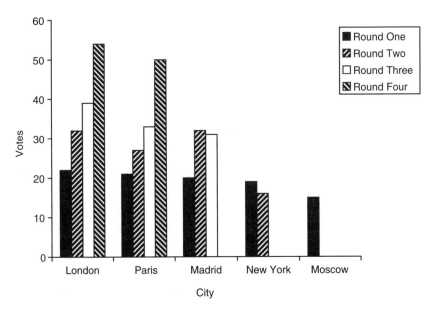

Figure 4.1 Election of the Host City for the 2012 Olympic Games, Singapore, 6 July 2005 (source: IOC 27 October 2005).

and the Olympic movement (IOC 6 July 2005). On the latter, under *Olympism and Culture*, the IOC reported how London had 'proposed an extensive and varied programme of activities, including theatre, music, carnival performances and exhibitions in museums during the Games' (*ibid.*). This programme would begin 'immediately after the Beijing Olympic Games with the launch of the "Olympic Friendship" (an oceangoing clipper) which would tour the world conducting an Olympic educational programme' (*ibid.*). Most important, the bid by London for the 2012 Games seemed to have a high level of 'local' (both candidate city and country-wide) popular support. According to the Report of the IOC Evaluation Commission for the Games of the XXX Olympiad in 2012 (REC 2012):

> The bid enjoys strong support and commitment from the Queen, the national government and the [Greater London Authority]. This was demonstrated through the participation of various ministers throughout the Commission's visit. The bid is also supported by all major political parties. This was underlined to the Commission during a meeting with the Prime Minister and the leaders of the two main opposition parties. A public opinion poll commissioned by the IOC shows the following levels of support to host the 2012 Olympic Games: 68% support in London and 70% support throughout the country.
>
> (IOC 6 June 2005)

On the other hand, while there was a high level of all-round local support for the London bid, the level of popular support appears to have fallen quite a long way short of that enjoyed by other candidate cities for the 2012 Games, just as it appears to have fallen quite a long way short of the local popular support given to several of the candidate cities for the 2008 Games. As noted in REC 2012 (Appendix D), the IOC commissioned MORI to conduct public opinion polls in the five candidate cities 'and their respective countries regarding support for hosting the Games of the XXX Olympiad in 2012' (IOC 12 November 2005), with all five polls being carried out in December 2004. The pollsters posed the question: 'To what extent would you support or oppose [Candidate City] hosting the Olympic Summer Games?' (*ibid.*), and the results are given in Table 4.1. The polls suggest that while local popular support for London was greater than that for New York, it was slightly less than that for Moscow and Paris, but considerably less than that for Madrid. Furthermore, the local popular support given to London seems to be much less than that which was given to Beijing when, four years earlier, it was a candidate city for the 2008 Games. According to the Report of the IOC Evaluation Commission for the Games of the XXIX Olympiad in 2008 (REC 2008):

> There is very strong support from national and local levels of government

Table 4.1 Local popular support for the candidate cities for the 2012 Olympic Games

	Opposed	Neutral	Support
Madrid	3	6	91
Spain	3	12	85
Paris	7	8	85
France	5	16	79
Moscow	8	15	77
Russia	10	14	76
London	18	15	68
UK	12	19	70
New York	24	17	59

Source: IOC 12 November 2005.

Notes
'All figures are expressed in percentage terms. Where they do not add up to 100%, this is due to computer rounding' (IOC 12 November 2005). The areas of the candidate cities were defined as follows: Paris: UDA (Union des Annonceurs); New York: Brooklyn, Queens and Manhattan Counties, the Bronx and Staten Island; Moscow: The City of Moscow; London: UK Government Office Region for London; Madrid: Madrid Metropolitan Area' (*ibid.*).

> as shown by the financial guarantee provided jointly by the Chinese Central and Beijing Municipal governments guaranteeing the funding of any shortfall, the construction of infrastructure and venues and working capital for the OCOG. The Commission also received strong personal assurances of support from the President of China and the Mayor of Beijing. The Bid Committee claimed 95% public support. The IOC poll showed 96% support in Beijing and other urban areas.
>
> (IOC 13 March 2002)

Among the candidate cities for the 2008 Olympics, at the other end of the scale, it seems that the local popular support for the Japanese city of Osaka was relatively poor:

> The Osaka bid is a City-driven bid and has received Japanese Government approval and statements of support. Both Osaka Prefecture and Osaka City will provide sports facilities and the City will construct many additional facilities. The Commission requested clarification of the apparent differences between the statements made in the Candidature File and the actual written guarantees from the Government, Prefecture and City particularly in respect of the stated financial commitments in the Candidature File. The existence of satisfactory guarantees was confirmed. The Bid Committee claimed 76% public support in Osaka. The IOC poll showed 52% support in Osaka and 51% in Japan.
>
> (*ibid.*)

The degrees of local popular support which appear to have been given to the remaining three candidate cities fell between that given to Beijing and that to Osaka. As with the 2012 Games, the IOC commissioned MORI to conduct public opinion polls in the five candidate cities and their respective 'countries regarding the hosting of a 2008 Games', and the responses to the 'question: To what extent would you support or oppose [Candidate City] hosting the Olympic Games?' can be seen in Table 4.2.

The IOC notes that the results of the opinion polls 'assisted the Commission in compiling its evaluation' of the five candidate cities. Indeed, the results may well have been highly persuasive when it came to the IOC finally electing the host city for the 2008 Games, with Beijing beating its rivals by a wide margin, as shown by the figures in Figure 4.2. The way in which Beijing clearly won in its bid to host the 2008 Olympics contrasts sharply with the outcome of the city's previous bid for the Games. Beijing failed in its bid in the early 1990s to host the 2000 Games, but only just. On 4 December 1991, Beijing became the first ever applicant city from China (Games Bids 29 July 2005) when it submitted a formal application to the IOC to host the 2000 Games. On that day, Zhang Baifa, the Executive Vice-President of the Beijing Bid Committee, handed Beijing's application to Juan Antonio Samaranch, the IOC's President at the IOC's headquarters in Lausanne, Switzerland (COC 27 March 2004). The submission included a formal letter of application from Chen Xitong, the Mayor of Beijing, a recommendation from He Zhenliang, President of the Chinese Olympic Committee (COC), and a letter to the IOC President from Chinese Premier Li Peng (*ibid.*). Early in 1993, all eight cities bidding for the 2000 Games submitted candidature files to the IOC. Beijing's file 'expressed the Chinese people's sincere wish to develop

Table 4.2 Local popular support for City Bids for 2008 Olympic Games

	Opposed	Neutral	Support
Beijing	+	4	96
PRC	1	3	96
Istanbul	6	4	86
Turkey	5	5	86
Toronto	14	11	71
Canada	12	19	67
Paris	5	28	66
France	5	30	55
Osaka	23	24	52
Japan	15	33	51

Source: IOC 13 March 2002.

Notes
'+' indicates that the figure (percentage) was 'too low to register'. The country-wide poll in the case of the PRC was conducted in urban areas only (IOC 13 March 2002).

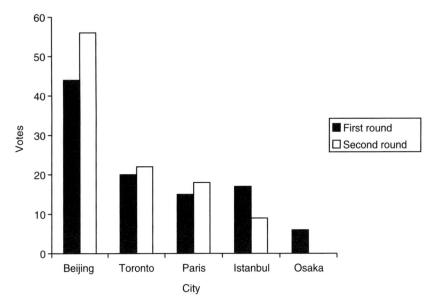

Figure 4.2 Election of the Host City for the XXIX Olympic Games, Moscow, 13 July 2001 (source: IOC 12 January 2006).

the Olympic movement and Beijing's enthusiasm and plans for hosting the Games' (*ibid.*). On 20 June 1993, 'Chinese President Jiang Zemin wrote a letter to members of the IOC, reaffirming that the Chinese government and the whole Chinese people' supported Beijing's bid for the 2000 Games (*ibid.*). However, on 23 September 1993, at the 101st IOC Session held in Monte Carlo, Sydney rather than Beijing was finally chosen from the six candidate cities – the other four being Berlin, Brasilia, Istanbul and Manchester – to host the Games (*ibid.*), but by only two votes over Beijing, and even though Beijing had attracted more votes than all the other candidate cities in each of the three earlier rounds of voting (Games Bids 28 July 2005) (see Figure 4.3).

In spite of the twists and turns in the way Sydney managed to grasp victory from Beijing at the finishing line, the COC commented: 'as a saying goes, bidding for the Olympic Games is a competition without losers, as no competition can compare with the Olympic bid as an opportunity for a city, even for the whole country, to display and assert itself before the world' (COC 27 March 2004a). The COC's sanguine response to losing to Sydney in the race to host the 2000 Games is worthy of such sentiments attributable to Pierre de Coubertin as *the most important thing in the Olympic Games is not winning but taking part; the important thing in life is not to triumph but to compete; the important thing in life is not victory but combat, it is not to have vanquished but to have fought well*; and *the essential thing in life is not conquering but fighting well*

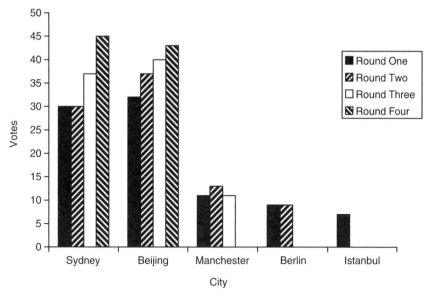

Figure 4.3 Election of the Host City for the 2000 Olympic Games, 23 September 1993 (source: COC 27 March 2004; Games Bids 28 July 2005).

(BQ 2005). However, under the circumstances, it is difficult to imagine the COC's disappointment being anything other than considerable, and even to have become more acute later when, in January 1999, it was revealed that officials of the Sydney Organising Committee for the Olympic Games (SOCOG) had employed dubious tactics in securing victory:

> An investigation into Sydney's successful bid for next year's Olympic Games says officials broke rules set by the International Olympic Committee, but fell short of corruption. The head of the independent inquiry, Mr Tom Sheridan, says Sydney might not have won the bid if hospitality and red carpet treatment given to IOC delegates had been less extravagant. According to his report, members of the Sydney Olympic Committee and the IOC were in 'technical breach' of the rules. The value of gifts given to Olympic Committee delegates and assistance given to their families were found to have exceeded IOC limits. Some of the international delegates' trips to Sydney were described as holidays in five-star hotels at popular resorts.
>
> (BBC 15 March 1999a)

None the less, the inquiry report came to the conclusion that 'there was no bribery or corruption, and described the Olympic Committee's guidelines as unclear and ambiguous' (*ibid.*). The investigators decided that there was 'no need for further action by police or other authorities' (*ibid.*). In response, Michael Knight, the President of SOCOG, declared that 'there was no comparison with the scandal surrounding Salt Lake City's bid for the winter Games' of 2002 (*ibid.*).

The inquiry report's conclusions, exonerating SOCOG of corrupt practices in trying to secure the right to host the 2000 Games, came despite attempts by SOCOG officials to garner the support of IOC members by offering monetary incentives right to the finishing line, the vote in Monte Carlo. One SOCOG official admitted offering 'tens of thousands of dollars to members of [the IOC] the night before' the election of the host city:

> John Coates, President of the Australian Olympic Committee and a leader of the Sydney 2000 bid, said he had offered $35,000 apiece to two African members of the IOC. The money was pledged to the National Olympic Committees of Kenya and Uganda, through their respective IOC members, Charles Mukora and Major-General Francis Nyangweso. The offers were made in Monte Carlo [. . .], the night before Sydney won the 2000 Games by two votes. After making the disclosure in a newspaper interview, Mr Coates told a news conference on Saturday that he pledged the money because he felt Sydney's chances were 'slipping away'. Mr Coates said the payments were within IOC guidelines and similar to plans used by bidding competitors from Beijing and Manchester. He denied the money was a bribe and said it would go toward helping sports in Kenya and Uganda.
>
> (BBC 23 January 1999; see also BBC 12 December 1998;
> BBC 25 November 1998)

SOCOG's tactics were defended by Kevan Gosper, an Australian member of the IOC's Executive Board, the *supreme authority* of the Olympic movement (IOC 11 January 2006):

> 'As far as I'm concerned Sydney won on merit and Sydney acted appropriately and acted in line with the rules,' Mr Gosper told Australian Broadcasting Corporation radio from Lausanne, where he is attending an inquiry into alleged bribery during Salt Lake City's successful bid for the 2002 Winter Games.
>
> (BBC 23 January 1999)

But, not everyone accepted the legitimacy of SOCOG's actions. The BBC reported how 'Manchester lost out on the bid and now wants Sydney stripped of the Games' (*ibid.*), with Graham Stringer of the Manchester Organising Committee for the Olympic Games declaring, "I think the IOC should take a very serious look at whether the Games can be removed from Sydney [and] because the IOC have presided over a corrupt process, at least

once, if not several times, I think they should pay the bidding cities money
that they spent on bidding" ' (*ibid*.). Here is an allusion to what is probably
the biggest ever scandal surrounding a city's bid to host an Olympic Games –
Salt Lake City's bid for the 2002 Winter Games. Shortly before the 1999
report on the inquiry into SOCOG's actions in helping secure the 2000
Games, 'a Libyan delegate became the second IOC member to resign amid
vote-buying allegations in Salt Lake City's selection as host of the 2002
Winter Games' (*ibid*.). Bashir Mohamed Attarabulsi withdrew from the IOC
because it had emerged that 'his son had received college scholarships at
schools in Utah paid for by the bid committee' (*ibid*.). Earlier, a Finnish IOC
member, Pirjo Haeggman, resigned, 'despite protesting her innocence of any
wrongdoing' (*ibid*.). It was expected that the report into the Salt Lake City
scandal would reveal that 'the US city spent more than £400,000 on gifts and
payments during the bidding for and after winning the 2002 Winter Games',
and that moreover 'bribery within the Olympic movement [had] been going
on for decades' (*ibid*.; see also Chapter 1 of this book; BBC 25 January 1999;
McLaughlin 1999; Simson and Jennings 1992).

On hearing about the questionable tactics by SOCOG officials, it was
reported that 'China alleges unfair treatment during Olympics bid' (BBC
14 December 1998). COC officials claimed that Beijing 'may have lost the
right to stage the Games in 2000 because of unfair treatment during the
bidding process' (*ibid*.). The BBC reported how one COC official, 'speaking
at the Asian Games in Bangkok, said issues unrelated to sport became a factor
in the selection' (*ibid*.). In spite of this muted response, the BBC claimed that
'Beijing obviously thinks it lost the race to hold the Olympics because it
may have been the victim of corruption' (*ibid*.).

In contrast to the conclusion of the inquiry report into Sydney's victory
for the 2000 Games, it was decided that Salt Lake City's success in gaining
the 2002 Winter Olympic Games was due to corrupt practices, and that
consequently major reforms were needed in the selection procedure:

> The International Olympic Committee should undergo a thorough
> reform 'at all levels', following the corruption scandal over the way the
> 2002 Winter Games were awarded to Salt Lake City. The changes are
> called for in the report of an inquiry by the United States Olympic
> Committee into the million dollar corruption scandal. The inquiry
> blamed a 'culture of gift-giving', which encourages cities wanting to host
> the Games to try to buy the votes of International Olympic Committee
> members. An earlier investigation found that two top officials who led
> Salt Lake City's 2002 bid, paid more than $1m to 24 members of the
> IOC panel which chooses the venue.
>   (BBC 1 March 1999; see also BBC 15 March 1999b)

Here, we can recall Short's argument (see Chapter 1) that the 'increasing importance of major corporations to the IOC has affected IOC policies', as exemplified in particular by the way in which the IOC's 'response [. . .] to the scandals emanating from the Salt Lake City corruption charges was in large part due to [the IOC's] need to reassure corporate sponsors' (Short 2003):

> The Olympics is a brand with a high value because of its positive associations; corruption charges undermined the value of the brand. The corporate sponsorship has also influenced the siting of the Games. The major corporations have been very eager to get the Games into China as a strategy of promoting their products and name recognition to one of the largest faster growing markets in the world.
>
> (*ibid.*)

For Short, the Salt Lake City corruption scandal can be understood in terms of the way in which, with globalization, for both the sponsoring corporations and the host cities 'the benefits of the Games seem [increasingly] secure' (*ibid.*). This is an important factor in making sense of the growing intensity of, what might be called, *the host city bidding war* which precedes each Olympic Games. Even inside a particular country, there can be keen competition among several aspirant cities. This applies when, for instance, the United States National Olympic Committee (USNOC) was required to choose between eight cities that had put themselves forward for selection as the USA's bid city for the 2012 Games – Cincinnati, Dallas, Houston, Los Angeles, New York, San Francisco, Tampa and Washington – a competition eventually won by New York.

In Short's view, the 'structural context' in which the Salt Lake scandal was played out entailed 'cities desperate to land the Games' and a 'bidding system under which IOC delegates would visit bid cities, ostensibly to check out the site, and then vote in a secret ballot', a recipe for cities being 'lavish with their hospitality' and delegates being 'eager to cash in on their voting power' – to exploit the fact that they were not subject to either any IOC 'ethical guidelines' or any IOC checks on their city visits (*ibid.*). As a result of the scandal, the IOC set up an Ethics Committee and introduced changes to the host city bid and election process. According to Short, the IOC was not so much interested in making the process any more democratic or, for that matter, any more transparent, as responding to 'the bad publicity and the fear of corporate withdrawal. As the head of McDonald's German subsidiary noted, "If the corruption suspicions are confirmed, McDonald's will ask itself if sponsorship of the Games still has a place on the group's image" [Korporaal and Evans 1999]' (*ibid.*).

When, on 13 July 2001 at the 112th IOC Session in Moscow, Beijing was elected the host city for the Games of the XXIX Olympiad in 2008, it was the first city to be chosen under the 'new two-phase host city election procedure', as adopted by the IOC Session in December 1999 (IOC 12 January

2006). The second city to be chosen under this new election procedure was London in 2005 for the 2012 Games. According to this procedure, 'cities must pass an initial selection phase during which basic technical requirements are examined by a team of experts', clearing them to be put forward to the IOC Executive Board (*ibid.*). The ten selected cities for the 2008 Games were Bangkok, Beijing, Cairo, Havana, Istanbul, Kuala Lumpur, Osaka, Paris, Seville and Toronto. On being approved by the Executive Board, the applicant cities become official candidate cities and, as such, 'are authorised to go forward into the full bid process' (*ibid.*). On 28 August 2000, the five candidate cities for the 2008 Games that were accepted by the Executive Board were (in the order of drawing of lots) Osaka, Paris, Toronto, Beijing and Istanbul. The process then requires each candidate city to submit a Candidature File to the IOC and afterwards to be visited by the IOC Evaluation Commission. The Evaluation Commission 'studies the candidatures of each candidate city, inspects the sites and submits a written report on all candidatures to the IOC two months before the Session which will elect the host city' (*ibid.*).

The IOC claims that the reforms 'have created an improved host city election process' that clarifies 'the qualifications necessary to bid for the Games and the responsibilities and obligations of all parties involved in the process' (IOC June 2005; see also IOC 14 November 2005). In the first place, 'the two-step process (applicant city/candidate city) is designed to ensure that only interested cities that the IOC judges to be capable are approved to proceed to the candidature phase, thereby avoiding unnecessary expenditure for those cities which are judged to be insufficiently prepared at the time' (IOC June 2005). In addition, there is the elimination of the visits by IOC members to the candidate cities on the grounds that 'members will have the benefit of knowledge gained from a strengthened Evaluation Commission Report and the additional assessment of cities made during the bid acceptance procedure' (*ibid.*). Furthermore, the obligation of a National Olympic Committee (NOC) 'to serve as a full partner with the bid committee' has been strengthened to help ensure 'that the application meets the IOC's requirements'. Finally, there is 'the signing of a contract between the IOC and each candidate city, along with their respective NOC, outlining the obligations of each party, the applicable code of conduct, and the sanctions for breaches of these terms' (*ibid.*).

The response within China itself, and especially of the people of Beijing, to the outcome of the election for the 2008 Games impressed many observers (see Chapter 6). Jim Hoagland of *the Washington Post* has noted 'the uplifting reaction to [the] event by the Chinese public, which emerges [. . .] as justifiably proud and joyous over an opportunity to show that their country can meet modern international standards of sportsmanship, hospitality and openness' (Hoagland 2001). Hoagland adds:

The last time you saw Chinese crowds on television was probably when they were menacing the U.S. Embassy, or otherwise being manipulated into the streets by their rulers for short-term political gain. Think of the light-years that separate last weekend's spontaneous, globally televised festival in Beijing from Mao's xenophobic and self-destructive China.

(*ibid.*)

A similarly buoyant response to Beijing's election came from the IOC, which noted how the 'vote followed in line with the recommendation of the IOC Evaluation Commission that "a Beijing Games would leave a unique legacy to China and to sports. The Commission is confident that Beijing could organise an excellent Games" ' (IOC 12 January 2006). The IOC's confidence over its choice of Beijing echoes the way in which the Chinese delegation to Moscow promoted the city's bid to host the 2008 Games. He Zhenliang, who as well as being Chairman of the Chinese (National) Olympic Committee (COC), had been a member of the IOC since 1981, a member of the Executive Committee of the IOC since 1985, and a Vice-President of the IOC since 1989, not to mention being Vice-Minister in charge of the State Commission for Physical Culture and Sports of the PRC since 1985, gave the delegation's *Opening Speech*. He Zhenliang recalled how eight years had elapsed since Beijing's bid for the 2000 Games, during which time China had 'made tremendous strides on the road to modernisation and social progress', and noted how the Evaluation Commission had declared, 'Beijing has the capacity to organize an excellent Olympic Games which will hand down a unique heritage to China and to sport' (BOCOG 30 July 2005). Following He Zhenliang, Li Lanqing, the PRCs Vice Premier,[1] gave a speech reaffirming that the PRC's government stood 'firmly behind Beijing in its bid for the 2008 Olympic Games', and would 'honor each and every commitment it [had] made in Beijing's Candidature File and [would] do whatever it [could] to assist Beijing to fulfill its promises' (*ibid.*). Li Lanqing declared, 'China embraces the Olympic spirit and has always been a staunch supporter behind the IOC initiatives', and:

China has been one of the fastest growing economies in the world over the past 20 years since its reform and opening-up. It has enjoyed continued political stability, social progress and economic prosperity. An Olympic Games in Beijing will not only serve the interests of the Chinese people, but also promote the Olympic spirit and contribute to peace and friendship, stability and development in the world.

(*ibid.*)

Next, Liu Qi, the Mayor of Beijing,[2] spoke and announced that the 'three themes' of the Beijing bid were 'Green Olympics, Hi-tech Olympics and the People's Olympics' (*ibid*). Liu Qi continued:

Our goal is to spread the Olympic Ideals among our people, especially 400 million young people. Over 95% of our population supports the bid – because they believe that hosting the 2008 Olympic Games will help raise their quality of life. Over half a million people have volunteered to assist in any and all Olympic projects. Our citizens, both young and old, are actively learning foreign languages to welcome you in friendly and familiar voices. As you may notice, I am learning English now. In 1998, we began a 10-year program of 12 billion US dollars to improve the environment. We will use the most advanced and reliable technology for all Olympic projects. The Beijing Organizing Committee will have full power to comply with all of the obligations of the Host City Contract and to meet all of the needs of the Olympic Family. We are committed to meet each of the challenges cited in the Evaluation Commission report. I want to say that the Beijing 2008 Olympic Games will have the following special features: [they] will help promote our economic and social progress and will also benefit the further development of our human rights cause; [they] will promote an exchange of rich Chinese culture with other cultures; [and they] will mark a major step forward in the spreading of the Olympic Ideals [. . .]. I am very confident that Beijing will organize an excellent Games in 2008 and [that] the Games [. . .] will leave a unique legacy to China and to sport.

(*ibid.*)

Among the remaining Chinese delegation speeches, that by Wang Wei, the Secretary General of Beijing's Bid Committee, is notable.[3] Wang Wei reassured his audience that Beijing 'possesses a modern infrastructure to ensure the smooth operation of a truly great Olympic event', including a well 'developed transportation network' (*ibid.*); and that the 'Olympic family will be serviced by a dedicated fleet of vehicles with English speaking local drivers' (*ibid.*). Turning to the environment, Wang Wei claimed that Beijing had 'come a long way since its last bid in 1993'; that the 'city has taken giant steps to fight pollution caused by industrialization and economic growth'; that there had been a 'remarkable improvement in air-quality through vehicle emission controls and greater use of clean energy sources'; and that the bid for the Games had 'further stimulated support among the people, business and government for a united approach to environmental improvement', so that 'the 2008 Olympic Games will leave a great environmental legacy – with new standards and benchmarks for developing cities' (*ibid.*). The Chinese delegation's presentation was rounded off by He Zhenliang, who was 'convinced that the Olympic values are universal and the Olympic flame lights up the way of progress for all humanity' (*ibid.*). He pointed out that by voting for Beijing, the IOC would 'bring the Games for the first time in the history of Olympism to a country with one fifth of the world's population and give to this billion people the opportunity to serve the Olympic movement with creativity and devotion'. The selection of Beijing would 'signal the beginning of a new era of global unity' (*ibid.*).

The Chinese delegation's Moscow speeches emphasized certain themes in support of Beijing's bid for the right to host the 2008 Olympics, including those of *the Green Olympics, Hi-tech Olympics and the People's Olympics*. During the speeches, it was pointed out that Beijing's bid enjoyed high levels of local popular support, enthusiasm and commitment; and, moreover, that the state *stood firmly behind Beijing in its bid for the 2008 Olympic Games*, such as by guaranteeing to financially underwrite the event. It was pointed out that the Games had yet to be held in China, a country with a fifth of the world's population. Beijing could boast an *ancient culture*, while being the capital city of a country which had made *tremendous strides on the road to modernization and social progress*, and which was continuing to develop, economically and otherwise, at great speed. It was claimed that there had been substantial *environmental improvement*, and that there would be yet more to come, especially if inspired by the staging of the Olympics. The Games, moreover, would *not only serve the interests of the Chinese people, but also promote the Olympic spirit and contribute to peace and friendship, stability and development in the world*. The Beijing Games would be conducive to the Olympic movement's spirit, ideals and values, these being *universal values*, and the promotion of which would contribute to ensuring *global unity*. This unity would be further fostered by the way the Beijing Games would not only help consolidate English as the global *lingua franca*, but also 'benefit the further development of [China's] human rights cause', and consequently the *global human rights cause* through the strengthening of the *global human rights regime* (see below; see also Close and Askew 2004a).

These themes have been further clarified by the Beijing Organizing Committee for the Games of the XXIX Olympiad (BOCOG) in its *Olympic Action Plan* (OAP) for the 2008 Games (BOCOG 14 January 2006a), which opens by declaring that the award of the Games to Beijing 'has added fresh impetus to the development of Beijing and that of China as a whole', so that from 'now on, Beijing will see a period of rapid development, and the preparation for the Olympic Games will greatly facilitate the implementation of the 10th "Five-year Plan" and the "Strategy of Three-phased Development" for Beijing' (*ibid.*). The OAP covers the development of Olympic venues and related facilities; ecological environment and infrastructure development; social environment development; strategic support (speeding up the economic development of Beijing; advancing the development of new technologies; developing sound commanding and decision-making systems; being market-oriented in financing and improving fund management; developing human resource backup; and setting up supervision and auditing mechanisms); Olympic Action Plan for Beijing Sports; transport construction and traffic management plan; a plan for *High-Tech Olympics* construction; a programme for the construction of *Digital Olympics*; the development of the cultural environment; energy development and energy mix readjustment; and environment protection (*ibid.*).

In the OAP's section on *Being Market-oriented in Financing and Improving Fund Management*, BOCOG pledges to 'stick to the principle of market orientation in financing activities, which shall be organised and guided by the government' (*ibid.*), and says:

> Monopoly by departments and sectors must be broken and, instead, market-oriented operation in the infrastructure project development shall be promoted and non-governmental investment shall be encouraged. Continued efforts shall be made to regulate the prices for infrastructure products and services and to put into practice the governmental compensation and repayment mechanisms for some commercial infrastructure projects. 'The Bidding Law' shall be further enforced, and the selection of project proprietors and contractors for all the important construction stages, including planning and designing, construction, project management, procurement of equipment and materials, shall be made open for national and international bidding. Successful fund raising experience should be drawn from the previous Olympic host cities and new approaches to fund raising developed.
>
> (*ibid.*)

This stance on financing (or funding) the 2008 Games reflects BOCOG's determination to comply with the IOC's requirement on all host cities – at least since the 1980s (under the direction of Juan Antonio Samaranch as President of the IOC between 1980 and 2001) – entailing 'the marketing of sport [. . .] through a highly managed programme and balanced partnership with the private sector' (IOC July 2001b). This approach has allowed the IOC to 'achieve its goals' (*ibid.*), not least that of ensuring the survival of the Games, the Olympic movement and Olympism:

> In 1980, many questioned whether the Olympic movement and the Games were financially viable. The IOC, the NOCs and the [International Federations (IFs)] had few sources of independent revenue, and potential bid cities feared the financial risks involved in staging the Games. President Samaranch understood, from the outset of his Presidency in 1980, that unless the Olympic movement could develop an independent financial base and revenue source, it would not survive. Since then, the Olympic movement has experienced a remarkable financial turnaround.
>
> (*ibid.*)

If so, then it will not be surprising to find that the IOC closely scrutinizes and monitors each Organizing Committee's (OCOG's) commitment in principle and in practice to a market-oriented, private-sector partnership approach to the financing of any Games. In the case of the 2008 event, over the six months prior to 12 July 2001 selection of the host city, the IOC worked 'closely with each of the five candidate cities to prepare the necessary foundations for the development of a successful Games marketing programme' (*ibid.*). The purpose was to 'ensure that revenue expectations [were] feasible [. . .] and that clear protocols and [. . .] agreements [were] in place prior to election to ensure protection of the Olympic image and partner rights' (*ibid.*) – that is, the rights of the Olympic Games' corporate, or *big business*, sponsors. As of January 2006, the sponsors of the 2008 Games included 11 Worldwide Olympic Partners: Coca-Cola, Atos Origin, GE, Kodak, Lenovo, Manulife, McDonald's, Omega, Panasonic, Samsung and Visa; ten Beijing 2008 Partners: Bank of China, CNC, Sinopec, CNPC, China Mobile, Volkswagen, Adidas, Johnson and Johnson, Air China, and PICC; and nine Beijing 2008 Sponsors, among them Haier, Budweiser, Tsingtao, and Yanjing Beer (BOCOG 14 January 2006b).

Significantly, as noted by the IOC, the 'selection of the Host City has little, if any, impact on the revenue to be generated from the Olympic marketing programmes' (IOC July 2001b). For instance, 'many of the worldwide sponsorship agreements [were] already in place for 2008' before the host city had been selected, as were 'all broadcast agreements' (*ibid.*). As of July 2002, the IOC already had 'under contract for the benefit of the Host City more than US$1,200 million – approximately 60% of most of the bid budgets' (*ibid.*). As part of the host city election process, each of the five candidate cities for 2008 was 'required to enter into a number of agreements prior to selection', the purposes of which were to 'protect the fundamental marketing principles' that had been developed and 'ensure the orderly development of the Olympic marketing plan'; 'provide the strongest possible protection for the exclusivity of all Olympic partners'; and 'take steps to maximise the promotion of the Olympic brand in the host city'; *inter alia* (*ibid.*). Furthermore, each Candidate City was required to enter 'into a single marketing programme agreement with its NOC, whereby all marketing rights of the NOC and the Olympic team' were ceded to BOCOG for the period 2001 to 2008, and whereby the Games sponsors would 'also be sponsors of the 2008 national Olympic team for 2004, 2006 and 2008'; obtain 'a binding option for the IOC and the OCOG to purchase all outdoor advertising throughout the city, and at the main transportation access points, for the two-month period surrounding the Games, at pre-agreed rates, linked to 2000 indexed pricing'; review 'with the government the necessary steps to further improve the protection of Olympic marks and rights'; and develop a *Marketing Plan* (*ibid.*).

BOCOG's marketing plan states that the Beijing 2008 Olympic Games Sponsorship Programme, would 'provide a unique Olympic marketing platform for both Chinese and foreign enterprises and encourage the broad participation of Chinese business entities to enhance their corporate image and brand awareness through their Olympic association, and provide quality services to sponsors and maximize the return on their investments while helping them forge long-term partnerships with the Olympic movement in China' (BOCOG 14 January 2006a). It follows that the IOC's commitment to a market-oriented, private-sector partnership approach to financing the Olympics together with BOCOG's determination to satisfy the IOC's expectations in this regard have major implications for the Olympics in general and the Beijing Games in particular, along with the Olympic movement, Olympism and all the sports associated with the Olympics. They have implications for the way in which the latter relate to, mediate between, are shaped by, and in turn help shape a range of other matters, including economic activity, processes and trends within and beyond China; *business entities* based in and outside of China; the state within China; China's political economy development as an integral, but central, part of its overall social development; the advance of market capitalism, perhaps in conjunction with liberal democracy, within China and elsewhere; the evolution and spread of market capitalism at the global level; and the progress of globalization along its economic, political and cultural dimensions.

Both Chinese and foreign *business entities* will have responded favourably to the choice of Beijing for the 2008 Games, and will have remained favourably disposed as China's economy continued to grow by an average 9.6 per cent annually from 1990 (Bloomberg 2006), so that in 2004 it accounted for 13 per cent of global growth (*ibid.*), and by 2005 had become 'the world's fourth biggest, behind the US, Japan and Germany' (BBC 19 December 2005; see also Finfacts 2005b; Pesek 16 January 2006); as the 'private sector' continued to expand so as to account for 'over two thirds of the country's economy' by the end of 2005 (Finfacts 2005a); and as its integration into the world economy continued apace (see Prasad 2004).[4] In other words, the response of the local (China's), regional (East Asia's), and global *business communities*,[5] and above all *business elites*, will have been at one with the way in which the IOC seemed to be convinced by the Chinese delegation's presentation and promises at the IOC's Session in Moscow on 13 July 2001.

What comes to mind here is how Juan Antonio Samaranch, on retiring as President of the IOC in 2001, was congratulated by Yutaka Narita, President of Dentsu, for steering the Olympic movement towards its 'close co-operation with the private sector' (*Marketing Matters* July 2001), and by Juergen E. Schrempp, Chairman of the Board of Management of Daimler Chrysler, for ensuring that during the 1980s and 1990s 'the creative collaboration of sports and business was expanded and intensified' into an *alliance* (*ibid.*) (see Chapter 7). In turn, the use here of such terms as co-operation, collaboration and alliance brings to mind further terms, in particular those of pact, compact and social compact, where a pact or compact is 'an act or state of agreeing between parties regarding a course of action'

(AC 15 January 2006). The phrase 'social compact' has a long and illustrious history, starting with its appearance in Jean Jacques Rousseau's *The Social Contract: the Principles of Political Right* in 1762, and subsequently 'in the Massachusetts Constitution of 1780 and in numerous other [US] founding-era documents' (Ellmers 2003; see also West and Pestritto 2003). In recent years, the term has been employed in various contexts, including as the title for 'a coalition of business leaders from across the [USA] who are promoting successful business investment in lower-income communities for the benefit of current residents' (Social Compact 15 January 2006). At the same time, the UN has put in place *The Global Compact*, which 'asks companies to embrace, support and enact, within their sphere of influence, a set of core values in the areas of human rights, labour standards, the environment, and anti-corruption' (UN 15 January 2006). In January 1999, Kofi Annan, the UN's Secretary-General, addressed the World Economic Forum (WEF) and 'challenged business leaders to join an international initiative – the Global Compact – that would bring companies together with UN agencies, labour and civil society to support universal environmental and social principles' (*ibid.*). In July 2000, the Global Compact's 'operational phase was launched', and subsequently, according to the UN, 'many hundreds of companies from all regions of the world, international labour and civil society organizations' became involved, 'working to advance ten universal principles in the areas of human rights, labour, the environment and anti-corruption' (*ibid.*). The 'ten principles' of the Global Compact are derived from the Universal Declaration of Human Rights, the International Labour Organization's Declaration of Fundamental Principles and Rights at Work, the Rio Declaration on Environmental Development, and the United Nations Convention Against Corruption (*ibid.*). Essentially:

> Through the power of collective action, the Global Compact seeks to promote responsible corporate citizenship so that business can be part of the solution to the challenges of globalization. In this way, the private sector – in partnership with other social actors – can help realize the Secretary-General's vision: a more sustainable and inclusive global economy.
>
> (*ibid.*)

Just as the UN might claim that any advances in responsible corporate citizenship and in a more sustainable and inclusive global economy are in part due to its Global Compact, so it can be claimed that the Beijing Olympiad is in part, and perhaps largely, due to a global social compact – that between the leaders of the Olympic movement and of business enterprises around the world; and in turn between these leaders and a set of political leaders at various levels, including the local (nation-state), regional and global. The form (as a mega-event) and content – or particulars of the character, course and consequences – of the Beijing Olympiad can be largely accounted for in terms of *the power of collective action* enjoyed and exercised by this global social compact.

At the same time, however, far from all observers, and especially those representing *civil society*, have welcomed the IOC's choice of Beijing, with many being critical and opposed, and some being antagonistic and downright hostile (see Beichman 2001; *FEER* 23 May 2001; Jacoby 2001; Jones 2001; Li Thian-hok 2001; *Washington Post* 2001a, 2001b). For example, the *Far Eastern Economic Review* tells us, 'Domestically, Beijing constitutes a fearful regime; internationally, it is a threat to regional stability', and questions whether it is 'a fit thing for' the IOC 'to appear to sanction repression, belligerence and naked territorial ambitions' (*FEER* 23 May 2001). Li Thian-hok has been similarly troubled, while accepting that the Games will have *positive* results internally, in particular in the field of human rights:

> The critics of the International Olympic Committee's decision to award the 2008 summer Games to Beijing are worried that the decision may enhance the legitimacy of the repressive Communist Party government, leading it to accelerate its policy of military modernization and territorial expansion. The 1936 Berlin Games and the subsequent launching of World War II by Germany [are] often cited in this connection. Optimists, on the other hand, cite the 1988 Seoul Games and the positive effect it had in moving South Korea towards greater pluralism. China will be put under a microscope and, the optimists say, will have no choice but to improve its human rights record. These two views appear to conflict, but actually they may not. China could improve its human rights record sufficiently to ward off any possible boycott of the 2008 Olympics, and yet at the same time exploit the prestige and commercial gains brought by the Games to further its goal of becoming a wealthy nation with a powerful military.
>
> (Li Thian-hok 2001)

In contrast to Li Thian-hok's top-down perspective on the relationship between the Beijing Olympiad, on the one hand, and China's internal and external social relations, processes and development, on the other, Jim Hoagland of the *Washington Post* draws on a bottom-up perspective, with particular reference to the Olympiad's internal impact. Hoagland is more optimistic, albeit cautiously so, than Li Thian-hok. He thinks there is a good chance he will *see an Olympic victory for China's people* (Hoagland 20 July 2001). For Hoagland, there 'was much to be said against choosing China, or any other nation ruled by a corrupt dictatorial mob, to host the 2008 Olympics' (*ibid.*), but 'those who have made it possible and for whom the decision will count the most [are] the Chinese people' (*ibid.*). In his view:

Once again they are standing up, overcoming burdens of their closed, misbegotten past. Their awakening to the world forces their rulers to run ever faster and to take gigantic risks that will bring cataclysmic change.

(*ibid.*)

Hoagland looks forward to the changes that 'will be brought by China's nearly simultaneous preparations for the Olympics and the severe adjustments in the economy that membership in the World Trade Organization will force China to make' (*ibid.*); and has speculated on the possibility that 'holding the Olympics in China will inexorably liberalize Chinese Communist rule out of existence' (*ibid.*). He is aware of 'the road China and its people have been traveling', recalling, in contrast to the crowds that had gathered spontaneously to celebrate the choice of Beijing for the 2008 Olympics:

the crowds that [had] gathered [also spontaneously] in Tiananmen Square [in the spring of 1989 in] demonstrations that began as a simple, eloquent demand that China's rulers behave decently, only to end in a state-ordered massacre. The students, workers, journalists and foreign ministry personnel who dared to hold their government to account by demonstrating in the square were among the bravest, most honorable [of] people [. . .]. Those people have not gone away. They have been repressed by more than a decade of brutal counterrevolution condoned by two American presidents. They have paid a heavy price for their commitment to decency. But that commitment still inspires fear in their masters and respect from democrats everywhere. May the 2008 Olympics become theirs, and add to their freedom and honor.

(*ibid.*)

Also on the other side of the Pacific, Human Rights Watch (HRW), the US-based *global civil society organization* (GCSO), was similarly troubled by the Chinese state's human rights record, but perhaps more doubtful about the prospect of any improvement under the influence of the Beijing Olympiad. HRW has noted that when Beijing was elected the host city for the 2008 Games, the IOC 'said that this would leave a "unique legacy to China and to sports" ' (HRW 2004). But, asks HRW, *what will that legacy be in practice?* With this question in mind, and in a similar way to Hoagland, HRW has declared 'for the sake of China's people, the Olympics movement, and human rights, we hope that the 2008 Olympics will be an impetus for China to demonstrate greater respect for the human rights guaranteed to all under international law'; and suggests that as China 'enters the global arena, the 2008 Beijing Olympics will provide an opportunity for China to come into compliance with international legal standards that protect human rights' (*ibid.*). But, as of 2004, the signs in HRW's view were far from encouraging:

While recent leadership changes have sparked some optimism that respect for human rights in China will improve, in fact this has not happened. The government actively limits expressions of dissent by all Chinese citizens, especially in Tibet and Xinjiang. China's ruling Communist Party bans opposition political parties and religious organizations independent of government control. Although the government permits a few non-governmental organizations (NGOs) to operate, most other 'non-governmental' organizations are actually government-controlled. China prohibits domestic human rights groups and bars entry to international human rights groups. The state continues to engage in Internet surveillance and media censorship. Arbitrary forced evictions are frequent, including in Beijing where construction of Olympic sites is underway. International human rights law guarantees everyone such rights as freedom of expression, due process and legal redress during eviction from their homes, and the right to organize independent labor unions. The 2008 Beijing Olympics will shine a global spotlight on these rights in China.

(*ibid.*)

Human Rights Watch has listed three key human rights issues that are likely to *shine under the global spotlight* during the Beijing Olympiad, especially when 'thousands of international journalists descend on Beijing' for the Games of the Olympiad (*ibid.*): China's pervasive censorship and control of domestic and international media and the Internet (see HRW 13 November 2005; Ward 8 March 2005); the way in which the Olympic Games had been used to justify the violent forced evictions of thousands of people from their homes to make way for Olympics-related construction (see HRW 14 November 2005); and China's restrictions on labour rights, including the rights of workers to organize independent trade unions (see HRW 15 November 2005). For HRW, these particular human rights issues directly relate to, or spring from, the preparations for and staging of the Games themselves. However, these issues are far from being the only ones of concern to HRW, along with other CSOs among a broad range of interested observers. As indicated already (above), HRW's concerns extend to how, contrary to international human rights law that guarantees freedom of expression, the Chinese 'government actively limits expressions of dissent by all Chinese citizens, [but] especially in Tibet and Xinjiang'; how 'China's ruling Communist Party bans opposition political parties and religious organizations independent of government control'; how 'the government permits [only] a few non-governmental organizations (NGOs) to operate', with 'most other "non-governmental" organizations [being] actually government-controlled'; and how the government 'prohibits domestic human rights groups and bars entry to international human rights groups' (HRW 2004).

According to what is probably the leading GCSO in the human rights arena, Amnesty International (AI):

> [During 2004, there] was progress towards reform in some areas, but this failed to have a significant impact on serious and widespread human rights violations perpetrated across the country. Tens of thousands of people continued to be detained or imprisoned in violation of their fundamental human rights and were at high risk of torture or ill-treatment. Thousands of people were sentenced to death or executed, many after unfair trials. Public protests increased against forcible evictions and land requisition without adequate compensation. China continued to use the global 'war on terrorism' to justify its crackdown on the Uighur community in Xinjiang. Freedom of expression and religion continued to be severely restricted in Tibet and other Tibetan areas of China.
>
> (AI 25 May 2004)

If so, then China's human rights record, not only before the Beijing Olympiad, but also during the first few months of this period, does not auger well for subsequent developments. On the other hand, perhaps there are grounds for anticipating that what HRW and AI would regard as human rights progress in China will be irresistible, at least in the longer run. After all, there is one human rights issue which AI and HRW appear to sideline, if not ignore, but that draws attention to a complex set of considerations, factors and forces which may be, in something of a combined fashion, driving China inevitably along the path of human rights progress and so further into the arms of the *global human rights regime* (GHRR), assisted by AI and HRW and facilitated by the award of the 2008 Games to Beijing. This issue is about the relationship between human rights matters and the GHRR, on the one hand, and the parts played by culture and power in social life in general, on the other. It can be examined by treating China's human rights record during the Beijing Olympiad as but one, albeit an especially useful, case study among many (see Close and Askew 2004a).

In this regard, during the early years of the twenty-first century, taking in the Beijing Olympiad, China was one among a raft of other countries and territories both nearby and far away that were the target of particular human rights concerns and general, worldwide human rights campaigns (AI 4 July 2004). HRW's list of global human rights issues includes free expression on the Internet, press freedom, prison conditions and the treatment of prisoners, refugees, religious freedom, repression in the name of anti-terrorism, the International Criminal Court (HRW 1 July 2004), and the United Nations (HRW 3 July 2004). The treaty (Statute) setting up the International Criminal Court (ICC) was adopted on 17 July 1998 at a conference in Rome, when 120 UN Member State government delegations voted in favour of proceeding, seven voted against (including those from China and the USA) and 21 abstained (*ibid.*). By 11 April 2002, 66 governments – or six more than were required to establish the court – had ratified the treaty (*ibid.*), as a result of which, on 1 July 2002, 'the ICC's jurisdiction commenced' (*ibid.*). By 14 May 2003, 90 governments had ratified the Rome Statute (HRW 14 May 2003); and by 3 May 2004, 94 governments had done so (CICC 2004). In other words, less than half the eligible 194 nation-state governments in the world had actually ratified the Rome Statute, with such major countries as China, Japan, Russia and the USA having opted not to do so (CICC 4 July 2004; HRW 14 May 2003). However, the split over the ICC has been accompanied by a more fundamental division, or (as some might say) *clash* (Huntington 1993, 1996), within the so-called *global community* in relation to global human rights issues, and concomitantly to the evolving global human rights regime (GHRR). The GHRR is being constructed around what Jack Donnelly labels the *Universal Declaration model* of human rights, 'in recognition of the central role of the Universal Declaration of Human Rights in establishing the contours' of what Donnelly tells us is the 'contemporary consensus on internationally recognized human rights' (Donnelly 2003: 22). That is, the Universal Declaration of Human Rights (UDHR), adopted by the UN General Assembly on 10 December 1948, is 'the basis of global efforts to promote and protect human rights', serving as 'the foundation on which all other global human rights instruments are built' (Moore and Pubantz 2002: 358; see also Close and Askew 2004a, Chapters 2 and 3).

The GHRR is being constructed mainly under the aegis of the UN and so around UN human rights provisions, with the assistance especially of the UN Office of the High Commissioner for Human Rights (OHCHR). The UN's weighty and highly effective contribution in this respect has been variously celebrated, not least in October 2001 when the Norwegian Nobel Committee awarded the Nobel Peace Prize for 2001, 'in two equal portions', to the UN and to the UN's Secretary-General, Kofi Annan, 'for their work for a better organized and more peaceful world' (Norwegian Nobel Committee 2001). Apart from such endorsements, however, in its task of constructing a GHRR, the UN is able to rely on the support of many bodies around the world and at all levels, including a pack of CSOs and GCSOs, to the fore of which are AI and HRW. At the same time, however, in view of the character of these bodies, quite a lot of unease has been expressed concerning the implications of the GHRR, especially with respect to the way in which it may well reflect and reinforce one particular package of values, ideals and principles at the expense of others. For some, more specifically, the GHRR embodies above all Western culture, which it then underscores as the prevailing *dominant global culture*. According to this argument, the GHRR has been constructed largely by the most powerful global political economy (GPE) players principally in accordance with their own values, and in a manner which suits their own, self-serving interests. For these critics and detractors, the progress of the GHRR can be largely understood in terms of how it serves the interests of those who have most influence, power and control over the GHRR and concomitantly over global developments more generally, such interests being largely centred upon the preservation of this influence, power and control. Among those who have attacked the GHRR along these lines are a number of East Asian political leaders, including the former Prime Minister of Singapore, Lee Kwan Yew, and the former Prime Minister of Malaysia, Mahathir bin Mohamad, as well as incumbents of high political office in China, at least up until China's *Open-door policy*, which first unblocked 'the country to foreign investment and encouraged development of a market economy and private sector' during the 1980s (BBC 13 October 2005; see also Close and Askew 2004a, Chapters 1 to 6; cf. Kim 1994, 1998, 1999).

Essentially, it has been argued that the general character, operation and development of the GHRR is best interpreted as the product of how culture and power are used at and between the local, regional and global levels of modern social life (Close and Askew 2004a: 9–11). The construction and reconstruction of the GHRR is the result of competition among cultures, or cultural representatives and entrepreneurs, within the *global culture market*. Within this market, some players are more able, forceful and successful than others in purveying their cultural ideas and items, goods and services; and consequently, some are more influential than others in the process whereby cultural products are installed and used at the global among other levels. Some players have more power and control than others over human rights matters, the unequal distribution of power and control involved being largely rooted in the development of the political economy, above all at the global level. Those with most power tend to be in or otherwise associated with *the North*, better placed as the players of the North are within the GPE. At the same time, the most powerful political economy – and so human rights – players tend to be aligned with Western cultures, ideas and values, there being a substantial overlap between the Northern core of the GPE and the Western sphere of global social life. Consequently, the GHRR is largely commensurate with the Western cultural account (Meyer et al. 1987), with its emphasis on such principles and practices as individualism, liberal democracy and market capitalism. The political economy players of *the South* are at a disadvantage in trying to promote and purvey their own distinctive cultural goods and services, as well as in trying to protect their own cultural ideas and items by resisting the advance of Western culture as embodied in, for instance, the GHRR. This particular human rights-focused struggle exemplifies a broader tussle which is taking place around the economic, political and cultural processes of globalization.

Within the so-called *global community* there is a hegemonic *sub-global community* of Western and Northern cultural, human rights and political economy players which is mainly responsible for determining the development of the GHRR, and for fashioning a world which is becoming increasingly homogenous over human rights matters. However, this is not to say that everyone, including everyone in the West, is content with this scenario. While Kofi Annan shared the Nobel Peace Prize with the UN in 2001 for their contribution to a peaceful world, an earlier winner, David Trimble, the Ulster Unionist leader, has poured scorn on, at least some aspects of, the GHRR. In January 2004:

> Trimble called human rights organisations a 'great curse' [. . .] and accused them of complicity in terrorist killings. 'One of the great curses of this world is the human rights industry,' he told the Associated Press news agency at an international conference of terrorism victims in Madrid. 'They justify terrorist acts and end up being complicit in the murder of innocent victims.' His words drew an angry reaction from Amnesty International and Human Rights Watch, two of the world's biggest human rights groups, with about 200,000 members in Britain and more than a million worldwide [. . .]. A spokeswoman for the Norwegian Nobel Institute in Oslo, which awarded Mr Trimble his prize in 1988, declined to say whether [the Institute] considered itself [to be] a member of the 'human rights industry'.
>
> (Tremlett 2004; see Close and Askew 2004a: 9–11)

David Trimble's view of the *human rights industry* has been applauded by Rajiv Malhotra, who in turn has compared human rights activism with money laundering. The latter involves 'channeling illegal funds through a complex web of transactions to make the money's character increasingly ambiguous, and eventually [. . .] through lawful business activities that turn it into "legal" money' (Malhotra 2004). Fortunately, Malhotra tells us, the money laundering industry is being fought by 'a worldwide movement led by the United States' (*ibid.*), distinguishing it from 'another kind of "laundering" that plays the same type of subterfuge, lacks transparency, but thrives unchallenged' (*ibid.*). He is 'referring to the vast network of "human rights" programs and activism involving globalized NGOs [. . .], government programs, religious institutions, and private funding sources that promote conflict and sometimes become fronts for insurgencies and separatist movements of various kinds' (*ibid*). Malhotra continues:

> One man's terrorists are another man's freedom fighters, and this turns into an opportunity for doublespeak [. . .]. There are many other kinds of conflicts-of-interest which are even harder to pin down, but which nevertheless entail great abuse of the power that comes from being 'givers' and 'helpers'. For example, National Public Radio broadcast a series on widespread sexual abuses of women in famine-stricken parts of Africa. The culprits were UN employees, contractors and local volunteers who

traded food for sex to desperate mothers and young women either through gross intimidation or through more ambiguous methods of 'persuasion'. The culprits used the 'moral authority' and power conferred by their position of being the 'givers' and 'human rights activists' in a fairly blatant way to violate the minds, values and bodies of the downtrodden they claimed to help.

(*ibid.*; see also Close and Askew 2004a: 9–11)

If NGOs, or CSOs, such as AI and HRW, along with governmental organizations, and above all the UN (or perhaps especially certain UN agencies, such as the UNHCHR), are members of a *human rights industry* and are engaged in *human rights laundering*, then presumably all other organizations that help promote human rights, if only tangentially, such as the IOC and the Olympic movement, will be also. If so, then the IOC and the Olympic movement will belong to a social network, or compact, which is using its *collective power* to contribute to the creation of a GHRR in conjunction with the global advance of Western cultural account, intimately tied as this is to the doctrines, principles and practices of individualism, liberal democracy and market capitalism.

The IOC and the Olympic movement, by virtue of their responsibility for and influence through the Olympic Games, probably currently the greatest series of sporting mega-events, and in particular the Beijing Olympiad, probably the greatest mega-event of any kind and of all time, will be not only furthering the cause of Olympism, but also playing a major role in the global social network, or compact, which is using its collective power to steer the processes of globalization. The latter is occurring along three basic dimensions – the economic, the political and the cultural – in a way which has so far largely reflected Western values combined with Northern power, or hegemony, increasingly rooted as this has become in the evolving GPE. Given recent developments in the GPE, however, it is possible, even likely, that a fundamental shift has been taking place since the early 1990s, in the distribution of GPE power – or, that is, in the configuration of GPE power players – towards East Asia and especially China, as signalled, symbolized and perhaps further secured by the award of the 2008 Olympic Games to Beijing.

The Beijing Olympiad and especially the concluding Games, as a global mega-event, will provide a major opportunity for CSOs and other purveyors of ideas, goods and services on the global human rights market to scrutinize, criticize and vilify the government of China for its human rights record. CSOs will do their job, help rationalize their existence, and further ensure their survival. The PRC's government will be placed in the glare of the human rights spotlight and put under pressure to improve, so to speak, its human rights record in accordance with GHRR principles and Western values. Another chance will be taken, if not wholly created, to strengthen the GHRR, and to promote not only Olympism, but also the Western cultural account, individualism, liberal democracy, and market capitalism, and thereby contribute to the progress of globalization. This is not to ignore the way in which it is not just CSOs and other organizations that find fault with China's human rights record. So do individuals, as indicated by a famous Western athlete's experience of how Chinese children are being trained as gymnasts for the 2008 Games:

> Olympic legend Sir Matthew Pinsent has been left stunned by the treatment of young gymnasts in Beijing. The four-times gold medallist assessed China's preparations for the 2008 Olympic Games for BBC Radio Five Live. Pinsent, who described children in pain while training and claimed a boy had been beaten by his coach, said: 'It was a pretty disturbing experience' [. . .]. Pinsent, a former IOC and current British Olympic Association member, felt children were being pushed beyond acceptable limits in pursuit of excellence. He was disappointed that it appeared to be regarded as necessary. Pinsent said: 'I know it is gymnastics and that sport has to start its athletes young, but I have to say I was really shocked. I was wondering whether the western approach compared to the eastern approach is a bit different, but I do think those kids are being abused. When I talked to the vice-principals, they said hitting was against the law, but then there were parents who want you to do it. They said this is what they needed to do to make them hard.' The choice of Beijing to host the Games has been condemned in some quarters because of the country's poor human rights record.
>
> (BBC 17 November 2005)

Perhaps the Olympic Games were awarded to Beijing in the belief that this would help with the progress of human rights in China. If so, then perhaps the IOC can claim some success, in that on 14 March 2004, an amendment to the Constitution was adopted by the Second Session of the Tenth National People's Congress (NPC), 'which stipulates clearly that "the state respects and safeguards human rights" ' (Dong Yunhu 2004). As pointed out by Dong Yunhu, a Vice-President and the Secretary-General of the China Society for Human Rights Studies (CSHRS),[6] this is 'the first time that the concept of "human right" has been included in the Constitution – a major event in the development of China's democratic constitutionalism and political civilization, and an important milestone in human rights progress in China' (*ibid.*). Here, Dong Yunhu is celebrating a landmark event in the history of human rights in the PRC and the world as a whole. At the same time, moreover, if the groundbreaking inclusion of human rights in the PRC's Constitution is not momentous enough, it was accompanied by yet another major revision. For the first time since the 1949 socialist revolution, private property rights were enshrined in the Constitution. This is remarkable if only because as recently as 4 December 1982 the NPC approved a Constitution which

declared the PRC to be 'a socialist state under the people's democratic dictatorship led by the working class and based on the alliance of workers and
peasants' (*People's Daily* 18 May 2004). The 1982 Constitution stated 'the
socialist system is the basic system' of the PRC, and declared: 'Sabotage of
the socialist system by any organization or individual is prohibited' (*ibid.*).[7]

The Chinese government's political economy policies, principles and practices have undergone revolutionary change since the early 1980s, so that as of
the 2004 opening of the Beijing Olympiad not only had the PRC's Constitution been amended to include the right to own private property, but also
China had joined the World Trade Organization (WTO), the body which
'deals with the rules of trade between nations at a global or near-global level'
(WTO 16 November 2005). The WTO describes itself as an 'organization
for liberalizing trade'; and, to this end, as a 'forum for governments to nego-
tiate trade agreements' and 'to settle trade disputes'. The WTO 'operates a
system of trade rules', the 'overriding purpose of which is 'to help trade flow
as freely as possible', something which 'means removing obstacles' to trade
(*ibid.*). But, it would seem, this is not the only thing it means. As otherwise
summarized, the WTO 'is an international body whose purpose is to promote free trade by persuading countries to abolish import tariffs and other
barriers', and as 'such, it has become closely associated with globalisation'
(BBC 16 November 2005). The WTO's main purpose, at least in effect, is to
promote, boost and expand market capitalism at the global level in a manner
commensurate with the processes of globalization. As such, the WTO 'has
been the focal point of criticism from people who are worried about the
effects of free trade and economic globalisation' (*ibid.*). Criticisms of the
WTO focus on four main concerns:

> the WTO is too powerful, in that it can in effect compel sovereign states
> to change laws and regulations by declaring these to be in violation of
> free trade rules; the WTO is run by the rich for the rich and does not
> give significant weight to the problems of developing countries. For
> example, rich countries have not fully opened their markets to products
> from poor countries; the WTO is indifferent to the impact of free trade
> on workers' rights, child labour, the environment and health; and the
> WTO lacks democratic accountability, in that its hearings on trade
> disputes are closed to the public and the media.
>
> (*ibid.*)

Still, doubts of this kind seem not to have deterred China from joining the
WTO. The PRC joined on 11 December 2001 after 15 years of negotiations,
the longest in the WTO's history, a move which perhaps more than any other
has ensured the PRC's integration into the global economy, centred on the
principles and practices of market capitalism (see Prasad 2004).[8] Cynics
might claim that any indifference to the *negative impact* of free trade and lack

of democratic accountability on the part of the WTO will not trouble the PRC's government, which was very keen to sign up. It would seem that the consequences for the PRC of its accession to the WTO will be considerable. According to Jim Hoagland, as already noted (above), accession to the WTO will help force China to make severe adjustments in its economy (Hoagland 2001), modifications which are being introduced alongside those 'brought by China's nearly simultaneous preparations for the Olympics' (ibid.).

It is reasonable to assume that the impact on China of its membership of the WTO, on the one hand, and of China's preparation for the Beijing Olympics, on the other, will be in many ways mutually consistent and supportive. Or, to put it another way, it is reasonable to assume that both China's accession to the WTO and Beijing's success in winning the right to host the 2008 Olympic Games reflect and, in turn, reinforce certain underlying, pivotal developments in China's political economy relationships with the rest of the world; or, that is, in China's inclusion and place within the evolving GPE in accordance with the processes of globalization (see Prasad 2004).

Just as PRC's admission to and acceptance by the WTO can be understood in terms of the government's decision to have China move on by pruning state socialism and embracing market capitalism, so Beijing's election as the host city for the 2008 Olympic Games can be understood in terms of the same epochal adjustment. The IOC will have selected Beijing for the Games, not so much with the aim of encouraging China to make progress in the area of human rights, as to reward the PRC for its switch to market capitalism and to encourage it to progress rapidly as a player within the global market-capitalist system, perhaps at the expense of human rights – although human rights organizations, purveyors and entrepreneurs are likely to have something to say about this particular ramification.

Certainly, the IOC's selection of Beijing to host the 2008 Games in recognition of and support for the PRC's market-capitalist development and progress as a political economy player on the world stage is consistent with the IOC's previous selection of the only other Asian cities to have hosted the Olympics, Tokyo in 1964 and Seoul in 1988. It might also be seen as consistent with the IOC's decision against selecting Beijing to host the 2000 Games on the grounds that in the early 1990s, China was still in the rudimentary and uncertain stages of its progress as a market-capitalist society. Thus, He Zhenliang, who – as already mentioned (above) – was a leading figure in the Chinese Olympic Committee (COC) as well as the IOC during the PRC's bids for the 2000 Olympics and the 2008 Games, has recalled:

> One influential IOC member told me 'I have to tell you frankly that last time when I voted for Sydney instead of Beijing, it was because I was a little concerned about political stability in China, as your senior Leader Deng Xiaoping was very old. I didn't know what would happen after

Deng. And in my continent there are many former socialist countries that have problems. So I was concerned about China, but what [has] happened in China during these eight years [has] showed that I was wrong, so this time I will vote for Beijing.'

(Xinhua News Agency 9 October 2003)

While this particular IOC member had a change of mind about Beijing's suitability as an Olympics host, others retained major misgivings about its candidacy for the 2008 Games. He Zhenliang, who by July 2001 had become honorary chairman of the PRC's National Olympic Committee, recalls:

During the bidding process, [. . .] the main difficulty [was] that the out-side world didn't understand how fast both economic and social pro-gress [was] being achieved in China. They always look at China from an old angle, an old view. But according to new IOC rules, we couldn't invite IOC members to China. So the only way was to send them VCDs and magazines. And how were we to make the western [sic] press aware of the progress we had made? We invited the sports press, which is more objective, to come to China. This strategy was very useful. Besides, I'm allowed to visit our colleagues in the IOC, so I use every opportunity to exchange views with them, telling them how fast we are developing; this convinced them that China really was capable of staging a wonderful Olympic Games.

(ibid.)

According to the Xinhua News Agency, as a member of the IOC, He Zhenliang 'acted as a bridge connecting Chinese sport with the rest of the world', and in this regard recalls:

An IOC member said they had some concerns, for instance the environ-ment, and traffic. These are problems everybody is aware of because Beijing is growing so fast. My approach is not to avoid [. . .] problems. You can just tell them, 'Yes, we have this problem, those are big chal-lenges for us but we have invested a lot, we have done a lot to improve.' And as for the traffic problem, I told them about the measures we would take over the coming years. [Most] IOC members are highly respected people, and with them, a frank and honest attitude is always the best way.

(ibid.)

If so, then He Zhenliang's approach seems to have worked. Eventually, the 2008 Games themselves will provide in a direct way an opportunity for China to progress yet further as a player within the global market-capitalist system, just as the Games will provide an opportunity for external political economy players to take advantage of and make further moves into, by investing in, the PRC's deepening market-capitalist economy. The result will be further boosts to globalization, especially along its economic dimension, and the PRC's political economy presence and standing on the world stage.

As already noted (above), for Jim Hoagland, the award of the 2008 Games to Beijing was made possible by the people of China through their efforts *in breaking free from the past and building a new China*, in particular towards a market-capitalist and perhaps liberal-democracy future. At the same time, the award was made that much easier by the way in which the people of China appeared highly supportive of, not to say enthusiastic about, Beijing's bid. With this in mind, it is notable how the figures in Table 4.3 vary by other, underlying differences between the candidate cities and their respective countries, and in particular according to differences in their *economic development*.

The figures in Table 4.3 suggest that there is a rough correlation between, on the one hand, the differences in local popular support given to the candidate cities for the 2008 Games and, on the other hand, the differences in the rankings of these cities along *economic development indicators*, as the World Bank refers to them (World Bank 15 July 2005), with the least popular support tending to be given to the cities in the most economically developed countries. Equally striking is the way in which the greatest popular support was given to those candidate cities which were least developed while, none the less, exhibiting the greatest economic growth rates, at least as indicated by increases in gross domestic product (GDP).

In this way, indirectly, the fast pace of China's economic growth during the 1990s, albeit from a relatively low starting point, will have come to the aid of Beijing's bid for the 2008 Games, at least in so far as the IOC's decision was influenced by the evidence on local popular support for the bid. Of course,

Table 4.3 Local popular support for the candidate cities for the 2008 Olympics and Economic Development Indicators (2004) for the Respective Countries

City	Total support, as in Table 4.2	Country	Gross Domestic Product (PPP) (2004)	GDP per capita (2004)	GDP growth rate (2001) (%)	GDP growth rate (2002) (%)	GDP growth rate (2004) (%)	GNP per capita (PPP) (2004)
Beijing	96 (96)	China	7,123,712	5,600	7.5	8.0	9.1	5,530
Istanbul	86 (86)	Turkey	552,990	7,400	7.5	7.8	8.2	7,680
Toronto	71 (67)	Canada	993,079	31,500	1.5	3.3	2.4	30,660
Paris	66 (55)	France	1,744,352	28,700	2.1	1.2	2.1	29,320
Osaka	52 (51)	Japan	3,774,086	29,400	0.4	0.3	2.9	30,040

Source: CIA 31 March 2006; World Bank 15 July 2005; World Bank 2004.

Note:
PPP refers to measurements on a purchasing power parity basis (see Note 9).

China's economic growth has continued at an even faster pace since Beijing won the right to host the 2008 Games, including into the period of the Beijing Olympiad. The starting point for the growth surge can be pinned down to 1978, when 'the Chinese leadership began moving the economy from a sluggish, inefficient, Soviet-style centrally planned economy to a more market-oriented system' (CIA 1 November 2005). While the economy continues 'to operate within a political framework of strict Communist control', the 'influence of non-state organizations and individual citizens has been steadily increasing' (*ibid.*). The government has introduced 'a system of household and village responsibility in agriculture in place of the old collectivization, increased the authority of local officials and plant managers in industry, permitted a wide variety of small-scale enterprises in services and light manufacturing, and opened the economy to increased foreign trade and investment' (*ibid.*). As a result, as already noted (above), by the end of 2005 the 'private sector' had expanded to account for 'over two thirds of the country's economy' (Finfacts 2005a); and the economy had expanded 'by an average 9.6 percent annually' since 1990 (Bloomberg 2006), so that by 2005 it had become 'the world's fourth biggest, behind the US, Japan and Germany' (BBC 19 December 2005; see also Finfacts 2005b; Pesek 2006).

Over the quarter of a century between 1978 and the opening of the Beijing Olympiad in 2004, there was 'a quadrupling of GDP', so that when measured on a purchasing power parity (PPP) basis (CIA 1 November 2005), China 'stood as the second-largest economy in the world after the US, although in per capita terms the country [was] still poor' (*ibid.*).[9] Indeed, the World Bank still counts China as a developing country: *a low- to middle-income country* in which 'most people have a lower standard of living with access to fewer goods and services than do most people in high-income countries' (World Bank 2003a). It would seem that while both *agriculture and industry* 'have posted major gains', these have been 'especially [evident] in coastal areas near Hong Kong and opposite Taiwan and in Shanghai, where foreign investment has helped spur output of both domestic and export goods' (CIA 1 November 2005). Consequently, China's economic development has been neither even, whether between economic sectors or between geographical areas and regions, nor smooth and uninterrupted. In particular, the 'economic disparity', or *wealth gap*, 'between urban China and the rural hinterlands is among the largest in the world', the results being that many 'impoverished rural dwellers are flocking to the country's eastern cities', and that there has been considerable social discontent and 'protests by farmers and workers' (BBC 24 November 2005; see also Luard 2005). At the other end of the social, economic and political ladder, *the leadership* has 'experienced – as a result of its hybrid system – the worst results of socialism (bureaucracy and lassitude) and of capitalism (growing income disparities and rising unemployment)', and has responded by having 'periodically backtracked, retightening central controls at intervals' (CIA 1 November 2005).

The government has been faced with a number of especially difficult country-wide economic and social challenges that are rooted in or, at least, have been exacerbated by the transition from a state socialist to a market-capitalist economy. In particular, the government 'has struggled to (a) sustain adequate job growth for tens of millions of workers laid off from state-owned enterprises, migrants, and new entrants to the work force; (b) reduce corruption and other economic crimes; and (c) keep afloat the large state-owned enterprises, many of which had been shielded from competition by subsidies and had been losing the ability to pay full wages and pensions' (*ibid.*). Crucially, the transition from a state socialist to a market-capitalist economy is responsible for the way in which between 100 and 150 million 'surplus rural workers are adrift between the villages and the cities, many subsisting through part-time, low-paying jobs' (*ibid.*).

Another notable effect of, as well as prospective 'long-term threat to', economic growth is 'the deterioration in the environment – notably air pollution', especially in the cities (*ibid.*). While, as already noted (above), Wang Wei, the Secretary General of Beijing's Bid Committee for the 2008 Games, has claimed that Beijing 'has taken giant steps to fight pollution caused by industrialization and economic growth', entailing for instance 'remarkable improvement in air-quality through vehicle emission controls' (BOCOG 30 July 2005), 'the economic boom' has brought considerable 'environmental degradation' and left China with 'many of the world's most-polluted cities' (BBC 24 November 2005). In response, the government has pledged its determination to control and contain China's 'rapid economic growth', such as through reducing 'somewhat its spending on infrastructure' (CIA 1 November 2005) – although, presumably, this strategy will not apply to the Beijing area during the Olympiad.

In spite of the downside, difficulties and doubts, it seems certain that 'China's remarkable economic growth' (*ibid.*) will continue during the Beijing Olympiad and beyond. China's growth will probably remain high relative to that of all other political economy players on the world stage, including Brazil, Russia and India, which together with China comprise the BRIC economies. According to the BRIC thesis (Wilson and Purushothaman 2005), during the first half of the twenty-first century, 'China is likely to surpass the US as the world's largest economy and, together with Brazil, Russia, and India – [also known as] the BRICs – will overshadow the economic might of the seven leading industrialized nations of today' (*Business Week* 27 October 2003). In particular, in 'its rivalry with India as an economic power', China has certain advantages. For instance, it 'has a lead in the absorption of technology, the rising prominence in world trade, and the alleviation of poverty' (CIA 1 November 2005). While currently, India 'has one important advantage in its relative mastery of the English language', even here 'the number of competent Chinese English-speakers is growing rapidly' (*ibid.*). Indeed, as already noted (above), the 2008 Olympic Games may be a spur to the expansion of the PRC's English-speakers, especially in and around Beijing, at least if the enthusiasm of Liu Qi, the Mayor of Beijing, for learning and having others learn English is anything to go by (BOCOG 30 July 2005).

China's rise (Brown 2000; Kokubun and Wang 2004; Sutter 2005; Yong Deng 2004), peaceful rise (Zheng Bijian 2005), emergence (Goldstein 2003; Johnston and Ross 1999), or re-emergence (Davies, E. 10 March 2005; Frank 1998; Lei Guang 2002; Nye 1997–8; Shambaugh 2006) as a powerful political economy player both in East Asia and globally is widely recognized (see also Goldstein 2005; Kitazume 2004), well documented, and increasingly celebrated, including by Beijing having been awarded the right to host the 2008 Olympic Games, the first time China will have staged a mega-event, sporting or otherwise. The PRC's development has occurred in the context of, and latterly at the forefront of, the rise of East Asia (see Berger and Borer 1997), or of *the East Asian miracle* (World Bank 1993). What underlines China's outstanding economic ascendancy is that originally it was not counted as part of this miracle:

> East Asia has a remarkable record of high and sustained economic growth. From 1965 to 1990 the twenty-three economies of East Asia grew faster than all the other regions of the world. Most of this achievement is attributable to seemingly miraculous growth in just eight economies: Japan; the 'Four Tigers' – Hong Kong, the Republic of Korea [or South Korea], Singapore, and Taiwan [. . .] – and the three newly industrializing economies (NIEs) of South-east Asia, Indonesia, Malaysia, and Thailand. These eight high-performing Asian economies (HPAEs) are the subject of this study.
>
> (World Bank 1993: 1)

The way in which China's economy has recently – especially from around the time of Beijing's first bid for the Olympic Games – expanded at a faster rate than any of the other countries and territories of East Asia indicates that it is steadily but surely regaining the dominant position it enjoyed over several millennia and until just a few centuries ago as a political economy player at both the regional and global levels. China has 'a long and illustrious past', and 'has usually been a rather bigger player in the global economy than it' has been in recent years (Davies, E. 10 March 2005). However, 'the growth in living standards in the two decades after market reforms in China were launched, is greater than the cumulative progress in the previous two millennia' (*ibid.*), an indication of how 'in a generation or two', when China is producing around 20 per cent of total world output, 'normal service will have been resumed' (*ibid.*; see also Maddison 2005).

Even so, the process is likely to encounter obstacles and pitfalls, not least those alluded to by the suggestion that accession to the WTO 'helps strengthen [the PRC's] ability to maintain strong growth rates but at the same time puts additional pressure on the hybrid system of strong political controls and growing market influences' (CIA 1 November 2005). That is, the rate of economic change has not 'been matched by political reform, with the Communist Party – the world's biggest political party – retaining its monopoly on power and maintaining strict control over the people. The authorities still crack down on any signs of opposition and send outspoken dissidents to labour camps' (BBC 24 November 2005). So far China has been suffering from, in effect, an *uneven development* imbalance or disjunction within its hybrid political economy between its rapid economic progress and its slow pace of political change, so much so that the latter may have been inhibiting the former. Eventually, however, economic progress, or more accurately the constrained potential for economic progress, may become a source of irresistible pressure for commensurate political change – for more *even development* across the political economy arena of Chinese society. A re-alignment between the economic and political spheres of Chinese social life may be forged, albeit accompanied, and indeed assisted, by social unrest, as perhaps presaged by the 1989 Tiananmen Square incident (see Miles 1996; Mooney 2004; Perry and Selden 2003). For Enver Can, the exiled Vice President of the World Uyghur Congress (based in Germany), the PRC's 'government ultimately will not be able to change the tide of globalization and keep its people immune [. . .]. It [will] try to regain the confidence of the people by introducing democratic reforms [. . .]. If the Party does not face [. . .] reality, and delays introducing radical reforms, no one can guarantee that the people will continue to be as docile as they used to be' (quoted in Mooney 2004).[10]

A re-alignment between the economic and political spheres of Chinese society may be inevitable and already well underway. This may be because there is an *elective affinity* between the ideals and tendencies of market capitalism, on the one hand, and those of liberal democracy, on the other, something which means that eventually the economic and political spheres will become aligned, congruent and harmonious around these ideals and tendencies in spite of attempts by the Chinese state to prevent this from happening. The state will find it increasingly difficult to control and contain the impact of the elective affinity between market capitalism and liberal democracy on Chinese society by way of the mutually supportive development of the economic and political spheres. Under the sway of an elective affinity, the political sphere is straining to fall into line with the economic sphere by operating in an unconstrained liberal democratic manner, not least because market capitalism and liberal democracy are similarly infused with and driven by the doctrine, principles and practices of individualism.

There are grounds for assuming that the Beijing Olympiad will act as a catalyst in the re-alignment, or re-configuration, process within the political-economy arena of Chinese society. After all, the Olympiad will be a convergence point, focal event or meeting place for a cluster of major developments at and between the local, regional and global levels of social life, and between which there is a formidable array of elective affinities. The developments involved include the deepening institutionalization of Olympism at the global level; the global spread of the Western cultural account around the doctrine of individualism; the advance of market capitalism and liberal democracy on the global plane; the progress of globalization in conjunction with the consolidation of global society; and the rise of China as a regional and GPE player and superpower. It is because of the way in which the Beijing Olympiad has drawn together in a highly concentrated, dense and intense fashion these developments along with their elective affinities that the 2008 Games are likely to be not just another sporting mega-event, but instead the greatest mega-event, sporting or otherwise, of all time.

An elective affinity entails an *extraordinary convergence*, or mutual attraction, between the ideals and tendencies, or principles and practices, that are associated with a set of social developments, and which accordingly provide each other with support, strength and impetus. It is with these connotations in mind that 'elective affinity' has been used most famously by Max Weber to make sense of the relationship between *the Protestant Ethic and the Spirit of Capitalism*, primarily to account for the development of market-capitalist social formations in the West. While a suitable synonym for 'elective affinity' is 'mutual attraction', another is 'irresistible mutual desire', at least when the term is used in relation to human and social affairs as distinct from the material world, in relation to which the term was originally coined towards the end of the eighteenth century (see German Historical Museum 2005; MacLeod September 2005; Smith, P. 2001). This is not to imply that an elective affinity between two or more developments – or *elective affinity partners* – will necessarily guarantee that these developments will unfold in a completely smooth and untroubled manner, facilitated by *convergence events* that proceed in a wholly harmonious fashion.

An Olympic Games is a convergence event on a grand scale or, that is, a convergence mega-event. Any convergence event can be viewed as if it were, figuratively speaking, a marriage, or perhaps a wedding which launches a marriage, and the event which is scheduled to round off the Beijing Olympiad is likely to resemble a blockbuster of a wedding. However, whatever the degree of mutual attraction and desire between the (elective affinity) partners, a marriage may turn out to be a difficult affair and a wedding a far from perfect prologue. Apart from anything else, an elective affinity in human and social affairs, while necessarily entailing mutual attraction and desire, may also entail a degree of aversion and repulsion.[11] After all, an elective affinity between a set of developments in human and social affairs, or more precisely between the packages of ideas associated with these developments, will bring together not only similar and compatible ideas, but also dissimilar and perhaps somewhat contradictory, conflicting and confusing ones. This applies where elective affinities and convergence events entail Olympism, a package of ideas that simultaneously affirms both individualism and collectivism – a source of internal tension; that promotes individualism in principle, but in conjunction with tight restrictions on individuality in practice; and that through elective affinities and convergence events will be confronted by other packages of ideas which to some extent encourage a rejection of individualism.

The somewhat contradictory character of Olympism, as reflected in the Olympic Charter for instance, is perhaps not surprising given that the origins of the Olympic movement lie in the West, which far from merely coincidently is also the source of both liberal democracy and individualism, on the one hand, and such collectivisms as socialism and communism, on the other. Liberal democracy alone is renowned for lending itself to the problem of how to balance in practice individualism and individuality with collectivism and social collectivities (or social formations), especially in so far as a collectivity's cohesion depends upon the state, and so on a degree of top-down authority, control and regulation. Still, while Olympism contains ideas that are compatible with collectivism – as indicated by the IOC's declaration that the 'goal of Olympism is to place sport at the service of the harmonious development of man, with a view to promoting a peaceful society concerned with the preservation of human dignity' (IOC 1 September 2004) – it also emphasizes ideas that are consistent with individualism. Olympism emphasizes above all, or at its core, ideas that are consistent with that doctrine, which is closely associated with the global advance of the Western cultural account, market capitalism and liberal democracy; the progress of globalization in conjunction with the consolidation of global society; and the rise of China as a GPE player and superpower. In the run up to the 2008 Games, the participants in the Olympiad – the athletes, coaches, NOCs, Organizing Committee for the Olympic Games (BOCOG), and sponsors among many others – will be subjected to a profusion of somewhat competing, conflicting and confusing ideas, while none the less experiencing an intense barrage of ideas favouring an individualistic approach to life in general and the Games in particular. The result may well be an Olympiad in which the participants by no means fully conduct themselves in accordance with 'best practice' as judged with reference to the principles, rules and laws surrounding the event, the requirements of a harmonious event, or both.

The rough handling of children in training as gymnasts, the use of financial and other inducements in soliciting support from IOC members for a particular candidate city's bid to host an Olympic Games, the corruption which appears to be a prominent feature of any Games,[12] the use of performance enhancing drugs (see BBC 21 April 2005; *Sydney Morning Herald* 2004),[13] and a range of other questionable activities may be mainly explicable in terms of how an Olympiad draws together in a grand fashion a cluster of major social developments, in particular at the global level, their associated ideas, and their elective affinities, but which nonetheless draws on above all the doctrine, principles and practices of individualism. The dubious activities of athletes, coaches and other participants in the Beijing Olympiad will reflect an overwhelming urge to succeed and win, scoop Olympic gold and glory, and enjoy any other rewards that flow from an Olympic championship, and doing this at whatever the cost to Pierre de Coubertin's *golden rule*, according to which *the most important thing in the Olympic Games is not winning but taking part*. The idea of winning may turn out to be much more attractive and far more compelling for most Olympiad participants than the ideas of friendship, fellowship and fraternity, of a wholly harmonious event, and so on. If so, then of course these participants will be demonstrating their complicity in that global social compact which is largely responsible for the Beijing Olympiad, and the *collective power* of which lies increasingly in the global political economy.

Chapter 5

The Olympic Games as a 'coming out party'

Tokyo, Seoul, Beijing and the Asian Olympic discourse

[T]he coming of the Olympic Games to Beijing realizes a goal which for more than a century Chinese people have increasingly yearned for; recognition, respect and acceptance as an equal by the rest of the world.

(Collins 2002: 135)

As can be seen in Table 5.1, for the first sixty years of modern Olympic history, the host cities of the Olympic Games were located solely in Europe and the USA.[1] The Games bounced back and forth across the Atlantic, from Athens (1896) to St Louis (1904), from Paris (1924) to Los Angeles (1932), and so on. The Games were a Western revival of something with European origins, and members of a *Western-based club* centred on the IOC recognized each other's ability and suitability for the task of hosting the Games. Contrary to the declared universalist aspirations of the Olympic dream, the club was and remained for a long time solidly and exclusively Western. That the host cities were always located in the West reflected the West's domination of the Olympic host city selection procedure along with, hegemonically, the world in general, and in turn contributed to the perpetuation of the West's domination of these things.

The Western domination of the Olympic movement and Games has, of course, not been limited to determining the geographical spread of the host cities. Most of the sports included in the Games, among them relatively new ones such as beach volleyball, are either Western in origin or Western versions of non-Western sports. There are exceptions, perhaps the most notable example being judo. Even the exceptions, however, if anything lend credibility to the rule whereby the *what, where and how* of the Games will be acceptable to the Western-based club which runs the Games and will conform to a set of basic Western values, conventions and standards which underpin both the Games and Western social life in general.

The operating languages of the Olympic Games – English and French – signify the way in which the founding of modern Olympic movement occurred while Europe still enjoyed economic, political and cultural domination at the global level, followed by the way in which the movement

Table 5.1 Olympic Games Host Cities

Year	City
1896	Athens, Greece
1900	Paris, France
1904	St Louis, USA
1906	*Athens, Greece (Intercalated)*
1908	London, UK
1912	Stockholm, Sweden
1920	Antwerp, Belgium
1924	Paris, France
1928	Amsterdam, Holland
1932	Los Angeles, USA
1936	Berlin, Germany
1948	London, UK
1952	Helsinki, Finland
1956	Melbourne, Australia
1960	Rome, Italy
1964	Tokyo, Japan
1968	Mexico City, Mexico
1972	Munich, Germany
1976	Montreal, Canada
1980	Moscow, Soviet Union
1984	Los Angeles, USA
1988	Seoul, South Korea
1992	Barcelona, Spain
1996	Atlanta, USA
2000	Sydney, Australia
2004	Athens, Greece
2008	Beijing, China
2012	London, UK

evolved while the mantle of domination remained with the West, albeit more specifically with the USA. The West is the font of a range of sports which the Olympic movement has helped turn into what has become *global sporting practice*. In particular, as Allen Guttmann has mentioned, from 'the British Isles, modern sports went forth to conquer the world' (Guttmann 1994: 2). Concomitantly, the 'modern Olympic Games began as a European phenomenon and it has always been necessary for non-Western peoples to participate in the Games on Western terms' (*ibid.*: 120).[2]

It is no mere coincidence that both those sports that have acquired a global reach and the greatest multi-sports event, the Olympic Games, are almost wholly Western in their origins. Each development can be traced to how the nineteenth century was in an important sense *the British century*. While Baron Pierre de Coubertin (1863 to 1937), the founder of the modern Olympic movement, was a French nobleman, he was also a deeply committed anglophile.[3] The birth of the modern Olympic movement is indebted not only to

Coubertin's organizational flair, but also to the prevailing Western fascination with the glories of *classical antiquity* (the period of history from the seventh century BC to the fifth century AD which was centred on the Mediterranean Sea, and which opened roughly with the ancient Greek poetry of Homer and ended with the fall of the Western Roman Empire), the influence of continental anglophilism, and French anxiety about a perceived decline in French masculinity as manifested on the battlefield.

The driving force behind the creation of the movement lay in the combined influence of Western liberal democratic values (see Chapters One to Four of this book), nationalism – with its origins in Western Europe – and the English aristocratic emphasis on amateurism. The latter is an ethic which was closely associated with the English public (or leading, independent, fee-paying) school system, and in this regard Coubertin was strongly influenced in his worldview by the 'powerful figure' of Thomas Arnold (1795 to 1842), a notable English historian and author, and the renown head of Rugby School from 1828 to 1841.[4]

Public school athleticism, and in particular that developed under the guidance of Thomas Arnold, firmly linked physical endeavours such as individual athletics and team sports with classical and religious education, character building, and such gender-skewed notions as *manly piety* and *good sportsmanship*. The *real athlete* was an amateur, male and Christian. He was, essentially, a *Christian gentleman*. He practised a code of ethics which can be distinguished as 'Muscular Christianity' *à la* Thomas Hughes (1822 to 1896), who attended Rugby School and is famous for his semi-autobiographical novel *Tom Brown's Schooldays* (1857) and lesser-known sequel *Tom Brown at Oxford* (1861); and Charles Kingsley (1819 to 1875), who – apart from being appointed Regius Professor of Modern History at the University of Cambridge in 1860 – was the author of *The Heroes* (1856), a children's book about Greek mythology, and several historical novels, including *Hypatia* (1853), *Hereward the Wake* (1865) and *Westward Ho!* (1855).[5] Those physical, athletic and sporting activities which were honed by the underlying *Muscular Christianity* code of ethics (as reflected in the best known of all Olympics-related cinema film, *Chariots of Fire*, 1981), emerged as enhanced purity. That cultural ethic, or 'physical morality' (Knowlton, cited in Lucas 1975: 459), which was constructed around such principles and practices as 'fair play' and 'cricket' was exclusively embodied in the vigorous, athletic, and honourable gentleman-sportsman.

The introduction of Physical Education (PE) or Training (PT) into schools in the United Kingdom and elsewhere in Europe during the nineteenth century was closely entwined with the militarization of European societies, and as such assumed the appearance of military drills, just as the introduction of similar activities in China from the latter half of the century under Western influence did (see Chapter 6 of this book). Physical endeavours, such as through PE, was an expression of the Western celebration and idealization of the male physique, enshrined as this was within the dominant Western discourse (account, argument, narrative or treatise) concerning masculinity. The dominant Western discourse on masculinity and idealization of the male physique drew heavily on images of and myths about Europe's Hellenistic roots – where the Hellenistic period of ancient Greek history and culture stretched from the death of Alexander the Great to the accession of Augustus.

During the nineteenth century and well into the twentieth century, those born into the working classes of European societies faced almost insurmountable barriers to becoming gentlemen-sportsman, not least given the financial constraints and demands surrounding amateurism, and consequently to becoming Olympians. But even more so, especially in the early stages of the development of the modern Olympic movement, females faced exclusion. Thus, it 'is true that the first Olympic Games of the modern era in 1896 were not open to women. Baron Pierre de Coubertin, who revived the Games, was very much a man of his time' (IOC 8 September 2006b). However, women were allowed to take part in the 1900 Games (IOC 8 September 2006a), since when 'the participation of women in the Olympic movement at all levels has changed considerably' (IOC 8 September 2006b), albeit with the exception so far of the highest level, that of the President of the IOC. Over the course of the twentieth century, and especially since the 1960s, the gender-skewed character of the Olympic movement and Games was greatly reduced, although perhaps significantly even during the 2008 Games there will be only a small number of sports (led by equestrian events) in which men and women will be allowed to directly compete against each other.[6]

Yet another group who have experienced exclusion from the Olympic Games, and have had to fight longer and harder to be included, is made up of those variously called disabled and handicapped, whether physically or intellectually or both. An 'Olympic Games' for athletes with disabilities were staged in 1960, and these have subsequently become known as the first Paralympic Games, where the use of the Greek 'para' (meaning 'beside' or 'alongside') here indicates that the event took place in parallel with the Rome Summer Olympic Games. The first Winter Paralympics were staged in 1976 in Sweden, in parallel with the Winter Olympic Games which took place in that year at Innsbruck in Austria. Since 1988, when the Summer Games were hosted by Seoul, the Summer Paralympics have been held in conjunction with the Olympic Games in the same city, a practice which was extended to the Winter Paralympics in 1992, and which became the official policy of the IOC (and so of the International Paralympic Committee, or IPC) in June 2001. The Paralympics are held three weeks after the close of either the Summer Games or the Winter Games, and in each case use precisely the same facilities. The cities which bid for the right to host an Olympic Games are required to include a provision for the Paralympic Games, and typically the same organizing committee runs both events. In 1996, athletes with intellectual disabilities were allowed for first time to compete in the Atlanta Paralympic Games. However, as a result of cheating at the 2000 Sydney Paralympic Games, when it was discovered that non-disabled athletes had been included in Spain's intellectually disabled basketball team, athletes with intellectual disabilities have been excluded from the Paralympic Games. The IPC has said that it will re-assess the participation of athletes with intellectual abilities after the 2008 Beijing Paralympic Games.

In a manner variously resembling the experiences of the working class, women and the disabled, the athletes, people and nations of the non-Western 'Other' (see Said, 1978) have faced barriers to participating, competing and succeeding in the Olympic Games and movement. There have been restrictions on their inclusion in and influence over the Western-based club which has governed the Olympic movement and Games, just as there have been similar and not unrelated restrictions on the inclusion of non-Western nation-states in that Western-based club which in a hegemonic fashion has dominated the world's economic, political and cultural affairs for at least two centuries. This is poignantly reflected in the fact that during the four decades spanning the 1896 Athens Games and the 1936 Berlin Games, only three Asian countries – India, Japan and the Philippines – gained any medals (see Nam-Gil and Mangan 2003: 213). In 1932, Japan came fifth in the final, overall medals table (behind the USA, Italy, France and Sweden), India came nineteenth and the Philippines came twenty-fifth. Indeed, Japan's achievement at the 1932 Games is made all the more notable by the way its athletes won 11 of the 16 swimming medals. Nonetheless, if anything, exceptional successes of this kind merely underline the conclusion that there is a general tendency for the non-Western *Other* to be largely prevented from making its mark on the highly Westernized Olympic movement.

Many cultural items with political-economy ramifications were diffused around the world in conjunction with the spread and governance of Western empires. This applies to a range of sports, including cricket and football (otherwise known as soccer), and connectedly to the Olympic Games, steered by the Olympic movement and IOC as a vehicle of cultural imperialism (Guttmann 1994); of, that is, the global march of the *Western cultural account* (Axford, 1995; Meyer et al., 1987) in a manner consistent with the advance of globalization around Western (economic) market capitalism and (political) liberal democracy. World domination by Western sports emerged in the shadow of Western imperialism, colonialism and domination of the world's production, exchange and distribution of goods, sporting and otherwise. Western hegemony has been so successful that even in those locations within the non-Western world where strong nationalist sentiments and movements are to be found there has been little or no effective resistance against the encroachment by Western sports, sports goods, and the Olympics. Indeed, the global spread of the West's sporting paraphernalia may have been greatly assisted by the presence of nationalism in the non-Western world. It may have been facilitated by the way it has been presented, promoted and purveyed as a means by which national identity can be asserted with internal benefits (around social cohesion and stability) and external advantages in relation to regional rivals and even to Western imperialist nation-states. J. A. Mangan suggests that sports are a key element in an evolving 'global consumer culture' which boasts 'an international symbolic language – tracks, fields, arenas, medals, cups – even more widespread than the English language' (Mangan 2002: 7).

The principal discourse on the modern Olympic Games and movement has reflected the Western domination of these things and the world as a whole, and concomitantly has reflected above all Western interests and concerns. The latter cover everything from those preoccupations which lay behind the founding of the modern Games and movement, to those matters which troubled and divided Western peoples, nations and nation-states in the run-up to the Second World War, to the factors which underpinned the Cold War schism, to the attention which has been given in recent years to gender, disability, human rights, environmental and developmental issues, and to the anxieties about terrorism during the period of the Beijing Olympiad. However, alongside the Western discourse on the Games there are other, alternative and contending narratives, including a distinctively Asian discourse which focuses upon Japan as the most successful and trailblazing Asian nation-state in relation to the Games. For instance, between the 1896 Games and the end of the 2004 event, Japan won more Olympic medals than any other Asian nation-state (333 medals), although the PRC was not far behind (with 286 medals), followed by the People's Republic of Korea (or South Korea) with 184 medals, the Democratic People's Republic of Korea (or North Korea) with 35, Indonesia with 20, India and Thailand both on 17, Chinese Taipei and Mongolia with 15 medals each, and Pakistan with 10.

Not unrelated to its position at the start of the 2004–8 Beijing Olympiad in the overall Olympic medals table, Japan was the first Asian nation-state to host the Games. The 1964 Games was a breakthrough, a watershed not only in the Japanese experience, but also in the Asian experience. The Tokyo Games helped inform, shape and sharpen the latter, providing a model for the purpose, whereby Asia's relationship with the rest of the world by way of sport, the Olympic movement and mega-events could be re-assessed and enhanced. The Japanese experience of hosting the Games was perceived in terms not just of the country's sporting agendas, aims and achievements *per se*, but also of its underlying social, political and economic (or political economy) and associated internal (or domestic) and external (or international, regional and global) agendas, aims and achievements. The Tokyo Games clearly provided the Japanese people, nation and state with a window for showcasing its great economic strides, for gaining prestige on the world stage, and for boosting domestic confidence and cohesion, in particular around the government and governing political party.

Throughout modern Olympic history, hosting the Games has been about much more than simply putting on a sporting event as such, no matter how impressive. They have usually been seen as a useful means for pursuing a political agenda, perhaps most notoriously in the case of the 1936 Berlin Games, but also palpably during the Cold War period, the opening of which coincided more or less with the 1948 London Games and the close of which occurred in the middle of the 1988 to 1992 Barcelona Olympiad. They first assumed also, however, a highly evident and somewhat blatant economic propaganda purpose during the 1960 to 1964 Olympiad, when the Games first passed to Asia, when Japan could boast having made astonishing economic strides, and when the Japanese government had firmly committed the country to a course of yet further, rapid economic growth. While this is not to ignore the accompanying political agenda underlying the Tokyo Games, it is to suggest that the strong emphasis on the economic purposes and benefits was new and provided the hallmark of a distinctive, emerging Asian discourse on the Olympics. Certainly, subsequently, and no doubt influenced by the Japanese experience, or model, the motive behind and agenda underlying the return of the Games to East Asia appears to have been primarily economic, albeit intimately linked to political considerations. Indeed, perhaps the economic dimension of the Asian discourse on the Games has become yet more pronounced over the years as first South Korea followed by the PRC have followed Japan's example by growing enormously in economic stature while wanting to outperform in this regard their regional political-economy rivals, and especially Japan itself.

Interestingly, while the Asian discourse on the Olympics may well have emphasized the economic agendas, aims and advantages of the Games in a way which has distinguished it from the dominant Western discourse, it would appear that the latter has recently acquired a similar emphasis in the aftermath of the Cold War. This perhaps makes sense in terms of how the major confrontations which afflict the post-Cold War new world order are more about economic distributions and divisions (in particular between the North and the South) than they used to be; and, not unconnectedly, how globalization is spearheaded primarily by its economic patterns, processes and trends in favour of the global reach of market capitalism (see Chapter 1 of this book). Again, this is not to ignore the salience of various political, not to mention cultural, confrontations, clashes and conflicts, most notably those associated with the *War on Terror* since 2001. But, there would seem to have been something of a convergence between the Western discourse on the Olympics and the Asian discourse around a greater emphasis on economic matters, an emphasis which until the 1990s set the Asian discourse apart from the Western. In a sense, the Asian discourse would seem to have been more advanced that its Western counterpart, at least when judged in terms of the latter's relatively recent modification under the influence of the transition to the *new world order* and, perhaps above all, the thrust of globalization.

In 1956, the Olympic Games travelled for the first time beyond the geo-political terrain of Western Europe and the USA, or of what might be called the *North Atlantic community*, while none the less remaining in the West. They were staged in the southern hemisphere, or antipodes, in Melbourne, Australia. After returning to Western Europe in 1960 (Rome), they travelled for a second time outside the North Atlantic community in 1964 when they were hosted by Tokyo, and so for the first time in a non-Western, non-Caucasian and non-Christian country – a twelve-year-long hosting pattern which was to be roughly repeated several decades later when Sydney 2000 was followed by Athens 2004 and then by Beijing 2008.

While the West monopolized the Games until 1964, as can be seen in Table 5.1, the Tokyo Games opened the door to a notable change. To begin with, Mexico City, the capital city of what may be described as a peripheral Western country (see the writings of Immanuel Wallerstein), hosted the Games; next, Moscow, the capital of the Soviet Union and principal city of the Soviet (or Eastern) bloc, staged the Games; and eight years later, Seoul became the second East Asian city to act as hosts. In the aftermath of a series of Olympic disasters – including those involving the Palestinian terrorist attack on Israeli athletes at Munich in 1972, the widespread African boycott of the Montreal Games in 1976, and the Cold War debacles of 1980 (when only 80 teams participated in Moscow due to the non-attendance of over 60 NOCs in protest at the Soviet Union's invasion of Afghanistan) and 1984 (when fourteen Eastern bloc NOCs did not go to Los Angeles in retaliation for the 1980 boycott) – South Korea was determined to host a successful Games by ensuring as close to full, global participation as possible. The Seoul organizing committee did well in this respect. While the Cold War confrontation left its mark, it did so only marginally. Only four National Olympic Committees (NOCs) refused to attend on political grounds: those of North Korea and, in support, those of Cuba, Ethiopia, and Nicaragua. These NOCs denied that their non-attendance was a 'boycott' in order to avoid IOC censure; and, the affect of the absence of the Cuban athletes aside, their failure to turn up was hardly noticed. Instead, attention at the Seoul Games became firmly fixed on another issue, that of the abuse of performance enhancing drugs, in particular by one Canadian athlete. As a result, the Seoul Games have come to be known as 'Ben Johnson's Games'.

During the death throes of the Cold War confrontation between the West (or the First World) and Western market capitalism and liberal democracy, on the one hand, and the Eastern bloc (Soviet Empire or Second World) and state socialism on the other, the South Korean government saw the Japanese approach to staging the 1964 Games as offering a useful model for pursuing its own purposes, concerns and interests. The Tokyo Games, after all, had been the occasion when Japan had débuted on the world stage as a fully 'developed' nation-state on a par with most of the advanced industrial, market-capitalist nation-states of the West. Indeed, the Games had been awarded, if only in effect, in recognition of the way Japan had achieved economic parity with much of the West in conjunction with, moreover, the way it had remained fully alligned (politically) with the West and had become sufficiently Westernized (culturally) to be accepted by the club which controlled the Olympic movement and Games primarily on behalf of the West. Japan had received the West's seal of approval for membership (economically, politically and culturally) of the West, to the point of being admitted to that club centred on the IOC which had responsibility for controlling, organizing and awarding the Games in accordance with Western values, conventions and standards. The IOC-centered club assumed the role of a gate-keeper to the West. At the same time, however, by admitting Japan, the club had introduced the prospect of opening up the dominant discourse on the Olympics to change. After all, Japan was still in a number of fundamental ways a non-Western society; was the source of the specifically Japanese model for approaching the Games; and was the inspiration behind a distinctive Asian discourse on the Games. In granting Tokyo the right to host the Games, the IOC had created a conduit which provided an early illustration of how the processes of globalization are accompanied by various complicating factors, and in particular those which stem from the processes of localization, playback and glocalization (see Chapter 1 of this book).

In the light of the Japanese model for approaching the Olympic Games, South Korea saw the Olympics as a way of showcasing its own impressive rate of economic development, modernization, and Westernization. Accordingly, the 1988 Seoul Games firmed up the Asian discourse on the Olympics whereby the economic dimension involved was emphasized above all, while none the less the political and cultural ramifications were far from lost to sight, and the Games were to be used as a *rite de passage*, or a coming of age celebration, or a 'coming out party' (Espy 1979: 76). Subsequently, the 2008 Beijing event is being approached within the PRC in a similar fashion, to celebrate what is perhaps the most astonishing economic upturn and about turn in East Asian social history, centred as these developments are on the transformation of the PRC from a rigid state socialist society organized around a command economy to a rapidly evolving market-capitalist society which embraces a range of pivotal principles and practices that had previously been rejected and condemned by the state as Western. As a result, the PRC is emerging as a leading player on the world stage in the drive towards the construction of a global society which in the first instance is market capitalist in character, but which eventually will probably operate in accordance with the practices and principles of Western individualism, Western liberal democracy, and the Western cultural account. The IOC has colluded with the PRC in its decision to opt for the Japanese model and

Asian discourse approach to the Olympics by granting Beijing the right to host the 2008 Games as the third East Asian *coming out party*, the prospective result being that the Beijing Olympiad will turn out to be the greatest mega-event of any kind that has ever been staged not only in Asia, but also anywhere (see Chapter 1 of this book).

While in the past the PRC may well have adopted an approach to the Olympics which it shared with other state socialist societies and was largely concerned with boosting the image, credibility and legitimacy of state socialism,[7] the ideological driving force behind the PRC's enthusiasm for the Games is not so much socialism as nationalism. As discussed in Chapter Three of this book, guided by Shaun Narine, the PRC's 'commitment to capitalism is actually a commitment to economic nationalism' (Narine, 2005: 2), a commitment which shines through in its approach to the 2008 Games. Narine argues that economic nationalism 'characterizes the approach of all other regional states to development, providing a common ground on which China and its neighbours can meet and organize institutional arrangements' (*ibid.*: 3), something which is evident in the Asian discourse on the Olympics as manifested in the approach to the 1964 Games and 1988 Games adopted by Japan and South Korea respectively. Of course, the success of the economic nationalism approach to capitalism, like the success of being guided by the (Japanese model informed) Asian-discourse approach to the Olympics, will be heavily dependent upon effectively harnessing and promoting *popular nationalism*.

In 1964, Japan finally staged an event which originally had been scheduled for 1940. The Tokyo Games were officially opened by the head of state, the Shôwa Emperor, and in this way provided a symbolic means for confirming and celebrating Japan's admittance into the post-War world community. By accepting that the sole surviving leader of a Second World War *axis power* would open an Olympic Games, the bulk of the world community was signalling that as far as it was concerned the Second World War could finally be put to rest a decade and half after the allies had dropped atomic bombs on Hiroshima and Nagasaki followed by Japan's formal surrender. It is notable, however, that the PRC did not attend the 1964 Games due to the suspension of ties between the PRC and the IOC in 1958 over the 'two Chinas' problem (see Chapter 6 of this book), and that the Chinese people retain a considerable degree of deep-seated animosity towards Japan and its people, something which has surfaced in various ways, including at sporting events (see Chapters 2 and 6 of this book). At the 2008 Games, it will not be surprising to see demonstrations of popular nationalism sharpened by strong anti-Japanese feelings, although the Games' organizers in unison with the PRC's governing regime will want to contain these as much as possible.

In a highly potent symbolic act, and in order to underscore the wish to bring about Second-World-War closure, the person chosen as the final torchbearer at the 1964 Games, Sakai Yoshinori, was born in Hiroshima on the day in 1945 when the atomic bomb was dropped on that city. Yoshinori and Japan had survived, and since 1945 Japan had come a long way. The *shinkansen*, or 'bullet train', had been constructed specifically for the Games, and it sent a clear message to the both the people of Japan and the rest of the world that Japan had been developing at great speed its technological prowess, industrial might and economic output. Japan was well on the way to creating the second largest economy in the world, and the 1964 Games served as the *mega-means* (see Chapter 1 of this book) by which its rapid and formidable progress to this end could be showcased and, moreover, further fuelled. The people, government and industrialists of Japan wanted to make their mark on the world, and the Games provided the greatest opportunity in this respect. The resulting impact was not confined to the economic sphere. Thus, at the 1964 Games, the martial art of judo (meaning *gentle way*) which originated in Japan became an Olympic sport, and thereby became the best known and most successful example of a non-Western sport which had been introduced into the modern Olympics and onto the world stage. In the wake of the Second World War, Japan had continued to modernize and Westernize at an accelerating pace, while the moment had arrived for the West to be re-shaped to some extent by Japan, that country which had achieved economic parity with most of the West, but which had retained much that still set it apart from the West in cultural terms. Perhaps it was no mere coincidence that the 1964 Tokyo Games took place at that moment in world history when, it is widely agreed, globalization took off (see Chapter 1 of this book) while none the less being tempered by localization, playback and glocalization, whereby the distinctive 'local' culture of Japan was being far from simply swept aside and away by globalization and the Western cultural account; but instead would be played back on – influencing – globalization and thereby the West.

The Tokyo Olympic Games were harnessed to promote Japan's internal and external credibility, and connectedly to help shore up the Japanese government and state. In 1964, Japan was thoroughly embroiled in the Cold War standoff, including by virtue of its close economic, political and military ties with the West, and especially with the USA, combined with its close proximity to the most powerful state socialist societies in the world, the PRC and Russia, not to mention their supporting cast, in particular in South East Asia, and most notably North Vietnam. The country was in the front line of the Cold War confrontation, and facing directly a number of regimes whose hostility towards Japan in particular was made all the greater by the collective memory of Japan's atrocious activities during the 1930s and 1940s. Moreover, the Cold War division around the world was replicated at the level of internal, domestic politics, with a basically right-wing, pro-market-capitalist and pro-American faction, the Liberal Democratic Party (LDP), in government and a left-wing, socialist and pro-Soviet faction, the Japan Socialist Party (JSP), as the main opposition. Both the LDP and the JSP were founded in 1955, the result being the '1955 System', with the LDP continuously in government and the JSP continuously in opposition right up to the end of the Cold War and the resulting 1990s' implosion of the JSP.

After the end in 1952 of the US-led allied occupation of Japan, there were moves within the country to revise the security arrangement it had established in 1951 with the USA. Following negotiations during the second half of the 1950s, the LDP decided to impose upon Japan's strongly anti-militaristic population a new security treaty with the USA – the Japan–US Mutual Cooperation and Security Treaty – with far-reaching military and external implications. This provoked violent anti-government and anti-LDP demonstrations during 1959 and 1960, especially by students, in response to which the Prime Minister, Kishi Nobusuke, resigned to be replaced on 15 July 1960 by Ikeda Hayto. Subsequently, the LDP government sought to smooth troubled waters by diverting the domestic debate from political issues to economic considerations, something it managed to do with much skill and success. In 1960, Ikeda introduced the Income-Doubling Plan with the promise of increasing the country's GNP by at least a hundred percent by the end of the decade. Eight years later, Japan's GNP had doubled, although it is widely assumed that this would have occurred without the Income-Doubling Plan. Wily Ikeda may have had the foresight to anticipate and exploit what was going to happen anyway.

The Japanese economy had expanded markedly prior to 1960, but then proceeded to display an even greater rate of growth throughout the 1960s and into the 1970s, feeding the process whereby the attention of the Japanese people, including students, was indeed re-directed onto economic agendas, aims and achievements. By 1968, Japan had overtaken Germany to become the world's second largest economy after the USA; the LDP had ridden out the political storms of the late 1950s and early 1960s; and as a reward, the LDP went on to beat the JSP in election after election over the next 25 years.[8]

What became known as 'the Japanese miracle' was revealed to the world at the 1964 Tokyo Games. This event served to focus the internal and external limelight on Japan's post-War economic achievements, to help assuage domestic political anxieties, to promote among the Japanese people an emphasis on their roles as economic producers and consumers rather than as political activists, and to unify the Japanese people and nation around the prospect of yet greater economic success, the enjoyment of domestic harmony and tranquility, and growing external, world-wide prestige. That Japan had already achieved considerable economic success which it was on the way to surpassing became the perception both at home and abroad, including among its nearby Asian neighbours. The idea caught on among the people and rulers around East Asia that they could and should follow in the footsteps of Japan, taking clues from the Japanese experience, approach and model. South Korea was the first among Japan's Asian neighbours to go some way towards emulating Japan's economic development, and in the process was the first to attract the Olympic Games. In 1981, South Korea was awarded the right to host the 1988 Games, and what is more to do so while – just as Japan had been two decades earlier – the country was in the grips of a tumultuous period in its post-War history.

In May 1980, just 15 months before the IOC selected Seoul for the 1988 Games, the South Korean governing regime had brutally suppressed the Kwangju pro-democracy uprising by turning its guns on its own people with much loss of life.[9] At the time, the head of state was President Chun Doo Hwan, a military general who had seized power in December 1979 through a *coup d'état*. In 1987, Chun was replaced as head of state by his handpicked successor, Roh Tae Woo, another military general, who then proceeded to oversee the Seoul Games. In view of the Kwangju incident – an event which has been called 'Korea's Tiananmen' (Scott-Stokes and Lee 2000) – human rights activists expressed profound dismay at the IOC's decision to award the 1988 Games to Seoul (Larmer 2001), a precursor to the similar reaction evoked two years after the Tiananmen Square massacre by the prospect of the IOC selecting Beijing for the 2000 Games, as well as to that which followed the July 2001 election of Beijing to host the 2008 Games.

Securing the 1988 Games was of great value to the South Korean government in its struggle with North Korea for international legitimacy. In 1981, a swathe of left-leaning people around the country and governments around the world did not recognize the South Korean government at all, but instead recognized the North Korean regime as the legitimate one for the whole of the Korean Peninsula. According to Woong-Yong Ha (1998: 12), as many as 37 National Olympic Committees (NOCs) did not have any sporting ties with South Korea. But, in November 1987, the North Korea government in Pyongyang made a major diplomatic error to the benefit of the South Korean government. It unleashed a terrorist attack on a civilian aircraft which killed all 115 passengers and crew onboard, as a result of which the 'weird and violent' character of the North Korean regime was amply revealed to the world (Walker 1988). Furthermore, in a twist of fate, one of the terrorists who had been responsible for planting the bomb which had brought down the aircraft failed to commit suicide, was captured while travelling on a fake Japanese passport, and subsequently informed on North Korea's state-run programme of kidnapping Japanese civilians in order to teach North Korean secret agents how to pass themselves off as Japanese.

All of this helped to ensure that the South Korean government could harness the 1988 Games in its diplomatic negotiations aimed at improving its relations with North Korea and other state socialist countries through its policy of *nordpolitik*. Consequently, the Seoul Olympics are notable for marking a turning point in South Korea's relations with, among others, the Soviet Union and the People's Republic of China (PRC). The use of the Games in this way can be viewed as an extension of the ping-pong diplomacy

(Meyer 2003) which was instrumental in breaking the ice in Sino-US relations in 1971, and which resulted in President Richard Nixon of the USA visiting the PRC for a summit meeting with Mao Zedong in February 1972 (see Chapter 6 of this book). At the same time, however, the South Korean government showed how a sporting event could be exploited to even greater effect in that it had managed to use the Seoul Olympics to 'outflank' (Bedeski 1994: 194) a third party, the North Korean regime, in its attempt to improve its relations with the Eastern bloc as a whole, not to mention the rest of the world (see Middleton 1997, especially 162–6, on the Olympic Games and *nordpolitik*).

Like Japan, South Korea sought to demonstrate and celebrate its graduation into a society which had achieved economic parity with a number of Western countries, and which was on its way to yet greater advances in this regard. The opening and closing ceremonies of the Seoul Games were used to draw the world's attention to the Korean 'economic miracle' (Manheim 1990: 281), to convey messages and images about the 'unknown Korea', and to establish links between the incumbent government and the various examples of Korean success and sources of Korean pride. National pride had been stimulated by Seoul's successful bid for the 1988 Games, especially in that this had been achieved at the expense of a challenge from Nagoya, Japan. A further injection was to follow as a result of the Games' final overall medal table, with South Korea gaining fourth place behind the Soviet Union, the German Democratic Republic (East Germany) and the USA, well ahead of the PRC in eleventh place and Japan in twenty-fourth place. The South Korean governing regime was keen to be associated with these successes, and as far as possible to be regarded as being responsible for them.

However, the ensuing sense of national euphoria and enhanced national confidence helped facilitate the process by which South Korea subsequently made the transition from a military dictatorship to a Western-style liberal democracy. The authoritarian regime now found it more difficult to resist the internal demands and pressures for change, especially given the accompanying and reinforcing presence of considerable external interest under the gaze of the world's mass media. The government had been teased by an unrelenting stream of widespread and violent opposition, protests and demonstrations, culminating in the June Popular Rising of 1987. The latter in particular posed a major dilemma for the regime: 'The Chun government was confronted with a painful choice between bringing in the army to quell those demonstrations just a few months before the scheduled Summer Olympics and making a wholesale concession to the demands of anti-government forces' (Shin 1999: 3). A refusal by the government to accede to the demands for fundamental political change would have provoked an onslaught of world-wide mass media criticism and condemnation (Manheim 1990: 292), and crucially may have led to a disastrous Seoul Olympics. In other words, the up-coming Games became a 'hostage to political instability' (Bedeski 1994: 69). They served as a brake on state repression and, if only indirectly, as a vehicle for the promotion of liberal democracy on the Korean Peninsula, not to mention for the advance of globalization entailing the spread of the Western cultural account. On 29 June 1987, Roh Tae Woo's government passed the Declaration of Democratic Reform which prepared the way for South Korea's transition to a Western-style liberal democracy, and thereby its passage towards not only greater economic parity with the West, but also greater political and cultural endorsement by the West as befits a country which, after all, had already been trusted with the Games and all that these reflect and represent.

As summarized by Han Sung-Joo:

> Internally, the Games played a pivotal role in bringing democracy to South Korea, if only because intensifying world scrutiny made it difficult for the government to deal harshly with those demanding expanding freedoms. The people, for the most part, felt satisfaction with what they thought was proof that the country had arrived among the developed nations of the world after much hard work and suffering. Externally, the Games have established for South Korea unofficial but increasingly lucrative trade ties and expanding trade contacts with China, the Soviet Union, and East Europe.
>
> (Hang Sun-Joo 1989: 34)

The President of South Korea, Roh Tae Woo, who earlier had been the Minister of State for Sport (Nam-Gil and Mangan 2003: 232), sharpened the view of the Seoul Games as South Korea's *coming out party* when he declared:

> Our national sense of confidence and advanced national conscience, given the success of the Olympics, pose on us a new challenge and obligation that we should fulfill [the] task of joining the advanced nations and achieving full democracy in the country.
>
> (cited in Woong-Yong Ha 1998: 11)

In spite of the longstanding and deep-seated enmity which the South Korean people shared with the Chinese people towards Japan, the South Korean government opted for the Japanese approach to its political economy development along with the Japanese model of the Olympics, underscoring in the process the distinctive Asian discourse on the latter. The fact that the 'Japanese experience' played a large part in South Korean government programmes, policies and practices in general and in relation to the Seoul Games in particular was clearly revealed through research at the time as being 'by far the most common recurring theme in interviews with government officials' (Manheim 1990: 283). Moreover, what is equally evident is how the *Japanese experience* has been subsequently adopted by those in charge of the Beijing Games. As with the Tokyo and Seoul Olympiads, the 2004 to 2008 Olympiad is being harnessed to shine the limelight on yet a third East Asian economic success story. The PRC has its own economic miracle about which to boast and on which to build, including by enhancing the world's familiarity with PRC-based companies, brands and products (see Chapter 1 of this book; see also Taylor 2005a, 2005b).[10] At the same time, intimately wrapped up with the pursuit of economic agendas, is the government's interest in certain political aims. Just as the Japanese government and ruling political party used the 1964 Games to help bring to a close the events leading up to and surrounding the Second World War, and the South Korean regime used the 1988 Games to paper over the 1979 military coup and the 1980 Kwangju massacre, so the PRC government will use the 2008 Games to help bury the ghost of the 1989 Tiananmen Square disaster. In each case, the underlying purpose is to be as full a member of the world community as possible, in particular on equal (economic) terms with the West, and in a way which entails (political and cultural) acceptance by the West.

Faced with the fading appeal and grip of socialism, the Communist Party of China (CPC) has increasingly turned to economic nationalism and concomitantly to promoting popular nationalism as the way forward and around which to perpetuate its social control (on economic nationalism, see Chapters 3 and 4 of this book). This strategy, however, has its downside and dangers, as indicated by those expressions of popular nationalism which spilled over into anti-Japanese violence during the Asian Cup football tournament in the PRC in 2004 (see Chapter 2 in this book). This among other incidents has served to expose the virulent racism and xenophobia which lurks not far below the surface of Chinese society, if only primarily towards the Japanese, at the expense of the *master narrative* which is designed to focus the attention of people at home and abroad on the more complimentary and attractive features of the Chinese national character, Chinese national endeouvours, Chinese national achievements, and the like (Alford 2004: 11; McGregor and Pilling 2004: 2). The PRC regime may turn to such devices as sport and sports competitions, the Olympic Games and other mega-events, and the world's mass media in order to disseminate the *master narrative* and highlight the PRC's highly successful economic performance in the interests of social cohesion and of achieving even greater economic advances, but such devices are a double-edged sword. The result may just as easily be less rather than more social control. Here, of concern to the government is how *public nationalism* – as sanctioned by the state – may feed *popular nationalism* to the point that it gets out of hand, becomes uncontrollable. For instance, many young Chinese citizens brought up on a diet of anti-Japanese education are also sophisticated Internet users – or *netizens* – enabling them to organize anti-Japanese protests, such as at sports competitions, in a way which threatens to escape constraint by the state (see Yardley 2005). This opens up the prospect of considerable damage to the PRC's image, in particular if the Beijing Games are blighted.

It is to be expected that a large, and probably an exceptional, number of the PRC's athletes will triumph in the 2008 Games; and indeed that the PRC will go one better than at the 2004 Games by heading the final medals table. This will be a major boost to national pride and identity, and connectedly to the governing regime's internal credibility and security. But, the question arises, how will the Chinese people respond to any failures, and especially to any defeats of its athletes by their Japanese rivals? Doubts have been raised about the Chinese people's ability to cope with failure, especially if it is at the hands of the Japanese, in particular by managing to respond in a non-violent manner even at the Olympic Games in spite of the likely deleterious external impact and the controlling efforts of the state. The PRC's governing regime will be keen to ensure that as far as possible the Games will have no damaging repercussions for the country's international relations, and instead will be wholly beneficial and constructive in this regard. Just as the South Korean government was anxious to take advantage of the Seoul Games in order to make headway in its relations with North Korea in particular and with the Soviet bloc in general, so the PRC's governing regime will be poised to exploit the Beijing Games to make progress in overcoming the main source of its international difficulties, that of the Taiwan (or two Chinas) problem, and more specifically of the PRC's claim over Taiwan. In contrast to the anxiety in South Korea during the Seoul Olympiad surrounding its relations with North Korea, there would seem to be no need for the PRC to be troubled by the possibility of a military or terrorist attack from Taiwan. But, there will be a well-founded concern about displays of distinctive Taiwanese symbols and other expressions of the territory's separation and independence, and about how the state should respond to any such gestures. There is a sense in which, in comparison with South Korea in relation to North Korea, the PRC's hands are firmly tied in relation to Taiwan, whereby its freedom of manoeuvre and chances of a breakthrough are greatly restricted, at least for the short term. Although unlike North Korea, Taiwan does not enjoy extensive international recognition as an independent, sovereign nation-state (in particular at the United Nations), unlike North Korea also, Taiwan has a highly developed (market-capitalist) economy, a well-established liberal-democratic political system, and receives much sympathy and support from the West – and crucially from the USA – not least of the military kind. The PRC withdrew from the 1956 Melbourne Olympic Games and then in 1958 from the Olympic movement over of the Taiwan problem (Hill 1992: 42), and although the PRC returned the Olympic fold in the 1970s, Taiwan's relationship with – or within – the PRC remains far from resolved, a highly sensitive matter, and an issue which threatens to surface with troublesome consequences at any time. The opportunity provided by the greatest mega-event in history may prove too tempting and useful to be missed by Taiwanese nationalists for resolving the Taiwan problem in a way which is more conducive to their aims than to those of the PRC (see also Chapters 1, 2, 3 and 6 in this book).[11]

Alongside its external agenda, the PRC's governing regime faces various internal issues, difficulties and threats, including certain fundamental ones stemming from Deng Xiaoping's 1970s' economic reforms, with their uneven-development consequences for the economic system, on the one hand, and the political system, on the other (see Chapter 4 of this book). In sum, the PRC has undergone a remarkable, even revolutionary, process of liberalization, but one which has been almost wholly confined to the economic sphere to the exclusion of the political sphere. Consequently, there may be considerable pressure building up for more even development entailing substantial political change in favour of liberal democracy. Any internal social demands for change in this direction will be accompanied and encouraged by external sympathy and support, especially from the West; and the Beijing Games will provide an unprecedented opportunity for attention to be drawn, with the help of the world's mass media, to these demands and the political circumstances within which they are being made. Still, in formulating a response to the threat posed to the country's image, cohesion and stability, the PRC's governing regime can turn for guidance to the solution adopted by Ikeda Hayto, the Liberal Democratic Party (LDP) prime minister of Japan, in similar circumstances in the run-up to the 1964 Tokyo Games. We can recall how, in 1960, Ikeda introduced the Income-Doubling Plan with the promise of doubling Japan's GNP by the end of the decade; how eight years later, Japan's GNP had doubled; and how this helped to divert the Japanese people's attention away from political issues to economic considerations.

In a similar way, in the PRC, the Chinese Communist Party (CPC) could try to defuse the unease, demands and tensions surrounding the absence of political freedoms, of liberal democracy, of human rights (in particular of the political and civil, or first-generation, kinds), and of civil society by persuading the bulk of the Chinese people that this is the necessary and acceptable price to be paid for the benefits of stupendous economic growth, ever higher productivity, and of a Western-style consumer society. In a manner consistent with post-War Japan's approach to governing society and the 1964 Olympic Games as a social, economic, political and cultural mega-event, and following the way in which South Korea adopted a similar approach during the build-up to the Seoul Games, the PRC's governing regime will use the Beijing Olympiad to enhance its internal credibility and control, showcase the PRC's economic miracle, impress the outside world, take responsibility for the PRC's achievements (including its successes in hosting and taking part in the 2008 Games), tighten its hold in principle and in practice over 'rebellious' Taiwan, improve its international relations, move on beyond the legacy of the Tiananmen Square incident, and establish the PRC as a full member of the world community.

While the Asian discourse on the Olympics can be distinguished from the Western discourse in terms of its consistent emphasis on 'the economic' as distinct from 'the political', as will have become clear the Asian discourse also has running through it notable political and cultural dimensions. Indeed, the Asian discourse has become modified somewhat under the stewardship of South Korea and the PRC, even to the point that a distinct continental Asian discourse has emerged. The continental Asian discourse (or CAD) on the Olympic Games is largely, if not primarily, political in character, and is certainly highly nationalistic and acutely anti-Japanese in focus.

The PRC and South Korea, as well as Taiwan and North Korea, have consistently shown a steadfast determination to beat and, as far as possible, to defeat and humiliate Japan – above all Japan due to historical con-siderations – in all areas of social life, including those concerned with sport. Not content with seeing off Nagoya in the competition for the 1988 Olympic Games, the Seoul organizing committee rubbed salt into the wound by choosing Lee Hak-rae, a judo athlete, to read the Olympic Oath at the opening ceremony. Japanese success and signs of 'superiority' in sport and at the Olympic Games have long been recognized and resented around North East Asia. In 1936, one Chinese observer wondered at the performance of the Japanese athletes in Berlin: 'Their physique is no better than ours; they are usually shorter in height. There are one hundred and one things that can be said to be similar between these two nationalities. Why are they so far ahead of us?' (*The China Critic*, cited in Morris 1999: 560). Certainly Japan's success in Berlin was outstanding relative to not only other Asian countries, but also to Western ones. Japan achieved eighth place in the final overall medals table (behind Germany, the USA, Hungary, Italy, Finland, France, and Sweden), well ahead of Turkey (nineteenth), India (twenty-first) and the Philippines (thirty-second), the three other Asian NOCs to feature. The motivation to emulate the Japanese was considerable in that it was thought throughout East Asia that there is a close association between physical, or bodily, strength and social, or national, strength. It was assumed that this association was not merely metaphorical or symbolic; that rather bodily prowess was an important foundation on which to build a proficient nation-state. Consequently, considerable anxiety was widely express about the con-tinental Asian physique (Hong 1998; Mangan and Hong 2003), which was viewed as relatively small, sickly and weak. There seemed to be an obvious link between how China had succumbed to foreign (Western and Japanese) invasion, imperialism and subjugation and how Chinese athletes were no match for their Western and Japanese counterparts. Accordingly, in response to foreign imperialism, 'In China, physical training [has been] pursued for the goal of establishing a new state' (Hwang and Jarvie 2001: 15), in a manner resembling similar assumptions about the importance of physique to the construction of the nation-state which have prevailed at various points in the histories of Japan and Korea.

Western and Japanese imperialism and domination in East Asia, not to mention (at least in the Western case) throughout the world, together with such Western notions, worldviews and narratives as Orientalism contributed to a *racialized* discourse on Asia and Asians which fed a sense of (Asian) inferiority and the perceived limits to the (Asian) Self. In the aftermath of the effort put into expelling foreign imperialists, which by the end of the Second World War boiled down to the Japanese, the official view to emerge was that the individual physique, the Chinese nation and the PRC as a nation-state could and should be made more robust in a dialectical fashion. In and only in this way could the Chinese people stand up to, resist and, if necessary, repel the West with its persistent imperialist tendencies and ambitions, as indicated by its militaristic belligerence and ventures during the Cold War and its economic, political and cultural campaigns since. For Hwang and Jarvie (2001: 15), the 'control and ordering of physical bodies in time and space was the goal in establishing a new regime, and sports provided a potent metaphor for the process.' The highly muscular and deeply bronzed Chinese athletes, especially swimmers, that have become increasingly apparent at sports events since the PRC's 1970s' re-entry into the international sporting arena are a sign of the considerable effort which has been put into enhancing the Chinese people's physical appearance and national confidence on the world stage along with the PRC as a nation-state within international relations, and there can be little doubt that they will be more evident than ever at the 2008 Games.

The deeply troubled relationship between the PRC and Japan has been fuelled for a decade or more in the run-up to the Beijing Games by two especially prominent issues rooted in Japan's military adventures on the continent during the 1930s and 1940s: the picture presented by Japan of its actions at that time in its history textbooks for current use in Japanese schools; and the continuing visits by Japan's political leaders, including its prime minister, to the country's national war memorial, the Yasukuni Shrine. The relationship has been further aggravated by a range of long-standing difficulties and occasional incidents, stretching from territorial disputes to the sexual exploits of Japanese businessmen during their visits to the PRC, a reminder of the Japanese imperial army's notorious abuse of several hundred thousand Chinese, Korean and other women who were turned into sex slaves (euphemistically referred to as comfort women) during the Second World War. The territorial disputes, which also involve Taiwan, centre on the uninhabited islands of Diaoyu Tai – otherwise known to the Japanese as Senkaku-shoto – and Japan's unilaterally declared *equidistance line* in the East China Sea (CIA 1 November 2005), although it may be noted that the PRC's territorial disputes are from being confined to those it has with Japan:

> in 2005, China and India began drafting principles to resolve all aspects of their extensive boundary and territorial disputes [. . .]; recent talks and confidence-building measures have begun to defuse tensions over Kashmir, site of the world's largest and most militarized territorial dispute with portions under the de facto administration of China (Aksai Chin), India (Jammu and Kashmir), and Pakistan (Azad Kashmir and Northern Areas); India does not recognize Pakistan's ceding historic Kashmir lands to China in 1964 [. . .]; China asserts sovereignty over the Spratly Islands together with Malaysia, Philippines, Taiwan, Vietnam, and possibly Brunei [. . .]; China occupies some of the Paracel Islands also claimed by Vietnam and Taiwan; certain islands in the Yalu and Tumen rivers are in an uncontested dispute with North Korea and a section of boundary around Mount Paektu is considered indefinite [. . .]; China and Russia prepare to demarcate the boundary agreed to in October 2004 between the long-disputed islands at the Amur and Ussuri; demarcation of the China-Vietnam boundary proceeds slowly and although the maritime boundary delimitation and fisheries agreements were ratified in June 2004, implementation has been delayed [. . .].
>
> (*ibid.*)

Each dispute has potentially dangerous political and economic ramifications, not least that in the East China Sea, 'the site of intensive hydrocarbon prospecting' (*ibid.*) in the extensive oil and gas fields.[12]

The troubled relationship between China and Japan has often surfaced in the sporting arena, and not just at the Asian Cup in 2004 (see Chapter 2 of this book). For instance, the antagonistic relationship between China and Japan was instrumental in persuading the Kuomintang (KMT, or Chinese Nationalist Party) to underwrite the dispatch of the athlete Liu Changchun to the 1932 Los Angeles Games, as a result of which Liu became the first Chinese national ever to actually participate in an Olympic Games (see Chapter 6 of this book; see also Hong Hua 2003: 203–4; Morris 1999). Indeed, for some observers, the long-standing and deep-seated anti-Japanese sentiments that pervade Chinese society have provided the bedrock on which the PRC's governing regime has been able to stoke Chinese nationalism, including in the pursuit of its economic aims, and so have been deliberately fanned by the regime. According to Ian Buruma, the regime has poured a hefty amount of money into the construction of a large number of *sacred sites of memory* around the country which have helped to keep alive specifically anti-Japanese feelings, something which Baruma finds highly 'disturbing', devious and hypocritical (2005: 23). Baruma claims:

That the truth of Chinese butchery of its own citizens is still suppressed, while anti-Japanese feelings are continually stoked, smacks of self-serving hypocrisy. Many more Chinese died at the hands of Chairman Mao than at the hands of the Imperial Japanese Army. But there is something else too. Patriotic education is full of a type of nationalism, born in Europe and transplanted, often through Japan, to China and Korea, which has had lethal consequences: ethnic nationalism combined with social Darwinism. It is the struggle for survival of the fittest nations and races. The weak must perish [. . .]. Now the Chinese are being told that only discipline, vigilance and ever greater national strength will save China from future humiliations. Civic patriotism of the French republican or traditional US kind has no place in an authoritarian system such as that of the People's Republic of China, let alone the vague post-national idealism of the European Union. Japan's official pacifism, which is fast crumbling anyway, certainly has little appeal. Ideologically, the PRC, like North Korea, and to a much lesser extent South Korea, is firmly stuck in the late 19th century, when Darwinist ideas made their first impression.

(*ibid.*)

The style and content of Baruma's account needs to be treated with considerable circumspection. But the argument that the withering of the appeal of socialism, Marxism, Leninism and even Maoism in the PRC has been accompanied by the compensatory elevation of nationalism, and in particular that nationalism that draws heavily on the experience, resentment and hatred which is rooted in the 'War of Anti-Japanese Resistance' (as the Second World War is known in China; see Chapter 6 of this book), along with the pride which is derived from the role the PRC has persuasively claimed for itself (with the help of the education system) in driving out the Japanese from China is laudable. Perhaps the success of the Beijing Games will be judged in part by the degree to which the PRC's governing regime is able to rein in the genie it has so ably managed to unleash in demonizing the Japanese, who are variously referred to in official propaganda as 'Eastern Devils', 'Eastern Dwarves', 'Runty Japanese Lackies', 'Runty Japanese Pigs', 'Beastly Japanese Devils', and 'Japanese Bandits'.

P. H. Gries has noted how, according to the Western mass media, the anti-Japanese racism which has been increasingly expressed by Chinese people and especially by Chinese youth is a product government policy and practice:

The Chinese government [is said to have] encouraged the anti-Japanese protests for both domestic and international purposes. Domestically, the Chinese Communist Party is seen as using Japan as a scapegoat to pre-empt popular criticisms of the Chinese government itself.

Internationally, the party is seen as using popular anti-Japanese protests to achieve specific foreign policy goals, such as denying Japan a permanent seat in the U.N. Security Council. Such arguments tell an important part of the story. With the decline of the legitimating appeal of communist ideology following the 1989 Tiananmen Massacre, the Communist Party initiated a Patriotic Education Campaign in the early 1990s to bolster its nationalist credentials. There is no question that the party has deployed its educational and propaganda systems to inculcate anti-Japanese views.

(Gries 2005: E–1)

Gries goes on to note, however, that while the state played a significant role in producing nationalism:

it would be a mistake to attribute complete control over Chinese nationalism today to the Communist Party. The genie is now out of the bottle. With the emergence of the Internet, cellphones and text messaging, popular nationalists in China are increasingly able to act independently of the state [. . .]. The real concern, in other words, may not be the party's ability to manipulate popular nationalism, but its inability to fully control it.

(*ibid.*)

Modern Chinese national identity has been re-formed around a new narrative:

The Maoist 'victor narrative,' about heroic Chinese victories over Western and Japanese imperialism from the mid-19th to the mid-20th centuries, has been challenged since the mid-1990s by a new 'victim narrative' about Chinese suffering during the 'Century of Humiliation.' This traumatic re-encounter with long suppressed suffering has understandably generated anger. This anger has been directed primarily at Japan. Why? To most Chinese, the Japanese are the paradigmatic 'devils' – not just because of the brutality of the Japanese invasion of China and the sheer numbers of Chinese killed by Japanese troops but also because of an ethical anger with earlier origins [including a] perceived injustice of 'little brother' Japan's impertinent behavior toward 'big brother' China.

(*ibid.*)

In addition to anti-Japanese outbursts, the Beijing authorities will be worried about a number of other threats to the sparkling image and unified face they will want to present to the outside world through the 2008 Games. These include possible demonstrations in favour of political liberalization, greater adherence to (especially political and civil) human rights, more religious freedom (as demanded by Falun Gong, for example), and independence for Taiwan, Tibet and even for other territories, such as the Xinjiang Uygur Autonomous Region (XUAR). Whether the PRC's governing regime will manage to use the 2008 Games to present an image of a highly unified and increasingly successful nation-state to the world, or whether instead the PRC's unification will be revealed as a facade, not to mention further diminished, is yet to be seen.

Chapter 6

China's long march for the Olympics

Sport has acquired an influential role in the development of nation-states, the relationships among nation-states, and the evolving global political economy (GPE). 'Sport' is a contested notion, but for current purposes can be defined as 'gamelike activity having rules, a competitive element, and requiring some form of physical exertion' (Blanchard 1995: 9). This is not to ignore the way in which sport is inseparable from the encompassing social – cultural, political and economic – circumstances within which it will always be firmly and deeply embedded. Sport is a social construct, a creation of the cultural, political and economic patterns, processes and trends within which it is found, while in turn (or dialectically) being an area of activity which variously contributes to, helps shape and to some extent determines these patterns, processes and trends. To put it another way, sport is necessarily a social activity with cultural, political and economic ramifications that extend well beyond the immediate *fields of play*. This is especially the case in the current era of globalization (see Chapter 1).

While there is a sense in which sport is universal, what can be distinguished as 'modern sport' – that associated with, for instance, the modern Olympic Games – is socially and historically specific, at least in its origins. Modern sport is rooted in the evolution of Western, and more precisely of European, society, while nonetheless having been subsequently transported around the world by way of such vehicles as Western imperialism, colonization and globalization (LaFeber 1999; also see Chapter 5 of this book). Sport of the specifically modern, Western kind is now without doubt a global phenomenon, something which helps account for the status of certain sporting occasions being themselves global-reach phenomena or *mega-events*. Indeed, given the transportability of sport combined with certain underlying universal tendencies, such as those reflected in nationalism, it is perhaps not surprising that the greatest, least ambiguous, and perhaps only mega-events are of the sports kind.

According to one notable account, the development of modern sport can be traced to – and so in its formative stages is largely explicable in terms of – the rise of nationalism during the eighteenth and nineteenth centuries in Europe

(Brownell 1995: 46); and certainly the subsequent development and spread of modern sport beyond Europe and the West is linked to the presence and rise of nationalistic sentiments, identities and aspirations. At the same time, however, the history of modern sport in East Asia, for instance, can only be understood in terms of Western imperialist expansion, whereby modern sport in general, certain sports in particular (such as football), together with sporting mega-events, symbolize Western imperialism's achievements during the nineteenth century, and perhaps its persistence during the twenty-first century by way of globalization (see Horne 2004; see also Horne and Manzenreiter 2002, 2004, 2006; Manzenreiter and Horne 2004).

The origins and progress of modern sport in China is broadly indicative of the wider, global pattern, even though the details entailed are to some extent local. In China, the introduction of modern sport occurred during a period when concerted efforts were being made to turn the dynastic Chinese Empire into a modern, Western-style nation-state (Brownell 1995: 46). During this period, the development of sport in particular, on the one hand, and of the process of *modernization* in general, on the other, closely mirror each other. One indication of *both* the relatively recent spread of modern sport to China *and* of the social construction of sport wherever it occurs is the novelty of the word 'sport' itself:

In pre-modern China physical activity, exertion (Blanchard 1995: 9), or exercise was associated with, and treated as an incidental aspect of, a range of other pursuits, including productive labour, military training and scholarly zeal:

> In ancient times, there were no words in the Chinese vocabulary entirely equivalent to the Western terms of 'sport' and 'physical education'. Such physical exercises as wrestling, swordplay, archery, charioteering and horse-racing were all included in military training and therefore came under the general term of '*wuyi*', or 'martial arts'. Thus a scholar was required 'to be versed in both polite letters and martial arts'. It was not until the [nineteenth] century that sport in the modern sense of the word found its way into China, first in the form of military drills, and then as part of the curricula of Western-type schools. Correspondingly, 'sport' was first translated [as] 'ticao', or 'physical training' [. . .]. Modern sport was introduced into China as a result of the modernization of sport in the West on the one hand, and of the Westernization movement in China on the other.
>
> (COC 27 March 2004)

While the early development of modern sport in China is attributable primarily to Western imperialist expansion, it was assisted by the 'Westernization movement' (*yangwu yundong*) among the Chinese themselves. Beginning with the Opium War of 1840, China was subjected to 'imperialist invasion', with 'large areas of her territory [being] annexed by the Western powers' (*ibid.*). Faced with the threat posed by the West, many intellectuals and government officials – notably Li Hongzhang and Zhang Zhidong – became *reformists*, advocating fundamental change in Chinese society along Western lines. By the 1870s, *yangwu yundong* was officially sanctioned by the Manchu Qing Dynasty (1644–1911); and by the end of the century, the country had embarked on a process of adopting 'Western technology and [had] even built a new army and navy after the Western fashion' (*ibid.*). Accordingly, the Qing government engaged instructors from abroad 'to teach "foreign drills" and opened physical training courses in some military academies, including gymnastics, fencing, boxing, athletics, football and swimming' (*ibid.*). In addition, in 'the new-type public schools established by the reformists on the pattern of Western education, great attention was paid to physical training' in an attempt to decisively counter 'the prevailing "cult for frail-looking scholars" ' (*ibid.*). Furthermore, the introduction of modern sport was assisted through a third influential channel, that of 'the missionary schools and colleges and YMCA organizations founded in various parts of the country by British, American and other Churches to disseminate Christianity. The schools had no physical training courses, but they promoted athletics and ball games as extracurricular activities' (*ibid.*).

By the start of the twentieth century, all public schools were required to have *ticao courses*, in which, for between two and three hours each week, the students would do physical training 'with military formations as the main content "for an even-balanced development of the body, agility of the four limbs, a cheerful frame of mind, and the cultivation of bravery, esprit de corps and sense of discipline" ' (*ibid.*). However, these highly regimented, rigid and monotonous physical training sessions, 'mostly conducted by low-ranking army officers', failed to inspire, were not appreciated by the students involved, and quickly 'fell into disfavour with the general public' (*ibid.*). During 1922–3, 'the *ticao* (physical training) courses' were replaced with '*tiyu* (physical education) activities; military-style drills with Western-style, competitive ball games and athletics' (*ibid.*).

In this way, one of the vestiges of the Manchu Qing Dynasty was removed. The various modernizing reforms that had been pursued during the nineteenth century into the start of the twentieth had failed to salvage the Qing Empire – the 'sick man of East Asia' (*Dong Ya bingfu*). Reformist strategies appeared to have been exhausted, and the idea of revolution began to take hold. Consequently, in 1911, the Qing Dynasty was overthrown by a movement led by Sun Yat Sen, and the Republic of China was created. However, China continued to suffer both internal discord and external aggression due to the divisive rule by warlords at home and the pressure of imperialism from abroad. In response, 1919 saw the creation of the revolutionary 4 May Movement, a major event in Chinese history. Inspired by the 1917 Bolshevik revolution in Russia, the 4 May Movement revolutionaries declared themselves in favour of fundamental change, entailing the creation of an independent, sovereign nation-state around the principles and practices of anti-imperialism, nationalism and democracy. The movement provided the basis of two subsequent political formations, each with its own distinctive agenda for constructing a modern nation-state. On the one side, there was the moderate Chinese nationalist party, the Kuomintang (KMT);[1] and, on the other side, there was the radical Communist Party of China (CPC). Between 1924 and 1927, the KMT and the CPC were aligned in waging a 'northern expedition' to oust the incumbent warlord government. Following the alliance's victory in 1927, it disintegrated, opening the way for the *Nanjing Decade* of KMT rule under the leadership of Chiang Kai-shek.

The CPC was purged and went underground, but retained control of some areas. In particular, the 'most successful group settled in the countryside near the border between Jiangxi and Fujian provinces in an area they called the Jiangxi Soviet' (MSN Encarta 7 April 2006). Crucially, this group managed to attract considerable local support and to build a peasant army (*ibid.*), helped by the fact that one of its leaders was Mao Zedong:

> Mao was from a peasant family in Hunan but was educated through the new school system [. . .]. In the 1920s, when most of the early [CPC] members were organizing workers in the cities, Mao worked in the countryside, developing ways to mobilize peasants.
>
> (*ibid.*)

Chiang made several attempts at destroying Jiangxi Soviet, each of which failed. In October 1934, Chiang's forces encircled the Jiangxi base, threatening to obliterate Mao's forces. But, 80,000 Communists succeeded in breaking out and to undertake what has become known as the Long March. For about a year, the Communists were hounded by the KMT, until just 8,000 survived. After a trek of almost 9,600 kilometres (6,000 miles), the Communists eventually reached Shaanxi province, where they made their new base and from where, undaunted, they were to achieve final victory.[2]

There seem to be notable similarities between Mao's *Long March* and that of China's long-haul pursuit of and struggle for the Olympic Games, eventually won by Beijing to host the 2008 event.

While the KMT had managed to force the CPC into a retreat in the mid-1930s, persistent domestic fragmentation, disorder and weakness was an invitation for further imperialist incursions from abroad, especially by the Japanese in the North and North East of the country. Japan had a firm and expanding grip over Manchuria, and, following the Manchurian Incident, installed a pro-Japanese puppet regime in Manchuria, or *Manchukuo*, nominally headed by Henry Pu Yi, the last emperor of the

Qing Dynasty. In 1933, the eastern part of Inner Mongolia was incorporated into Manchukuo. In the face of unrelenting pressure, Chiang eventually agreed to unite again with the Communists, this time against the Japanese; and in 1937 the *Nanjing Decade* was brought to a close when, at the Marco Polo Bridge, shots were fired at the Japanese military, an incident which escalated into a full-scale war between China and Japan, the Sino-Japanese War of 1937–45.

Chaos, revolution and war were the backdrop to the continuing attempts to reform, modernize and Westernize sport in China. In 1924, the All-China (Amateur) Athletic Association (AAA) was founded, the first country-wide sports organization (COC 27 March 2004). Its tasks included hosting the Far Eastern Championship Games, organizing international sporting exchanges, deciding on the teams for various international sports tournaments, such as the Davis Cup in tennis, and selecting the athletes for participation in the Olympic Games. In 1931 (according to the Chinese Olympic Committee), the AAA was formally recognized by the International Olympic Committee (IOC) as China's National Olympic Committee: CNOC, or simply COC (Chan 1985: 473).[3] During the 1930s, the KMT government tried to impose school physical education programmes based on Western models, but unsuccessfully, not least because of the dearth of supporting human and financial resources. This culminated during the 1940s in a low ebb in the process of developing physical education and modern sport in China, not helped by the way in which the country was in the grip of devastating wars, although 'the "Fighting" basketball team under the 120th Division became a backbone in promoting sports among the troops. Its commander, General He Long, was later appointed Vice-Premier and concurrently Minister in charge of the State Commission for Physical Culture and Sports' following the founding in 1949 of the People's Republic of China (PRC) (COC 27 March 2004). Moreover, the 'Westernization of physical education', which had been taking place over half a century or so, proved immensely valuable in laying a 'solid social foundation for the later development of the Olympic movement in China' (*ibid.*).

It is unclear if China was invited to send a team of athletes to the first modern Olympic Games held in Athens from 6 to 15 April 1896. Contrary to the claim that China was not, some suggest that the IOC sent a letter of invitation as early as 1894, but that the Qing government simply failed to respond (Li Xiao 2004). Certainly, the Prime Minister, Li Hongzhang, had undertaken an extensive diplomatic mission to Europe and the USA during 1896, and it would seem was informed by France's Foreign Minister about the forthcoming Games (COC 27 March 2004). Still, the fact is that China did not send a team to the 1896 event, nor for that matter to any Games prior to the 1932 Los Angeles Games. This does not, however, mean there was no relationship between China and the Olympic movement. In 1920, the International Olympic Committee (IOC) formally recognized the Far Eastern

Amateur Athletic Federation (FEAAF) and its flagship event the Far Eastern Championship Games. Indeed, the FEAAF was the very first specifically regional sports organization to receive the IOC's endorsement in this way.[4] In 1922, Wang Zhengting, the Chancellor of the China University and a sponsor of the Far Eastern Championship Games, became the first Chinese to be elected as an IOC member.[5] In 1928, the government sent a diplomat, Song Ruhai, as an observer to the opening ceremony of the Olympic Games of the IXth Olympiad in Amsterdam. What is more, it would seem that an overseas Chinese, He Haohua, registered to compete in these Games in cycling on behalf of China. Although He Haohua was prevented by injury and hospitalization from actually getting to the Games, he carved a place for himself in history as the first ever Chinese Olympian (COC 27 March 2004). Four years later, for the first time ever, China's government positively responded to an IOC invitation by having the COC send a team of athletes to an Olympic Games.

Earlier, the KMT government had decided against sending a team to the Los Angeles Games. However, a rumour emerged that Manchukuo was intending to dispatch two representatives, including Liu Changchun. Liu declared in a statement published in the newspaper *L'Impartial* that he would refuse to represent Manchukuo in Los Angeles. However, in response to the prospect of the Manchukuo making use of the Games to gain international credibility, Zhang Xueliang[6] offered to sponsor Liu Changchun and his coach, Song Junfu, so that they could go to Los Angeles. Zhang announced during the North Eastern University's graduation ceremony that Liu and Song would be attending the 1932 Games on behalf of China, the KMT government having finally given way under the pressure of popular Chinese nationalism. While Liu was eliminated in the preliminary heats of the 100 m and 200 m sprint competitions, clocking 11.1 and 22.1 seconds respectively, he pioneered the way for China's actual presence at the modern Olympic Games.

In 1935, having become aware of the domestic and international importance of China's involvement in the Olympic movement, the KMT government appropriated almost 200,000 *yuan* to help fund the preparations for the next Games. Consequently, a concerted attempt was made to select the best athletes and to conduct serious training with the intention of doing well in 1936. Thus, China sent a 117-strong delegation to the Berlin Games, including 69 athletes for seven events, 39 observers, and nine demonstrators of the traditional Chinese martial art of *wushu*. The Chinese delegation was accompanied by an entourage of 150 journalists, sports teachers and scholars, and other interested people. However, only one Chinese Olympian, Fu Baolu, made it to a final round of competition, having cleared 3.80 m in the pole vault. The Chinese delegation was more than disappointed. It felt humiliated, stating in the concluding report: 'We were a far cry from many countries in the results and athletic abilities. We were ridiculed as having brought back nothing but a "duck's egg" ' (COC 27 March 2004). Still, taking advantage of the opportunity, after the Games, the *wushu* players visited a number of European countries as envoys of Chinese culture, and some of the observers embarked on a six-week tour of Europe, visiting sports facilities, witnessing physical education and training in schools and colleges, and studying sports management.

In 1947, China began its preparations for the Olympic Games of the XIV Olympiad, to be hosted by the city of London in July 1948.[7] However, plagued by the civil war which had once again broken out between the KMT and the Communists following the conclusion of the Second World War and the expulsion of the Japanese, plus a considerable financial crisis, the KMT government managed to allot merely US$25,000 towards the Chinese delegation's total expenses of around US$100,000, leaving the delegation to try to cover the shortfall from other sources. Part of this was raised by donations from the general public at home, and another part came from the proceeds of games played by the basketball and football teams during tours of Hong Kong, Saigon, Manila, Bangkok, Singapore, Rangoon and Calcutta on their way to London (*ibid.*). Despite all their efforts, the Chinese Olympians fared no better at the 1948 Games than they had at the 1936 event. Moreover, to add greatly to their embarrassment, the Chinese delegation had to borrow money for their travel and subsistence all the way back home!

In 1949, the KMT government was overthrown by the Communists and fled to Taiwan, marking the opening of a division in China with major domestic and international political-economy ramifications that persist in the run up to the 2008 Beijing Olympic Games. Each incumbent government – that on the mainland of the People's Republic of China (PRC) and that of the Republic of China (ROC) in Taiwan – has claimed, sought and variously demanded domestic and international recognition, legitimacy and rights at the expense of the other. The competition involved has been highly confrontational, intense and dangerous, both within the East Asian region and well beyond, especially in so far as it has drawn in superpower involvement, in particular during the 1947–91 Cold War.

Along the way, the project of building and securing a strong and sound nation-state has played a decisive role in shaping the development of sport in China, with the state's perceived political-economy interests at home and abroad proving crucial. In a manner consistent with communist ideology, following the founding of the PRC, Mao Zedong rejected 'elitist, competitive sport' in favour of 'mass sport'. Mass sports, sports activities and sports events were staged around the country in accordance with the way in which body culture was to play a part in China's socialist transformation. However, it did not take long for the state to recognize that sport could otherwise be used for internal and external purposes, in particular through the PRC's representation in international sporting events, including the Olympic Games. Hence, at the behest of the state, China's keen and, in the end, highly rushed and somewhat messy attempt to participate in the 1952 Helsinki Games.

Following the overthrow of the KMT government and the founding of the PRC in 1949, the AAA was reformed as the All-China Sports Federation (ASF), its headquarters being moved from Nanjing to Beijing. Subsequently, a dispute flared up over the ASF's status within the IOC given its claim to represent the whole of China and the rival claim of Taiwan's Olympic committee. The PRC insisted on its right to send a team to Helsinki, while the IOC wanted to resolve the issue of the precise status of the ASF within the Olympic movement. After considerable wrangling, the IOC issued an invitation to the PRC to send a team while also inviting Taiwan to do the same, and doing so just two days before the Games' opening ceremony. In spite of the fact that it had failed to have the issue of the status of the ASF resolved and therefore would be participating in the Games alongside a separate Taiwan team, the Beijing government decided that there were more important political considerations at stake and so that it was best to send a team. A 40-member delegation was hurriedly pulled together and, at midnight on the eve of its departure for Helsinki, leaders asked to meet Zhou Enlai, the Prime Minister. Zhou Enlai declared that the value of the team's attendance at the Games would lay not so much in the competition results as in what had already been gained and what was yet to be gained from the achievement of simply getting there. In Zhou's words: 'It will be a victory once our five-starred red national flag is hoisted at the Games' (ibid.).

On 19 July 1952, when the PRC's team arrived in Helsinki, most of the preliminary heats of the various sports competitions had been completed. Only one athlete, swimmer Wu Chuanyu, managed to compete in a heat. While Wu got no further, he managed to set a new national record in the 100 m backstroke. The rest of the athletes, however, made use of the opportunity to engage in friendly competitions, in particular with athletes and sides from the host country, Finland (ibid.). What is more, the Helsinki Games otherwise had a major impact on the PRC's approach to sport by virtue of the way in which it revealed to the Chinese delegation the astonishing sports progress that had been made by athletes from other socialist countries, in particular the Soviet Union and several Eastern European nations (Li and Su 2004). In view of the assumed political importance of sport and sporting achievements, especially in the international arena, the Beijing government decided that a major change of strategy and input of resources were necessary. In the process, in connection with its domestic and foreign policy agendas, the state would come to play a far more dominant and determined role in the development of sport. So it was that, in 1955, the government established a centralized sports system based on the Soviet model. It set up the State Commission for Physical Culture and Sports (SPCS), appointing He Long, the Deputy Prime Minister and one of the People's Liberation Army's (PLA) ten marshals, as the SPCS's first chairman.

Since then, sport has been thoroughly enmeshed in the PRC's political-economy struggle for recognition, legitimacy and prestige on the world stage. Sport has been used not only symbolically, but also more concretely to achieve the state's ambitious goals – to break through various externally – especially Western – imposed political and economic barriers. In a manner resembling the mission which has been assigned to PLA soldiers, athletes have been expected to strive in international sports arenas on behalf of socialism, the homeland and national identity. Thus, athletes have been trained, disciplined and generally organized like soldiers, in a military fashion. They have been assigned a major role in helping transform the 'sick man of East Asia' into a strong, vibrant and highly respected modern nation-state. There is no doubt that, during the countdown to the 2008 Beijing Games, the intimate, state-centred link between sport, the military and *national salvation* remains firmly in place (see Brownell 1995: 22; Li and Su 2004).

It was somewhat paradoxical, therefore, that in 1958 the 'two Chinas' problem led to the severing of ties between the PRC and the IOC, something which more or less totally blocked the possibility of the PRC's athletes participating in international competitions. It was not until the 1970s that the first signs of a re-emergence occurred as the PRC engaged in a diplomatic courtship of the Third World. The state used sport and athletes under the guise of 'cultural diplomacy' to serve as the PRC's ambassadors to Third World countries. In recognition of the importance of their activities in this regard, the PRC's athletes were granted especially generous privileges with respect to travel, including that of being allowed to remain abroad for greatly extended periods (Li and Su 2004). In their tasks, they were to be guided by the maxim 'Friendship First, Competition Second' (*youyi diyi, bicai dier*), with gaining friends and recognition for the PRC taking precedence over winning. Not unconnectedly, much of the PRC's enhanced economic assistance to Third World countries entailed helping with the construction of sports facilities, stadiums and gymnasiums.

It was during this period that the famous ping-pong diplomacy (Meyer 2003) that helped break the ice in Sino-US relations took place. Sport has variously been harnessed by the state in the PRC to facilitate a *soft power* approach to diplomacy, including at critical moments, but perhaps no more so than during the opening year of the 1970s. Early in 1971, the PRC's Foreign Ministry was deliberating the delicate question of how to re-open the country's relations with the USA, by considering for instance who to invite first, when to invite them, and through which channels. Then a totally unexpected opportunity arose. It just happened that from 28 March until 7 April 1971, the 31st World Table Tennis Championships were scheduled for Nagoya, Japan. In the run-up to the event, on 11 March, a special State Council meeting was held concerning the PRC's participation. The meeting was attended by officials from the Foreign Ministry and the State Commission for Physical Culture and Sports (SCPCS), with the Prime Minister, Zhou

Enlai, presiding. Zhou remarked: 'Our table tennis team represents our country and our people. It will come into contact with many teams from other countries including the United States' (COC 27 March 2004).

In Nagoya, Song Zhong, the leader of the PRC's table tennis delegation, met Graham Steenhoven, the manager of the US delegation. Steenhoven informed Song that on the eve of the US delegation's departure, the State Department had lifted all restrictions on travel by US passport holders to the PRC. Song remarked that this meant that he and Steenhoven would meet someday in Beijing; and Steenhoven responded by suggesting that the US players could learn much from the Chinese players if they were provided with the opportunity to visit the PRC. The exchange between Song and Steenhoven was reported back to the PRC, where a daily news bulletin from Nagoya was being published, with copies being sent to the Foreign Ministry, Zhou and Mao.

On 1 April, on the other side of the Pacific, Henry Kissinger read a memorandum from the State Department in which Zhou is reported to have told Japan's former Foreign Minister, Fujiyama Aiichiro, that there appeared to be the chance of a sudden turn for the better in the relations between the PRC and the USA, signalled in particular by President Nixon's use for the first time of mainland China's formal name, the *People's Republic of China*. However, the State Department concluded that, because of the escalating war in Indochina, there was no prospect of an immediate thaw in Sino-US relations. In Beijing, the Foreign Ministry proposed that when it came to inviting visitors to China from the USA, priority should be given to influential politicians and journalists; and, accordingly, in a 4 April report prepared jointly by the Foreign Ministry and the State Commission for Physical Culture and Sports (SCPCS), it was suggested that the PRC's table tennis delegation in Nagoya should tell the US team that the time had not arrived for it to visit the PRC. This report was sent to Zhou and Mao.

By then, PRC and US table tennis players had not only come into contact on several occasions, but also had exchanged souvenirs, something which had drawn considerable worldwide media attention. The US players emphasized their wish to visit the PRC, and Mao responded by deciding that an invitation for them to visit should be immediately dispatched. On 7 April, the PRC's delegation received a directive from home: 'considering that the American team has made the request many times with friendly enthusiasm, approval has been given to invite it, including its leaders, to visit our country' (COC 27 March 2004). On receiving the invitation, Steenhoven informed the US Ambassador to Japan; and upon reading the ensuing cable from Tokyo, President Nixon decided that the US team should go. Nixon recognized the invitation as an opportunity that should not be missed for a long-awaited and much sought-after diplomatic breakthrough.

As Zhou Enlai put it, *a ball bounced over the net and the whole world was shocked*. On 14 April 1971, Zhou received the US table tennis delegation along with visiting teams from several other countries in the Great Hall of the People, Beijing. He told his American guests: 'The Chinese and American people used to have frequent exchanges. Then came a long period of severance. Your visit has opened the door to friendship between the peoples of the two countries' (COC 2004) Within a few hours, Nixon had announced a relaxation of the US embargo on China (*ibid.*), which in turn paved the way for Nixon to visit the PRC in February 1972, when he held a summit meeting with Mao Zedong, thereby demonstrating how a *small ball* (ping-pong) had set in motion the *big ball* (the globe).

The 1970s marked a major turning point in the PRC's integration in the international community. Starting in 1971 with the PRC's entry into the UN and concluding in 1979 with the normalization of US–China diplomatic relations, the PRC emerged onto the world stage as a rising regional and global political-economy player. The PRC's integration was further consolidated by the country's *second revolution*, that entailing the fundamental shift from the *genocidal madness* under Mao to the *four modernizations* under Deng. The PRC's sports development in general and the country's links with the Olympic movement in particular reflect this transformative process. It is no accident that the *Dengist shift* in conjunction with the re-working of national identity along reformist modernizing lines as opposed to revolutionary socialist lines coincided with the PRC's 1979 re-entry into the movement.

The first international sports organization to take action was the Asian Games Federation (AGF). China sent observers to the first Asian Games held in New Delhi in 1951, but was barred from the second to the sixth events due to, as with the Olympic Games, the 'two Chinas' problem. When it came to the seventh Asian Games, to be held in Tehran in 1974, the majority of the 21 member states of the AGF had indicated their support for the PRC's membership, even though the governments of only ten had established diplomatic relations with the PRC, and in spite of the risk of the AGF being sanctioned by the IOC and its affiliated international federations (IFs). In September 1973, at an Executive Meeting of the AGF in Bangkok, two members – Iran and Japan – proposed that China should be represented within the AGF by the PRC's All-China Sports Federation (ASF), and that consequently Taiwan should be expelled. Two months later, a resolution to this effect was passed at a special Council Meeting by 38 votes in favour, 13 against, and five abstentions (COC 27 March 2004; Hill 1992: 44).

In 1972, Lord Killanin (or Michael Morris) of Ireland succeeded Avery Brundage as the President of the IOC. Like many others in the IOC, Killanin held that China should be reinstated in the organization in conjunction with a resolution of the *Taiwan problem*. Both Killanin and the IOC's Vice-President, Juan Antonio Samaranch, made visits to the PRC in September 1977 and April 1978, respectively, to explore ways of ironing out China's representation in the Olympic movement. On 1 January 1979, the Standing Committee of the PRC's National People's Congress (NPC), constitutionally the country's highest organ of state power, promulgated a 'Letter to Com-patriots in Taiwan', which called on the Chinese people as a whole to strive for peaceful reunification, and to re-establish navigation, trade and postal communications as well as cultural and scientific exchanges across the Taiwan Strait. It was this move by the PRC that was pivotally instrumental in preparing the ground for the country's restoration as a member of the IOC.

In March 1979, representatives of the PRC's Chinese Olympic Committee (COC) were invited to attend an IOC Executive Board meeting, at which they declared their willingness to have talks with their Taiwan counterparts on the issue of the participation of Taiwanese athletes in the Olympic Games. If the Taiwanese would not go to Beijing, then the COC's representatives were prepared to go to Taipei, or indeed any other place, for a meeting. This suggestion aroused strong interest among Executive Board members (COC 27 March 2004). At the Executive Board meeting, President Killanin made two especially significant observations. He noted that the IOC had recog-nized the All-China Sports Federation (ASF) as the 'Chinese (National) Olympic Committee'; but that there was no record of the IOC having recog-nized Taiwan's so-called 'Olympic Committee' as a National Olympic Committee (NOC) (Hill 1992: 41). With this in mind, the Board decided that a roundtable conference would be held at the IOC's headquarters in Lausanne to try to resolve the problem of China's representation in the IOC (COC 27 March 2004). While the Taiwanese indicated that they had reservations and wanted further clarification about the conference, the COC's representatives enthusiastically agreed.

In April 1979, at the 81st IOC session held in Montevideo, the COC's representatives dealt with questions raised by IOC members who wanted to be sure about the PRC's approach and policies in relation to Taiwan's participation in the Olympic movement. The COC reaffirmed the basic principle that there is only one China, it being the People's Republic of China (PRC). Taiwan, it was declared, is part of the PRC's territory. In view of this affirmation, the COC urged the IOC to recognize just one NOC for the whole of China, this being the Chinese Olympic Committee (COC), with its headquarters in Beijing. The COC argued that its position in this regard was consistent with the Olympic Charter, according to which each country can be represented in the Olympic movement by only one National Olympic Committee (see, however, ANOC October 2005; IOC 26 October 2005; Chapter 3 of this book). The COC drew the attention of the IOC's members to the way in which, in 1954, Taiwan's 'Olympic Committee' had been included as an NOC by default, in that its inclusion had occurred without a vote, without being discussed at any meeting, and without undergoing any formal affiliation procedure of any kind (COC 27 March 2004).

However, in order to ensure that Taiwan's athletes could take part in international competitions, the COC agreed that the Taiwanese 'Olympic Committee' could remain affiliated with the IOC under certain conditions. It would not be allowed to attach 'Republic of China' to its name or use the appellation 'Taiwan'. Nor would it be allowed to use its 'national flag' or 'national anthem', or for that matter anything else symbolizing the 'Republic of China'. The COC's initiative was welcomed by many IOC members (COC 27 March 2004), and was used a few months later as the basis for the PRC's accession to an IOC-affiliated sports organization. In mid-October 1979, the Federation International de Football Association (FIFA) passed a resolution that the PRC be re-admitted as a member and that Taiwan's football organization be allowed to remain under the name of 'Chinese Taipei'.

In late October 1979, at a meeting in Nagoya, Japan, Lord Killanin made it clear that there was a determination to re-admit the PRC into the IOC while allowing 'Taipei' to stay, as he put it, 'if they wished, on our terms' (Hill 1992: 49). After the meeting, a vote by mail was taken on a proposal that recognition of the PRC's All-China Sports Federation (ASF) be re-affirmed as the Chinese Olympic Committee (COC), using the PRC's national flag and anthem, while Taiwan's 'Olympic Committee' would remain under the name 'Chinese Taipei Olympic Committee', using an amended flag and anthem to be approved by the IOC. The proposal was passed with 62 votes in favour, 17 against and two abstentions. At the cost of revealing once more the IOC's moral ambiguity, the PRC's long-haul quest to be re-instated within the IOC had been achieved at last (Chan 1985: 481; COC 27 March 2004; Hill 1992: 49). The PRC claimed the *Nagoya Resolution* reflected, on the one hand, the PRC's adherence to its one-China principle but, on the other hand, the PRC's flexibility in allowing Taiwan's organization to remain in the IOC (see, however, Chapter 3). This aside, there was certainly all-round relief that the 21-year-long 'two Chinas' impasse had been put to rest.

China's aspiration to make a bid to host the Olympic Games can be traced back to 1908, when the *Tianjin Youth* magazine posed three questions to the people of China: when can China send an athlete to participate in the Olympic Games?; when can China send an athletic team to participate in the Olympic Games?; and when can China host the Olympic Games (COC 27 March 2004; see also Li Xiao 2004). However, it was not until the Second World War was in its final stages that the possibility of China hosting an event gathered momentum. In 1945, during a China Sport Promotion Committee meeting held in Chongqing, Dong Shouyi, an IOC member and well-known sports expert, proposed that China should bid to host the XVth Olympic Games scheduled for 1952. Dong's proposal was unanimously approved. However, the outbreak of civil war in 1946 followed by the 'two Chinas' problem after the founding of the PRC in 1949, thwarted China's ambition to host the Games. It was to take another 30 years, following the PRC's re-admission to the IOC in 1979, before the possibility of China hosting the Olympic Games could be seriously considered again.

It was Deng Xiaoping who first charged Chinese sports officials with the mission to bid for the Games. Coinciding with the IOC's decision to re-admit the PRC, Deng declared that the PRC would bid for the Games when the moment was appropriate (*ibid.*). In 1984, the President of the IOC, Juan Antonio Samaranch, stated that the IOC would like to see the PRC host not only the 1990 Asian Games (otherwise known as Asiad) but also the Olympic Games; and when, in July 1990, Deng inspected the Asian Games Village in Beijing, he made it clear that the time had indeed arrived for the PRC to make a bid (*Lianhe Zhaobao*) (COC 2004; Kentupa 14 July 2001). During the 1990 Asiad in Beijing, Yang Shangkun, the President of the PRC, told Samaranch that the PRC was committed to bidding for the Games; and at the 7 October closing ceremony, there appeared among the spectators a huge banner which read, 'With the success of the Asiad, we look forward to hosting the Olympic Games' (*ibid.*).

On the completion of the 1990 Asian Games, the Beijing Asiad organizing committee was promptly turned into a preparatory body for Beijing to bid for the Games of the XXVII Olympiad scheduled for 2000. Then, in February 1991, at a special session held in Beijing, the COC unanimously approved the Beijing municipal government's application to bid (COC 27 March 2004). The decision evoked considerable popular support and nationalist sentiment at a time when the PRC was in the grips of trying to both overcome its so-called *Tiananmen complex* and handle its 'second revolution', inspired by Deng's *four modernizations*.[8] In the wake of the 1989 Tiananmen Square massacre, the government faced the daunting task of sustaining its credibility at home and improving its damaged image and diplomatic relations within the international community, and the Beijing bid presented a major opportunity in this regard. However, while the bid was backed by high levels of enthusiasm from both the government and the general public at home, it proved to be hugely controversial abroad.

While the campaign for the Games appeared to be boosting popular support for the bid and, not unconnectedly, the government at home, it inspired and mobilized various 'anti-China' forces abroad. These forces were united in their disapproval of the PRC's totalitarian regime, governance and policies, especially with respect to certain areas of social life and within certain sections of the international community. For instance, as far as a broad range of human rights organizations and Western governments were concerned, the PRC did not deserve the Games in view of its human rights record and general oppression (see Chapters 2, 3 and 5). On the other hand, it can be noted, the gap between the internal cohesion surrounding the Beijing bid and the display of external disapproval especially in the West meant that the government could anticipate winning whatever the outcome. It could claim credit if Beijing was elected, and blame anti-Chinese Western 'hostile forces' if Beijing was not elected, thereby garnering in its interests the popular nationalism evoked in either case.

Of importance in the government's cause were two particular demonstrations of Western hostility: a resolution by the US Congress and a statement by British Foreign Secretary, Douglas Hurd. In expressing opposition to the Beijing bid, these were indicative of the highly politicized character of the issue. In September 1993, when Beijing lost to Sydney by just two votes as the host of the 2000 Games, Chen Xitong, the Mayor of Beijing and President of the Beijing bid committee, said in his homecoming speech that, 'in fact, as everyone knows, we suffered from some obstacles and interference that crudely trampled the Olympic spirit' (Chanda and Kaye 1993: 12).

Following this setback, Beijing decided against trying for the 2004 Games, but carefully examined how it might launch a successful bid for a subsequent event. In September 1999, with the approval of the PRC's State Council, the Beijing 2008 Olympic Games Bid Committee (BOBICO) was established, with Liu Qi, the Mayor of Beijing, as the President and Yuan Weimin, the COC's President, as the Executive President. The guiding motto of Beijing's 2008 bid was 'New Beijing, Great Olympics', the connotation being that Beijing's 3,000-year history in conjunction with its modernization under the PRC meant that the city would be an ideal choice for a twenty-first century Games.

In spite of evident and even increasing strain in some areas of social life, there is no doubt that Beijing's bid for the Games led the people of the city and of the PRC more widely to rally together in support of the bid and the government. The effect was consistent with what had been observed in other cases, as summarized by one sports commentator: 'Historically, the Olympic process has tended to provide legitimacy to host governments and their policies' (Wamsley 2002; see also Wamsley et al. 2002). Thus, according to the results of an opinion poll conducted by the Gallup organization in November 2000 in the run up to the bid outcome, 94.9 per cent of Beijing's residents were in favour of the city's bid for the 2008 Games. On whether Beijing would actually be elected, 62.4 per cent of those polled were confident that Beijing would be successful (COC 27 March 2004; see also IOC 2001a). In view of these and other, encouraging findings (see Chapter 4 of this book; IOC 13 March 2002), the IOC's Evaluation Commission concluded: 'There is significant public support for the prospect of organizing the Olympic Games and a feeling that a successful bid would bring recognition to the nation' (IOC 2001a).

Significantly, on this occasion, the US Congress chose not to criticize Beijing's bid. Moreover, the newly elected US President, George W. Bush, openly expressed his support. In the build up to the vote on 13 July 2001 in Moscow, Beijing was widely regarded as the front-runner, and so it came as no surprise when the city was elected with a handsome majority in the second-round secret ballot (Osaka, Japan, having been eliminated in the first round). Of the 105 IOC members, 56 voted for Beijing, well ahead of Toronto with 22, Paris with 18 and Istanbul with nine votes, respectively. A *Beijing Review* journalist, Tang Yuankai, reported:

What happened on July 13 could best be summed up as a 'sleepless night'. An instant in history became everlasting happiness. When the news came that Beijing won the Olympic bid, millions of Beijingers were elated. More than 400,000 people gathered at Tiananmen Square – the heart of China – to celebrate the fulfillment of their long sought dream. In the meantime, shouts of joy throughout the nation made the world feel the heartbeat of the Chinese nation. Samaranch excited 1.3 billion Chinese people.

(Tang 2001).

Tang added poignantly:

Gaining the right to host the Olympics is a great success for any city because it forebodes long-standing honor, reputation and unlimited potential for economic development. But for Beijing, there is even more significance. After a long isolation and nearly 200 years of humiliation brought about by foreign invasion and oppression, the action of bidding for the Olympics serves as a demonstration that China is actively seeking integration with the world.

(ibid.)

Apart from a protest meeting by Falun Dong practitioners, the 13 July 2001 gathering at Tiananmen Square in celebration of the election of Beijing to host the 2008 Games was the first since the infamous 1989 massacre, and can be taken as a sign of how much the political scene in China had changed. The movement for fundamental political reform and democratization had been pushed to one side, and in its place in Tiananmen Square there was a huge outpouring of popular nationalistic sentiment, pride and hope. If what happened on 13 July had been anything else, then the government would have responded very differently from the way it did. Instead, the government not only let it happen, it joined in. Unexpectedly, Jiang Zemin, along with other political leaders, appeared on the balcony of Tiananmen Gate to rejoice with the huge crowds in the square below.

China has slowly emerged as a sporting power. The PRC has participated in five Summer Olympic Games since its 1979 re-admission to the Olympic movement,[9] as a result of which 85 Chinese, on 108 occasions, have won 80 gold medals in 55 events of ten sports. In 1984, China dispatched a delegation of 353 members to the XXIII Olympics in Los Angeles. At these Games, Xu Haifeng, a marksman, won the PRC's first gold medal – not only its first of these particular Games, but also its first in Olympic history. In Los Angeles, the PRC's athletes took 15 gold, eight silver and nine bronze medals altogether, a remarkable Olympic debut (COC 27 March 2004), albeit somewhat tarnished by the effect of the boycott of the Games by the Soviet Union and a number of other Soviet bloc countries.

China did not fare so well in 1988 at the XXIV Games in Seoul as far as its overall medals standing is concerned, gaining just five gold, 11 silver and 12 bronze medals. However, the PRC's delegation picked up again in 1992 at the Games of the XXV Olympiad in Barcelona, when it collected 16 gold, 22 silver and 16 bronze medals, coming fourth in the overall medals table behind the Commonwealth of Independent States (the ex-Soviet Union), the USA and Germany. In 1996, at the Centennial Games in Atlanta, the PRC retained its fourth place – with 16 gold, 22 silver and 12 bronze medals – behind the USA, Russia and Germany. In 2000, at the XXVII Games in Sydney, the PRC surged ahead to win 28 gold medals, coming third in the overall gold medal standings, and thereby realizing the strategic plan which had been laid down in the 1980s. In 2002, at the IXX Winter Games held in Salt Lake City, short-track speed skater Yang Yang ended the PRC's Winter Olympics gold medal drought by winning the women's 500 m and 1000 m races (*ibid.*). Then, in 2004, at the Summer Games of the XXVIII Olympiad in Athens, 83 PRC competitors set six world records; 235 qualified for the finals in 107 events of 23 sports; and overall, the delegation won 32 gold, 17 silver and 14 bronze medals in 55 events of 18 sports, as a result of which the PRC ranked second to the USA (with its 35 gold, 39 silver and 29 bronze medals) in the final, overall medals table (*ibid.*).

In that the PRC is committed to fully embracing and participating in global society, and in particular the global political economy, as an essential element of its overall developmental strategy, the *culture of international competitive sport* has penetrated the PRC, and has been making headway at a faster pace in recent years with the unfolding of the Beijing Olympiad. So-called 'champion-ism' (*jinbiao zhuyi*), which Mao and Zhou harshly denounced as a corrupt, capitalist notion, has become a 'rule of thumb', motivating both athletes in their pursuit of personal glory (not to mention wealth) and state officials in their promotion of modern sport. In the process the 'Friendship First, Competition Second' motto would seem to have lost its place in the new China.

More broadly, modern sport has emerged as an important instrument for helping maintain the legitimacy of the state and the stability of society as the older sources of these things have been removed with the transition from state socialism to market capitalism. The state has turned to nationalism for support, and to the country's athletes as agents of the PRC's reformed national identity on the world stage. Projecting itself as outstanding at sport in the international arena has become an essential component of the PRC's external rise and concomitantly of the country's internal cohesion. Accordingly, the chance followed by the right to host *the* sporting mega-event has considerable importance for the state and meaning for the people.

The slogan 'break out of Asia and advance on the world' (*chongchu Yazhou, zouxiang shijie*) expresses the PRC's 'great power dream' (*qiangguo meng*), revitalized by the Dengist 'new long march' towards joining the global community of nation-states with confidence. This is the backdrop against which the PRC began its quest to host the Olympic Games, fuelled by the momentum which came from staging a successful Asian Games. In effect, the determination to host the Games gives 'the overall impression of an attempt to symbolically link economic modernization, Chinese nationalism, and Communist Party legitimacy into a meaningful and even moving totality' (Brownell 1995: 110).

The PRC's accomplishment at the 2004 Games is indicative of the way in which the PRC and Chinese people have managed to launch themselves in a quite dramatic fashion onto the world stage through their highly successful participation in sports, international sports organizations and international sports events, and moreover it is symptomatic of the way in which they have managed to do similar things more broadly, including above all in the global political economy (GPE) arena. Indeed, the case of China clearly demonstrates how the development of sport can be intimately linked to, dependent upon and a determinant of other areas of social development, such as those of the political economy kind. It is of interest to speculate on whether, however, the holding of the 2008 Games in Beijing will turn out to be little more than symbolic given the PRC's now well-established achievements and foothold within the GPE; or whether the anticipated greatest mega-event of all time will turn out to have more substantial political-economy value, of the kind that the 31st World Table Tennis Championships had almost four decades before. There is now not far to go on China's long march for the Olympics, and in the wait to see what impact the Beijing Games will have on China, East Asia and the rest of the world.

Chapter 7

Conclusion

For decades, human rights were a useful, if minor, tool of Chinese diplomacy. Placing its emphasis on the rights of self-determination and development, Beijing used human rights advocacy to strengthen friendships with revolutionary movements and Third World nations [which] shared its interest in opposing domination by the big powers. Since the 1970s, however, and especially after 1989, the issue of human rights has turned from a shield of China's sovereignty into a spear pointed against it.

(Nathan 1994: 622)

The starting point of any reflection on contemporary China – especially with regard to the human-rights question – should be the obvious yet unpopular observation that the Peking [Beijing] regime is a totalitarian system.

(Leys 1978)

The 1936 Berlin Olympic Games have been identified and vilified as the 'most controversial Olympics' (Guttmann 1992/2002: Chapter 4). When the Games opened on 1 August, Adolf Hitler (1889 to 1945) had been Chancellor (or head of government) of Germany for precisely three years and *Führer* (*Leader*, or head of state) of Germany for precisely two; Germany had violated the 1919 Treaty of Versailles by reintroducing conscription to the armed forces (March 1935) and reoccupying the Rhineland (March 1936); the Spanish Civil War had begun (July 1936), with General Francisco Franco receiving support from Germany's armed forces; and the German Olympic team – contrary to the German NOCs' reassurances – had been divested (or ethnically cleansed) of Jewish athletes.

Germany went on to win by far the largest overall number of medals at the Games – 89 compared with the USA's second place total of 56 and Hungary's third place tally of just 16 – although not without some significant defeats, in particular those at the hands (or the *feet*) of Jesse Owens, the black US athlete who by winning four gold medals in the 100 metres sprint, the 200 metres sprint, the four by 100 metres relay, and the long jump did much to undermine Hitler's myth of Aryan superiority (IOC 13 September 2006). Still, Hitler had achieved a considerable propaganda coup simply by having the IOC select Berlin to host the Games, which he and the *Nationalsozialistische Deutsche Arbeiterpartei* (NSDAP, National Socialist German Workers Party, or Nazi Party) proceeded to exploit to the full specifically for the purpose of enhancing the image of the Third Reich (1933 to 1945) at home and abroad.

For some observers, the way in which seventy years later the IOC awarded the 2008 Games to Beijing in spite of the PRC's undemocratic political system, territorial claims (including over Taiwan and Tibet), and harsh treatment of its own people is an indication of the IOC's persistently questionable ethics, morality and purpose (see Hunt 1993). For many observers, what Simon Leys asserted three decades before the 2008 Games remains largely applicable today: 'the historical record of the regime could be characterized as a continuous and ruthless war waged by the Communist government against the Chinese people' (Leys 1978). Of considerable concern around the world in this regard is evidence of the widespread use in the PRC of torture, as reflected in both broad brush data and individual cases, such as that of Zhou Jianxiong, as revealed by Amnesty International in 2001:

> Zhou Jianxiong, a 30 year-old agricultural worker from Chunhua township in Hunan province, died under torture on 15 May 1998. Detained on 13 May, he was tortured by officials from the township birth control office to make him reveal the whereabouts of his wife, suspected of being pregnant without permission. Zhou was hung upside down, repeatedly whipped and beaten with wooden clubs, burned with cigarette butts, branded with soldering irons, and had his genitals ripped off.
>
> (AI 2001)

What is disturbing about such cases is not just the details of the torture itself, but also the 'crime' for which Zhou was tortured and killed, that of refusing to betray *his wife, suspected of being pregnant without permission.*

Zhou's experience would seem to be far from isolated. In December 2005, well into the Beijing Olympiad, it was reported that 'Immersion in sewage, ripping out fingernails, sleep deprivation, cigarette burns and beatings with electric prods — these are some of the torture methods used by China's police and prison officers to extract confessions and maintain discipline, a United Nations investigation has found' throughout the PRC (Watts 2005).

The widespread use of torture in the PRC is accompanied by the frequent use of the death penalty.[1] Amnesty International (AI) has estimated that on average 15,000 people were executed each year between 1997 and 2001. AI explains:

In China, the death penalty targets poor and marginalized groups including ethnic minorities, migrant communities, political dissidents, and so called 'separatists'. Since the 'war on terrorism' began, Muslims in the Xinjiang Uighur Autonomous Region have been the target of intense crackdowns, and political dissidents may be labeled as 'terrorists' and sentenced to death, regardless of whether they have used or advocated violence, and regardless of whether they have been implicated in any crime.

(AI 2006)

What is more, even death does not bring an end to practices which have caused widespread consternation, with the executed having their organs harvested for sale to be implanted in the bodies of other people.[2] The PRC authorities have acknowledged that organ harvesting has been taking place, but have claimed that the law has now been tightened up to bring the practice to an end (Toy 2006). It remains to be seen what will happen here, although monitoring progress on this and other activities for which the police and prison officers are responsible is likely to be severely hampered by at least one factor, that of the PRC's extensive chain of prison and labour camps, or gulags (*laogai* in Chinese), a reminder of the similar ways in which Stalin's Soviet Union and Hitler's Germany dealt with and disposed of their undesirables and unwanted.[3]

As was the case in the Soviet Union under Stalin, when gulags were places to which government opponents, critics or dissenters were sent, so in the PRC dissent from state orthodoxy has been criminalized and leads to not only incarceration, but also the administration of remedial psychiatry.[4] As pointed out by Robin Munro, this PRC practice makes possible the 'simultaneous criminalization and medicalization of certain forms of dissenting activity', including that of 'so-called "political maniacs", whistleblowers and exposers of official corruption, persistent complainants and petitioners, and also unconventional religious sectarians' (Munro 2000: 7–8). Treatment can go as far as to entail lobotomies, with 'dozens' of such operations being performed each year in each institution (Munro 2000: 25–6).

In the PRC, the old statutes in the Criminal Law which criminalized counter-revolutionary activities (or freedom of expression and association) have been re-labelled 'crimes of endangering state security', with political dissidents, independent labour unionists, and non-conformist religious adherents being the major targets (*ibid.*: 69–70). In the PRC, it is dangerous to 'express opinions on important domestic and international affairs' or to 'make anti-government speeches in public' given that these activities are defined as the acts of a 'political maniac' (*zhengzhi fengzi*) (Munro 2000: 75). Those engaging in them can be found guilty of 'endangering state security' and of being mentally ill. The result will be incarceration and compulsory hospitalization in a country where torture appears to be endemic.

As summarized by Munro, along with those who genuinely pose a *serious danger* to the physical well-being of themselves and others:

> China [. . .] applies its 'serious danger' criteria to those whom the govern-ment deems a political threat to 'social order'. As a result, thousands of political and religious dissenters, including urban dissidents, exposers of official corruption, persistent complainants and petitioners, and unconventional religious sectarians, have in recent decades been forcibly and unjustifiably incarcerated in mental asylums. Under inter-nationally agreed standards of legal and medical ethics defined by the United Nations and the World Psychiatric Association, peaceful religious or political dissidents are emphatically not considered as belonging to this highly select category of the criminally insane. While these abusive practices seemed to have declined since the late 1980s, there has been a conspicuous resurgence lately in the case of detained adherents of the Falun Dafa [Falun Gong] spiritual movement and others.[5]
>
> (*ibid.*)

Falun Gong members, it would seem, are routinely detained and tortured, and suffer and consequently die in sizable numbers in prisons, camps, hospitals and mental institutions around the PRC.[6] According to Human Rights Watch, while there are difficulties in obtaining reliable information:

> There is evidence of a range of serious abuses against Falungong members in custody, including beatings, electric shock and other forms of torture, forced feeding and administration of psychotropic drugs, and extreme psychological pressure to recant [. . .]. As of June 27, 2001, Falungong claimed that some 234 practitioners had died suspicious deaths in custody or immediately following release, and that countless others were victims of torture and mistreatment.
>
> (HRW 2002)

Frequent comparison are made between Nazi Germany and the PRC, in particular by Western commentators (see for instance, Chaudhary 2001; Cyphers 1993; The Economist, 1993; The Independent 2001; Larmer 2001; Lilley 2001; Mackay and Chaudhary 2001; Murphy 2001; National Review 2001; Nordlinger 2000; Weekly Standard 2001), and indeed the argument is occasionally trotted out that the PRC's governing regime is fascist, at least of the 'soft' variety.[7,8] For instance, Brandt Ayers (2005: 3c) claims that 'China is communist in name only. A more accurate title would be Fascist China', which, he continues, consists of 'state control and citizen subordination in a dynamic capitalist economy' (Ayers 2005: 3c). In Michael A. Ledeen's view, the PRC is 'a maturing fascist regime'. Leeden asserts:

Like the earlier fascist regimes, China ruthlessly maintains a single-party dictatorship; and although there is greater diversity of opinion in public discourse and in the media than there was a generation ago, there is very little wiggle room for critics of the system, and no toleration of advocates of Western-style freedom and democracy. Like the early fascist regimes, China uses nationalism – not the standard communist slogans of 'proletarian internationalism' – to rally the masses. And, like the early fascisms, the rulers of the People's Republic insist that virtue consists in sublimating individual interests to the greater good of the nation. Indeed, as we have seen recently in the intimidation and incarceration of overseas Chinese, the regime asserts its right to dominate all Chinese, everywhere. China's leaders believe they command a people, not merely a geographic entity.

(Leeden 2002)

Of course, the greatest care and caution should be exercised over the argument, or rhetoric, that the PRC's governing regime is fascist, not least given the underlying political, not to say mischievous, agenda at work. This agenda reflects and helps to reinforce Western discourses on both the PRC and the 2008 Beijing Olympics, while, perhaps relatedly, being far from universally and consistently accepted in the West.

Following the end of the Cold War, the West's need for the PRC as an ally in its confrontation with and attempt to contain the Soviet Union dissipated; and in the post-Cold War new world order, what had been an emphasis on nation-state independence, sovereignty and non-interference was soon to be questioned in favour of that on human rights as the main organizational principle of international relations. New fault lines emerged in international relations as *realpolitik* gave way to a heightened interest on the part of the West in the internal, domestic activities of the governing regimes of nation-states both within the West itself and elsewhere. Accordingly, the PRC's human rights record among other continental East Asian countries has been greatly scrutinized and heavily criticized by the West in line with the Western discourse on the role and responsibilities of the state, with one result being the claim that the PRC's position in the world is that of 'a human rights pariah' (Nathan 1994: 631). At the same time, however, the PRC's governing regime has been far from uniformly condemned, especially due to what some see as its successes in the area of so-called second-generation (or social, economic and cultural) rights as distinct from that of first-generation (or civil and political) rights (on the PRC's human rights record in the past and the West's responses, see Chang and Halliday 2005). In this regard, such Western-based global civil society organization (GCSOs) as Amnesty International (based in London) and Human Rights Watch (based in New York) have been in the vanguard of the attack, as has the US government. The denunciation of the PRC over its human rights practices from Europe and

Japan has been relatively muted, albeit matched as such by the response at times by the USA, depending upon it would seem its prevailing international relations considerations, concerns and interests (on the various responses to the PRC's human rights record, see also Ming Wan 2001). In other words, the USA's approach to human rights undulates over time, just as it varies between target locations, including between itself in comparison with other – perhaps especially non-Western – countries. The USA has been widely condemned for being highly selective and hypocritical over human rights; and for how it appears to use, exploit and abuse human rights manipulatively and cynically in pursuit of its underlying hegemonic agenda. The case of the USA's approach to human rights suggests the need for caution in assessing the degree and decisiveness of the shift away from *realpolitik* in the international relations arena, at least so far (see Close and Askew 2004).[9]

As Laura Tyson, the Dean of the London Business School, put it shortly after Beijing had been awarded the right to host the 2008 Games:

> The International Olympic Committee awarded the Games to China despite relentless pressure from Beijing on disciples of the Falun Gong, a recent crackdown on newspapers, and the high-profile arrests of foreign scholars. Does the IOC decision, like the decision to grant normal trading relations to China and to accept China into the World Trade Organization, mean that the U.S. and the rest of the world are condoning human-rights violations in China? Are moral concerns taking a backseat to greed in foreign policy as global companies vie for a share of China's markets?
>
> (Tyson 2001)

As has been made clear at various points throughout this book, the USA by no means resisted and rejected the IOC's choice of Beijing for the 2008 Games on the grounds of the PRC's human rights record or any other grounds. Nor, of course, did other Western nation-states. It is likely that every NOC which has been invited to attend the 2008 jamboree will turn up, and that they will tend do so not just in the interests of sport and Olympism, but also – and perhaps primarily – in the interests of a range of other considerations, factors and forces, including international relations and security, the War on Terror, political stability and progress, economic gains at the micro and the macro levels, economic development on the local, regional and global planes, and (if only in effect) globalization around market capitalism, liberal democracy and the Western cultural account. If all goes to plan, there will be many more winners during the Beijing Olympiad than those athletes who gain bronze, silver and gold medals at the Games.

This is not to ignore the view that there will be plenty of losers too:

Human rights advocates, supporters of a free Tibet and members of the banned spiritual group Falun Gong, however, sought to prick Beijing's bubble by warning that the eyes of the world would be trained on the Government for seven years. Pro-Tibet groups condemned the IOC decision and vowed to intensify their opposition, despite statements by the Dalai Lama that the Games could bring greater prosperity to Chinese people. 'We are disappointed that the IOC has chosen to overlook the systematic destruction of Tibetan culture and human rights abuses committed by the Chinese Government', Australia Tibet Council president Alex Butler said. [The human rights NGO] Human Rights in China echoed concerns that the Communist Party will use the Olympics as Adolf Hitler did in 1936 as a fascist nation-building exercise.

(O'Donnell 2001: 10)

Opposition to the IOC awarding the Olympics to Beijing stretches back to the days when the city was bidding for the 2000 Games (see Cyphers 1993: A4H; Greenberger 1993: A7; Hunt 1993: A1; Mackay and Chaudhary 2001: 1), and was inspired by not just the PRC's human rights record (see The Age 1993). On the other hand, Western human rights advocates and activists, or purveyors and entrepreneurs (see Chapter 4 of this book), have been far from unified over the Beijing Games issue. There are those who have been strongly opposed to the award of the Games to Beijing on moral grounds (the moralists), such as within the Free Tibet Campaign. Thus: 'Since the IOC's controversial decision to award the 2008 Olympic Games to Beijing in July 2001 Free Tibet Campaign has condemned its decision and vowed to intensify its opposition through intense lobbying and campaigning in the run-up to the event' (Free Tibet Campaign 2006; see also 2008 – Free Tibet 2006). Of course, it is far from just Tibet, or more to the point the Tibetan minority, which has felt the weight of the PRC's state machine, policies and practices on their backs. As with the people of Tibet, so with the people of other regions within the PRC, including the Xinjiang Uygur Autonomous Region (XUAR), with the result that some observers have drawn a parallel between the PRC and the Soviet Union, especially under Stalin. In each case, it has been claimed, the 'moulding and destruction of ethnic groups [can be viewed as] part of a complex, and often brutal, process of trying to create a [single] nation from a conglomerate of peoples under their control' (Bartov 2006).

Still, there are also those who are not opposed to the award of the Games to Beijing in so far as the Games will help improve the PRC's human rights practices (the pragmatists). For the pragmatists, just as the awarding of the 1988 Games to Seoul contributed to South Korea's transition to a Western-style liberal democracy, so the Beijing Olympiad is likely to ease the PRC's development not only economically, but also politically (see Tyson 2001).

With this prospect in mind, specialist civil society organizations (CSOs), such as Olympic Watch: Human Rights in China and Beijing 2008 (which also describes itself as the Committee for the 2008 Olympic Games in a Free and Democratic Country), have been established to monitor human rights in practice in the PRC in the run up to the 2008 Games. Olympic Watch will be conducting its 'mission [. . .] to monitor the human rights situation in the People's Republic of China and to campaign for its improvement before Beijing is to host the 2008 Summer Olympics' (Olympic Watch 2006), along-side such organizations as Amnesty International (AI), Freedom House, and Human Rights Watch (HRW), whose Beijing 2008 campaign is concentrating on such issues as the PRC's censorship of the media, eviction of people from their homes, and labour rights (Human Rights Watch 2004; see also Chapter 4 of this book).

It might be argued, however, that what the moralists and pragmatists clearly have in common with not only each other, but also the Olympic movement is their role in facilitating Western cultural imperialism – in the 'colonial subjugation of non-Western [sports and their] cultures' (Giulianotti 2004: 358) – with the ramifications which this process has for the political economy of the PRC and of the world as a whole. In this regard, it is pertinent to note Dong Jinxia's observation that in the run up to the 2008 Games, the financial and other rewards enjoyed by individual athletes can be spectacular. In particular, elite athletes are granted 'huge material incentives and political rewards' (Dong Jinxia 2001: 4). For instance, the winners of gold medals at the 1992 Barcelona Games typically received bonuses of between 700,000 and 800,000 yuan, which was equivalent to '400 years of income for an ordinary Chinese' (ibid.: 4); while, at the top of the ladder, one athlete was given 1.16 million yuan plus an apartment worth 400,000 yuan. What these rewards reflect is the way in which the state's funding of sport is heavily tipped towards supporting and encouraging elite activities and athletes (ibid.: 4). In 1990, on average 14,000 yuan per year was spent on training a professional athlete compared with the typical 800 yuan per year which was allocated for the sports budget of each primary school in Beijing (Fan Hong 1998: 161; 2004: 340). During the 1990s, of the state's total annual sports budget of around a billion yuan, all but 13 million yuan was spent on professional sports activities (Fan Hong 1998: 161), and there is no evidence to suggest that this pattern of sports funding has changed (see Fan Hong 2004).

It has been claimed that the improvement in the PRC's sporting prowess has been built upon the intensive exploitation of 'child labour' (ibid.). According to Fan Hong's estimates in 2004, two thirds of the PRC's 80,617 professional athletes were child athletes (ibid.: 338). What is more, another 400,000 children were enrolled in 3,000 specialist sports schools, in which children as young as five would spend between six and eight hours (and up to ten hours in the case of older children) per day in training (ibid.: 340). Fan

Hong tells us that 'child athletes are obliged to devote all their energy and life to their training and performance. They work long hours, train under physical, social and psychological strain and carry much responsibility [to achieve] glory for the nation, the Party, the coaches and their parents' (*ibid.*: 341). In the PRC, the intensive training techniques used on children from a young age mean major educational deficiencies and post-retirement (from professional sporting activities, usually in the 20 to 30 years age-range) difficulties (Dong Jinxia 2001: 19; Giulianotti 2004: 361).

In the PRC, there is a close relationship between the exploitation of children in sports and the experience of women. On the one hand, there has been notable progress in the participation and success of women, a development which has mirrored the general process of emancipation from which women have benefited.[10] There is evidence of the way in which women have been increasingly able to use professional sport in order to achieve upward social mobility (Dong Jinxia 2001: 1). On the other hand, however, the intensive training techniques used on children have been especially harsh and troublesome for females. As Fan Hong has pointed out, it is not only that 'young Chinese female athletes [in particular] have been trained under cruel and inhumane circumstances since the 1960s', but also that they are particularly vulnerable to sexual abuse (Fan Hong 2004: 342). Among the most notorious cases of the harsh treatment of young female athletes is that surrounding Ma Junren. As Riordan and Jinxia have noted, 'Even some Chinese critics accused [infamous running coach] Ma [Junren] of "cruelty and inhumanity" in regard to his charges' (Riordan and Jinxia 1996: 144).[11] Famously, Ma's runners burst onto the world stage in the early 1990s, variously rewriting the women's track and field record book. However, most of Ma's charges soon left him, citing cruelty. Eventually, Ma was axed after 'suspicious' drug testing results. Citing Zhao Yu's *Majiajun diaocha* (an examination of Ma's army), Fan Hong writes:

> Ma Junren acted not as a modern athletics coach, but as an ancient gladiator trainer. Girls under his training were 14–16 years old. They had to run 220 km a week – almost a marathon a day. He beat them whenever he wanted to. Wang Junxia, the holder of world records from 1,500 m to 10,000 m and recipient of the prestigious Jesse Owns Trophy in 1994, was beaten by Ma every week, sometimes even in front of TV crews and her parents for her 'inappropriate behaviour'. The same things happened to the other female athletes. Zhao Yu claimed that all girls were subjected to verbal and physical abuse regularly.
>
> (Fan Hong 2004: 342)

However, subjecting young female athletes to verbal insults and physical violence has by no means been confined to the case of Ma Junren. For instance, according to Brook Larmer (2005):

> Far from being a chance creation, Chinese basketball giant Yao Ming
> was knowingly bred for the sport, forced into it against his will and
> subjected to years of dubious science to increase his height. [He] also
> went through years of punishing training. The revelations [. . .] are likely
> to raise further disquiet over China's Soviet-style sports system ahead of
> the 2008 Beijing Olympics.
>
> (Australian 2006)

It would seem that Yao Ming's father, one of the tallest men of Shanghai,
was 'paired off' with a tall woman: 'The two were encouraged to marry in a
system with undertones of eugenics, the gene-pool manipulation espoused
by the Nazis and previously trumpeted by Beijing'; and their son 'was
recruited for basketball despite his parents' objections and his own hatred
for the sport' (ibid.; see also Larmer 2005).

While the sexual exploitation of female athletes is not covered in the state-
controlled mass media, it is widely discussed. As Fan Hong mentions, stories
about sexual liaisons between athletes and athletic coaches are common (Fan
Hong 2004: 342), as are 'rumours about some female athletes running away
or taking early retirement to avoid their coaches' sexual abuse' (ibid.: 342).[12]
Similarly, the topic of the use of performance enhancing drugs is given only
restricted space in the media, although stories do often emerge, as in the case
surrounding Ma Junren. After the fall of the Berlin Wall in 1989, many East
German sports coaches and physicians moved to the PRC, as a direct result
of which the performances of the country's female athletes improved
remarkably, in particular in running and swimming.[13] For instance, at the
Seventh World Swimming Championships in Rome in September 1994,
PRC women won 12 of the 16 swimming and diving world titles, in stark
contrast to PRC men, who failed to win a single medal. These results are
widely explained partly if not wholly in terms of the use by the women of
performance enhancing drugs in a manner similar to the use by female
athletes in East Germany for decades prior to 1989. During 1994, 11 PRC
swimmers tested positive for performance enhancing drugs (Riordan and
Jinxia 1996: 130–1), including 1 who had won 4 gold medals and 2 silver
medals at the Rome championships and who, with 6 other PRC swimmers,
tested positive at the subsequent Asian Games held in November 1994 in
Hiroshima, Japan. Of the 23 gold medals won by PRC swimmers at the 1994
Asian Games, 9 had to be relinquished as a result of unfavourable drugs
tests. Four years later, PRC swimmer, Yuan Yuan, was caught at Sydney
international airport on her way to the 1998 World Swimming Championships in Perth, Western Australia, with 13 vials of prohibited human growth
hormone in her luggage, prior to four further swimmers failing drugs tests at
the championships themselves (see Australian: 4; Litsky 1998).

Of course, these incidents of PRC athletes using banned performance
enhancing drugs are far from the whole story covering their use among

athletes around the world as a whole. It is likely that many athletes from many, if not most, countries and territories occasionally or regularly use such substances, and of considerable interest when it comes to the Beijing Games will be the number of PRC athletes compared with athletes from elsewhere who will be revealed as having used drugs in breach of the rules, to cheat, and to deviate from the basic principles of Olympism; and the reaction of their respective NOCs and compatriots (see also Chapters 2 and 4 of this book).

East Germany provides what remains the most notorious example of the near automatic, blanket and long-term abuse of drugs, with costs which have since become palpably obvious. In 2000, J. Hammer and J. Biehl reported:

> Manfred Ewald, 75, longtime director of East Germany's Olympic program, and his head physician, Manfred Hoppner, 66, stand accused of helping cause 'grave bodily damage' to 142 female swimmers and track-and-field stars given massive doses of steroids between 1974 and 1989. Prosecutors say the women were victims of a state-sponsored 'doping' campaign carried out in pursuit of Olympic gold as proof of communism's supremacy. The costs were appalling: many of the women suffered ovarian cysts, infertility and miscarriages. Some gave birth to children with terrible handicaps.
>
> (Hammer and Biehl 2000: 23)

In the East German case, the state was heavily involved in the manufacture and distribution of performance enhancing drugs, the use of which was as close to being compulsory as makes little difference, and in the administration of these substances to *wunderkind* as young as seven years old (Riordan and Jinxia 1996: 131). More recently, it has been claimed, the PRC has been engaging in similar practices:

> An urgent issue of the protection of child athletes in China is doping. In the medal-crazy atmosphere that has existed since the 1980s, the rights of athletes in general and the rights of child athletes in particular are ignored. Coaches and sports authority figures forced young athletes to take drugs in order to get medals at national and international competitions.
>
> (Fan Hong 2004: 351)

Fan Hong indicates the scale of the problem in the PRC: 'In 2000, at the National Junior Sports Championships, 25 per cent of athletes tested positive' (Fan Hong 2004: 351). If so, then the signs are that among athletes as a whole, the use of performance enhancing drugs will involve millions of people, either directly (as athletes) or indirectly (as coaches, administrators and so on). If so, then will this be revealed during the 2008 Beijing Olympic

Games, and will it spoil the show? Will drug abuse or other – such as nationalist or terrorist – incidents spoil the image of the PRC and, yet again, that of the Olympic movement?

What will be the legacy of the 2008 Beijing Games? What, if anything, will be the impact of these Games on such things as sport and drugs, sport in general, the Olympic Games in general, the Olympic movement, the city of Beijing, the People's Republic of China, human rights in the PRC, the PRC's international relations, international relations in general, the political economy sphere of social life at and between the local, regional and global levels, and the processes of globalization? For pragmatists, crucially, the Games offer hope, as suggested by Laura Tyson:

> Refusing China's Olympic bid might have been a dramatic expression of moral outrage over the human-rights abuses of China's government. Yet it would have done nothing to improve either the economic or political prospects of average Chinese citizens. Paradoxically, hosting the Games is likely to be a boon for China's citizenry and a headache for their leaders. Preparation for the Games will require infrastructure and environmental upgrading that will improve the lives of millions of Chinese. Indeed, these investments will be so large that they may well add nearly half a percentage point to China's annual growth rate over the next several years. The timing of this additional growth couldn't be better, as it coincides with the painful economic adjustments confronting China upon its accession to the WTO.
>
> (Tyson 2001)

For Tyson, staging the 2008 Games will bring not just *economic rewards* to the PRC and its people, but also political benefits. She notes in this regard how well in advance of the Games – throughout and even before the four-year period of the Beijing Olympiad – the PRC and especially the PRC's governing regime will be 'in the glare of the international spotlight':

> Thousands of journalists from around the world will be scrutinizing all aspects of life in China, including human-rights practices that violate both the country's laws and international norms. Chinese leaders will have difficulty hiding from this scrutiny, and if they try to do so they will sacrifice a historic opportunity to bolster China's reputation and strengthen its links with the rest of the world.
>
> (*ibid.*)

Tyson notes how those who criticize the IOC's decision to award Beijing the right to host the 2008 Games 'point to the ill-advised decision to award Germany the 1936 Olympics' (*ibid.*). But, Tyson argues, this comparison 'is misleading' in that the PRC's 'current leaders are reformers who sought the

Olympics to promote economic and political change' (*ibid.*). Accordingly, she claims that a 'better comparison is the IOC's selection of South Korea for the 1988 Olympics, which proved to be a major catalyst for democratic transformation there' (*ibid.*; see also Cummings 2001).

Clearly, Laura Tyson, like many other observers, accepts and applauds the decision to allow Beijing to stage the 2008 Games in spite of the PRC's human rights record and political system in that, in her view, it is likely to have welcome consequences for this record and this system, as well as for connectedly the PRC's participation in the global political economy. Perhaps, but still it may be asked, at what cost? In Fan Hong's account, the most striking and significant of all the performances that contributes to any Olympic Games and Olympiad 'is the relay of the flame from its Greek sanctuary, which may be interpreted as symbolizing the light of Western civilization spreading out from its Greek origins, bringing enlightenment to the rest of the world' (Fan Hong 1998: 149). Certainly, the Olympic flame is a potent symbol of the Olympics, of everything associated with them, and of everything for which they stand. The flame purportedly commemorates the theft of fire from the Greek god Zeus by Prometheus for use by mere mortals, and its origins lie in the ancient Olympics (*circa* 776 bc to 393 ad), when a fire was kept burning throughout each of the Games. The fire was introduced into the modern Games in 1928. However, interestingly, the torch relay – which now gets underway with a torch being lit at Olympia, Greece, several months before an opening ceremony – was introduced by Carl Diem, the president of the committee which organized the 1936 Berlin Games. Ostensibly, the torch relay was intended to signify *unity among nations*, but in practice was part and parcel of the effort to glorify Germany under the Nazi Party (the Third Reich), and far from merely coincidently displayed the logo of the steel and munitions manufacturer Krupp, which was primarily responsible for arming Germany during each of the twentieth century's two world wars (see New York Times 2004).

Of course, the Third Reich origins of the torch relay need not detract from the current symbolism and significance of the performance. Perhaps the relay can be interpreted *as symbolizing the light of Western civilization spreading out from its Greek origins, bringing enlightenment to the rest of the world* (Fan Hong 1998: 149). Perhaps, in other words, the relay symbolizes how the world is being re-shaped primarily around so-called Western civilization, or what might be otherwise referred to as *the Western cultural account*, and concomitantly Western liberal democracy and, above all, Western market capitalism. Perhaps the relay symbolizes how the world is converging towards a single global society under the sway and hegemony of, if only for the time being, the West and principally the USA.

Readers of utopian fiction will know that projected future utopias are often set in a relatively small city. Utopias set in the future are places where global practices and beliefs have emerged; where historical experiences have been distilled to produce a single model of the good life; and where the lives, activities and thinking of human beings in any one place almost identically replicate the lives, activities and thinking of human beings in all other places. If nothing else, future utopias reflect the unrelenting onward march of universalism.

The models of the good life in fiction, social thought and political philosophy tend to share the same bedrock of ideas, beliefs and values. While there are exceptions (such as that of Robert Nozick's meta-utopia, 1974), proponents of idealized models of social organization – including of the utopian, socialist or capitalist varieties – generally assume that human societies will converge towards some common, stable social order in which the problem of economic scarcity will have been overcome, and in which material abundance will have brought an end to serious conflict. This view can be seen running through the debates surrounding the processes of globalization, whereby the principal driving forces behind the dynamics of the modern world are conspiring, for better or for worse, to create a single global and homogeneous social (economic, political and cultural) formation.

With the end of the Cold War and so the collapse of the Soviet Union and empire, the theoretical possibility (as flagged in the works of such thinkers as Hayek and Mises) of the eclipse of the philosophies and ideologies of socialism and communism as alternatives to capitalism was turned into a real, concrete certainty. Famously, in 1989 Francis Fukuyama wrote: 'What we may be witnessing is not just the end of the Cold War, or the passing of a particular period of post-war history, but the end of history as such: that is, the end point of mankind's ideological evolution and the universalization of Western liberal democracy as the final form of human government' (Fukuyama 1989: 4; also see Fukuyama 1992). The end of 'ideological evolution', Fukuyama assumed and hoped would mean an end to the major sources of political confrontation, clashes and conflict, heralding a new era of peace and prosperity.

By way of a challenge to Fukuyama's thesis and prognosis, Samuel Huntington presented an alternative scenario. Huntington rejected the view of the end of the Cold War bringing about an end to major political schisms, struggles and battles:

> It is my hypothesis that the fundamental source of conflict in this new world will not be primarily ideological or primarily economic. The great divisions among humankind and the dominating source of conflict will be cultural. Nation states will remain the most powerful actors in world affairs, but the principal conflicts of global politics will occur between nations and groups of different civilizations. The clash of civilizations will dominate global politics. The fault lines between civilizations will be the battle lines of the future.
>
> (Huntington 1993: 22)

Huntington's civilizational fault lines involve China, which in so far as it is anti-Western could become allied with an anti-Western Islam faction, the result being what Huntington calls the 'Confucian-Islamic connection' (*ibid*: 45–48).

The Fukuyama–Huntington debate draws attention to the question of the future trajectory of the PRC. Will the country converge with Western societies around market capitalism, liberal democracy and the Western cultural account? Will it converge with Western societies through economic, political and cultural globalization, but towards a global social formation which significantly diverges from what the West has to offer? Will the PRC and the West converge towards a social formation which is substantially shaped by the distinguishing features of Chinese society, or of more than one of the BRICSAM group of leading developing societies and regions: Brazil, Russia, India, China, South Africa, ASEAN and Mexico? Will the PRC and the West remain fundamentally, different? Will the PRC and the West provide the focal points of disparate blocs within a mosaic, or dystopia, of ideational, cultural and civilizational particularisms? Will the persistent differences and diversity between the PRC and the West mean that they will remain not just highly competitive, but also diametrically opposed in certain areas of global social life? Are the PRC and the West on a collision course which will end in open conflict over such things as scarce economic resources, territorial claims and disputes, the political status of Taiwan and Tibet, and civilizational and ideological issues? What about the possibility of the West being increasingly confronted not so much by a Confucian-Islamic axis, as by an alliance within the BRICSAM group, perhaps centred on a China, Russia, India and ASEAN (or a CRIA) arrangement? Are there signs already of a CRIA arrangement emerging to the exclusion of and in opposition to the West through such regional and inter-regional social constructions as ASEAN Plus Three (the PRC, South Korea and Japan), the South Asian Association for Regional Co-operation (SAARC), and the Shanghai Cooperation Organization (SCO), which groups China, Russia, Kazakhstan, Kyrgystan, Tajikistan and Uzbekistan (see Kang San Jung 2006; see also Close 2000; Close and Ohki-Close 1999. On the prospect of a post-modern future for the Olympic movement, see Real 2002).

There is no doubt that due to its territorial and demographic features (see for instance, Walker 2006: 60–1), economic importance, and political clout, the PRC will become an increasingly powerful player on the world stage and within the global community, in shaping human and social life, relationships and experiences at and between all planes, from the global to the personal. This is reasonable to anticipate if only due to the implications of the country's astonishing economic growth for the world's scarce and non-renewable resources, the environment, and global warming. But, will the PRC pull its weight in responding to such considerations in the interests of not just itself, but of the global community and humanity as a whole?

On balance, in line with Laura Tyson's pragmatic approach, the 2008 Beijing Olympic Games give cause for optimism about the future of the PRC, the relationship between the PRC and the rest of the world, the Chinese people among others, Chinese society and other social formations, of the global political economy, and of global developments. The Games provide good grounds for assuming that the PRC is on its way to using its growing global weight and clout to help shoulder the burden of ensuring the best all-round future for the planet and its people. The doubts surrounding the benefits of globalization as it is currently taking place – given in particular the way in which the processes involved are being directed mainly by the West and in the interests of the West, Western hegemony and Westernization – could be confirmed and compounded by the how the PRC responds to its emerging superpower status. But, there is a good chance that the PRC will respond not only by ensuring more even development internally, but also more even and equitable development between the West and the rest and the North and the South externally.

The enthusiasm which the PRC's leaders and people have shown for the Games is a sure sign of the PRC's commitment to being a full member of the global community. What remains to be seen is whether this enthusiasm will be translated into not only the greatest but also the most successful mega-event ever; and whether this commitment will be translated into serving the common interests of humankind, sporting and non-sporting alike. Our optimism in these respects makes us think that selecting Beijing for the 2008 Games is commendable. Now, we are left to look forward to the Games and their results, to participating in the spectacle (as onlookers), to comparing what we have written in this book with what actually unfolds during and following the Games, and to writing about the Beijing Olympiad again at some point in the near future.

Notes

1 Toward an analytical framework

1 There are competing claims as to which are the most recognizable images. For instance: 'The golden arches of McDonald's are among the world's three most recognisable images. Only the Coca-Cola logo and the crucifix are better known' (*Guardian* 14 October 2004).

2 See also Andranovich and Burbank June 2004; Burbank et al. 2001.

3 'The Olympic Games consist of the Games of the Olympiad and the Olympic Winter Games. Only those sports which are practised on snow or ice are considered as winter sports' (IOC 8 August 2004: 16). The Games of the Olympiad (see Note 9 below) are otherwise known as the Summer Games. The Olympic Winter Games were launched in 1924. Until 1992, the Winter Games took place in the same year as the Summer Games, but since then they have taken place in the second year of their respective Olympiads. On the Winter Olympics, see Gerlach 2004.

4 By and on Baron Pierre de Coubertin, see Coubertin, 1898, 1967, 1978, 1979, 1986a, 1986b, 1986c, 1988a, 1988b, 2000, 2002a, 2002b, 2002c, 2002d; Gafner 1994; MacAloon 1981.

5 To cite de Coubertin in his own words: 'De plus les six couleurs ainsi combines reproduisent celles de toutes les nations sans exception. Le bleu et jaune de Suéde, Ie bleu et blanc de Gréce, les tricolores français, anglais, américain, allemand, belge, italien, hongrois, le jaune et rouge d'Espagne voisinent avec les innovations brésilienne ou australienne, avec le vieux Japon et la jeune Chine. Voilá vraiment un embléme international' (Coubertin 1913: 6, quoted in Barney 1992a).

6 Robert Knight Barney adds: 'Circles, after all, connote wholeness (as we are told by the psychologist Karl Jung), [and] the interlocking of them [connotes] continuity' (Barney 1992a: 629).

7 A huge amount has been written on the history of the Olympics. Among the best historical accounts during recent years are Adams and Gerlach 2002; Buchanan and Mallon 2006; Guttman 1992, 2002; Toohey and Veal 2000; Young, D. 2002, 2004.

8 For our purposes, an Olympiad is the four-year period between the close of one modern Summer Olympic Games and the close of the next, as exemplified by the interval between the closing ceremony of the 2004 Athens Games and the closing ceremony of the 2008 Beijing Games. We are aware of how the IOC has defined an Olympiad as 'a period of four consecutive calendar years, beginning on the first of January of the first year and ending on the thirty-first of December of the fourth year. The Olympiads are numbered consecutively from the first Games of the Olympiad celebrated in Athens in 1896. The XXIX Olympiad will

begin on 1 January 2008 (IOC 8 August 2004: 17). However, this approach is probably explicable in terms of administrative convenience more than anything else; results in an otherwise arbitrary delineation of the boundaries between Olympiads; and ignores convention. With regard to the latter, according to one overview, an Olympiad is 'a period of four years between two celebrations of the Olympic Games' (AC 11 February 2006). The definition given by the *Concise Oxford Dictionary of Current English* is of the *conventional* kind: 'a period of four years between Olympic Games, used by the ancient Greeks in dating events; a four-yearly celebration of the ancient Olympic Games; a celebration of the modern Olympic Games' (Allen 1990: 827).

9 Olympic icons, otherwise referred to by the IOC as 'Olympic properties', include the 'Olympic symbol, flag, motto, anthem, identifications (including but not limited to "Olympic Games" and "Games of the Olympiad"), designations, emblems, flame and torches, as defined in Rules 8–14' in the Olympic Charter (IOC 8 August 2004).

10 On Olympism, see Adams and Gerlach 2002; Andrews 1975; Anthony 1992; Berlioux 1972; Brundage 1966, 2002a, 2002b; Chang 1996; Clarke 1976; Colwell 1981; Coubertin 1967; Czula 1975, 1978b, 1978c, 1980; Czula et al. 1976; Da Costa 1992; Davenport 1996; Diem 1970; Donnelly, P. 1996; Durantez et al. 1996; Dyreson 1998; Loland 1995; Segrave 1988. On so-called *Post-Olympism*, see Bale and Christensen 2004.

11 In these ways, NOCs may be playing a major role in the process of 'localization', whereby cultural globalization, and so in particular the Western cultural account, is mediated by 'local' cultures and so modified at the 'local' level. On globalization, localization and glocalization in general, see Short 2003, 2004. On the example of McDonald's in East Asia, see Watson 1997. On the processes of globalization, localization and glocalization in relation to football (soccer), see Bellos 2002; Horne 2004; Horne and Manzenreiter 2002, 2004, 2006; Manzenreiter and Horne 2004. See also Bernstein and Blain 2003; De Moragas Spa et al. 2004; Cox 1997; Hendry 2000; Maguire 1999; Miller et al. 2001; Short 2004.

12 On the 2006 Winter Games, see the Organising Committee of the XX Torino 2006 Olympic Winter Games 21 February 2006; IOC 21 February 2006.

13 According to Tom Van Riper, the 'economic Olympic gold standard – the 1984 Los Angeles Summer Games – made a £114 million profit thanks to the fact that the city was already filled with plenty of stadiums, arenas, parks and roads' (Van Riper 2006).

14 The International Federations (IFs) are 'international non-governmental organisations recognised by the International Olympic Committee (IOC) as administering one or more sports at world level. The national federations administering those sports are affiliated to them' (IOC 17 February 2006).

15 On the Paris Congress, see Paillou 1997; Roukhadzé 1997.

16 Jacques Rogues became the eighth President of the IOC in 2001 following the retirement of Juan Antonio Samaranch.

17 On Riga's hopes for hosting the 2009 Congress, see Riga Convention Bureau 20 December 2005.

18 On the reaction in Copenhagen, see Wonderful Copenhagen 8 February 2006.

19 On the cities that have made bids for the 2016 Games, see Games Bids 20 February 2006. As of February 2006, the following cities and countries had indicated they were interested in making bids: Baltimore, USA; Chicago, USA; Chile; Dubai, United Arab Emirates; Hamburg, Germany; Houston, USA; New Delhi, India; Fukuoka, Japan; Kenya; Los Angeles, USA; Madrid, Spain; Milan or Rome, Italy; Montreal, Canada; Moscow, Russia; Philadelphia, USA; Portugal; Rotterdam,

Netherlands; Rome, Italy; St Petersburg, Russia; St Paul/Minneapolis, USA; San Francisco, USA; San Diego, USA, together with Tijuana Mexico; Tel Aviv, Israel; Thailand; Tokyo, Japan.

20 'The Olympic Games are the exclusive property of the IOC which owns all rights and data relating thereto, in particular, and without limitation, all rights relating to their organisation, exploitation, broadcasting, recording, representation, reproduction, access and dissemination in any form and by any means or mechanism whatsoever, whether now existing or developed in the future. The IOC shall determine the conditions of access to and the conditions of any use of data relating to the Olympic Games and to the competitions and sports performances of the Olympic Games. The Olympic symbol, flag, motto, anthem, identifications (including but not limited to "Olympic Games" and "Games of the Olympiad"), designations, emblems, flame and torches [. . .] shall be collectively or individually referred to as "Olympic properties". All rights to any and all Olympic properties, as well as all rights to the use thereof, belong exclusively to the IOC, including but not limited to the use for any profit-making, commercial or advertising purposes. The IOC may license all or part of its rights on terms and conditions set forth by the IOC Executive Board [. . .]. The Olympic symbol, the Olympic emblems and any other Olympic properties of the IOC may be exploited by the IOC, or by a person authorised by it, in the country of an NOC, provided that the [certain strict] conditions are [. . .] fulfilled' as spelled out in the Olympic Charter (IOC 8 August 2004: 17–25).

21 The prefix *mega-* derives from the Greek word 'megas', which means large, very large or great. It denotes large, very large, great, extraordinary, or surpassing other examples of its kind; as well as one million (10 to the power of 6), as in *megahertz*.

22 On Juan Antonio Samaranch, see Samaranch 2002.

23 On mega-events, see Anderson et al. 1999; Andranovich et al. 2001; Beate 1996; Burbank et al. 2001; Cashman et al. 2004; De Moragas Spa 1999; Elstad 1996; Hall and Hodges 1996; Hiller 1998, 1999; Horne and Manzenreiter 2004; Jeong 1999; Kang and Perdue 1994; Mount and Leroux 1994; Olds 1998a, 1998b; Persson 1999; Ritchie 1990; Ritchie and Hall 2000; Ritchie and Smith 1991; Roche 1992, 2000, 2003, 2004; Veale and Toohey 2005.

24 On the relationship between the Olympic movement and business, the Olympic movement as a business, and the economic dimension of the Olympic Games as a mega-event, see Barney et al. 2002; Cai and Yang 2004; Cicarelli and Kowarsky 1973; FEER 1997; Ferrand and Torrigiani 2005; Harvey and Saint Germain 2001; Lenskyi 2002; Lenskyi and Burstyn 2000; Levine and Thurston 1992; Milton-Smith 2002; Preuss 2004; PriceWaterhouseCoopers 2000; Renson and den Hollander 1997; Silk 2004; Slack 2003; Veale and Toohey 2005; Westerbeek and Smith 2003; Wilson, N. 1988.

25 According to Maurice Roche, since the late nineteenth 'century when they first made their appearance the two main mega-event genres have been Expos and great sport events, initially on the Olympic Games, but in the postwar period also joined by the soccer World Cup event' (Roche 2003: 101). However, a question mark hangs over Expos as mega-events for reasons outlined later in this chapter.

26 On the political and cultural dimensions of mega-events, the Olympics and sport in general, see Boyle and Haynes 2000; Cai and Yang 2004; Hill 1992; Houlihan 1994; Lechner ad Boli 2005; Pound 2004; Senn 1999; Spots 1994; Sugden and Tomlinson 2002; Tomlinson 2002; Tomlinson and Young 2005.

27 See Roche 1992, 2000, 2003, 2004.

28 On the Expo genre, see Greenhalgh 1988; Hendry 2000; Ley and Olds 1999; Pred

1991; Roche 2000, 2003; Rydell 1984, 1993; Rydell and Gwinn 1994; Spillman 1997.

29 Similarly, but with a somewhat different emphasis, John Short tells us: 'The IOC and major media present the Olympics as a "pure" global event above national politics and grubby commerce. The dominant narrative is of an event born in purity and full of innocence. National politics and commercial considerations are often contrasted to the mythical narrative of the sacred quality of the Olympic tradition, and the pure Olympic ideal. This attempted distancing of the Olympics from the mundane world of politics and money is fictitious but nevertheless an important Olympic myth. There never was any innocence [. . .]. But this still leaves the question of why and how this discourse persists. It exists in part because we want it to be true. In a rapidly changing world where commerce and politics produce a necessary pragmatism it is important to have an unchanging reference point. The more things are changing the more important it is to have a fixed perspective. A once pure Games is a case in point. In part, it also exists because it is a message reinforced by those selling the Games at the global, national and local levels. As the world becomes more politicized and more commercial the "purity" of the Games becomes an important political and commercial product' (Short 2003).

30 The literature on globalization is vast and the stances on, discourses about and debates surrounding it are complex, to the point where one school of thought raises doubts about the existence of 'globalization', at least in so far as regarding it as a recent phenomenon worthy of a new name (see Hirst and Thompson 2000). A highly commendable survey of stances – including that according to which globalization took off and proceeded on a significantly higher plane during the 1960s, which therefore mark the start of a distinctive *era of globalization* – is to be found in Baylis and Smith's *The Globalization of World Politics* (1997, 2004); see also Bryane 2002; Held et al. 1999; Held and McGrew 2001, 2003a, 2003b. Other writings which either illustrate stances on globalization or provide helpful introductions, overviews, surveys and critiques include Axford 1995; Robertson 1992, 2000; Scholte 2000; Sklair 1999, 2000a, 2000b, 2000c, 2001b, 2001c, 2002c, 2002d, 2003a, 2003b, 2003c, 2004; Stilglitz 2003; Waters 1995.

31 At the very first Olympic Games in Athens in 1896, around 250 competitors from up to 15 countries and territories took part. This compares with the 11,100 competitors from 202 countries and territories that took part in the Games in Athens in 2004. At the 1960 Rome Olympics, there were 5,348 competitors from 83 countries and territories. At the 1964 Tokyo Games, there were 5,140 competitors from 93 countries and territories. Still, the 1964 Games were the first to be able to exploit major breakthroughs in the development of telecommunications. In particular, aided by the advent of communication satellites, they were the first to be broadcast live on television.

32 It is frequently claimed that the FIFA World Cup is the most widely-viewed and otherwise followed sporting event in the world, attracting even greater interest than the Olympic Games. The cumulative audience for the 2002 World Cup held in Japan and Korea is estimated to have been 28.8 billion viewers; and the audience for the final match of this tournament is estimated to have been 1.1 billion. Around 300 million viewers watched the draw to decide the distribution of the teams for the 2006 World Cup in Germany.

33 On the World Cup, FIFA and (association) football, see Giulianotti 1999; Horne and Manzenreiter 2002; Manzenreiter and Horne 2004.

34 See Gramsci 1971, 1978; Sklair 1999, 2000a, 2000b, 2000c, 2001a, 2001d, 2001e, 2002b, 2002d, 2002e, 2003a, 2003c.

35 Also on globalization and sport, see Bairner 2001; Bellos 2002; Bernstein and Blain 2003; Cox 1997; Hargreaves 2002; Harvey et al. 1996; Hendry 2000; Houlihan 2003; Horne and Manzenreiter 2002, 2004; Maguire 1999, 2003; Manzenreiter and Horne 2004; Miller et al. 2001; Rose 2003; Rowe 2000; Silk and Andrews 2001.

36 On globalization and the Olympics, see Bernstein 2000; Brundage 2002b; Cochrane et al. 1996; De Moragas Spa et al. 2004; Gillen 1994; Gordon and Sibson 1998; Larson and Park 1993; Lechner and Boli 2005; Maguire 2003; Milton-Smith 2002; Pujik 2000; Roche 2000; Rowe 2000; Short 2001, 2003, 2004; Spots 1994; Tomlinson and Young 2005.

37 On the victory and vindication of the West thesis, see Fukuyama 1992, 2004, 2006.

38 On sport, the Olympics and international relations, law and regimes, see Levermore and Budd 2004; Nafziger 2004.

2 Olympism, individualism and nationalism

1 On sport, the Olympics and human rights, see Amnesty International 1996; Bass 2002; Edwards 1979; Jewell and Kilgour 2000; Miah 1999; Ritchie and Hall 2000; Sen 1999; and Taylor 2000. A good deal of interest has been shown in the topic of China and human rights in view of Beijing's bid and then election to host the Olympics. See, for example, Amnesty International 8 May 2004, 5 August 2005; Gittings 2001; Human Rights Watch 9 March 2006, 24 August 2004; Labor Rights Now 9 March 2006; LoBaido 2001; Olympic Watch 9 March 2006.

2 Also on China, Tibet and the Beijing Olympiad, see Canada Tibet Committee 9 March 2006; Olympic Watch 7 March 2005.

3 On Olympism and the Beijing Olympics, see Amnesty International 13 July 2001.

4 A discourse is a stance on, or an argument about, an issue among a range of diverse, perhaps conflicting, stances, as reflected in for example the adage 'one man's terrorists are another man's freedom fighters' (Malhotra 2004). There are, for instance, several distinct discourses on the issue of globalization (see Baylis and Smith 2004), each of which has its own particular implications for studying, analyzing and making sense of the Beijing Olympiad as a mega-event. See the writings of Michael Foucault (1926–84). See also Connolly 1974.

5 In critical theory, and most notably in post-modern critical thinking, a metanarrative is a grand, over-arching account, or all-encompassing story about some aspect of human and social life. The notion is associated above all with the work of Jean-François Lyotard, who defines 'postmodern as incredulity towards metanarratives' (Lyotard 1984). For Lyotard, the post-modern era, or condition, is distinguishable by a widespread and growing scepticism towards metanarratives as tools for imposing meaning, order and control during the era of modernity.

6 Maximilian Weber (21 April 1864 to 14 June 1920) was a German sociologist whose best known work is probably *The Protestant Ethic and the Spirit of Capitalism*, but whose most acclaimed work among fellow sociologists is *The Theory of Social and Economic Organization* (1997). See Weber 1958, 2002, 2003.

7 Weber's use of the term 'elective affinity' derives from Goethe's earlier use. See Goethe 1978. See also Elliott 1998; Kent 1983. The term implies *mutual attraction*, perhaps of an overwhelming irresistible kind.

8 In *Modernization, Cultural Change, and Democracy*, Ronald Inglehart and Christian Welzel draw on 'survey data from eighty-one societies containing 85 [per cent] of the world's population, collected from 1981 to 2001, that demonstrates that [. . .] values are changing [. . .] as socio-economic development takes place [. . .]

promoting' individual autonomy, gender equality, and democracy (Inglehart and Welzel 2005: 1).

9 The suffix -ism carries ideational connotations. It implies such things as a system of beliefs, a doctrine, an ideology, a philosophy, a school of thought, a theory, and the like (see Benzi 2005).

10 See, however, the arguments of those who have contributed to the school (or schools) of thought known as 'post-modernism', such as those of Jean-Francois Lyotard, the 'recently deceased, French philosopher, most famous for defining postmodernism as an incredulity towards metanarratives' (PMTH 1 July 2005). See, in particular, Lyotard 1984. Post-modernism has been neatly summarized by David Coughlin: 'Postmodernism, therefore, is anti-essentialist and anti-foundationalist; it sees as problematic the question of universal truths, true representation, or absolute reality; it does not hold with the autonomous, rational subject; it questions the notion of non-gendered, non-historical, non-ethnocentric reasoning; it interrogates Enlightenment ideology; it views historicism favourably; it rejects the labels of relativism or nihilism; it posits heterogeneity, difference, fragmentation, and indeterminacy as positive forces in cultural discourse. But more needs to be said about the way in which this cultural postmodernism emerges with social, economic, and political postmodernity, also known as "postindustrial society" (Daniel Bell), "the society of the spectacle" (Guy Debord), multinational capitalism, media society, consumer society, or globalisation. In this, three theorists in particular are significant, Jean-François Lyotard, Jean Baudrillard, and Fredric Jameson' (Coughlan 1 February 2006).

11 On performance enhancing drugs and the like, see Miah 2004.

12 Albert Camus (1913–1960) is quoted as saying, 'All I know most surely about morality and obligations, I owe to football' (Camus, quoted in George 2005). As explained by Eduardo Galeano: 'In 1930, Albert Camus was Saint Peter guarding the gate for the University of Algeria's soccer team. He had been playing goalkeeper since he was a child, because in that position your shoes don't wear out as fast. From a poor home, Camus couldn't afford the luxury of running the fields; every night, his grandmother examined the soles of his shoes and gave him a beating if he found them worn. During his years in the net, Camus learned many things: "I learned that the ball never comes when you expect it to. That helped me a lot in life, especially in large cities where people don't tend to be what they claim." He also learned to win without feeling like God and to lose without feeling like rubbish, skills not easily acquired, and he learned to unravel several mysteries of the human soul, whose labyrinths he explored late on in a dangerous journey on the page' (Galeano 2003, quoted in George 2005).

13 According to Marketing Matters (July 2001): 'Interest in the Games has grown dramatically: Everyone in the world who has access to television now has access to Olympic Games coverage. It is estimated that during the past two decades the global television audience has grown from fewer than 1.5 billion viewers to more than 3.7 billion. Cumulative global television viewing hours for the combined Olympic and Olympic Winter Games combined now exceed 60 billion TV Viewing Hours.' With regard to the Internet, the BBC has reported: 'In less than 10 years China has gone from a net newcomer to the country with the world's second-largest online population. The first international internet data from China started travelling across the net in 1994, yet now the country has more than 100m net users. That puts its second only to the US with its 185m web users. But China looks set to pass that within a few years – especially when you consider that China's net users represent barely 8% of its population. If Chinese net use grows to the levels seen in many Western nations, it could end up with 750m people

regularly going online. But currently the experience of the average Chinese net user differs greatly from that of many in the West. Part of the net's allure to Western users is the sense of freedom it gives them to look at, read, and say almost anything they want. By contrast, Chinese net use is much more circumscribed. Much has been made of the so-called Great Firewall of China that censors what people see using technology built in to the country's basic net infrastructure. The Chinese authorities have used several methods to "sanitise" what people see online, according to a report from US firm Dynamic Internet Technologies, which watches net use in the country' (BBC 8 March 2005; see also Jackson and McPhail 1989; McDaniel 2002; McKay and Kirk 1992; Meadow 1989; Miller 2000; Min 1987; Mitchell and Yeates 2000; *Olympic Review* 1996; Pollock et al. 1997; Pope 1997; Pujik 2000; Ware 1999).

3 The Olympics, the nation-state and capitalism

1 'The International Olympic Committee is the supreme authority of the Olympic movement [. . .]. The Executive Board, founded in 1921, consists of the International Olympic Committee (IOC) President, four Vice-Presidents and ten other members. All the members of the Executive Board are elected by the Session, by secret ballot, by a majority of votes cast, for a four-year term' (IOC 31 July 2005).
2 See the official websites of the Olympic movement and for the Sydney, Athens, Beijing and London Games at:
<http://www.olympic.org/uk/index_uk.asp>
<http://www.gamesinfo.com.au/home.html>
<http://www.olympics.com.au/>
<http://www.athens2004.com/en/>
<http://en.beijing2008.com/>
<http://www.london2012.org/en>
3 On world system theory, see Wallerstein 1974, 1979, 1980, 1982a, 1982b, 1983, 1984, 1989a, 1989b, 1990, 1991, 1995, 2003, 2004.

4 Beijing and the Olympic social compact

1 Li Lanqing retired as Vice Premier in 2003. See Miller, H. 2004.
2 The *People's Daily* has provided the following description of Liu Qi: 'Han nationality, native of Wujin, Jiangsu Province, was born in [November] 1942. He joined the Communist Party of China (CPC) in September 1975 and began to work in June 1968. He graduated from the Metallurgical Department of Beijing Institute of Iron and Steel Engineering, majoring in iron smelting. With a postgraduate education, he holds the professional title of senior engineer (professor in rank). He is now a member of the Political Bureau of the CPC Central Committee; secretary of the CPC Beijing Municipal Committee; mayor of Beijing' (*People's Daily* 30 July 2005).
3 For all the speeches, see BOCOG 30 July 2005.
4 According to the IMF, China accounted for 13 per cent of 'global growth in 2004', and its economy expanded by an average 9.6 per cent per year in the 15 years to 2004' (Bloomberg 15 January 2006). Towards the end of 2005, China announced 'that its economy was significantly bigger than previous official measures following a national economic census that showed its booming and mainly private service sector, had been underestimated. The National Bureau of Statistics (NBS) increased the estimate for gross domestic product in 2004 to Rmb15,987bn (US$1,930bn), 16.8 per cent higher than the previous calculation of Rmb13,688bn.

Of the increase of Rmb2,299bn, Rmb2,130bn had come from the tertiary sector, the bureau said, with services making up 40.7 per cent of GDP. The NBS said China's economy had surpassed the size of Italy's last year, making it the world's sixth-largest economy. The revision also showed that the economy was less reliant on investment and more driven by consumption than had been assumed, trends the Chinese government has been trying to encourage. The NBS said that although the revision leads to "some increase in the total size of GDP", the ranking of China's per capita GDP is still beyond 100 in the world. The census added the equivalent of Austria's annual output to the world's fastest-growing major economy, vaulting it over the UK, as the world's fourth largest economy in 2005. Chinese output of $2.16 trillion in 2005, based on a government forecast of 9.4 per cent growth, compares with UK's $2.13 trillion economy. America's, the world's biggest, is valued at about $11.7 trillion, more than twice that of Japan's, the second largest. Germany is in third place. Among the reasons given for the revision, the NBS referred to the country's increasingly diverse "economic constituents" and particularly, the expanding role of the private sector in the transport, storage, telecommunications, wholesale, retail, trade, food and beverage industries. The bureau said it would gradually revise GDP figures published since 1993 based on the new methodology used for last year's figures. The revision was in line with market expectation but Song Guoqing, a professor at Peking University, was reported as saying that a revision of up to 20 per cent would still be insufficient to capture the size of the economy. "Private companies may continue to understate the size of their business in order to escape tax," he said' (Finfacts 2005b). See also BBC 3 March 2006.

5 On the notions of 'business community' and 'community' in general, see Anderson 1983; Mason 2000.

6 Dong Yunhu (or Dong Yun hu) has been identified in The *People's Daily* newspaper as 'Vice-president and secretary-general of the China Human Rights Research Society' (Dong Yunhu 2004). However, he was actually one of the six Vice Presidents and the Secretary-General of the China Society for Human Rights Studies (CSHRS). The CSHRS was founded in January 1993 and has become 'the largest academic organization specializing in human rights studies in China' (CSHRS 2003). CSHRS tells us that it is 'sponsored by scholars and experts concerned with human rights at nine Beijing-based schools of higher learning and research institutes, the All-China Federation of Trade Unions and the All-China Women's Federation, the China Society for Human Rights Studies (CSHRS)' (*ibid.*). CSHRS describes itself as 'a non-government organization that is in consultative status with the United Nations Economic and Social Council'; a 'non-profit organization' which 'relies on financial aid and donations to maintain its operations'. As for its aims, the 'society devotes itself to research of the theories, history and current conditions of human rights, study of theoretical and practical issues concerning the development of human rights knowledge, and international exchanges in the human rights arena. It aims at promoting mutual understandings between the Chinese people and people of the world on the question of human rights, and helps China and the world ensure a sound development of the human rights cause' (*ibid.*). While the CSHRS claims to be a non-governmental organization, it has been categorized by outside observers as a 'Chinese government controlled organization seeking to expand dialogue about human rights in China' (Asiaco 2004).

7 These amendments are to the constitution of 1982, the fourth constitution adopted by the PRC since the end of the Second World War. The PRC adopted its first constitution in 1954, although many of its provisions were not recognized

during the Cultural Revolution of the 1960s. A new constitution was adopted in 1975 during the Cultural Revolution, and yet another in 1978 following the Cultural Revolution. The 1982 constitution has proved the most enduring, while nonetheless having been amended four times, most recently in 2004 (Ching 2004).

8 On 1 January 2002, the Republic of China (Taiwan) joined the WTO under the name 'Separate Customs Territory of Taiwan, Penghu, Kinmen and Matsu'.

9 Purchasing power parity (PPP) is a 'method of measuring the relative purchasing power of different countries' currencies over the same types of goods and services. Because goods and services may cost more in one country than in another, PPP allows us to make more accurate comparisons of standards of living across countries. PPP estimates use price comparisons of comparable items but since not all items can be matched exactly across countries and time, the estimates are not always "robust" ' (World Bank 2003b). More technically, 'PPP is purchasing power parity; an international dollar has the same purchasing power over GDP as a U.S. dollar has in the United States' (ibid.). GNP (gross national product) is the 'value (in U.S. dollars) of a country's final output of goods and services in a year. The value of GNP can be calculated by adding up the amount of money spent on a country's final output of goods and services, or by totaling the income of all citizens of a country including the income from *factors of production* used abroad. Since 2001, the World Bank refers to the GNP as the GNI, gross national income' (World Bank 2003c; see also World Bank 2003a).

10 According to James Miles, for instance, China's 'economic transformation is fueling instability', so that ten years later, the country was 'at least as unpredictable and volatile as it was at the outset of the Tiananmen Square protests' (Miles 1996): Miles adds: 'China's economic boom has enthralled the world and brought unprecedented prosperity to millions of Chinese. But [also,] it has aggravated social tensions and weakened the party's grip. The gap between rich and poor and between rural and urban areas is widening. Corruption is flourishing among officials who, seeing [the] collapse of communism elsewhere, have lost faith in their party's future [. . .]. China [. . .] is a country deeply unsure of where it is going. Politicians and public alike are asking themselves whether China is emerging as a new economic superpower with global influence to match, or if it is heading toward the chaos they so much fear. In the coming years, the answer to this question will have major implications for the outside world' (ibid.). More recently, attention has been drawn to a string of protests that has 'deeply worried central government leaders' (Mooney 2004). In October 2004, around '50,000 demonstrators lined up in front of government offices in a small town in Sichuan province and set a police van on fire to protest [against] the beating of a migrant worker, allegedly by a government official' (ibid.). A few days later, in Hanyuan county, also in Sichuan, 'an estimated 100,000 farmers stormed a government building and battled police over land lost to a dam project and what they called inadequate compensation' (ibid.). On this occasion, order 'was not restored until martial law was declared and paramilitary forces were scrambled to the scene' (ibid.). At the end of October 2004, 'hundreds of heavily equipped security forces imposed a curfew on university campuses in Inner Mongolia after a planned concert by a popular Mongolian rock band was canceled' (ibid.); and in November 2004, 'when security guards [. . .] stopped Uighur Muslims in Guangzhou selling fried mutton from a street mall, fighting erupted between riot police and angry Uighurs, leaving several people injured' (ibid.). According to James Miles, it is the way in which 'income disparities are growing and corruption is spiraling' that largely accounts for 'mounting anger and a sharp rise in the number of disturbances around the country' (ibid.). China 'experienced more than 58,000 major

incidents of social unrest' in 2003, 15 per cent more than the figure for 2002, and involving 'more than 3 million people' (*ibid.*).

11 It is to be expected that the Beijing Olympiad, culminating in the 2008 Games, will exemplify how the playing out of elective affinities involving human and social life in general is unlikely to be completely smooth, harmonious and trouble free. Joel Elliott tells us that the term 'elective affinity' (*Wahlverwandtschaft*) 'derives from Goethe' (Elliott 1998: 14). Here, Elliott is alluding to one particular novel by Johann Wolfgang von Goethe (1749–1832), as otherwise described by Peter Smith: '*Elective Affinities* is [. . .] the title of Goethe's classic novel published in 1809 [. . .]. Goethe's work is a landmark both in the history of the novel and relations between science and literature. His depiction of the interaction of science and human relationships sets a high standard for subsequent literary engagements with science. Its central theme is human desire represented as "an indescribable, almost magical force of attraction" that overcomes social and moral bonds. By exploring this theme through contemporary chemical theories of affinity, Goethe establishes links between the scientifically described material world and the realm of human desires, setting in motion a debate about the role of science in our lives that remains topical to this day' (Smith, P. 2001). Goethe's novel was first published in 1809 (see Goethe 1978), but as Smith points out, 'Goethe's interest in theories of chemical affinity can be dated back to at least 1769', the title of his novel being taken from the work and ideas of 'the Swedish chemist Torbern Olof Bergman (1735–84)' (*ibid.*). The term 'elective affinity' was coined in 1775 by Bergman with chemical processes in mind, but as a result of being borrowed by Goethe became associated with 'human and cultural sympathies and aversions' (German Historical Museum 2005). In Goethe's 1809 novel, 'the chemical term "elective affinities" [is extended] to human relationships, both intimate and political' (MacLeod September 2005); and, as with 'the alkalis and acids of which Goethe's characters speak, words and images, though apparently opposed, may have a remarkable affinity for one another' (*ibid.*). Thus, in the case of social life, in the first instance, the notion of elective affinity between two ideas or packages of ideas necessarily implies mutual attraction, so that while neither side is the *cause* of the other, each gives support and sustenance to the other, and in particular to each side's progress. Hence, the appeal of the notion of elective affinity for Max Weber: 'Elective affinity [was used] by Max Weber to conceptualize [the] nondeterministic [. . .] interaction of components [of] different sociocultural systems [. . .]. The [main] case study [. . .] in Weber's work is *The Protestant Ethic and the Spirit of Capitalism* [. . .]. According to Weber, there was an *elective affinity* between Puritan ethical norms and emerging capitalist business [principles and] practices in [the first instance in] seventeenth-century England [. . .]. [Thus,] a particular [package of] economic [ideas,] along with a particular [package of] religious [ideas] coincide [and interact in a highly] favorable [way with each] other, and [consequently, together] form a [cultural] or civilizational complex [. . .] that is especially powerful for the advancement of [the] sociocultural spheres combined [. . .]. Elective affinity is not restricted to the single case, [. . .] and can be considered [as a cornerstone of] a general theory of social [change. When a] favorable coincidence of sociocultural spheres occurs, there can be a quantum leap forward [. . .] on the part of [the resulting] sociocultural system' (Swatos 2005).

12 For instance, as reported during the Beijing Olympiad: 'China's auditor general has found that money for Olympic projects has been siphoned off from China's 2003 budget, the state-run media reported. Auditor General Li Jinhua's report also uncovered widespread embezzlement by officials of poverty relief funds

intended to aid farmers. He also catalogued inefficiency in constructing infrastructure projects, and tax evasion by state enterprises. Altogether, Mr Li's report
found 1.4bn yuan ($170m; £93.7m) missing [. . .]. Mr Li's report, which was
delivered to the Standing Committee of the National People's Congress, found
malpractices at the majority of departments it investigated – 41 out of 55, the
China Daily newspaper reported. "Most of the money [. . .] has gone into the
hands of staff members or to office building construction," *China Daily*'s report
said. Since 1999, the General Administration of Sports has appropriated 131m
yuan ($13.2m) earmarked for the Beijing 2008 Olympics organising committee.
The bulk of this – 109m yuan – was spent on building homes for the organising
committee's staff, the auditor general's report found' (BBC News 24 June 2004).
Subsequently, Bi Yuxi, a 'senior official in charge of building a massive new road
network' in Beijing was 'questioned over corruption': Bi Yuxi 'was described on
the front page of the *Beijing Youth Daily* as "morally degenerate", with a "decadent and dissolute" lifestyle. He has been handed over to the judicial authorities
for further investigation. The case comes soon after an official audit report
exposed widespread government corruption. As head of the Capital Road Development Corporation in Beijing, Bi Yuxi was in charge of building one of the
world's largest networks of ring-roads. China's capital city is undergoing rapid
development, partly because of the country's economic growth, and partly in
preparation for the Olympics, which are due to be held in the city in 2008. The
Beijing Youth Daily accused Mr Bi of taking huge bribes and abusing his position
to help acquaintances' (BBC News 9 August 2004). This particular case, while
concerned with the Beijing Olympiad, is just one among many, the explanation
for which lies outside anything directly linked, or at least solely confined, to the
Games, the Olympic movement or Olympism. That is, 'corruption is rife in
China's rapidly-growing economy. According to official figures, more than 20,000
cases have been investigated in the first half of 2004. It is also an issue which the
ruling Communist Party fears could undermine its authority' (*ibid.*).

13 But, perhaps the issue of the role of science in our lives through sport rages
especially around its application in the form of *performance-enhancing drugs*,
including at and in preparation for the Olympics. The problem is, in a sense,
relatively recent. In the early years, 'many Olympic athletes used drugs to enhance
their performance', including for instance 'the winner of the marathon at the
1904 Games, Thomas Hicks, [who] was given strychnine and brandy by his coach,
even during the race' (Wikipedia 21 October 2005). However, as the performance-
enhancing 'methods became more extreme, gradually' perceptions changed. The
first recognized Olympic Games 'death caused by doping occurred in 1960', when
'the Danish Knut Enemark Jensen fell from his bicycle and died' having been
'doped with amphetamines' (*ibid.*). During the 1960s, 'sports federations' started
to ban performance-enhancing drugs, and 'the IOC followed suit in 1967' (*ibid.*).
The first Olympic athlete 'to test positive' and be punished for the use of banned
drugs was Hans-Gunnar Liljenwall, a Swedish pentathlete at the 1968 Summer
Olympics. He 'lost his bronze medal for alcohol use' (*ibid.*). Following that case,
over 50 athletes, including several medal winners, have suffered a similar fate
(*ibid.*). Perhaps the 'most publicised doping-related disqualification' is that of Ben
Johnson, the Canadian sprinter, who won the 100 metres track race at the 1988
Seoul Olympics, 'but tested positive for stanozol' (*ibid.*). On a different scale, in
1990, documents came to light which showed that 'many East German athletes,
especially women, had been administered anabolic steroids and other drugs by
their coaches and trainers, as a [matter of] government policy' (*ibid.*). In 1999, in
response to evidence of the unabated use of banned substances, 'the IOC took

The initiative in a more organised battle against doping [. . .] leading to the formation of the World Anti-Doping Agency (WADA)' (*ibid.*). Even so, at the 2000 and
2002 Games, several athletes 'were disqualified after doping', including 'weight-
lifting and cross-country skiing' medalists (*ibid.*). In the build-up to the 2004
Games, the use by athletes of tetrahydrogestrinone (THG) and modafinil was the
source of considerable 'controversy throughout the sporting world, with many
high profile cases' and protests by athletes who were punished for using modafinil
when it had not been specifically prohibited. In response, WADA declared
modafinil to be 'a substance related to those already banned', and therefore that
the punishments for modafinil's use would stand. On 3 August 2004, just ten
days before the start of the Athens Games, modafinil was added to the list of
prohibited substances (*ibid.*). However, while the IOC and other sporting bodies
have been adopting an increasingly tough and co-ordinated approach to the use of
performance-enhancing drugs, athletes have been resorting to new, less detectable
methods, and in particular so-called 'gene doping' (*ibid.*; see Miah 2004). At
the 2004 Summer Olympics in Athens, several cases of alleged drug misuse for
performance-enhancing purposes surfaced, including those involving: two Greek
sprinters, Kosta Kederis and Katerina Thanou; Adrian Annus, the Hungarian
hammer throw champion; Maria Luisa Calle Williams, the Colombian cyclist;
Francoise Mbango Etone, the women's triple jump gold medalist from Cameroon;
Robert Fazekas, the Hungarian discus thrower; Ferenc Gyurkovics, the Hungarian
weightlifter; the Russian shot put winner, Irina Korzhanenko; the Hungarian,
weightlifter Zoltan Kovacs; and the Ukrainian team in the quadruple sculls rowing
competition (see *Sydney Morning Herald* 2004). China's answer to the *drugs in
sport problem* in the run up to the 2008 Games is to adopt a strict and strident
approach, as indicated by its announcement in early 2005 that it was 'planning a
big increase in drugs testing before it hosts the 2008 Olympics in Beijing' (BBC 21
April 2005): 'Shi Kangcheng, a top official in China's General Administration
of Sports, said: "We have set a target for raising anti-doping testing by 60%.
The campaign will start next year and continue through 2008." China conducted
5,000 drug tests in 2004, up from 165 in 1990 when its anti-doping drive began,
Shi said, adding the effort will go beyond 2008. China dropped 27 athletes from
its Olympic squads before the Sydney 2000 and axed some weightlifters and
others before last year's Athens Games for failing drug tests. David Howman,
director general of the World Anti-Doping Agency (Wada), also praised China
for setting up a well-equipped testing laboratory and putting effective sanctions in
place. China implemented its first anti-doping law in March 2004 to tighten controls over banned drugs and hand out criminal penalties to serious offenders'
(*ibid.*).

5 The Olympic Games as a 'coming out party'

1 On the history of the modern Olympic movement, see Guttmann 2002;
   Tomlinson 1984. See also the IOC 1994, 1995, 1997.
2 This is also the case with the Winter Olympics, where Western dominance is even
   more pronounced. As Paul Farhi notes: 'In the history of the winter competition,
   dating from its inception in 1924, competitors from only six countries – the
   Soviet Union/Russia, Germany (East, West and combined), Norway, the United
   States, Austria and Finland, in that order – have won almost two-thirds of all the
   medals awarded' (Farhi 2006).
3 On Coubertin, see in particular Coubertin 1989, 2000; Hill 1992: Chapter 1;
   IOC 1994.

4 The term 'powerful figure' is from Coubertin (cited in Tomlinson 1984: 89).

5 On *Muscular Christianity and the Olympic Movement*, see Lucas 1975, 1976. Lucas examines Coubertin's philosophy of sport and in particular the influence of the British model and Thomas Arnold, claiming that Olympism is the 'first cousin' of Muscular Christianity (Lucas 1976: 51). See also Haley 1978; Mangan 1981; Mason 1980; Sandiford 1994.

6 On women and sport in general, see Guttmann 1991; Hall 1996; Hargreaves 1994; Hartmann-Tews and Pfister 2003; Mangan and Park 1987. On women and sport in China, see Hong, F. 1997. On women and the Olympic Games, see Daddario 1998; Hargreaves 1984.

7 On East Germany, see Carr 1974. On Romania's decision to ignore the Eastern Bloc's boycott of the 1984 Games, see Wilson 1994.

8 For a general history of modern Japan, see Nakamura 1998. On the Japanese economy, see Nakamura 1995.

9 On the Kwangju Uprising, see Lewis 2002; Shin and Kyung Moon Hwang 2003.

10 Michael Taylor, for instance, says: 'It is interesting to note that Japanese brands did not become household names outside the country until the Tokyo Olympics in 1964. The same was true [with Korean brands] after the Seoul Olympics in 1988' (Taylor 2005b: 6). Taylor claims that China hopes to emulate earlier Asian successes. See also Taylor 2005a: 1.

11 For a detailed discussion of the Olympic history of the 'two Chinas', see Chan 1985: 473–90; Guttmann 2002: 90–4; Hill 1992: 40–53; Hong and Xiaozheng 2003: 319–28.

12 On the Senkaku Islands, see Austin 1998: Chapter 6.

6 China's long march for the Olympics

1 There are two systems of Romanizing (Westernizing) Chinese. According to one, the Chinese Nationalist Party becomes Kuomintang (KMT); according to the other, it becomes Guomindang (GMD).

2 See, however, Chang and Halliday's (2005) alternative account of the Long March in which much of the official version is dismissed as misleading and incorrect.

3 There are competing accounts of the IOC's recognition of China's NOC. According to the Chinese Olympic Committee (COC), the NOC was first recognized by the IOC in 1931 (COC 3, December 2004), but according to another account, it was recognized early, in 1922 (Hill 1992: 40). The Olympic Directory gives the date of the foundation of China's NOC as 1910 (*ibid.*: 54).

4 As an active member of the Federation, China participated in the ten Far Eastern Championship Games held during the period of 1913–34. When Manchukuo applied to be admitted into the Federation, the Games came to an end.

5 Following Wang Zhengting, two more Chinese, Kong Xiangxi and Dong Shouyi, were elected IOC members in 1939 and 1947, respectively.

6 General Zhang Xueliang was the son of the northeastern warlord, Zhang Zuolin, who was killed by Japanese in 1931.

7 The XII and XIII Games were not held because of the Second World War.

8 During the 1992 Chinese New Year holidays, Deng, although having officially retired from all his official positions in the previous year, made an unusual 'inspection tour' to southern China, during which he urged the current leadership to take an even bolder move to transform China's economy along the 'socialist market' line and embrace the global capitalist economy.

9 China did not take part in the XXII Olympics held in Moscow in 1980, which was boycotted by two-fifths of the IOC-recognized NOCs in protest at the Soviet invasion of Afghanistan.

7 Conclusion

1 Human Rights in China (2006) has published a number of critical reports on torture in the PRC.

2 For a comprehensive account, see Amnesty International's report 'Organ harvesting', AI 22 March 2004, Section 9.

3 The gulag system in the PRC has been publicized through the writings of Harry Wu among others. See Wu 1992; Wu and Wakeman 1993. See also Laogai Research Foundation 2004, 2005; Seymour and Anderson 1998.

4 On judicial psychiatry, see Robin Munro's discussions (Munro 2000, 2001).

5 According to Human Rights Watch, 'a doctor with Beijing University's Mental Hygienics Institute' claims that Falun Gong followers 'suffer from "delusion-like subcultural beliefs", that their state of mind is not "normal", and that their "righteous choice is to seek help from psychiatrists in hospitals"' (HRW 2000). This report confirms that it is state practice to incarcerate Falun Gong adherents 'in mental institutions or psychiatric wards' (*ibid.*).

6 For reports on the governing regime's crackdown on Falun Gong, see Amnesty International 2000; and Human Rights Watch 2002. For a survey of research finds on Falun Gong, see Barend ter Haar's website (Haar 2006). Danny Schechter (2001) provides a useful journalistic account.

7 The Berlin case was also frequently referred to by critics of the award to Seoul of the 1988 Games.

8 On the notion of 'soft fascism', see Victoria De Grazia's *The Culture of Consent: Mass Organization of Leisure in Fascist Italy*, 1989.

9 On the PRC and human rights, see Close and Askew 2004; Copper and Lee 1997; Edwards, Henkin and Nathan 1986; Foot 2000; Kent 1993, 1999; Santoro 2000; Weatherley 1999.

10 Female athletes' experience with the outside world seems to have had beneficial consequences. Dong Jinxia's research with female athletes who had trained outside the PRC indicates that they had 'benefited [. . .] psychologically from these foreign experiences' (Dong Jinxia 2001: 14). That is, their 'views of the world, women and sport were expanded. With consequent greater self-assertion and individualism, they demanded more respect from coaches and wanted a more democratic relationship between coaches and athletes. These demands influenced the transformation of both sports management and sports culture in China' (*ibid.*).

11 Fan Hong uses the words 'Ma's cruelty and inhumanity' (Fan Hong 2004: 343).

12 For an examination of sexual exploitation in sport, see Brackenridge 2001.

13 See N. Jeffery, who refers to the resurfacing in the PRC of Helga Pfeiffer after she had disappeared for almost 13 years (Jeffery 2005: 20–2).

References

2008 – Free Tibet (2006) Online at: http://www.2008-freetibet.org (accessed 1 April 2006).

Abbs, M. (20 June 2005) 'Massacres and profits: a brief history of the Olympics', *Envisioning People's Struggles*, online at: http://users.resist.ca (accessed 20 June 2005).

Adams, W.L. and Gerlach, L.R. (eds) (2002) *The Olympic Games: Ancient and Modern*, Boston, MA: Pearson Custom Publishing.

Age (1993) 'The Chinese gulags', *Age*, 8 June: 17.

Alford, P. (2004) 'Asian Cup shocker another kick in a sensitive region', *Australian*, 9 August: 11.

Allen, J., Harris, R., Jago, L.K. and Veal, A.J. (eds) (2000) *Events Beyond 2000: Setting the Agenda*, Sydney: Australian Centre for Event Management.

Allen, R.E. (ed.) (1990) *Concise Oxford Dictionary of Current English*, 8th edition, Oxford: Oxford University Press.

American Heritage Dictionary (AHD) (2004a) 'Individualism', *American Heritage Dictionary of the English Language*, 4th edition, Boston, MA: Houghton Mifflin.

AHD (2004b) 'Laissez faire', *American Heritage Dictionary of the English Language*, 4th edition, Boston, MA: Houghton Mifflin.

Amnesty International (AI) (1996) *Ethiopia: Human Rights Trials and Delayed Justice*, London: Amnesty International Secretariat.

AI (2000) 'The crackdown on Falun Gong and other so-called "Heretical Organizations" ', online at: http://web.amnesty.org (accessed 1 April 2006).

AI (2001) 'Torture – a growing scourge in China – time for action', online at: http://web.amnesty.org (accessed 1 April 2006).

AI (13 July 2001) 'China: human rights and the spirit of Olympism', online at: http://www.amnesty.org (accessed 2 April 2006).

AI (22 March 2004) 'People's Republic of China. Executed "according to law"? – the death penalty in China', online at: http://web.amnesty.org.

AI (8 May 2004) 'Greece: Athens Olympic Games security raises human rights concerns', online at: http://www.amnesty.org (accessed 2 April 2006).

AI (25 May 2004) 'China', online at: http://web.amnesty.org/report2004 (accessed 3 July 2004).

AI (4 July 2004) 'Current campaigns', online at: http://web.amnesty.org/campaign (accessed 30 March 2006).

AI (5 August 2005) 'China: human rights – a long way to go before the Olympics', online at: http://www.amnesty.org (accessed 5 August 2005).

Amnesty International USA (2006) 'Campaign to abolish the death penalty in China', online at: http://www.amnestyusa.org (accessed 1 April 2006).

Anderson, B. (1983) *Imagined Communities: Reflections on the Origins and Spread of Nationalism*, London: Verso.

Anderson, T., Persson, C., Sahlberg, B. and Ström, L. (eds) (1999) *The Impacts of Mega-Events*, Östersund: European Tourism Research Institute.

Andranovich, G. and Burbank, M. (2004) 'Regime politics and the 2012 Olympic Games', *California Politics and Policy*, 8, 1: 1–18.

Andranovich, G., Burbank, M. and Heying, C. (2001) 'Olympic cities: lessons learned from mega-event politics', *Journal of Urban Affairs*, 23, 2: 113–31.

Andrews, J.C. (1975) 'Physical education and Olympism: concepts, problems and comments', *FIEP Bulletin*, 45: 65–74.

Answers.com (AC) (3 November 2005) 'Individualism', online at: http://www.answers.com (accessed 3 November 2005).

AC (15 January 2006) 'Compact', online at: http://www.answers.com (accessed 15 January 2006).

AC (11 February 2006) 'Olympiad', online at: http://www.answers.com (accessed 11 February 2006).

Anthony, D. (1992) 'The propagation of Olympic education as a weapon against the corruption and commercialisation of world-wide sport', *International Olympic Academy (IOA): Thirty-Second Session, 17 June–2 July*, Lausanne: International Olympic Committee: 157–64.

Arbena, J.L. (1996) 'Mexico City, 1968: the Games of the XIXth Olympiad', in J. Findling and K. D. Pelle (eds), *Historical Dictionary of the Modern Olympic Movement*, Westport, CT: Greenwood Publishing: 139–47.

Asiaco (2004) 'China: society and culture: human rights', online at: http://vip.asiaco.com (accessed 2 April 2006).

Association of National Olympic Committees (ANOC) (October 2005) 'National Olympic Committees', online at: http://www.acnolympic.org (accessed 23 October 2005).

Associated Press (2006) 'IOC Executive Board backs Olympic recognition for Pacific islands', online at: http://sports.yahoo.com/olympics/torino2006 (accessed 5 February 2006).

Athens 2004 (2005) 'Unforgettable Games, dream Games', online at: http://www.athens2004.com (accessed 23 October 2005).

Austin, G. (1998) *China's Ocean Frontier: International Law, Military Force, and National Development*, St. Leonards, NSW: Allen & Unwin.

Australian (1998) 'Early alerts on Beijing blooms were ignored', *Australian*, 16 January.

Australian (2006) 'Chinese "bred" basketball star', *Australian*, 19 January.

Axford, B. (1995) *The Global System: Economics, Politics and Culture*, Cambridge: Polity Press.

Ayers, B. (2005) 'China embracing Fascism', *Charleston Gazette*, 24 April.

Bairner, A. (2001) *Sport, Nationalism and Globalization*, Albany, NY: State University of New York Press.

Baker, N. (1994) 'The Games that almost weren't: London 1948', in R. K. Barney and K. V. Meier (eds), *Critical Reflections on Olympic Ideology, Second International*

Symposium for Olympic Research, London, Ontario: Centre for Olympic Studies, University of Western Ontario: 107–16.

Bale, J. and Christensen M. (eds) (2004) *Post-Olympism? Questioning Sport in the Twenty First Century*, Oxford: Berg.

Barney, R.K. (1992a) 'This great symbol: tricks of history', *Olympic Review*, 301: 627–41.

Barney, R.K. (1992b) 'The Olympics: a history of the modern Games', in A. Guttmann, *Olympika: The International Journal of Olympic Studies*, 3: 135–40.

Barney, R.K., Scott, M. and Moore, R. (1999) 'Old boys at work and play: the International Olympic Committee and Canadian co-option, 1928–1946', *Olympika: The International Journal of Olympic Studies*, 8: 81–104.

Barney, R.K., Wenn, S.R. and Martyn, S.G. (2002) *Selling the Five Rings: The International Olympic Committee and the Rise of Olympic Commercialism*, Salt Lake City, UT: University of Utah Press.

Barrett, N. (1980) *Olympics 1980*, London: Piper Books.

Bartov, O. (2006) 'Life and death in the Red Army', *Times Literary Supplement*, 25 January.

Bass, A. (2002) *Not the Triumph but the Struggle: The 1968 Olympics and the Making of the Black Athlete*, Minneapolis, MN: University of Minnesota Press.

Baylis, J. and Smith, S. (eds) (1997) *The Globalization of World Politics: An Introduction to International Relations*, Oxford: Oxford University Press.

Baylis, J. and Smith, S. (eds) (2004) *The Globalization of World Politics: An Introduction to International Relations*, 3rd edition, Oxford: Oxford University Press.

Beate, E. (1996) 'Volunteer perception of learning and satisfaction in a mega-event: the case of the XVII Olympic Winter Games in Lillehammer', *Festival and Event Management*, 4, 3/4: 75–84.

Beaverstock, J., Smith, R. and Taylor, P. (2000) 'World city network: a new metageography', *Annals of the Association of American Geographers*, 90, 1: 123–34.

Beck, U. and Beck-Gernsheim, E. (2002) *Individualization: Institutionalized Individualism and its Social and Political Consequences*, London: Sage.

Beck, U., Giddens, A. and Lash, S. (1995) *Reflexive Modernization: Politics, Tradition and Aesthetics in the Modern Social Order*, Stamford, CA: Stamford University Press.

Bedeski, R.E. (1994) *The Transformation of South Korea: Reform and Reconstitution in the Sixth Republic under Roh Tae Woo, 1987–1992*, London: Routledge.

Beeson, M. (1999) *Competing Capitalisms*, London: Macmillan.

Beichman, A. (2001) 'China's unworthy invitation', *Washington Times*, 10 July.

Beijing Organizing Committee for the Olympic Games (BOCOG) (30 July 2005) 'Beijing 2008', online at: http://en.beijing2008.com (accessed 30 July 2005).

BOCOG (29 October 2005) 'The Olympic emblem', online at: http://en.beijing2008.com (accessed 29 October 2005).

BOCOG (14 January 2006a) 'Beijing 2008 Olympic marketing plan', online at: http://en.beijing2008.com.

BOCOG (14 January 2006b) 'Sponsors of the Beijing 2008 Olympic Games', online at: http://en.beijing2008.com (accessed 14 January 2006).

BOCOG (21 February 2006), 'Beijing 2008 Olympic marketing plan overview', online at: http://en.beijing2008.com (accessed 21 February 2006).

BOCOG (22 February 2006) 'Marketing Beijing 2008', online at: http://en.beijing2008.com (accessed 22 February 2006).

BOCOG (4 March 2006) 'Goals and concepts', online at: http://en.beijing2008.com (accessed 4 March 2006).

Bell, D. (1996) *The Cultural Contradictions of Capitalism*, New York: Harper Collins (originally published 1976).

Bell, J. and Sumner, T. (2002) *The Complete Idiots Guide to Protestantism and the Reformation*, Indianapolis, IN: Alpha Books.

Bell, R. (2001) 'The Olympic creed', *Sports Journal*, 4, 1: 1.

Bellah, R., Madson, R., Sullivan, W., Swidler, A. and Tipton, S. (1985) *Habits of the Heart: Individualism and Commitment in American Life*, Berkeley, CA: University of California Press.

Bellos, A. (2002) *Futebol: The Brazilian Way of Life*, London: Bloomsbury.

Benzi, G. (ed.) (2005) *The Ism Book*, online at: http://www.ismbook.com.

Berger, M.T. and Borer, D.A. (1997) *The Rise of East Asia*, London: Routledge.

Berger, P. (2002) 'Introduction: the cultural dynamics of globalization', in P. Berger and S. Huntington (eds), *Many Globalizations: Cultural Diversity in the Contemporary World*, Oxford: Oxford University Press.

Berger, P. and Huntington, S. (eds) (2002) *Many Globalizations: Cultural Diversity in the Contemporary World*, Oxford: Oxford University Press.

Berlioux, M. (ed.) (1972) *Olympism*, Lausanne: International Olympic Committee.

Bernstein, A. (2000) 'Things you can see from there you can't see from here: globalization, media and the Olympics', *Journal of Sport and Social Issues*, 24, 4: 351–69.

Bernstein, A. and Blain, N. (eds) (2003) *Sport, Media, Culture: Global and Local Dimensions*, London: Frank Cass.

Black, D. and Bezanson, S. (2004) 'The Olympic Games, human rights and democratisation: lessons from Seoul and implications for Beijing', *Third World Quarterly*, 25, 7: 1245–61.

Black, D. and Van Der Westhuizen, J. (2004) 'The allure of global games for "semi-peripheral" polities and spaces: a research agenda', *Third World Quarterly*, 25, 7: 1195–214.

Blanchard, K. (1995) *The Anthropology of Sport: An Introduction*, Westport, CT: Greenwood Publishing.

Blecher, M. (2005) 'Inequality and capitalism in China', American Political Science Association Annual Meeting, Washington, DC, 2 September.

Bloomberg (15 January 2006) 'LVMH, President Chain shares may benefit from China's growth', online at: http://www.bloomberg.com/apps.

Blume, G. (2003) 'Capitalism, the Chinese way', *World Press Review*, 50, 1, online at: www.worldpress.org (accessed 30 March 2006).

Boland, L. (1995) *The Principles of Economics*, London: Routledge.

Boyle, R. and Haynes, R. (2000) *Power Play: Sport, the Media and Popular Culture*, London: Longman.

Brackenridge, C. (2001) *Spoilsports: Understanding and Preventing Sexual Exploitation in Sport*, London: Routledge.

Bragg, R. (1997) 'A year later, some Atlantans are asking: what Olympic legacy?', *New York Times*, 20 July.

Brainy Quote (BQ) (2005) 'Pierre de Courbertin quotes', online at: http://www.brainyquote.com (accessed 2 November 2005).

Brasher, C. (1972) *Munich '72*, London: Stanley Paul.

Brichford, M. (1996) 'Munich, 1972: the Games of the XXth Olympiad', in

J. Findling and K. D. Pelle (eds), *Historical Dictionary of the Modern Olympic Movement*, Westport, CN: Greenwood Publishing: 148–52.

BBC (25 November 1998) 'Sydney embarrassed by Games row', online at: http://news.bbc.co.uk (accessed 13 November 2005).

BBC (12 December 1998) 'Olympic "vote buying" scandal', online at: http://news.bbc.co.uk (accessed 13 November 2005).

BBC (14 December 1998) 'China alleges unfair treatment during Olympics bid', online at: http://news.bbc.co.uk (accessed 13 November 2005).

BBC (23 January 1999) 'Sydney sucked into Olympics scandal', online at: http://news.bbc.co.uk (accessed 13 November 2005).

BBC (25 January 1999) 'Olympics bidding shake-up', online at: http://news.bbc.co.uk (accessed 12 January 2006).

BBC (1 March 1999) 'Olympics must ban "gift-giving" ', online at: http://news.bbc.co.uk (accessed 31 March 2006).

BBC (15 March 1999a) 'Sydney Olympics bid "broke rules" ', online at: http://news.bbc.co.uk (accessed 30 March 2006).

BBC (15 March 1999b) 'Timeline: Olympics corruption scandal', online at: http://news.bbc.co.uk (accessed 13 November 2005).

BBC (24 June 2004) 'China uncovers Olympic corruption', online at: http://news.bbc.co.uk (accessed 2 April 2006).

BBC (9 August 2004) 'China road official "took bribes" ', online at: http://news.bbc.co.uk (accessed 2 April 2006).

BBC (8 March 2005) 'China's tight rein on online growth', online at: http://news.bbc.co.uk.

BBC (21 April 2005) 'China steps up anti-drugs effort', online at: http://news.bbc.co.uk (accessed 17 November 2005).

BBC (10 May 2005) 'China PC firm aiming for top sport', online at: http://news.bbc.co.uk.

BBC (27 July 2005) 'SNP's Olympics plea is rejected', online at: http://news.bbc.co.uk (accessed 30 March 2006).

BBC (22 September 2005) 'Country profile: Taiwan', online at: http://news.bbc.co.uk (accessed 23 October 2005).

BBC (13 October 2005) 'Timeline: China', online at: http://news.bbc.co.uk (accessed 30 March 2006).

BBC (16 November 2005) 'Profile: World Trade Oranisation', online at: http://news.bbc.co.uk (accessed 16 November 2005).

BBC (17 November 2005) 'Pinsent shocked by China training', online at: http://news.bbc.co.uk (accessed 30 March 2006).

BBC (24 November 2005) 'Country profile: China', online at: http://news.bbc.co.uk (accessed 30 March 2006).

BBC (19 December 2005) 'Chinese growth to top 10% in 2005', online at: http://news.bbc.co.uk (accessed 30 March 2006).

BBC (23 December 2005) ' "Voting error" gave London Games', online at: http://news.bbc.co.uk (accessed 30 March 2006).

BBC (5 March 2006) 'China "to dwarf G7 states by 2050" ', online at: http://news.bbc.co.uk (accessed 30 March 2006).

British Olympics Association (BOA) (3 November 2005) 'Olympic issues: drugs', online at: http://www.olympics.org.uk (accessed 3 November 2005).

BOA (18 November 2005) 'Olympic issues', online at: http://www.olympics.org.uk (accessed 18 November 2005).

BOA (21 February 2006) 'International Olympic Committee', online at: http://www.olympics.org.uk (accessed 21 February 2006).

Brohm, J.-M. (1978) *Sport: A Prison of Measured Time*, London: Ink Links.

Brown, M. (ed.) (2000) *The Rise of China*, Cambridge, MA: MIT Press.

Brownell, S. (1995) *Training the Body for China: Sports in the Moral Order of the People's Republic*, Chicago, IL: University of Chicago Press.

Brundage, A. (1966) 'The Olympic Movement: objectives, and achievements', *Gymnasion*, 3: 3–4.

Brundage, A. (2002a) 'Farewell address to the 73rd IOC Session in Munich, October, 1972', in W. L. Adams and L. R. Gerlach (eds), *The Olympic Games: Ancient and Modern*, Boston, MA: Pearson Custom Publishing: 157–62.

Brundage, A. (2002b) 'On global Olympism', in W. L. Adams and L. R. Gerlach (eds), *The Olympic Games: Ancient and Modern*, Boston, MA: Pearson Custom Publishing: 137–44.

Bryane, M. (2002) 'Theorising the politics of globalisation: a critique of Held et al.'s "transformationalism" ', *Journal of Economic and Social Research*, 4, 2: 3–17.

Buchanan, I. and Mallon, B. (2006) *Historical Dictionary of the Olympic Movement*, 3rd edition, Lanham, MD: Scarecrow Press, third edition.

Burbank, M., Andranovich, G. and Heying, C. (2001) *Olympic Dreams: The Impact of Mega-events on Local Politics*, Boulder, CO: Lynne Rienner Publishers.

Buruma, I. (2005) 'The rest is history: China's insistent portrayal of Japan as brutal aggressor shows how ethnic nationalism is still used to shore up authoritarianism', *Financial Times Weekend Magazine*, 22 January.

Buschmann, J. and Lennartz, K. (1998) 'Germany and the 1948 Olympic Games in London', *Journal of Olympic History*, 6, 3: 22–8.

Bush, R. (2005) *Untying the Knot: Making Peace in the Taiwan Strait*, Washington, DC: Brookings Institution Press.

Business Week (27 October 2003) 'The BRICs are coming', online at: http://www.businessweek.com (accessed 30 March 2006).

Cai, J. and Yang, Y. (2004) *Ao Yun Zan Zhu Mou Lüe* (The Strategy of Olympic Sponsorship), Beijing: Jing Ji Guan Li Chu Ban She.

Calvert, J. (2002) 'How to buy the Olympics', *Observer Sport Monthly*, 21: 32–7.

Camus, A. (1962) 'What I owe football', in B. Glanville (ed.), *The Footballers Companion*, London: Eyre and Spottiswoode.

Canada Tibet Committee (CTC) (9 March 2006) 'Home page', online at: http://www.tibet.ca/en (accessed 9 March 2006).

Carr, G. (1974) 'The use of sport in the German Democratic Republic for the promotion of national consciousness and international prestige', *Journal of Sport History*, 1, 2: 123–36.

Cashman, R. (1995) 'When the bid party's over: Sydney's problem of delivering the Games', *Australian Quarterly*, 67, 1: 49–54.

Cashman, R. and Hughes, A. (eds) (1999) *Staging the Olympics: The Event and its Impact*, Sydney: University of New South Wales Press.

Cashman, R., Toohey, K., Darcy, S., Simons, C. and Stewart, R. (2004) 'When the carnival is over: evaluating the outcomes of mega sporting events in Australia', *Sporting Traditions*, 21, 1: 1–32.

CIA (5 October 2005) 'Cook Islands', *World Fact Book*, online at: http://www.cia.gov/ cia/publications/factbook (accessed 23 October 2005).

Central Intelligence Agency (CIA) (1 November 2005) 'China', *World Fact Book*, online at: http://www.cia.gov/cia/publications/factbook (accessed 15 November 2005).

Centre for Civil Society (2004) 'Definition of civil society', *London School of Economics*, online at: http://www.lse.ac.uk/collections/CCS/introduction.htm (accessed 22 March 2004).

Chamerois, N. (2002) *The Globalisation of the Olympic Games – From Seoul (1988) to Sydney (2000)*, Lausanne: Library of the Olympic Museum.

Chan, G. (1985) 'The "Two-China" problem and the Olympic formula', *Pacific Affairs*, 58, 3: 473–90.

Chanda, N. and Kaye, L. (1993) 'Circling Hawks', *Far Eastern Economic Review (FEER)*, 7 October: 12–13.

Chandler, J. (2005) 'Address to the 2004 International Conference on Sport and Religion', *The Second International Conference on Sport and Religion*, Northfield Minnesota, October, online at: http://www.stolaf.edu/services (accessed 30 March 2006).

Chang, F.A. (1996) 'The universality of the Olympic Games', Olympic Message, 26, 1: 153–65.

Chang, J. and Halliday, J. (2005) *Mao: The Unknown Story*, New York: A. A. Knopf.

Chase, M. (2002) *You've Got Dissent*, Santa Monica, CA: Rand Corporation.

Chaudhary, V. (2001) 'Olympic reaction: "This decision will allow a police state to bask in reflected glory" ', *Guardian*, 14 July.

China Daily (20 October 2004) 'Chinese to have FBI training for Beijing Olympics', online at: http://www.chinadaily.com.cn (accessed 30 May 2006).

China Daily (25 March 2005) 'Olympics: Beijing stresses anti-terrorism', online at: http://www.chinadaily.com.cn (accessed 30 March 2006).

China Internet Information Center (CIIC) (20 November 2005) 'China's population mix', online at: http://www.china.org.cn (accessed 20 November 2005).

China Society for Human Rights Studies (CSHRS) (2003) 'China's human rights', online at: http://www.humanrights-china.org (accessed 2 April 2006).

China View (3 March 2006) 'Chinese lawmakers warn against extravagant Olympics', *Xinhua News Agency*, online at: http://news.xinhuanet.com.

Chinese Olympic Committee (COC) (27 March 2004) 'Bid for 2000', online at: http:// en.olympic.cn (accessed 30 March 2006).

COC (31 December 2004) 'Olympic Movement', online at: http://en.olympic.cn (accessed 31 December 2004).

COC (2006) 'Olympic Movement', online at: http://en.olympic.cn (accessed 24 March 2006).

Ching, F. (2004) 'Removing the thorn from Japan–China ties', *Japan Times*, 19 September.

Chorbajian, L. and Mosco, V. (1981) '1976 and 1980 Olympic boycott coverage', *Arena Review*, 5, 3: 3–28.

Cicarelli, J. and Kowarsky, D.J. (1973) 'The economics of the Olympic Games', *Business and Economic Dimensions*, 9: 1–5.

Clarke, S.J. (1976) 'Amateurism, Olympism and pedagogy', in M. Hart (ed.), *Sport in the Sociocultural Process*, 2nd edition, Dubuque, IA: William C. Brown.

Close, P. (1995) *Citizenship, Europe and Change*, Basingstoke: Macmillan.

Close, P. (2000) *The Legacy of Supranationalism*, Basingstoke: Macmillan.

Close, P. and Askew, D. (2004a) *Asia Pacific and Human Rights: A Global Political Economy Perspective*, Aldershot: Ashgate Publishing.

Close, P. and Askew, D. (2004b) 'Globalisation and football in East Asia', in W. Manzenreiter and J. Horne (eds), *Football Goes East: Business, Culture and the People's Game in China, Japan and South Korea*, London: Routledge: 243–56.

Close, P. and Ohki-Close, E. (1999) *Supranationalism in the New World Order: Global Processes Reviewed*, Basingstoke: Macmillan.

Coalition for the International Criminal Court (CICC) (4 July 2004) 'The Statute of the ICC, signatories and ratifications', *International Criminal Court Now*, online at: http://www.iccnow.org (accessed 30 March 2006).

Cochrane, A., Peck, J. and Tickell, A. (1996) 'Manchester plays games: exploring the local politics of globalisation', *Urban Studies*, 33, 8: 1319–36.

Collins, M. (2002) 'China's Olympics', *Contemporary Review*, 280: 31.

Columbia University (1994) 'DeBary: Confucius joins modern Chinese hierarchy', *Columbia University Record*, 20, 12, online at: http://www.columbia.edu/cu (accessed 30 March 2006).

Colwell, J. (1981) 'Sociocultural determinants of Olympic success', in J. O. Segrave and D. Chu (eds), *Olympism*, Champaign, ILL: Human Kinetics: 242–61.

Concise Oxford Dictionary of Current English, 8th edition (1990), Oxford: Oxford University Press.

Connolly, W. (1974) *The Terms of Political Discourse*, Boston, MA: Heath, 1974; Princeton, NJ: Princeton University Press, 1984.

Copper, J.F. and Lee, T. (1997) *Coping with a Bad Global Image: Human Rights in the People's Republic of China, 1993–1994*, Lanham, MD: University Press of America.

Coubertin, P. de (1898) 'The Olympic Games of 1896', *Century*, 31: 39–53.

Coubertin, P. de (1913) *Revue Olympique*, August.

Coubertin, P. de (1967) *The Olympic Idea: Discourses and Essays*, Schorndorf: Karl Hofmann.

Coubertin, P. de (1978) 'The Olympic Games of 1896', in B. Lowe, D. Kanin and A. Strenk (eds), *Sport and International Relations*, Champaign, ILL: Stipes: 118–27.

Coubertin, P. de (1979) *Olympic Memoirs*, Lausanne: International Olympic Committee.

Coubertin, P. de (1986a) *Textes Choisis. Tome I: Revelation*, edited by G. Rioux, Zurich: Weidmann.

Coubertin, P. de (1986b) *Textes Choisis. Tome II: Olympisme*, edited by N. Müller, Zurich: Weidmann.

Coubertin, P. de (1986c) *Textes Choisis. Tome III: Pratique Sportive*, edited by N. Müller and O. Schantz, Zurich: Weidmann.

Coubertin, P. de (1988a) 'The Olympic Games of 1896', in J. Segrave and D. Chu (eds), *The Olympic Games in Transition*, Champaign, ILL: Human Kinetics: 179–90.

Coubertin, P. de (1988b) 'Why I revived the Olympic Games', in J. Segrave and D. Chu (eds), *The Olympic Games in Transition*, Champaign, ILL: Human Kinetics, 101–06.

Coubertin, P. de (1989) *Olympic Memoirs*, Toronto: University of Toronto Press.

Coubertin, P. de (2000) *Olympism: Selected Writings*, Lausanne: International Olympic Committee.

Coubertin, P. de (2002a) 'The charter of amateurism (1902)', in W. L. Adams and L. R. Gerlach (eds), *The Olympic Games: Ancient and Modern*, Boston, MA: Pearson Custom Publishing: 113–15.

Coubertin, P. de (2002b) 'The emblem and the flag', in W. L. Adams and L. R. Gerlach (eds), *The Olympic Games: Ancient and Modern*, Boston, MA: Pearson Custom Publishing: 119–20.

Coubertin, P. de (2002c) 'Why I revived the Olympic Games', in W. L. Adams and L. R. Gerlach (eds), *The Olympic Games: Ancient and Modern*, Boston, MA: Pearson Custom Publishing: 109–12.

Coubertin, P. de (2002d) 'The women at the Olympic Games', in W. L. Adams and L. R. Gerlach (eds), *The Olympic Games: Ancient and Modern*, Boston, MA: Pearson Custom Publishing: 117–18.

Coughlan, D. (1 February 2006) 'Postmodernism (1950–2005)', *Literary Encyclopedia*, online at: http://www.litencyc.com.

Cox, K.R. (1997) *Spaces of Globalization: Reasserting the Power of the Local*, New York: Guilford Press.

Crawford, K. (30 August 2004) 'NBC Universal rings in Athens profits', *CNN Money*, online at: http://money.cnn.com (accessed 24 March 2006).

Crossman, J. and Lappage, R. (1992) 'Canadian athletes' perceptions of the 1980 Olympic boycott', *Sociology of Sport Journal*, 9, 4: 354–71.

Cumings, B. (2001) 'China goes for the gold', *Nation*, 273, 5: 30.

Cyphers, L. (1993) 'U.S. activists try to put hurdles in way of Beijing's bid to host 2000 Olympics', *Wall Street Journal*, 2 April.

Czula, R. (1975) 'Pierre de Coubertin and modern Olympism', *Quest*, 24: 10–18.

Czula, R. (1978a) 'The Munich Olympics assassinations: a second look', *Journal of Sport and Social Issues*, 2, 1: 19–23.

Czula, R. (1978b) 'Social determinants of Olympic idealism', *Journal of Sport Behavior*, 1: 118–30.

Czula, R. (1978c) 'Sport and Olympic idealism', *International Review of Sport Sociology*, 13: 66–79.

Czula, R. (1980) 'Social determinants of Olympic idealism', *Review of Sport and Leisure*, 5: 46–69.

Czula, R., Flanagan, L. and Nasatir, D. (1976) 'A multidimensional analysis of Olympic idealism', *Review of Sport and Leisure*, 1: 1–14.

Da Costa, L. (1992) 'The central problems of Olympism in the face of the constraints of commercialisation, and possible solutions', in *International Olympic Academy: Thirty-Second Session, 17th June–2nd July*, Lausanne: International Olympic Committee: 77–84.

Da Costa, L. (2002) 'Olympic studies: current intellectual crossroads', Rio de Janeiro: University Gama Filho, Research Group on Olympic Studies (PPGEF), online at: http://www.cenesp.uel.br (accessed 24 March 2006).

Daddario, G. (1998) *Women's Sport and Spectacle: Gendered Television Coverage and the Olympic Games*, Westport, CN: Praeger.

Davenport, J. (1996) 'Olympism: foundation of the Olympic movement', *Journal of the International Council for Health, Physical Education and Recreation*, 32, 4: 26–30.

Davies, E. (10 March 2005) 'China's magnificent past', online at: http://news.bbc.co.uk (accessed 30 March 2006).

Davies, E.L. (1996) 'Rome, 1960: the Games of the XVIIth Olympiad', in J. Findling and K. D. Pelle (eds), *Historical Dictionary of the Modern Olympic Movement*, Westport, CN: Greenwood Publishing: 128–34.

De Grazia, V. (1989) *Yawarakai Fashizumu: Itaria Fashizumu to Yoka no Soshiki* (Soft Fascism: Italian Fascism and the Organization of Leisure), Tokyo: Yûhikaku (translation of De Grazia, V. *The Culture of Consent: Mass Organization of Leisure in Fascist Italy*).

De Moragas Spa, M. (1999) 'Functions and responsibilities of Olympic research: the experience of the Barcelona Olympic Study Centre', in T. Anderson, C. Persson, B. Sahlberg and L. I. Ström (eds), *The Impacts of Mega-Events*, Östersund: European Tourism Research Institute, 89–104.

De Moragas Spa, M., Rivenburgh, N. and Larson, J.F. (2004) 'Local visions of the global: some perspectives from around the world', in D. Rowe (ed.), *Critical Readings: Sport, Culture and the Media*, Maidenhead: Open University Press: 186–209.

Department for Culture, Media and Sport (2002) *London Olympics 2012: Costs and Benefits*, London: Department for Culture, Media and Sport.

Department of Economic and Social Affairs of the United Nations Secretariat (DESA) (2005) *The Millennium Development Goals Report 2005*, New York: United Nations.

Diem, C. (1970) *The Olympic Idea: Discourses and Essays*, Schorndorf: Verlag Karl Hoffmann.

Diem, L. and Knoesel, E. (1974) *The Games: The Official Report of the XXth Olympiad, Munich, 1972*, Munich: Munich Olympic Games Organising Committee.

Dong Jinxia (2001) 'Cultural changes: mobility, stratification and sportswomen in the new China', *Culture, Sport, Society*, 4, 3: 1–26.

Dong Yunhu (2004) 'Inclusion of human rights an important milestone', *People's Daily*, 4 March.

Donnelly, J. (2003) *Universal Human Rights in Theory and Practice*, Ithaca, NY: Cornell University Press.

Donnelly, P. (1996) 'Prolympism: sport monoculture as crisis and opportunity', *Quest*, 48, 1: 25–42.

Dunning J. (2003) *Making Globalization Good*, Oxford: Oxford University Press.

Durantez, D.C., Rosandich, T.P. and Haley, M. (1996) *The Atlanta Star – An Olympic Forest. A Study in Olympism: History, Art, Culture and Science*, Daphne, ALA: United States Sports Academy.

Durry, J. (1997) 'Le vrai Pierre de Coubertin', Paris: UP Productions, online at: http://www.coubertin.ch (accessed 24 March 2006).

Dyreson, M. (1998) 'Olympic Games and historical imagination: notes from the faultline of tradition and modernity', *Olympika: The International Journal of Olympic Studies*, 7: 25–42.

Dyreson, M. (1999) 'Selling American civilization: the Olympic Games of 1920 and American culture', *Olympika: The International Journal of Olympic Studies*, 8: 1–41.

Eastman, R. (1999) *The Ways of Religion: An Introduction to the Major Traditions*, Oxford: Oxford University Press.

Economist (1993) 'The Beijing Olympics?', *Economist*, 21 August.

Economist (2000) 'All to strive for', *Economist*, 16 September.

Edwards, H. (1979) 'The Olympic project for human rights', *The Black Scholar*, 6: 2–8.

Edwards, R., Henkin, L. and Nathan, A. (1986) *Human Rights in Contemporary China*, New York: Columbia University Press.

Elliott, J. (1998) 'The fate of reason: Max Weber and the problem of (ir)rationality', *University of North Carolina*, online at: http://www.unc.edu (accessed 20 October 2005).

Ellmers, G. (2003) 'Social compact, properly understood', *The Claremont Institute*, online at: http://www.claremont.org/writings (accessed 30 March 2006).

Elstad, B. (1996) 'Volunteer perception of learning and satisfaction in a mega-event: the case of the XVII Olympic Winter Games in Lillehammer', *Festival Management and Event Tourism*, 4, 1: 75–83.

Espy, R. (1979) *The Politics of the Olympic Games: With an Epilogue, 1976–1980*, Berkeley, CA: University of California Press.

Evans, G. (1998) *The Penguin Dictionary of International Relations*, Harmondsworth: Penguin.

Far Eastern Economic Review (FEER) (1997) 'Business aside: Sydney's Olympic dreams', *Far Eastern Economic Review*, 160, 48: 1.

FEER (23 May 2001) 'Should Beijing host the 2008 Olympics?', *Far Eastern Economic Review*, online at: http://www.taiwandc.org (accessed 30 March 2006).

Farhi, P. (2006) 'Where the rich and elite meet to compete', *Washington Post*, 5 February.

Ferrand, A. and Torrigiani, L. (2005) *Marketing of Olympic Sport Organisations*, Champaign, ILL: Human Kinetics.

Findling, J. and Pelle, K.D. (eds) (1996) *Historical Dictionary of the Modern Olympic Movement*, Westport, CN: Greenwood Publishing.

Finfacts (2005a) 'China's revolution: private sector controls 2/3 of economy', online at: http://www.finfacts.com (accessed 13 September 2005).

Finfacts (2005b) 'China becomes the world's fourth biggest economy overnight', online at: http://www.finfacts.com (accessed 20 December 2005).

Foot, R. (2000) *Rights Beyond Borders: The Global Community and the Struggle over Human Rights in China*, Oxford: Oxford University Press.

Fornäs, J. (1995) *Cultural Theory and Late Modernity*, London: Sage.

Fox-Genovese, E. (1992) *Feminism without Illusions: A Critique of Individualism*, Chapel Hill, NC: University of North Carolina Press.

Frank, G. (1998) *Reorient: Global Economy in the Asian Age*, Berkeley, CA: University of California Press.

Free Tibet Campaign (2006) 'Campaigns', online at: http://www.freetibet.org/campaigns/home.html (accessed 1 April 2006).

French, S.P. and Disher, M.E. (1997) 'Atlanta and the Olympics: a one-year retrospective', *Journal of the American Planning Association*, 63, 3: 379–92.

Fukuyama, F. (1989) 'The end of history?', *National Interest*, Summer: 3–35.

Fukuyma, F. (1992) *The End of History and the Last Man*, New York: Free Press.

Fukuyama, F. (2004) *State-Building: Governance and World Order in the 21st Century*, Ithaca, NY: Cornell University Press.

Fukuyama, F. (2006) *America at the Crossroads: Democracy, Power, and the Neoconservative Legacy*, New Haven, CT: Yale University Press.

Gafner, R. (ed.) (1994) *The International Olympic Committee: One Hundred Years: The Idea, the Presidents, the Achievements, 1894–1994*, Lausanne: International Olympic Committee, three volumes.

Galeano, E. (2003) *Soccer in Sun and Shadow*, London: Verso, new edition (originally, 1995).

Games Bids (28 July 2005) 'Past host city election results', online at: http://www.gamesbids.com (accessed 28 July 2005).

Games Bids (29 July 2005) 'Glossary', online at: http://www.gamesbids.com (accessed 29 July 2005).

Games Bids (4 February 2006) 'The election for the 13th IOC Olympic Congress', online at: http://www.gamesbids.com (accessed 4 February 2006).

Games Bids (20 February 2006) 'Bid profile and fact sheet – 2016 Summer Olympic bids', online at: http://www.gamesbids.com (accessed 20 February 2006).

Games Bids (22 February 2006) 'Past elections', online at: http://www.gamesbids.com (accessed 22 February 2006).

Gearing, J. (23 December 2003) 'Tibet and the Olympic factor', *Asia Times*, online at: http://www.atimes.com (accessed 30 March 2006).

George, C. (2005) 'Camus played in goal for Nigeria', *Football Poets*, online at: http://www.footballpoets.org (accessed 30 March 2006).

Gerlach, L.R. (2004) *Winter Olympics: From Chamonix to Salt Lake*, Salt Lake City, UT: University of Utah Press.

German Historical Museum (2005) 'Elective affinity', online at http://www.dhm.de/ausstellungen/wahlverwandtschaft/electiveaffinity.htm (accessed 20 December 2005).

Giddens, A. (1991) *The Consequences of Modernity*, Cambridge: Polity Press.

Gillen, P. (1994) 'The Olympic Games and global society', *Arena*, 4: 5–15.

Giller, N. (1980) *The 1980 Olympic Handbook: A Guide to the Moscow Olympics and a History of the Games*, London: Arthur Baker.

Gimenez, M. (2002) 'Connecting Marx and feminism in the era of globalization: a preliminary investigation', *Socialism and Democracy Online*, 19, 2, online at: http://www.sdonline.org/35/connectingmarxandfeminism.htm (accessed 4 November 2005).

Gissendanner, C.H. (1996) 'African American women Olympians: the impact of race, gender and class ideologies, 1932–1968', *Research Quarterly for Exercise and Sport*, 67, 2: 172–82.

Gittings, J. (2001) 'China shrugs off Olympic warning on human rights', *Observer*, online at: http://observer.guardian.co.uk (accessed 24 March 2006).

Giulianotti, R. (1999) *Football: A Sociology of the Global Game*, Cambridge: Polity Press.

Giulianotti, R. (2004) 'Human rights, globalization and sentimental education: the case of sport', *Sport in Society*, 7, 3: 355–69.

Gladney, D. (2000) 'China's national insecurity: old challenges at the dawn of the new millennium', *Institute for National Strategic Studies, National Defense University*, online at: http://www.ndu.edu (accessed 30 March 2006).

Glasius, M. and Kaldor, M. (2002) 'The state of global civil society', in M. Glasius, M. Kaldor and H. Anheier (eds), *Global Civil Society 2002*, Oxford: Oxford University Press.

Goethe, J.W. (1978) *Elective Affinities*, Harmondsworth: Penguin (originally published 1809).

Gold, J. and Gold, M. (2005) *Cities of Culture: Staging International Festivals and the Urban Agenda, 1851–2000*, Aldershot: Ashgate Publishing.

Goldman, M. and Lee, L. (2002) *An Intellectual History of Modern China*, Cambridge: Cambridge University Press.

Goldstein, A. (2003) 'An emerging China's emerging grand strategy' in C. Ikenberry and M. Mastanduno (eds), *International Relations Theory and the Asia-Pacific*, New York: Columbia University Press.

Goldstein, A. (2005) *Rising to the Challenge: China's Grand Strategy and International Security*, Stanford, CA: Stanford University Press.

Goodhart, P. and Chataway, C. (1968) *War without Weapons*, London: W. H. Allen.

Gordon, H. (2003) *The Time of Our Lives: Inside the Sydney Olympics: Australia and the Olympic Games, 1994–2002*, St Lucia, Queensland: University of Queensland Press.

Gordon, S. and Sibson, R. (1998) 'Global television: the Atlanta Olympics opening ceremony', in D. Rowe and G. Lawrence (eds), *Tourism, Leisure, Sport: Critical Perspectives*, Rydalmere, NSW: Hodder: 204–15.

Gramsci, A. (1971) *Selections from the Prison Notebooks*, New York: International Publishers.

Gramsci, A. (1978) *Selections from Political Writings (1921–1926)*, London: Lawrence and Wishart.

Greenberger, R.S. (1993) 'Washington insight: U.S., unhappy with Beijing's abuse of human rights, focuses on Olympics', *Wall Street Journal*, 23 August.

Greenhalgh, P. (1988) *Ephemeral Vistas: The Expositions Universelles: Great Exhibitions and World's Fairs, 1851–1939*, Manchester: Manchester University Press.

Gries, P.H. (2005) 'Anti-Japanese feeling among Chinese has historic roots', *Denver Post*, 22 May.

Grombach, J. (1980) *The Official 1980 Olympic Guide*, New York: Times Books.

Groussard, S. (1975) *The Blood of Israel: The Massacre of the Israeli Athletes, the Olympics, 1972*, New York: William Morrow.

Guardian (14 October 2004) 'Question mark hangs over golden arches brand', online at: http://www.smh.com.au (accessed 24 March 2006).

Gurevich, A. (1995) *Origins of European Individualism*, Oxford: Blackwell.

Guthrie, D. (1999), *Dragon in a Three-Piece Suit: The Emergence of Capitalism in China*, Princeton, NJ: Princeton University Press.

Guttmann, A. (1978) *From Ritual to Record: The Nature of Modern Sports*, New York: Columbia University Press.

Guttmann, A. (1984) *The Games Must Go On: Avery Brundage and the Olympic Movement*, New York: Columbia University Press.

Guttmann, A. (1988a) 'The Cold War and the Olympics', *International Journal*, 43.

Guttmann, A. (1988b) 'The Nazi Olympics', in J. O. Segrave and D. Chu (eds), *The Olympic Games in Transition*, Champaign, ILL: Human Kinetics: 201–20.

Guttmann, A. (1992) *The Olympics: A History of the Modern Games*, Urbana, ILL: University of Illinois Press.

Guttmann, A. (1994) *Games and Empires: Modern Sports and Cultural Imperialism*, New York: Columbia University Press.

Guttmann, A. (1998) 'The "Nazi Olympics" and the American boycott controversy', in P. Arnaud and J. Riordan (eds), *Sport and International Politics*, London: E. & F.N. Spon: 31–50.

Guttmann, A. (2002), *The Olympics: A History of the Modern Games*, 2nd edition, Urbana, ILL: University of Illinois Press.

Guttmann, A., Kestner, H. and Eisen, G. (2000) 'Jewish athletes and the "Nazi Olympics" ', in K. Schaffer and S. Smith (eds), *The Olympics at the Millennium: Power, Politics, and the Games*, New Brunswick, NJ: Rutgers University Press, 51–62.

Guttmann, A. (2002) *The Olympics: A History of the Modern Games*, 2nd edition, Urbana and Chicago: University of Illinois Press.

Ha, Woong-Yong (1998) 'Korean sports in the 1980s and the Seoul Olympic Games of 1988', *Journal of Olympic History*, Summer: 11–13.

Haar, B. (2006) 'Falun Gong', online at: http://website.leidenuniv.nl (accessed 1 April 2006).

Haley, B. (1978) *The Healthy Body and Victorian Culture*, Cambridge, MA: Harvard University Press.

Hall, C.M. and Hodges, J. (1996) 'The party's great, but what about the hangover? The housing and social impacts of mega-events with special reference to the 2000 Sydney Olympics', *Festival Management and Event Tourism*, 4, 1: 13–20.

Hall, M.A. (1996) *Feminism and Sporting Bodies: Essays on Theory and Practice*, Champaign, IL: Human Kinetics.

Hall, T. and Hubbard, P. (eds) (1998) *The Entrepreneurial City: Geographies of Politics, Regime and Representation*, New York: Wiley.

Hamilton, A. and Hoyle, B. (13 January 2005) 'The Queen puts boot into London bid with untimely approval of Paris', *Times*, online at: http://www.timesonline.co.uk (accessed 30 March 2006).

Hammer, J. and Biehl, J. (2000) 'The price of athletic glory', *Newsweek*, 29 May.

Han Sung-Joo (1989) 'South Korea in 1988: A revolution in the making', *Asian Survey*, 29, 1: 29–38.

Hargreaves, J. (1984) 'Women and the Olympic phenomenon', in A. Tomlinson and G. Whannel (eds) *Five-Ring Circus: Money, Power, and Politics at the Olympic Games*, London: Pluto Press: 53–70.

Hargreaves, J. (1994) *Sporting Females: Critical Issues in the History and Sociology of Women's Sports*, London: Routledge.

Hargreaves, J. (2002) 'Globalization theory, global sport, and nations and nationalism', in J. Sugden and A. Tomlinson (eds), *Power Games: A Critical Sociology of Sport*, London: Routledge, 25–43.

Hart-Davis, D. (1988) *Hitler's Olympics: The 1936 Games*, Sevenoaks: Coronet.

Hartmann-Tews, I. and Pfister, G. (eds) (2003) *Sport and Women: Social Issues in International Perspective*, London: Routledge.

Harvey, J., Rail, G. and Thibault, L. (1996) 'Globalization and sport: sketching a theoretical model for empirical analysis', *Journal of Sport and Social Issues*, 23, 3: 258–77.

Harvey, J. and Saint Germain, M. (2001) 'Sporting goods trade, international divisions of labour, and the unequal hierarchy of nations', *Sociology of Sport Journal*, 18, 2: 231–46.

Held, D. and McGrew, A. (2001) 'Globalization', in J. Krieger (ed.) *Oxford Companion to the Politics of the World*, Oxford: Oxford University Press.

Held, D. and McGrew, A. (2003a) *The Global Transformations Reader*, 2nd edition, Cambridge: Polity Press.

Held, D. and McGrew, D. (2003b) *Globalization and Anti-Globalization*, Cambridge: Polity Press.

Held, D., McGrew, A., Goldblatt, D. and Perraton, J. (1999) *Global Transformations: Politics, Economics and Culture*, Cambridge: Polity Press.

Helleiner, E. (2002) 'Economic nationalism as a challenge to economic liberalism: lessons from the nineteenth century', *International Studies Quarterly*, 46: 307–29.

Hendry, J. (2000) *The Orient Strikes Back: A Global View of Cultural Display*, Oxford: Berg.

Herz, D. and Altman, A. (1996) 'Berlin, 1936: the Games of the XIIth Olympiad', in J. Findling and K. D. Pelle (eds), *Historical Dictionary of the Modern Olympic Movement*, Westport, CN: Greenwood Publishing: 84–94.

Hill, C.R. (1992) *Olympic Politics*, Manchester: Manchester University Press.

Hill, C.R. (1999) 'The Cold War and the Olympic Movement', *History Today*, 49, 1: 19–25.

Hiller, H. (1998) 'Assessing the impact of mega-events: a linkage model', *Current Issues in Tourism*, 1, 1: 47–57.

Hiller, H. (1999) 'Mega-events and urban social transformation: human development and the 2004 Cape Town Olympic bid', in T. Anderson, C. Persson, B. Sahlberg and L. I. Ström (eds), *The Impacts of Mega-Events*, Östersund: European Tourism Research Institute: 109–20.

Hirst, P. and Thompson, G. (2000) *Globalization in Question*, 2nd edition, Cambridge: Polity Press.

Hoagland, J. (2001) 'Let's see an Olympic victory for China's people', *International Herald Tribune*, 20 July.

Hobermann, J. (1986) *The Olympic Crisis: Sport, Politics and Moral Order*, New York: New Rochelle.

Hoffman, S. (ed.) (1992) *Sport and Religion*, Champaign, IL: Human Kinetics.

Hong, F. (1997) *Footbinding, Feminism and Freedom: The Liberation of Women's Bodies in Modern China*, London: Frank Cass.

Hong, F. (1998) 'The Olympic Movement in China: ideals, realities and ambitions', *Culture, Sport Society*, 1, 1: 149–68.

Hong, F. (2004) 'Innocence lost: child athletes in China', *Sport in Society*, 7, 3: 338–54.

Hong, F. and Xiaozheng, X. (2003) 'Communist China: sport, politics and diplomacy', in J. A. Mangan and F. Hong, *Sport in Asian Society: Past and Present*, London: Frank Cass: 319–42.

Hornbuckle, A.R. (1996) 'Helsinki, 1952: the Games of the XVIth Olympiad', in J. Findling and K. D. Pelle (eds), *Historical Dictionary of the Modern Olympic Movement*, Westport, CN: Greenwood Publishing: 109–18.

Horne, J. (2004) 'The global game of football, the 2002 World Cup and regional development in Japan', *Third World Quarterly*, 25, 7: 1233–44.

Horne, J. and Manzenreiter, W. (eds) (2002) *Japan, Korea and the 2002 World Cup*, London: Routledge.

Horne, J. and Manzenreiter, W. (2004) 'Accounting for mega-events: forecast and actual impacts of the 2002 Football World Cup finals on the host countries Japan/Korea', *International Review for the Sociology of Sport*, 39, 2: 187–203.

Horne, J. and Manzenreiter, W. (eds) (2006) *Sports Mega-Events: Social Scientific Analyses of a Global Phenomenon*, Oxford: Blackwell.

Horton, P. (1998) 'Olympism in the Asia-Pacific region: a question of naïvety or pragmatism?', *Culture, Sport and Society*, 1, 1: 169–84.

Houlihan, B. (1994) *Sport and International Politics*, London: Harvester Wheatsheaf.

Houlihan, B. (2003) 'Sport and globalization', in B. Houlihan (ed.), *Sport and Society: A Student Introduction*, London: Sage: 345–63.

Human Rights in China (2006) 'Human Rights in China', online at: http://iso.hrichina.org/public (accessed 1 April 2006).

Human Rights Watch (HRW) (2002) 'Dangerous meditation: China's campaign against Falungong', online at: http://hrw.org (accessed 1 April 2005).

HRW (14 May 2003) 'Rome Statute ratifications', online at: http://www.hrw.org.

HRW (2004) 'China Olympics watch', online at: http://www.hrw.org (accessed 12 November 2004).

HRW (1 July 2004) 'Global issues', online at: http://www.hrw.org (accessed 30 March 2006).

HRW (3 July 2004) 'United Nations', online at: http://www.hrw.org (accessed 3 July 2004).

HRW (24 August 2004) 'Olympic spotlight shifts to China'. Online. Available HTTP: http://hrw.org (accessed 24 August 2004).

HRW (13 November 2005) 'Human rights and the 2008 Olympics in Beijing: media and Internet censorship', online at: http://www.hrw.org (accessed 13 November 2004).

HRW (14 November 2005) 'Beijing construction: forced evictions', online at: http://hrw.org (accessed 14 November 2005).

HRW (15 November 2005) 'Human rights and the 2008 Olympics in Beijing: business and labor rights', online at: http://www.hrw.org (accessed 15 November 2004).

HRW (9 March 2006) 'Beijing 2008: human rights and the Olympics in China', online at: http://hrw.org (accessed 9 March 2006).

Hunt, A.R. (1993) 'Use Olympics bid to pressure China on human rights', Wall Street Journal, 25 May.

Hunter, A. and Chan, K.-K. (2004) Protestantism in Contemporary China, Cambridge: Cambridge University Press.

Hunterformer, D. (2001) 'Olympism for the twenty first century: new life in a timeless philosophy', Sports Journal, online at: http;//www.thesportjournal.org/2001Journal (accessed 10 January 2006).

Huntington, S. (1993) 'The clash of civilizations?', Foreign Affairs, 72, 3: 22–49.

Huntington, S. (1996) The Clash of Civilizations and the Remaking of World Order, New York: Simon and Schuster.

Hutchinson, J. and Smith, A.D. (1994) Nationalism, Oxford: Oxford University Press.

Hwang, T. and Jarvie, G. (2001) 'Sport, nationalism and the early Chinese republic 1912–1927', The Sports Historian, 21, 2: 53–70.

Ignatieff, M. (2003) Human Rights as Politics and Idolatry, Princeton, NJ: Princeton University Press.

Independent (2001) 'China is not a suitable host for the Olympic ideal', Independent, 13 July.

Infantino, L. (1998) Individualism in Modern Thought: From Adam Smith to Hayek, London: Routledge.

Inglehart, R. and Welzel, C. (2005) Modernization, Cultural Change and Democracy, Cambridge: Cambridge University Press.

International Labour Organisation (ILO) (December 2004) 'Alphabetical list of other countries, territories and areas', online at: http://www.ilo.org (accessed 14 December 2004).

International Olympic Committee (IOC) (1994) The International Olympic Committee, One Hundred Years: The Idea, the Presidents, the Achievements, 1894–1994, The

Presidencies of Demetrius Vikelas (1894–1896) and Pierre de Coubertin (1896–1925),
The Presidency of Henri de Baillet-Latour (1925–1942), Volume 1, Lausanne: International Olympic Committee.

IOC (1995) *The International Olympic Committee, One Hundred Years: The Idea, the Presidents, the Achievements, 1894–1994, The Presidency of Sigfrid Edstrom (1942–1952), The Presidency of Avery Brundage (1952–1972),* Volume 2, Lausanne: International Olympic Committee.

IOC (1997) *The International Olympic Committee, One Hundred Years: The Idea, the Presidents, the Achievements, 1894–1994, The Presidencies of Lord Killanin (1972–1980) and of Juan Antonio Samaranch (1980–),* Volume 3, Lausanne: International Olympic Committee.

IOC (July 2001a) 'Moscow 2001', online at: http://www.moscow2001.olympic.org (accessed 24 March 2006).

IOC (July 2001b) 'Olympic marketing 1980–2001: two decades of unprecedented support for sport', *Marketing Matters: The Olympic Marketing Newsletter,* online at: http://multimedia.olympic.org (accessed 24 March 2006).

IOC (13 March 2002) 'Report of the IOC Evaluation Commission for the Games of the XXIX Olympiad in 2008', online at: http://multimedia.olympic.org (accessed 31 March 2006).

IOC (23 July 2004) 'Medical: the fight against doping and promotion of athletes' health', online at: http://multimedia.olympic.org (accessed 23 July 2004).

IOC (8 August 2004) *Olympic Charter,* online at: http://multimedia.olympic.org (accessed 24 March 2006).

IOC (1 September 2004) 'Preamble, Olympic Charter', online at: http://www.olympic.org (accessed 20 November 2005).

IOC (June 2005) 'Host city election: facts and figures', online at: http://multimedia.olympic.org (accessed 14 November 2005).

IOC (6 June 2005) 'Report of the IOC Evaluation Commission for the Games of the XXX Olympiad in 2012', online at: http://www.olympic.org (accessed 31 March 2006).

IOC (6 July 2005) 'Singapore 2005: London elected as the host city for the Games of the XXX Olympiad', online at: http://www.olympic.org (accessed 28 October 2005).

IOC (6–9 July 2005) '117th IOC Session', online at: http://www.olympic.org (accessed 28 October 2005).

IOC (31 July 2005) 'History and role of the Executive Board', online at: http://www.olympic.org/uk (accessed 31 July 2005).

IOC (26 October 2005) 'Fundamental principles of Olympism, Olympic Charter', online at: http://multimedia.olympic.org (accessed 26 October 2005).

IOC (27 October 2005) 'London 2012', online at: http://www.olympic.org (accessed 27 October 2005).

IOC (28 October 2005) 'Nine candidate cities competing to host the 13th IOC Congress in 2009', online at: http://www.olympic.org/uk (accessed 28 October 2005).

IOC (7 November 2005) 'Association of National Olympic Committees', online at: http://www.olympic.org (accessed 7 November 2005).

IOC (9 November 2005) 'Los Angeles 1984: Games of the XXIII Olympiad', online at: http://www.olympic.org (accessed 9 November 2005).

IOC (12 November 2005) 'Summary of IOC opinion poll results, report of the IOC Evaluation Commission for the Games of the XXX Olympiad in 2012', online at: http://www.olympic.org (accessed 12 November 2005).

IOC (14 November 2005) 'Past elections', online at: http://www.olympic.org (accessed 14 November 2005).

IOC (11 January 2006) 'Executive Board', online at: http://www.olympic.org/uk (accessed 11 January 2006).

IOC (12 January 2006) 'Beijing 2008: Games of the XXIX Olympiad', online at: http://www.olympic.org (accessed 12 January 2006).

IOC (8 February 2006) 'Copenhagen elected as host city for the 13th Olympic Congress in 2009', online at: http://www.olympic.org/uk (accessed 8 February 2006).

IOC (9 February 2006) 'Marshall Islands 203rd National Olympic Committee', online at: http://www.olympic.org/uk (accessed 9 February 2006).

IOC (17 February 2006) 'International Sports Federations', online at: http://www.olympic.org/uk (accessed 17 February 2006).

IOC (18 February 2006) 'NOCs in the front line of promoting Olympic values', online at: http://www.olympic.org/uk (accessed 18 February 2006).

IOC (19 February 2006a) 'Missions of the NOCs', online at: http://www.olympic.org/uk (accessed 19 February 2006).

IOC (19 February 2006b) 'There is a first time for everything', online at: http://www.olympic.org/uk (accessed 19 February 2006).

IOC (20 February 2006) 'How is Olympism disseminated throughout the world?', online at: http://www.olympic.org/uk (accessed 20 February 2006).

IOC (21 February 2006) 'Torino 2006', online at: http://www.olympic.org/uk (accessed 21 February 2006).

IOC (22 February 2006) 'Passion', online at: http://www.olympic.org/uk (accessed 22 February 2006).

IOC (23 February 2006) 'Coins', online at: http://www.olympic.org/uk (accessed 23 February 2006).

IOC (24 February 2006) 'Beijing 2008', online at: http://www.olympic.org/uk (accessed 20 February 2006).

IOC (25 February 2006) 'Members', online at: http://www.olympic.org/uk (accessed 25 February 2006).

IOC (11 March 2006) 'Athens 2004: medals by country', online at: http://www.olympic.org/uk.

IOC (8 September 2006a) 'Evolution of women and sport', online at http://www.olympic.org/uk/ (accessed 8 September 2006).

IOC (8 September 2006b) 'Promotion of women in sport', online at http://www.olympic.org/uk/ (accessed 8 September 2006).

IOC (13 September 2006) 'Berlin 1936', online at http://www.olympic.org/uk/ (accessed 13 September 2006).

Ishihara, S. (1991) *The Japan That Can Say No: Why Japan will be First Among Equals*, New York: Simon and Schuster.

Iton, J. (1978) *The Economic Impact of the 1976 Olympic Games, Report to the Organising Committee of the 1976 Games*, Montreal: Office of Industrial Research, McGill University.

Jackson, R. and McPhail, T. (eds) (1989) *The Olympic Movement and the Mass Media: Past, Present and Future Issues, International Conference Proceedings, University of Calgary*, Calgary: Hurford Enterprises.

Jacobsen, M. (2000) *Human Rights and Asian Values*, London: Routledge.

Jacoby, J. (2001) 'Hold the 2008 Olympics anywhere but in Beijing', *Boston Globe*, 10 May.

Jeffery, N. (2005) 'Stasi agent helping Chinese team', *Australian*, 16 February.

Jennings, A. (1996) *The New Lords of the Rings*, New York: Simon and Schuster.

Jennings, A. and Sambrook, C. (2000) *The Great Olympic Swindle*, New York: Simon and Schuster.

Jennings, R. (2004) 'China hardens stance on Japan protests', *Japan Times*, 24 September.

Jobling, I. (1996) 'Melbourne, 1956: the Games of the XVIth Olympiad', in J. Findling and K. D. Pelle (eds), *Historical Dictionary of the Modern Olympic Movement*, Westport, CN: Greenwood Publishing: 119–27.

Jeong, G.H. (1999) 'Residents' perceptions of the long-term impacts of the Seoul Olympics on the Chamsil Area development from a tourism perspective', in T. Anderson, C. Persson, B. Sahlberg and L. I. Ström (eds), *The Impacts of Mega-Events*, Östersund: European Tourism Research Institute: 169–78.

Jewell, B. and Kilgour, K. (2000) 'Sharing the spirit: the impact of the Sydney 2000 Olympics on human rights in Australia', in T. Taylor (ed.), *How You Play the Game: The Contribution of Sport to the Protection of Human Rights*, Sydney: Faculty of Business, University of Technology: 124–28.

Johnson, C. (2001) 'Economic crisis in East Asia: the clash of capitalisms', in H.-J. Chang, J. C. Palma and D. H. Whitaker (eds), *Financial Liberalization and the Asian Crisis*, New York: Palgrave: 8–20.

Johnston, A. (1999) 'Marketing and sponsorship', in R. Cashman and A. Hughes (eds), *Staging the Olympics: The Event and its Impact*, Sydney: University of New South Wales Press: 132–39.

Johnston, A.I. and Ross, R.S. (eds) (1999) *Engaging China: the Management of an Emerging Power*, London: Routledge.

Jonas, A. and Wilson, D. (eds) (1999) *The Urban Growth Machine: Critical Perspectives Two Decades Later*, Albany, NY: State University of New York Press.

Jones, D.M. (2001) *The Image of China in Western Social and Political Thought*, Hampshire and New York: Palgrave.

Jones, S. (2001) 'Require rights guarantees from Olympic hosts', *International Herald Tribune*, 11 July.

Kang San Jung (2006) 'Divisions, rivalries threaten new Cold War in East Asia', *Japan Times*, 3 January.

Kang, Y.S. and Perdue, R. (1994) 'Long-term impact of a mega-event on international tourism to the host country: a conceptual model and the case of the 1988 Seoul Olympics', in M. Uysal (ed.), *Global Tourist Behaviour*, New York: International Business Press/Haworth: 205–25.

Kang, Y.S. and Perdue, R. (1994) 'Long-term impact of a mega-event on international tourism to the host country: a conceptual model and the case of the 1988 Seoul Olympics', *Journal of International Consumer Marketing*, 6, 3/4: 205–25.

Kanin, D.B. (1981) *A Political History of the Olympic Games*, Boulder, CO: Westview Press.

Kass, D.A. (1976) 'The issue of racism at the 1936 Olympics', *Journal of Sport History*, 3: 223–5.

Kelle, U. (2001) 'Sociological explanations between micro and macro and the integration of qualitative and quantitative methods', *Forum: Qualitative Social Research*, 2, 1.

Kent, A. (1993) *Between Freedom and Subsistence: China and Human Rights*, Hong Kong: Oxford University Press.

Kent, A. (1999) *China, the United Nations, and Human Rights: The Limits of Compliance*, Philadelphia, PA: University of Pennsylvania Press.

Kent, H. and Merritt, J. (1984) 'The Cold War and the Melbourne Olympic Games', in A. Curthoys and J. Merritt (eds), *Better Red than Dead*, Sydney: Allen and Unwin.

Kent, S. (1983) 'Weber, Goethe, and the Nietzschean allusion: capturing the source of the "Iron Cage" metaphor', *Sociological Analysis*, 44: 297–319.

Kentupa (14 July 2001) 'Dentsu', online at: http://www.ketupa.net (accessed 31 March 2006).

Kim Dae Jung (1994) 'Is culture destiny? The myth of Asia's anti-democratic values', *Foreign Affairs*, 73, 6, online at: http://www.foreignaffairs.org/1994/6.html (accessed 10 January 2006).

Kim Dae Jung (1998) 'The government of the people: reconciliation and a New Leap Forward', Seoul: Presidential Inaugural Committee.

Kim Dae Jung (1999) 'Presidential address', *Democracy, Market Economy and Development*, *Korea Development Institute*, online at: http://www.idep.org (accessed 31 March 2006).

Kim, Sam (2003) *The International Relations of Northeast Asia*, Lanham, MD: Rowman and Littlefield.

Kim, S.H. (2004) *Max Weber's Politics of Civil Society*, Cambridge: Cambridge University Press.

Kingston, J. (2006) 'How does Japan say sorry? Accepting apologies is not so easy', *Japan Times*, 2 April.

Kitazume, T. (2004) 'Perception versus reality: China as a major power in progress', *Japan Times*, 8 October.

Kokubun. R. and Wang, J. (eds) (2004) *The Rise of China and a Changing East Asian Order*, Tokyo: Japan Centre for International Exchange.

Korporaal, G. and Evans, M. (1999) 'Games people play', *Sydney Morning Herald*, 11 February.

Kristof, N. (1998) 'Crisis pushing Asian capitalism closer to US-style free market', *Pacific Investment Research*, 17 January.

Krüger, A. and Murray, W. (2003) *The Nazi Olympics: Sport, Politics, and Appeasement in the 1930s*, Urbana, ILL.: University of Illinois Press, revised edition.

Labor Rights Now (LRN) (9 March 2006) 'Olympics 2008', online at: http://www.laborrightsnow.org (accessed 9 March 2006).

LaFeber, W. (1999) *Michael Jordan and the New Global Capitalism*, New York: W. W. Norton and Co.

Laogai Research Foundation (2004) *Laogai Research Foundation*, online at: http://www.laogai.org (accessed 1 April 2006).

Lapchick, R.E. (1978) 'A political history of the modern Olympic Games', *Journal of Sport and Social Issues*, 2: 1–12.

Larmer, B. (2001a) 'Beijing's Olympic moment', *Newsweek*, 137, 9, 26 February.

Larmer, B. (2001b) 'Olympic dreams', *Newsweek*, 137, 9, 26 February.

Larmer, B. (2005) *Operation Yao Ming: The Chinese Sports Empire, American Big Business, and the Making of an NBA Superstar*, New York: Gotham Books.

Larsen, J. and Park, H. (1993) *Global Television and the Politics of the Seoul Olympics*, Boulder, CO: Westview Press.

Lechner, F. and Boli, J. (2005) *World Culture: Origins and Consequences*, Oxford: Blackwell.

Lee, B. (2004) 'A philosophical anthropology of the communal person: a postcolonial feminist critique of Confucian communalism and Western individualism in Korean Protestant education', *Boston College*, online at: http://escholarship.bc.edu (accessed 4 November 2004).

Ledeen, M.A. (2002) 'From Communism to Fascism?', *Wall Street Journal*, 22 February.

Lehmann, L., Roth, G., Lazar, D. and Mauch, C. (1995) *Weber's Protestant Ethic*, Cambridge: Cambridge University Press.

Lei Guang (2002) 'Re-Orient: Andre Gunder Frank and a globalist perspective on the world economy', *Perspectives*, 3, 4, online at: http//www.ogcf.org/Perspectives (accessed 10 January 2006).

Lennartz, K. (2001) 'The story of the rings', *Journal of Olympic History*, 10, December: 29–61.

Lenskyi, H.J. (2002) *Best Olympics Ever? Social Impacts of Sydney 2000*, Albany, NY: State University of New York Press.

Lenskyi, H.J. and Burstyn, V. (2000) *Inside the Olympic Industry: Power, Politics, and Activism*, Albany, NY: State University of New York Press.

Leonard, E. (2005) *The Onset of Global Governance: International Relations Theory and the International Criminal Court*, Aldershot: Ashgate Publishing.

Levermore, R. and Budd, A. (eds) (2004) *Sport and International Relations*, London: Routledge.

Levine, J. and Thurston, K. (1992) 'The real marathon: signing Olympic sponsors', *Business Week*, 3 August.

Lewis, S. (2002) *Laying Claim to The Memory of May: A Look Back at the 1980 Kwangju Uprising*, Honolulu: Centre for Korean Studies, University of Hawaii at Manoa.

Ley, D. and Olds, K. (1999) 'World's Fairs and the culture of consumption in the contemporary city', in K. Anderson and F. Gale (eds), *Cultural Geographies*, 2nd edition, Melbourne: Longman: 221–40.

Leys, S. (1978) 'Human rights in China', in S. Leys, *The Burning Forest: Essays on Chinese Culture and Politics*, New York: Harold Holt, 1987.

Li, L. and Su, Y. (2004) 'The Chinese sportsworld bids farewell to the "Yuan Weimin era"', *Southern Weekend*, 16 December, online at: http://www.nanfangdaily.com.cn (accessed 17 December).

Li Thian-hok (2001) 'The Beijing Olympics and Taiwan', *Taipei Times*, 24 July.

Li Xiao (2004) 'China and the Olympic Movement', China Internet Information Center (CIIC), 5 January, online at: http://www.china.org.cn (accessed 9 April 2006).

Lianhe Zhaobao (13 July 2001) 'Ma Ying-joung favors Taiwan's co-hosting events', *Lianhe Zhaobao*, online at: http//www.zaobao.com (accessed 4 January 2005).

Liew, L. and Wang, S. (2003) *Nationalism, Democracy and National Integration in China*, London: Routledge.

Lilley, J.R. (2001) 'Beijing's risky game', *Newsweek*, 16 July.

Litsky, F. (1998) 'Swimming: new accusations aimed at Chinese swimmers', *New York Times*, 9 January.

LoBaido, A. (2001) 'China's human-rights public-relations scam: dissidents claim Beijing's "concessions" aimed at gaining 2008 Olympic Games', *WorldNetDaily.com*, 16 March, online at: http://www.worldnetdaily.com (accessed 24 March 2006).

Loland, S. (1995) 'Coubertin's ideology of Olympism from the perspective of the History of Ideas', *Olympika: The International Journal of Olympic Studies*, 4: 49–78.

Luard, T. (2005) 'China rethinks peasant "apartheid" ', *BBC News*, online at: http://news.bbc.co.uk (accessed 10 November 2005).

Lucas, J.A. (1975) 'Victorian "muscular Christianity": prologue to the Olympic Games philosophy' (part 1), *Olympic Review*, 97/98: 456–60.

Lucas, J.A. (1976) 'Victorian "muscular Christianity": prologue to the Olympic Games philosophy' (part 2), *Olympic Review*, 99/100: 49–52.

Lucas, J. (1983) 'American preparations for the first post World War Olympic Games, 1919–1920', *Journal of Sport History*, 10, 2: 30–44.

Lucas, J. (1992) *Future of the Olympic Games*, Champaign, ILL: Human Kinetics.

Lukes, S. (1973) *Individualism*, Oxford: Oxford University Press.

Lyotard, J.-F. (1984) *The Postmodern Condition: A Report on Knowledge*, Manchester: Manchester University Press (original 1979; reprint 2004).

Lyotard, J.-F. (1999) *Postmodern Fables*, Minnesota, MN: University of Minnesota Press.

MacAloon, J. (1981) *This Great Symbol: Pierre de Coubertin and the Origins of the Modern Olympic Games*, Chicago, ILL: University of Chicago Press.

McAvoy, A. (2004) 'Ra or realist, Ishihara vents his spleen', *Japan Times*, 6 October.

McClain, J.L. (1990) 'Cultural chauvinism and the Olympiads of East Asia', *International Journal of the History of Sport*, 7, 3: 388–404.

McDaniel, S.R. (2002) 'An exploration of audience demographics, personal values and lifestyles: influences on viewing network coverage of the 1996 Summer Olympic Games', *Journal of Sport Management*, 16, 2: 117–31.

McGeown, K. (9 November 2004) 'China's Christians suffer for their faith', *BBC World*, online at: http://news.bbc.co.uk (viewed 24 March 2006).

McGrath, A. and Marks D. (2004) *Blackwell Guide to Protestantism*, Oxford: Blackwell.

McGregor, R. and Pilling, D. (2004) 'Beijing crowd behaviour augurs ill for 2008', *Financial Times*, 9 August.

Machan, T. (1998) *Classical Individualism: The Supreme Importance of Each Human Being*, London: Routledge.

Mackay, D. and Chaudhary, V. (2001) 'Human rights alarm as Beijing wins race for 2008 games', *Guardian*, 14 July.

McKay, J. and Kirk, D. (1992) 'Sport and the media: Ronald McDonald meets Baron de Coubertin: prime time sport and commodification', *Australian Council for Health, Physical Education and Recreation (ACHPER) National Journal*, 136: 10–13.

McKay, M. and Plumb, C. (2001) *Reaching Beyond the Gold*, London: Jones Lang LaSalle.

McLaughlin, M. (13 January, 1999) 'Salt Lake City bribery scandal: the buying of the Olympic Games', *World Socialist Website*, online, at: http://www.wsws.org (accessed 12 January 2006).

McLean, I. and McMillan, A. (2003) *The Concise Oxford Dictionary of Politics*, 2nd edition, Oxford: Oxford University Press.

MacLeod, C. (September 2005) 'IAWIS/AIERTI 7th International Conference on Word and Image Studies: Elective Affinities', online at: http://ccat.sas.upenn.edu (accessed 21 October 2005).

Madden, J.R. (2002) 'The economic consequences of the Sydney Olympics: the CREA/Arthur Andersen study', *Current Issues in Tourism*, 5, 1: 7–21.

Maddison, A. (2005) *The World Economy: Historical Statistics*, Paris: OECD.

Magdalinski, T. and Chandler, T. (eds) (2002) *With God on Their Side: Sport in the Service of Religion*, New York: Routledge.

Maguire, J. (1999) *Global Sport: Identities, Societies, Civilizations*, Cambridge: Polity.

Maguire, J. (2003) 'Sport, globalisation, environmentalism and "green" issues', in *Leisure Issues: Official Publication of Research Committee 13 of the International Sociological Association*, 6, 3: 2–14.

Malhotra, R. (2004) 'Human rights' other face', *Redif.com*, 9 March, online at: http://www.redif.com (accessed 31 March 2006).

Maloney, L. (1996) 'Atlanta, 1996: the Games of the XXVIth Olympiad', in J. Findling and K. D. Pelle (eds), *Historical Dictionary of the Modern Olympic Movement*, Westport, CN: Greenwood Publishing: 194–200.

Mandell, R.D. (1991) *The Olympics of 1972: A Munich Diary*, Chapel Hill, NC: University of North Carolina Press.

Mangan, J.A. (1981) *Athleticism in the Victorian and Edwardian Public School*, Cambridge: Cambridge University Press.

Mangan, J.A. and Hong, F. (2003) *Sport in Asian Society: Past and Present*, London: Frank Cass.

Mangan, J.A. and Park, R.J. (eds) (1987) *From 'Fair Sex' to Feminism: Sport and the Socialization of Women in the Industrial and Post-industrial Eras*, London: Frank Cass.

Manheim, J.B. (1990) 'Rites of passage: the 1988 Seoul Olympics as public diplomacy', *Western Political Quarterly*, 43, 2: 279–95.

Manzenreiter, W. and Horne, J. (eds) (2004) *Football Goes East: Business, Culture and the People's Game in China, Japan and South Korea*, London: Routledge.

Marketing Matters (July 2001) 'Olympic marketing 1980–2001: two decades of unprecedented support for sport', *Marketing Matters: The Olympic Marketing Newsletter*, 19, online at: http://multimedia.olympic.org (accessed 31 March 2006).

Mason, A. (2000) *Community, Solidarity and Belonging*, Cambridge: Cambridge University Press.

Mason, T. (1980) *Association Football and English Society, 1863–1915*, Brighton: Harvester.

Matthews, G. (2005) *America's First Olympics: The St. Louis Games of 1904*, Columbia, MO: University of Missouri Press.

Maxwell, L. and Howell, R. (1976) 'The 1952 Helsinki Olympic Games: another turning point', in P. J. Graham and H. Ueberhorst (eds), *The Modern Olympics*, West Point, NY: Leisure Press: 187–98.

Meadow, R.G. (1989) 'The architecture of Olympic broadcasting', in R. Jackson and T. McPhail (eds), *The Olympic Movement and the Mass Media: Past, Present and Future Issues, International Conference Proceedings, University of Calgary*, Calgary: Hurford Enterprises.

Metcalfe, A. (1994) 'Review of Guttmann (1992), Hill (1992) and Lucas (1992)', *International Journal of the History of Sport*, 11, 1: 129–32.

Meyer, A. (2003) *Quiet Diplomacy: From Cairo to Tokyo in the Twilight of Imperialism*, Lincoln, NE: iUniverse Inc.

Meyer, J., Ramirez, F. and Boli, J. (1987) 'Ontology and rationalization in the Western cultural account', in G. Thomas, J. Meyer, F. Ramirez and J. Boli (eds), *Institutional Structure: Constituting State, Society and the Individual*, Beverley Hills, CA: Sage.

Miah, A. (1999) 'Human rights and sport', *Culture at the Olympics: Issues, Trends and Perspectives*, 1, 1: 1–14. online at: www.culturalolympics.org.uk (accessed 24 March 2006).

Miah, A. (2004) *Genetically Modified Athletes: Biomedical Ethics, Gene Doping, and Sport*, London: Routledge.

Microsoft Network (MSN) Encarta (4 November 2005) 'Confucianism', online at: http://www.connect.net (accessed 30 March 2006).

MSN Encarta (2006) 'Dissonance', online at: http://www.connect.net (accessed 31 March 2006).

MSN Encarta (7 April 2006) 'China', online at: http://encarta.msn.com (accessed 7 April 2006).

Middleton, L. (1997) 'South Korean foreign policy', in Dae Hwan Kim and Tat Yan Kong (eds), *The Korean Peninsula in Transition*, Basingstoke: Macmillan and New York: St. Martin's Press: 149–71.

Miles, J. (1996) *The Legacy of Tiananmen Square: China in Disarray*, Ann Arbor, MI: University of Michigan Press.

Miller, D. (2004), *Athens to Athens: The Official History of the Olympic Games and the IOC, 1894–2004*, Edinburgh: Mainstream Publishing Company.

Miller, H. (2004) 'Where have all the elders gone?', *China Leadership Monitor*, 10: 1–7.

Miller, T. (2000) 'Men of the game', in K. Schaffer and S. Smith (eds), *The Olympics at the Millennium: Power, Politics, and the Games*, New Brunswick, NJ: Rutgers University Press: 91–8.

Miller, T., Lawrence, G., McKay, J. and Rowe, D. (2001) *Globalization and Sport*, London: Sage.

Milton-Smith, J. (2002) 'Ethics, the Olympics and the search for global values', *Journal of Business Ethics*, 35, 2: 131–42.

Min, G. (1987) 'Over-commercialisation of the Olympics 1988: the role of US television networks', *International Review for the Sociology of Sport*, 22, 2: 137–41.

Mitchell, A. and Yeates, H. (2000) 'Who's sorry now? Drugs, sports and the media toward 2000', in K. Schaffer and S. Smith (eds), *The Olympics at the Millennium: Power, Politics and the Games*, New Brunswick, NJ: Rutgers University Press: 197–212.

Miyanaga, K. (1991) *The Creative Edge: Emerging Individualism in Japan*, New Brunswick, NJ: Transaction Publishers.

Molotch, H. (1993) 'The political economy of growth machines', *Journal of Urban Affairs*, 15: 29–53.

Mooney, P. (2004) 'China faces up to growing unrest', *Asia Times*, 16 November, online at: http://www.atimes.com (accessed 31 March 2006).

Moore, M. and Pubantz, J. (2002) *Encyclopedia of the United Nations*, New York: Facts on File Inc.

Morgan, N. and Pritchard, A. (1998) *Tourism Promotion and Power: Creating Images, Creating Identities*, Chichester: Wiley.

Morris, A. (1999) ' "I can compete!" China in the Olympic Games, 1932 and 1936', *Journal of Sport History*, 26, 3: 545–66.

Morris, B. (1991) *Western Conceptions of the Individual*, Oxford: Berg.

Mount, J. and Leroux, C. (1994) 'Assessing the effects of a mega-event: a retrospective study of the impact of the Olympic Games on the Calgary business sector', *Festival Management and Event Tourism*, 2, 1: 15–23.

Müller, N. (2004) *The International Olympic Academy Through its Lectures, 1961–2003*, Mainz: University of Mainz.

Munro, R. (2000) 'Judicial psychiatry in China and its political abuses', *Columbia Journal of Asian Law*, 14, 1: 1–128.

Munro, R. (2001) 'China's judicial psychiatry', *Asian Wall Street Journal*, 18 February.

Murphy, M. (2001) 'Beijing goes for the gold: will China in 2008 be a repeat of Berlin in 1936?', *Weekly Standard*, 19 March.

Murray, B. (1992) 'Berlin in 1936: old and new work on the Nazi Olympics', *International Journal of the History of Sport*, 9, 1: 29–49.

Murray, G.E. (2003) *The Nazi Olympics*, Urbana, ILL: University of Illinois Press.

Museum Lausanne (2002) *The Olympic Symbols* online at: http://multimedia.olympic.org (accessed 24 March 2006).

Nafziger, J. (2004) *International Sports Law*, 2nd edition, Ardsley, NY: Transnational Publishers.

Nakamura, T. (1995) *The Postwar Japanese Economy: Its Development and Structure, 1937–1994*, 2nd edition, Tokyo: University of Tokyo Press.

Nakamura, T. (1998) *A History of Showa Japan, 1926–1989*, Tokyo: University of Tokyo Press.

Nam-Gil, H. and Mangan, J.A. (2002) 'Ideology, politics, power: Korean sport – transformation, 1945–92', *International Journal of the History of Sport*, 19, 2–3: 213–42.

Narine, S. (2005) 'China and the United States: competing capitalisms and competing institutions?', *Regionalisation and the Taming of Globalisation?*, Centre for the Study of Globalisation and Regionalisation (CSGR), Centre for International Governance Innovation (CIGI), and UNU-Comparative Regional Integration Studies (UNU CRIS), University of Warwick, UK.

Nathan, A.J. (1994) 'Human rights in Chinese foreign policy', *China Quarterly*, 139: 622–43.

National Commission on Terrorist Attacks on the United States (22 July 2004) *The 9/11 Commission Report*, online at: http://www.9–11 commission.gov (accessed 31 March 2006).

National Review (2001) 'Editorial – China: a dangerous decision', *National Review*, 6 August.

New Zealand Olympic Committee (NZOC) (2005) 'Olympism – what is it?', online at: http://www.olympic.org.nz (accessed 19 October 2005).

New York Times (2004) 'Hitler's Berlin Games helped make some emblems popular', *New York Times*, 14 August.

News 24 (4 March 2006) 'Gypsies the big Olympic losers', News24.com, online at: http://www.news24.com (accessed 24 March 2006).

Nordlinger, J. (2000) 'Beijing 2008: The Olympics in the belly of the beast', *National Review*, 9 October.

Norwegian Nobel Committee (2001) 'The Nobel Peace Prize 2001', *Nobel e-Museum*, online at: http://www.nobel.se (accessed 12 October 2001).

Nozick, R. (1974) *Anarchy, State, and Utopia*, Oxford: Basil Blackwell and New York: Basic Books.

Nye, J. (1997) 'China's re-emergence and the future of the Asia-Pacific', *Survival*, 39, 4: 65–79.

O'Brien, J. and Newman, D. (2004) *Sociology*, Thousand Oaks, CA: Pine Forge Press.

O'Donnell, L. (2001) 'Euphoria turns to boasts and business', *Australian*, 16 July.

Office of the Prime Minister (of South Korea) (2005) 'Korean beliefs and religion', online at: http://www.opm.go.kr (accessed 4 November 2005).

Ohmae, K. (1990) *The Borderless World*, New York: HarperCollins.

Ohmae, K. (1995) *The End of The Nation State*, New York: HarperCollins.

Olds, K. (1998a) 'Hallmark events, evictions and housing rights: the Canadian case', in A. Azuela, E. Duhau and E. Ortiz (eds), *Evictions and the Right to Housing: Experience from Canada, Chile, the Dominican Republic, South Africa, and South Korea*, Ottawa: International Development Research Centre (IDRC): 1–45.

Olds, K. (1998b) 'Urban mega-events, evictions and housing rights: the Canadian case', *Current Issues in Tourism*, 1, 1: 2–46.

Olympic Review (1996) 'The Olympic Movement and the mass media', *Olympic Review*, 26, 1: 1–215.

Olympic Watch (7 March 2005) 'Free Tibet, save Tibet', online at: http://www.olympicwatch.org (accessed 7 March 2005).

Olympic Watch (2006) 'Mission', online at: http://www.olympicwatch.org (accessed 1 April 2006).

Olympic Watch (9 March 2006) 'Human rights in China and Beijing 2008', online at: http://www.olympicwatch.org (accessed 9 March 2005).

Organising Committee of the XX Torino 2006 Olympic Winter Games (21 February 2006) 'XX Olympic Winter Games 10–26 February 2006', online at: http://www.torino2006.org (accessed 21 February 2006).

Orru, M., Biggart, N.W. and Hamilton, G.G. (1996) *The Economic Organization of East Asian Capitalism*, London: Sage.

Orwell, G. (1945) 'The sporting spirit', *Tribune*, December.

Owen, J. (2005) 'Estimating the cost and benefit of hosting Olympic Games: what can Beijing expect from its 2008 Games?', *Industrial Geographer*, online at: http://www.findarticles.com (accessed 24 March 2006).

Paillou, N. (1997) 'Centennial Olympic Congress, congress of unity', in M. Roukhadzé (ed.), *The Centennial President*, Lausanne: International Olympic Committee: 141–46.

Patterson, E. (15 February 2005) 'Stadia China 2005 wrap-up', *Beijing This Month*, online at: http://www.btmbeijing.com (accessed 24 March 2006).

Paul, J. (1996) 'Nations and states', *Global Policy Forum*, online at: http://www.globalpolicy.org/nations/natstats.htm (accessed 31 March 2006).

Pempel, T. (2005) *Remapping East Asia: The Construction of a Region*, Ithaca, NY: Cornell University Press.

People's Daily (18 May 2004) 'Constitution of the People's Republic of China', online at: http://english.people.com.cn (accessed 31 March 2006).

People's Daily (30 July 2005) 'Lui Qi', online at: http://english.people.com.cn (accessed 31 March 2006).

Perry, E. and Selden, M. (2003) *Chinese Society: Change, Conflict and Resistance*, London: Routledge.

Persson, C. (1999) 'The structure of the host selection process for the 2002 Olympic Winter Games', in T. Anderson, C. Persson, B. Sahlberg and L. I. Ström (eds), *The Impacts of Mega-Events*, Östersund: European Tourism Research Institute: 121–32.

Pesek, W. (2006) 'China's conundrum', *Taiwan News*, 16 January.

Pingree, A. (1996) 'Atlanta', *Olympic Review*, 26, 10: 21–5.

Pollock, J.C., Kreuer, B. and Ouano, E. (1997) 'Comparing city characteristics and nationwide coverage of China's bid to host the 2000 Olympic Games: a community structure approach', *Newspaper Research Journal*, 18: 31–49.

Poole, L. and Poole, G. (1963) *The Ancient Olympic Games*, London: Vision Press.

Pope, S.W. (1997) 'Virtual games: the media coverage of the 1996 Olympics', *Journal of Sport History*, 24, 1: 63–73.

Postmodern Therapies (PMTH) (1 July 2005) 'Names to know when reading about Postmodernism', *Postmodern Therapies News*, online at: http://www.california.com (accessed 24 March 2006).

Pound, R. (2004) *Inside the Olympics: A Behind-the-Scenes Look at the Politics, the Scandals, and the Glory of the Games*, Toronto: Wiley (Canada).

Prasad, E. (ed.) (2004) *China's Growth and Integration into the World Economy: Prospects and Challenges*, Washington, DC: International Monetary Fund.

Pred, A. (1991) 'Spectacular articulations of modernity: the Stockholm Exhibition of 1897', *Geografiska Annaler*, 73: 45–84.

Preuss, H. (2000) *Economics of the Olympic Games: Hosting the Games 1972–2000*, Petersham, NSW: Walla Walla Press.

Preuss, H. (2004) *The Economics of Staging the Olympics: a Comparison of the Games, 1972–2008*, Cheltenham: Edward Elgar.

PriceWaterhouseCoopers (2000) *Business and Economic Benefits of the Sydney 2000 Olympics: A Collation of Evidence*, Sydney: NSW Government, Department of State and Regional Development.

Puijk, R. (2000) 'A global media event? Coverage of the 1994 Lillehammer Olympic Games', *International Review for the Sociology of Sport*, 35, 3: 309–30.

Quick, S.P. (1990) 'Black knight checks white king: the conflict between Avery Brundage and the African nations over South African membership of the IOC', *Canadian Journal of The History of Sport*, 21, 2: 20–32.

Real, M.R. (2002) 'The postmodern Olympics: technology and the commodification of the Olympic Movement', paper to the University of North Colorado, 14 March, online at http://www.royalroads.net/olympics/articles/MRpomoOlympics.php (accessed 16 September 2006).

Renson, R. (1985) 'From the trenches to the track: the 1920 Antwerp Olympic Games', in N. Müller and J. K. Rül (eds), *Olympic Scientific Congress, 1984 Official Report: Sport History*, Niederhausen, Germany: 234–44.

Renson, R. (1996) *The Games Reborn: The VIIth Olympiad – Antwerp 1920*, Ghent: Pandora.

Renson, R. and den Hollander, M. (1997) 'Sport and business in the city: the Antwerp Olympic Games of 1920 and the urban élite', *Olympika: The International Journal of Olympic Studies*, 6: 73–83.

Reuters (13 November 2004) 'Athens Games cost 9bn euros', *Dawn Group*, online at: http://www.dawn.com (accessed 24 March 2006)

Reuters (3 March 2006) 'China can't afford extravagant Games: Congress delegate', *Washington Post*, online at: http://www.washingtonpost.com.

Riga Convention Bureau (20 December 2005) 'Riga bids for the 2009 Olympic Congress', online at: http://www.inspirationriga.com (accessed 24 March 2006).

Riordan, J. and Dong Jinxia (1996) 'Chinese women and sport: success, sexuality and suspicion', *China Quarterly*, 145: 130–52.

Ritchie, J.R.B. (1990) 'Promoting Calgary through the Olympics: the mega-event as a strategy for community development', in S. H. Fine (ed.), *Social Marketing: Promoting the Causes of Public and Non-profit Agencies*, Boston: Allyn and Bacon: 258–74.

Ritchie, J.R.B. and Smith, B. (1991) 'The impact of a mega-event on host-region awareness: a longitudinal study', *Journal of Travel Research*, 30, 1: 3–10.

Ritchie, J.R.B. and Hall, C.M. (2000) 'Mega-events and human rights', in T. Taylor (ed.), *How You Play the Game: The Contribution of Sport to the Protection of Human Rights*, Sydney: Faculty of Business, University of Technology: 102–15.

Robbins, H. (1908) *Our First Ambassador to China: An Account of the Life of George, Earl of Macartney*, London: John Murray.

Robertson, R. (1992) *Globalization: Social Theory and Global Culture*, London: Sage.

Robertson, R. (2000) 'Globalization theory 2000+: major problematics', in G. Ritzer and B. Smart (eds), *Handbook of Social Theory*, London: Sage: 458–71.

Roche, M. (1992) 'Mega-events and micro-modernization: on the sociology of the new urban tourism', *British Journal of Sociology*, 43, 4: 563–600.

Roche, M. (2000) *Mega-Events and Modernity: Olympics and Expos in the Growth of Global Culture*, London, Routledge.

Roche, M. (2003) 'Mega-events, time and modernity: on time structures in global society', *Time and Society*, 12, 1: 99–126.

Roche, M. (2004) 'Mega-events and media culture: sport and the Olympics', in D. Rowe (ed.), *Critical Readings: Sport, Culture and the Media*, Maidenhead: Open University Press: 165–82.

Rose, D. (2003) 'Sport and the repudiation of the global', *International Review for the Sociology of Sports*, 38, 3: 281–94.

Rosenzweig, R. (1997) 'The Nazi Olympics: Berlin 1936', *Journal of Sport History*, 24, 1: 77–80.

Roukhadzé, M. (ed.) (1997) *The Centennial President*, Lausanne: International Olympic Committee.

Rowe, D. (2000) 'Global media events and the positioning of presence', *Media International Australia*, 97: 11–22.

Rozman, G. (2004) *Northeast Asia's Stunted Regionalism: Bilateral Distrust in the Shadow of Globalization*, Cambridge: Cambridge University Press.

Ryall, J. and Robertson, B. (2004) 'Football war engulfs Japan and China', *The Scotsman*, 6 August.

Rydell, R. (1984) *All the World's a Fair: Visions of Empire at American International Expositions, 1876–1916*, Chicago, ILL: Chicago University Press.

Rydell, R. (1993) *World of Fairs: The Century-of-Progress Expositions*, Chicago, ILL: Chicago University Press.

Rydell, R. and Gwinn, N. (eds) (1994) *Fair Representations: World's Fairs and the Modern World*, Amsterdam: VU University Press.

Saaler, S. (2005) *Politics, Memory and Public Opinion: The History Textbook Controversy and Japanese Society*, Munich: Deutsches Institut fur Japanstudien.

Safron, W. (1998) *Nationalism and Ethnoregional Identities in China*, London: Routledge.

Said, E.W. (1978) *Orientalism*, New York: Pantheon Books.

Samaranch, J.A. (2002) *Memorias Olimpicas*, Barcelona: Planeta Publishing.

Sandiford, K.A. (1994) *Cricket and the Victorians*, Aldershot: Scholar Press.

Santoro, M.A. (2000) *Profits and Principles: Global Capitalism and Human Rights in China*, Ithaca, NY: Cornell University Press.

Sassen, S. (1991) *The Global City*, Princeton, NJ: Princeton University Press.

Schaffer, K. and Smith, S. (eds) (2000) *The Olympics at the Millennium: Power, Politics, and the Games*, New Brunswick, NJ: Rutgers University Press.

Schechter, D. (2001) *Falun Gong's Challenge to China: Spiritual Practice or 'Evil Cult'?* New York: Akashic Books.

Scholte, J.A. (2000) *Globalization: A Critical Introduction*, London: Macmillan.

Scott-Stokes, H. and Lee Jai Eui (eds) (2000) *The Kwangju Uprising: Eyewitness Press Accounts of Korea's Tiananmen*, London: M. E. Sharpe.

Seevak, S. (2002) 'Pierre de Courbertin', *Learn To Question*, online at: http://www.learntoquestion.com (accessed 3 November 2005).

Segrave, J.O. (1988) 'Toward a definition of Olympism', in J. O. Segrave and D. Chu (eds) *The Olympic Games in Transition*, Champaign, ILL: Human Kinetics: 149–61.

Senn, A.E. (1999) *Power, Politics and the Olympic Games*, Champaign, ILL: Human Kinetics.

Seymour, J.D., and Anderson, R. (1998) *New Ghosts, Old Ghosts: Prisons and Labor Reform Camps in China*, Armonk, NY: M. E. Sharpe.

Shain, B.A. (1996) *The Myth of American Individualism: The Protestant Origins of American Political Thought*, Princeton, NJ: Princeton University Press.

Shambaugh, D. (2006) *Power Shift : China and Asia's New Dynamics*, Berkeley, CA: University of California Press.

Shanahan, D. (1992) *Toward a Genealogy of Individualism*, Cambridge, MA: University of Massachusetts Press.

Shao Da (17 September 2004) 'Beijing's Olympic economy', *China Internet Information Center*, online at: http://www.china.org.cn (accessed 25 March 2006).

Shi, Z. and Shih, C.-Y. (2002) *Negotiating Ethnicity in China*, London: Routledge.

Shin, Doh C. (1999) *Mass Politics and Culture in Democratizing Korea*, Cambridge: Cambridge University Press.

Shin, Gi-Wook and Kyung Moon Hwang (eds) (2003) *Contentious Kwangju: The May 18 Uprising in Korea's Past and Present*, Lanham, MD: Rowman and Littlefield.

Short, J. (1999) 'Urban imaginers; boosterism and the representation of cities', in A. Jonas and D. Wilson (eds), *The Urban Growth Machine: Critical Perspectives Two Decades Later*, Albany, NY: State University of New York Press.

Short, J. (2001) *Global Dimensions: Space, Place and the Contemporary World*, London: Reaktion.

Short, J. (2003) 'Going for gold: globalizing the Olympics, localizing the Games', *Globalization and World Cities (GaWC) Research Bulletin*, 10, online at: http://www.lboro.ac.uk/gawc/rb/rb100.html (accessed 31 March 2006).

Short, J. (2004) *Global Metropolitan: Globalizing Cities in a Capitalist World*, London: Routledge.

Short, J. and Kim, Y. (1999) *The City and Globalization*, Harlow: Longman.

Silk, M. (ed.) (2004) *Sport and Corporate Nationalisms*, Oxford: Berg.

Silk, M. and Andrews, D. (2001) 'Beyond a boundary? Sport, transnational advertising, and the reimagining of national culture', *Journal of Sport and Social Issues*, 25, 2: 180–201.

Simson, V. and Jennings, A. (1992) *Dishonored Games: Corruption, Money, and Greed at the Olympics*, New York: S.P.I. Books.

Sklair, L. (1999) 'Competing conceptions of globalization', in J. Schmidt (ed.), *Globalization, Regionalization and Social Change*, Aalborg: Research Centre on Development and International Relations, Part 1.

Sklair, L. (2000a), 'Social movements and global capitalism', in J. Roberts and A. Hite (eds), *From Modernization to Globalization*, Cambridge: Blackwell.

Sklair, L. (2000b), 'Sociology of the global system', in F. Lechner and J. Boli (eds), *The Globalization Reader*, Cambridge: Blackwell.

Sklair, L. (2000c) 'The transnational capitalist class and the discourse of globalization', *Cambridge Review of International Affairs*, 14, 1: 67–85.

Sklair, L. (2001a) 'Capitalism, global', in N. Smelser and P. Baltes (eds), *International Encyclopedia of the Social and Behavioral Sciences*, Amsterdam: Elsevier Science: 1459–63.

Sklair, L. (2001b) 'Globalization', in S. Taylor (ed.), *Sociology: Issues and Debates*, Basingstoke: Palgrave Macmillan.

Sklair, L. (2001c), 'Globalization and society', in M. Warner (ed.), *International Encyclopedia of Business and Management*, 2nd edition, Stamford, CN: Thomson Learning, 2389–98.

Sklair, L. (2001d) 'The transnational capitalist class', in R. Barry Jones (ed.), *Encyclopedia of International Political Economy*, London: Routledge.

Sklair, L. (2001e) *The Transnational Capitalist Class*, Cambridge: Blackwell.

Sklair, L. (2002a) 'Champions, losers and big business in China', *Asia-Pacific Business Review* 9, 1: 95–103.

Sklair, L. (2002b) 'Democracy and the transnational capitalist class', *Annals of the American Academy of Political and Social Science*, 581: 144–57.

Sklair, L. (2002c) *Globalization: Capitalism and its Alternatives*, 3rd edition, Oxford: Oxford University Press.

Sklair, L. (2002d) 'Globalization and management: the role of the transnational capitalist class', in P. Joynt and M. Warner (eds), *Managing Across Culture*, 2nd edition, Stamford, CN: Thomson Learning: 269–80.

Sklair, L. (2002e) 'The transnational capitalist class and global politics: deconstructing the corporate–state connection', *International Political Science Review*, 23, 2: 159–74.

Sklair, L. (2003a) 'Globalization, capitalism and power', *Developments in Sociology*, 10, 101–21.

Sklair, L. (2003b) 'The global system', in F. Lechner and J. Boli (eds), *The Globalization Reader*, Cambridge: Blackwell, 70–6.

Sklair, L. (2003c) 'Transnational practices and the analysis of the global system', in A. Hulsemeyer (ed.), *Globalization in the Twenty-First Century*, Basingstoke: Palgrave Macmillan: 15–32.

Sklair, L. (2004) 'The end of capitalist globalization', in M. Steger (ed.), *Rethinking Globalism*, Lanham, MD: Rowman and Littlefield: 39–49.

Slack, T. (ed.) (2003) *The Commercialisation of Sport*, London: Routledge.

Smith, A. (1995a) *Nations and Nationalism in a Global Era*, Cambridge: Polity.

Smith, A. (1995b) 'Nations and their pasts', *The Warwick Debates*, online at: http://members.tripod.com (accessed 6 November 2005).

Smith, P. (2001) 'Elective affinity', *Prometheus*, 4, online at: http://www.prometheus.demon.co.uk (accessed 21 October 2005).

Social Compact (15 January 2006) *Social Compact: Catalyzing Business Investment in Inner City Neighborhoods*, online at: http://www.socialcompact.org/aboutus.htm.

Soldatow, S. (1980) *Politics of the Olympics*, North Ryde, NSW: Cassell.

Sombart, W. (2001) *Economic Life in the Modern Age*, New Brunswick, NJ: Transaction.

Spillman, L. (1997) *Nation and Commemoration*, Cambridge: Cambridge University Press.

Spots, J.D. (1994) 'Global politics and the Olympic Games: separating the two oldest games in history', *Dickinson Journal of International Law*, 13, 1: 103–22.

Staun, J. (2003) 'The lure of the Olympics', *International Olympic Academy Participants Association (IOAPA), Denmark*, online at: http://ioapa.dk (accessed 20 July 2003).

Starr, S. (2004) *Xinjiang*, London: M. E. Sharpe.

Stilglitz, J. (2003) *Globalization and its Discontents*, Harmondsworth: Penguin.

Sugden, J. and Tomlinson, A. (eds) (2002) *Power Games: A Critical Sociology of Sport*, London: Routledge.

Sullivan, S. (15 January 2004) 'The Chinese and terrorism: a question of "proper candor" ', *Media Monitors Network*, online at: http://usa.mediamonitors.net (accessed 31 March 2006).

Sullivan, S. (26 February 2004) 'Beijing Olympics: opportunity or mockery', *Media Monitors Network*, online at: http://usa.mediamonitors.net (accessed 31 March 2006).

Sutter, R. (2005) *China's Rise in Asia: Promises and Perils*, Lanham, MD.: Rowman and Littlefield.

Swatos, W.H. (2005) 'Elective affinity', *Encyclopedia of Religion and Society*, Harvard Institute for Religion Research, online at: http://hirr.hartsem.edu/ency (accessed 20 October 2005).

Sydney Morning Herald (2004) 'Athens 2004: drugs testing', online at: http://smh.com.au (accessed 22 October 2005).

Tang Yuankai (2001) 'Beijing creates history', *Beijing Review*, online at: http://www.bjreview.com.cn/2001/200131/CoverStory–200131.htm (accessed 9 April 2006).

Taylor, M. (2005a) 'China's time to step into world spotlight: Asia has a handful of global brands, but more are emerging and the Beijing Olympics could provide a springboard', *South China Morning Post*, 21 November.

Taylor, M. (2005b) 'Beijing prepares to enter the branding games: Olympic exposure put Japanese and Korean firms on the world stage. Can China do the same?', *South China Morning Post*, 21 November.

Taylor, T. (ed.) (2000) *How You Play the Game: The Contribution of Sport to the Protection of Human Rights*, Sydney: Faculty of Business, University of Technology.

Tivey, L. (ed.) (1980) *The Nation-State*, Oxford: Martin Robertson.

Tomba, L. (ed.) (2002) *East Asian Capitalism: Conflicts, Growth and Crisis*, Milan: Fondazione, Giangiacomo, Feltrinelli.

Tomlinson, A. (1984) 'De Coubertin and the modern Olympics', in A. Tomlinson and G. Whannel (eds), *Five-ring Circus: Money, Power, and Politics at the Olympic Games*, London: Pluto Press: 84–97.

Tomlinson, A. (1996) 'Olympic spectacle: opening ceremonies and some paradoxes of globalization', *Media, Culture and Society*, 18: 583–602.

Tomlinson, A. (ed.) (2002) *Power Games: A Critical Sociology of Sport*, London: Routledge.

Tomlinson, A. and Young, C. (2005) *National Identity and Global Sports Events: Culture, Politics, and Spectacle in the Olympics and the Football World Cup*, Albany, NY: State University of New York Press.

Toohey, K. and Veal, A.J. (2000) *The Olympic Games: A Social Science Perspective*, Wallingford and New York: CABI Publishing.

Toy, M. (2006) 'China bans sale of body parts', *Sydney Morning Herald*, 29 March, online at: http://www.socresonline.org.uk/2/1/8.html (accessed 1 April 2006).

Treanor, P. (1997) 'Structures of nationalism', *Sociological Research Online*, 2, 1, online at: http://www.socresonline.org.uk (accessed 6 November 2005).

Tremlett, G. (2004) 'Human rights groups are complicit in murder, says Trimble', *Guardian Unlimited*, 29 January, online at: http://www.guardian.co.uk (accessed 31 March 2006).

Tyson, L. (2001) 'China: under the glare of the Olympic torch', *Business Week*, 13 August: 3745.

United Nations (UN) (15 January 2006) 'About the Global Compact', *Global Compact Office*, online at: http://www.unglobalcompact.org.

UN (31 October 2003) 'Sport for peace and development: building a peaceful and better world through sport and the Olympic ideal', 58th Session of the UN General Assembly, online at: http://multimedia.olympic.org (accessed 29 October 2005).

United States Sports Academy (2001) 'The fundamental principles of Olympism', *Sports Journal*, 4, 1:1.

Uygur Worlds (15 August 2005) 'The Uighur People: an introduction', *Uygur of Xinjiang*, online at: http://www.uygurworld.com (accessed 31 March 2006).

Van Harskamp A. and Musschenga A.W. (2001) *The Many Faces of Individualism*, Leuven, Belgium: Peeters Publishers.

Van Riper, T. (2006) 'The Olympic host city curse', Money UK MSN, online at: http://money.uk.msn.com (accessed 9 February 2006).

Veale, A.J. and Toohey, K. (2005) *The Olympic Games: a Bibliography*, Sydney: School of Leisure, Sport and Tourism, University of Technology.

Voeltz, R.A. (1996) 'London, 1948: the Games of the XVth Olympiad', in J. Findling and K. D. Pelle (eds), *Historical Dictionary of the Modern Olympic Movement*, Westport, CN: Greenwood Publishing: 103–8.

Wagner, J. (2006) 'Olympic Summer Games', *Virtual Museum of the Olympic Games*, online at: http://www.olympic-museum.de.(accessed 10 February 2006).

Walker, M. (2006) 'The geopolitics of sexual frustration', *Foreign Policy*, March/April 2006: 60–1.

Walker, R.L. (1988) 'The weird and violent regime in North Korea: terror as state policy', *Washington Post*, 2 March.

Wallerstein, I. (1974) *The Modern World-System, Vol. I: Capitalist Agriculture and the Origins of the European World-Economy in the Sixteenth Century*, New York: Academic Press.

Wallerstein, I. (1979) *The Capitalist World Economy*, Cambridge: Cambridge University Press.

Wallerstein, I. (1980) *The Modern World-System, Vol. II: Mercantilism and the Consolidation of the European World-Economy, 1600–1750*, New York: Academic Press.

Wallerstein, I. (1982a) *World-Systems Analysis: Theory and Methodology*, Beverly Hills, CA: Sage.

Wallerstein, I. (1982b) *Dynamics of Global Crisis*, Basingstoke: Macmillan.

Wallerstein, I. (1983) *Historical Capitalism*, London: Verso.

Wallerstein, I. (1984) *The Politics of the World-Economy: The States, the Movements and the Civilizations*, Cambridge: Cambridge University Press.

Wallerstein, I. (1989a) *The Modern World-System, Vol. III: The Second Great Expansion of the Capitalist World-Economy, 1730–1840s*, San Diego, CA: Academic Press.

Wallerstein, I. (1989b) *Antisystemic Movements*, London: Verso.

Wallerstein, I. (1990) *Transforming the Revolution: Social Movements and the World-System*, New York: Monthly Review Press.

Wallerstein, I. (1991) *Geopolitics and Geoculture: Essays on the Changing World-System*, Cambridge: Cambridge University Press.

Wallerstein, I. (2003) *Decline of American Power: The U.S. in a Chaotic World*, New York: New Press.

Wallerstein, I. (2004) *World Systems Analysis: An Introduction*, Durham, NC: Duke University Press.

Wamsley, K.B. (2002) 'The global sport monopoly: a synopsis of 20th century Olympic politics', *International Journal*, LVII, 3: 395–411.

Wamsley, K.B., Barney, R.K. and Martyn, S.G. (eds) (2002) *The Global Nexus Engaged: Past, Present, Future Interdisciplinary Olympic Research*, London, Ontario: Centre for Olympic Studies, University of Western Ontario.

Wan, M. (2001) *Human Rights in Chinese Foreign Relations: Defining and Defending National Interests*, Philadelphia, PA: University of Pennsylvania Press.

Wang, W. (2005) *Mega-Events, Urban Re-Imaging and Tourism Development: A Pilot Study of the 2008 Olympic Sailing Regatta in Qingdao, China*, Sheffield: School of Management, University of Sheffield.

Wang, Y. (2003) 'Civil society in China: concept and reality', *Japan Centre for International Exchange (JCIE)*, online at: http://www.iwep.org.cn (accessed 7 November 2005).

Ward, M. (8 March 2005) 'China's tight rein on online growth', *BBC News*, online at: http://news.bbc.co.uk (accessed 30 March 2006).

Ware, S. (1999) 'Technological progress and the Olympic Games', *Journal of Olympic History*, 7, 5: 45–8.

Washington Post (2001a) '2008 Olympics: a particular risk', *Washington Post*, 20 May.

Washington Post (2001b) 'China and the Olympics', *Washington Post*, 8 July.

Waters, M. (1995) *Globalization*, London: Routledge.

Watson, J. (ed.) (1997) *Golden Arches East*, Stanford, CA: Stanford University Press.

Watts, J. (2005) 'Torture still widespread in China, says UN investigator', *Guardian*, 3 December.

Weatherley, R. (1999) *The Discourse of Human Rights in China: Historical and Ideological Perspectives*, Basingstoke: Macmillan.

Weber, M. (1958) *The Protestant Ethic and the Spirit of Capitalism*, New York: Scribner (translated by Talcott Parsons; with a Foreword by R. H. Tawney).

Weber, M. (2002) *The Protestant Ethic and the Spirit of Capitalism and Other Writings*, Harmondsworth: Penguin.

Weber, M. (2003) *The Protestant Ethic and the Spirit of Capitalism*, New York: Courier Dover Publications.

Weekly Standard (2001) 'Beijing 2008 = Berlin 1936?', *Weekly Standard*, 4 June.

Wenshan, J. (2001) *The Remaking of the Chinese Character and Identity in the 21st Century: The Chinese Face Practices*, Norwood, NJ: Ablex/Greenwood.

West, T.G. and Pestritto, R.J. (eds) (2003) *The American Founding and the Social Compact*, Lexington, MA: Lexington Books.

Westerbeek, H. and Smith, A. (2003) *Sport Business in the Global Marketplace*, Basingstoke: Palgrave.

Wiggins, D.K. (1992) 'The year of awakening: black athletes, racial unrest and the civil rights movement of 1968', *International Journal of the History of Sport*, 9, 2: 188–208.

Wikipedia (21 October 2005) 'Doping', online at: http://en.wikipedia.org (accessed 22 October 2005).

Wikipedia (31 October 2005) 'Capitalism', online at: http://en.wikipedia.org (accessed 31 October 2005).

Wilson, D. and Purushothaman, R. (2005) 'Dreaming with BRICs: the path to 2050', *Global Economics, Goldman Sachs Global Economics Website*, online at: http://www.gs.com/insight/research/reports/99.pdf (accessed 1 October 2005).

Wilson, H. (1996) 'What is an Olympic City? Visions of Sydney 2000', *Media, Culture and Society*, 18: 603–18.

Wilson, H.E. (1994) 'The golden opportunity: Romania's political manipulation of the 1984 Los Angeles Olympic Games', *Olympika: The International Journal of Olympic Studies*, 3, 83–97.

Wilson, N. (1988) *The Sports Business: The Men and the Money*, London: Piakas.

Wishnich, E. (2005) 'China as a risk society', *Regionalisation and the Taming of Globalisation?*, Centre for the Study of Globalisation and Regionalisation (CSGR), Centre for International Governance Innovation (CIGI) and UNU-Comparative Regional Integration Studies (UNU CRIS), University of Warwick, UK.

Wonderful Copenhagen (8 February 2006) '13th Olympic Congress to Copenhagen', *Official Tourism Site of Copenhagen*, online at: http://www.visitcopenhagen.dk.

World Atlas (2006) 'The Olympic flag', *WorldAtlas.com*, online at: http://worldatlas.com (accessed 17 January 2006).

World Bank (1993) *The East Asian Miracle*, Oxford: Oxford University Press.

World Bank (2003a) 'Glossary', *World Bank Group* online at: http://www.worldbank.org/depweb/english/modules/glossary (accessed 17 November 2005).

World Bank (2003b) 'Gross national product', *World Bank Group*, online at: http://www.worldbank.org/depweb/english/modules/glossary (accessed 12 November 2005).

World Bank (2003c) 'Purchasing power parity', *World Bank Group*, online at: http://www.worldbank.org/depweb/english/modules/glossary (accessed 12 November 2005).

World Bank (15 July 2005) *World Development Indicators Database*, World Bank Group, online at: http://siteresources.worldbank.org (accessed 11 November 2005).

World Trade Organization (WTO) (16 November 2005) 'What is the World Trade Organization?', online at: http://www.wto.org (accessed 16 November 2005).

Wu, H. (1992) *Laogai: The Chinese Gulag*, Boulder, CO: Westview Press.

Wu, H. and Wakeman, C. (1993) *Bitter Winds: A Memoir of My Years in China's Gulag*, New York: Wiley.

Xinhua News Agency (9 October 2003) 'He Zhenliang: China's Mr Olympics', *China Internet Information Center* (CIIC), online at: http://www.china.org.cn/english/MATERIAL/115915.htm (accessed 31 March 2006).

Xu Yuan (2004) 'Minority rights and national development in the People's Republic of China', *IIAS Newsletter*, 35, November, online at: http://www.iias.nl (accessed 31 March 2006).

Yamazaki, J. (2005) *Japanese Apologies for World War II: A Rhetorical Study*, London: Routledge.

Yardley, J. (2005) 'A hundred cellphones bloom, and Chinese take to the streets', *New York Times*, 25 April.

Yeung, H. (2004), *Chinese Capitalism in a Global Era: Towards Hybrid Capitalism*, London: Routledge.

Yong Deng (2004) *China Rising: Power and Motivation in Chinese Foreign Policy*, Lanham, MD: Rowman and Littlefield.

Young, D. (2002) *Modern Olympics: A Struggle for Revival*, Baltimore, MD: Johns Hopkins University Press.

Young, D. (2004) *A Brief History of the Olympic Games*, Malden, MA: Blackwell Publishers.

Young, D.C. (1985) 'Coubertin and the Olympic logo', in J. A. Managan (ed.), *Proceedings of the XIth HISPA International Congress*, Glasgow: Jordan Hill College: 326–7.

Yu Keeping (2000) 'The emergence of Chinese civil society and its significance to governance', *Civil Society and Governance Programme*, online at: http://www.eldis.org/staticDOC10891.htm (accessed 31 March 2006).

Zhang Ye (2003) 'China's emerging civil society', *Center for Northeast Asian Policy Studies*, CNAPS Working Paper, Brookings Institute, August, online at: http://www.brookings.edu/fp/cnaps/papers/ye2003.htm (accessed 31 March 2006).

Zhang, M. (1996) 'The shifting Chinese public image of the United States', *Strategic Forum*, 89, online at: http://www.ndu.edu/inss/strforum/SF_89/forum89.html (accessed 10 January 2006).

Zheng Bijian (2005) 'China's peaceful rise and new role in East Asia', *Les Cahiers du Debat, Foundation Pour l'Innovation Politique*, May, online at: http://www.fondapol.org/pdf/CahierChineAnglais.pdf (accessed 31 March 2006).

Zheng Yongnian (2004) *Globalization and State Transformation in China*, Cambridge: Cambridge University Press.

Znamierowski, A. (2005) *The World Encyclopedia of Flags*, London: Lorenz Books.

Index